W9-CCP-129

DATE DUE

100 Most Popular African American Authors

Recent Titles in the Popular Authors Series

*The 100 Most Popular Young Adult Authors: Biographical Sketches and Bibliographies,
Revised First Edition*
Bernard A. Drew

Popular Nonfiction Authors for Children: A Biographical and Thematic Guide
Flora R. Wyatt, Margaret Coggins, and Jane Hunter Imber

100 Most Popular Children's Authors: Biographical Sketches and Bibliographies
Sharron McElmeel

*100 Most Popular Picture Book Authors and Illustrators: Biographical Sketches and
Bibliographies*
Sharron McElmeel

100 More Popular Young Adult Authors: Biographical Sketches and Bibliographies
Bernard A. Drew

Winning Authors: Profiles of the Newbery Medalists
Kathleen L. Bostrom

*Children's Authors and Illustrators Too Good to Miss: Biographical Sketches and
Bibliographies*
Sharron McElmeel

100 Most Popular Genre Fiction Authors: Biographical Sketches and Bibliographies
Bernard A. Drew

100 Most Popular
African American Authors

Biographical Sketches and Bibliographies

Bernard A. Drew

Popular Authors Series

LIBRARIES
UNLIMITED
A Member of the Greenwood Publishing Group

Westport, Connecticut • London

Library of Congress Cataloging-in-Publication Data

Drew, Bernard A. (Bernard Alger), 1950–
  100 most popular African American authors : biographical sketches and bibliographies /
by Bernard A. Drew.
    p. cm. — (Popular authors series)
  Includes bibliographical references and index.
  ISBN 1-59158-322-5 (pbk : alk. paper)
  1. American literature—African American authors—Bio-bibliography—Dictionaries.
  2. American literature—20th century—Bio-bibliography—Dictionaries. 3. African
American authors—Biography—Dictionaries. I. Title. II. Title: One hundred most popular
African American authors.
  PS153.N5D74   2007
  810.9'896073003—dc22   2006030669

British Library Cataloguing in Publication Data is available.

Library of Congress Catalog Card Number: 2006030669
ISBN: 1-59158-322-5

First published in 2007

Libraries Unlimited, 88 Post Road West, Westport, CT 06881
A Member of the Greenwood Publishing Group, Inc.
www.lu.com

Printed in the United States of America

The paper used in this book complies with the
Permanent Paper Standard issued by the National
Information Standards Organization (Z39.48–1984).

10   9   8   7   6   5   4   3   2   1

Contents

Introduction

African American fiction writers have achieved so much in the past decade and a half. Although never absent from the literary scene, now more than ever you will find on bookstore and library shelves a spectrum of black writers who excel in all genres, from romance to mystery, science fiction to historical, inspirational to urban, poetry and memoir to mainstream contemporary. They are wildly proclaiming their strong voices and rich vocabularies and have barely tapped their reserves of stories, themes, and characters.

Black authors have succeeded not only in all genres but in all literary levels within genres—from rough-grammared, violent street tales to polished, stellar-vocabularied literary novels. From Iceberg Slim to Edwidge Danticat, this reference book stresses "popular" authors. Selections were made with careful weight to genres and to authors within those genres. They are featured in harmony together in the same reference book because at heart they all have adored the written word, the power of communication, the opportunity to cry into the wilderness—and at last to be heard.

100 Most Popular African American Authors, the latest volume in Libraries Unlimited's Popular Authors series, carries brief biographical sketches of each writer with personal information, critical views from published sources, descriptions of writings, and pertinent comments from the authors about their craft. Profiles are based on a variety of sources, from existing reference works to trade and popular periodicals to author Web sites. The lists of author works are as current as possible at press time. Bibliographies and further sources of information round out the entries. Selected and documented quotations within profiles give readers—especially students—a flavor for what they might find should they wish to explore a particular author further. The sketches are arranged alphabetically by author name. The genre or genres that each authors writes in, along with a benchmark title, are listed at the beginning of each profile.

The work concentrates on 100 authors who have made their mark in the past quarter century. It stresses popular fiction writers (some also write poetry and memoirs, one crafts a newspaper comic strip), durability, and U.S. orientation (with a sprinkling of Canadian and Caribbean authors) in all genres. There are many, many "rising stars." Most of the writers covered are still active and are at or nearing the best of their careers. Partly in an attempt to show how many of these authors found their inspiration, a number of earlier, seminal popular fiction writers are included, such as Zora Neale Hurston, Alex Haley, Chester Himes, and Langston Hughes. Yes, some classic writers are omitted, to make way for this generation's scribes.

And this generation has produced some innovative and influential writers—to offer only a few shining examples: Terry McMillan, Walter Moseley, Maya Angelou, Tananarive Due, and John Edgar Wideman.

It's little surprise that African American writers face more than the usual market challenges of finding first a publisher and then an audience. They lack the depth of the same written literary tradition that white writers enjoy. They were displaced by slavery. They've had to rely on the African oral tradition to bridge the gap of the diaspora. Two words frequently emerge as these authors relate their upbringings and attraction to writing. Those words are *griot* (or African storyteller) and kitchen poets (urban gatherings of women who told stories or sang songs)—keepers of traditions.

It's also little surprise that so many African American authors are enflamed to confront the issues of American slavery and racism. Yet to do so and at the same time achieve a broad audience—within their own race as well as others—means they have to find an inner strength of expression.

And it is finally little surprise, too, that many African American writers have chosen either to delay confrontation with some matters of race until they have become better established or to work it into their words gradually, to strive for more universal themes of life and romance and death. Still, none has chosen to avoid it altogether.

— Bernard A. Drew

Rochelle Alers

Romance, Romantic Suspense, Contemporary Mainstream Literature

Benchmark Title: *All My Tomorrows*

New York, New York

1943

Photo credit: DeVito Studios

About the Author and the Author's Writing

Romance writer Rochelle Alers begins each book with a Bible verse in thanks to God for giving her the gift of storytelling. Readers and critics alike appreciate that gift. In a 1995–96 reader survey, she was voted Arabesque Books' Most Popular Author and has garnered other awards since.

The author was born in New York City in 1943, the daughter of James A. and Minnie L. Ford. With a double major in psychology and sociology, she earned a bachelor of arts degree from John Jay College of Criminal Justice of the City University of New York in 1974. Beginning in 1987, she worked as an executive assistant for Empire State Medical Equipment Dealers Association for four years, then became a community liaison specialist for state-contracted substance abuse programs with the Nassau County Department of Drugs and Alcohol Addiction Services. Now a resident of Freeport, New York, Alers is divorced with one daughter.

Although Alers began writing in 1984, it took four years before one of her manuscripts found a publisher. (The first book was eventually published as the initial title in her popular Hideaway series.)

Soon after, the author became known for depicting issues of significance to black women—domestic violence, single motherhood, infertility, and missing children. Although many of her books contain elements of suspense and danger and revolve around edgy themes, they usually have upbeat endings.

The heroines in Alers's books are independent and passionate. Quintin Lord in *Home Sweet Home* thinks nothing of marching into the apartment of her new neighbor and demanding he turn down the sound on his stereo. Summer Montgomery in *Renegade* works undercover for the Drug Enforcement Agency, in the guise of a drama teacher in a Massachusetts high school. Reporter Dana Nichols returns to Mississippi to ferret out the truth of her parents' murder/suicide many years before in *Homecoming*.

"Through my novels I show women and men the protocol of courting," the author said on her Web page. "I also want women to say, 'This is how I want a man to treat me.' "

In *Hidden Agenda*, Eve Blackwell and Matthew Sterling's marriage is one of convenience—made to free her abducted son from his spiteful father. The two never anticipate they will fall passionately in love. Jolene Walker in *No Compromise* is so dedicated to her work with victimized women, she doubts she has time for a romantic life—until she meets U.S. Army Captain Michael Kirkland.

"Alers paints such vivid descriptions that when Jolene becomes the target of a murderer, you almost feel as though someone you know is in great danger," commented reviewer Shelley Mosley in *Library Journal*.

No Compromise reflects the author's own life, in that she writes her novels while maintaining a full-time job. Alers has disciplined herself to write two hours every morning before going to her office. She seldom writes on weekends or at night, unless she needs to meet a deadline. *Private Passions* took longer—six months—for the author to write than most of her books because of the need to wrap up several plot strands. What's the most difficult part of the book to write? The first page, which has to be a grabber, she said in *Shades of Romance Magazine*.

Alers's other interests include travel, art, music, and gourmet cooking—activities that appear from time to time in the books she writes. She uses feng shui to create the imaginary furnishings of her characters' homes.

"Music plays a major role in my creative process because I always write to music," the author revealed to *Arabesque Romance News*. "I favor soundtracks that at times will convey the mood of the characters or their dilemma." Her broad musical taste runs the gamut of Mozart to Manhattan Transfer to Barry White.

The author takes her characters to diverse locations. *Hideaway* is set in Florida as acknowledgment of Alers's Southern roots, she said in an *Arabesque Romance News* interview, and it also afforded the opportunity to examine a multicultural locale. Serena Morris-Vega, the heroine of *Heaven Sent*, returns to her childhood home of Costa Rica to help her falsely convicted half-brother secure his release from prison. *Rosie's Curl and Weave* takes place in a Harlem hair salon, and *Summer Magic* finds its main character, Caryn Edwards, summering on North Carolina's Marble Island.

Alers's ambitious Hideaway Legacy series, with its floating cast of characters, took a good deal of organization. "Sometimes a series or family of characters take on a life of their own," Alers told Romantic Times Book Club. "I was caught off guard to learn my four-book series [Hideaway] wasn't going to end as I had planned. Readers were ready for the second generation to take shape, so I went back to work and further developed family trees."

Works by the Author

My Love's Keeper (1991)
Happily Ever After (1994)
Careless Whispers (1995)
Reckless Surrender (1995)
Home Sweet Home (1996)
Gentle Yearning (1998), reissued 2006
Summer Magic (1999)
Secrets Never Told (2003)
Lessons of a Lowcountry Summer (2004)
The Long Hot Summer (2004)
All My Tomorrows (2005)
Best Kept Secrets (2006)
A Time to Keep (2006), sequel to *Happily Ever After*
Pleasure Seekers (2007)

Hideaway Legacy Series

Hideaway (1995)
Heaven Sent (1998)
Harvest Moon (1999)
Just Before Dawn (2000)
Hideaway Saga (2004) (collects first three titles)

Hideaway Legacy Series: Sons and Brothers Trilogy

No Compromise (2002)
Homecoming (2002)
Renegade (2003)

Hideaway Legacy Series: Daughters and Sisters Trilogy

Vows (1997)
Hidden Agenda (1997)
Private Passions (2001)

Silhouette Desire Books

Blackstones of Virginia Series

1479. *A Younger Man* (2002)
1613. *Very Private Duty* (2004)
1649. *Beyond Business* (2005)

Anthologies

Holiday Cheer (1995), with Angela Benson and Shirley Hailstock

Love Letters (1997), with Donna Hill and Janice Sims
Rosie's Curl and Weave (1999), with Donna Hill, Felicia Mason, and Francis Ray
Island Magic (2000), with Shirley Hailstock, Marcia King-Gamble, and Felicia Mason
Della's House of Style (2000), with Donna Hill, Felicia Mason, and Francis Ray
Welcome to Leo's (2000), with Donna Hill, Brenda Jackson, and Francis Ray
Going to the Chapel (2001), with Gwynne Forster, Donna Hill, and Francis Ray
Tis the Season (2001), with Donna Hill and Candice Poarch
Twilight Moods (2002)
Island Bliss (2002), with Carmen Green, Marcia King-Gamble, and Felicia Mason
Living Large (2003), with Donna Hill, Brenda Jackson, and Francis Ray
Love at Leo's II (2004)
A Summer Place (2004)
Four Degrees of Heat (2004), with Reshonda Tate Billingsley, Brenda L. Thomas, and Crystal Lacey Winslow
Let's Get It On (2004), with Donna Hill, Brenda Jackson, and Francis Ray
Season of Miracles (2005), with Adrienne Byrd and Janice Sims

Written as Susan James

Reckless Surrender (1995)

For Further Information

"Meet the Author: Rochelle Alers," *Shades of Romance Magazine. http://www. sormag.com/alers3.html* (viewed April 22, 2003).

Mosley, Shelley, "No Compromise" review, *Library Journal* (Feb. 15, 2002).

Peacock, Scot, ed., Rochelle Alers entry, *Contemporary Authors*, volume 178. Detroit: Gale Research, 2000.

Rochelle Alers interview, *Arabesque Romance News* (May 1999). *http://authors. aalbc.com/rochelle.html* (viewed March 31, 2003).

Rochelle Alers Web page. *http://www.rochellealers.com/main.htm* (viewed April 22, 2003).

"Spin-Off Characters: Rochelle Alers' Secret Behind Her Hideaway Legacy Series," Romantic Times Book Club. *http://www.romantictimes.com/data/ tips/287.html* (viewed March 31, 2003).

Maya Angelou

**Poetry, Memoir, Drama,
Children's Literature**

Benchmark Title: *I Know Why the
Caged Bird Sings*

St. Louis, Missouri

1928

Photo credit: Steven Dunwell

About the Author and the Author's Writing

Maya Angelou is blessed with a deep memory, a keen eye for detail, and a way with words. Her latest memoir, *Hallelujah! The Welcome Table,* although not really a cookbook, recreates the bygone bustle in her mother's kitchen, complete with the aroma of smothered chicken.

It has been a long and fascinating journey from that kitchen through Angelou's far-ranging career in the performing arts and literature. She has sung, danced, and acted on stage. She has directed, produced, and crafted dramas and screenplays. A writer, editor, and civil rights activist, she was invited to read her poem, "On the Pulse of Morning," at Bill Clinton's inauguration in 1993. A few years later, the president presented her with the National Medal of Arts. She has written poetry that is accessible to younger readers. And she has compiled six volumes of rich memoir beginning with *I Know Why the Caged Bird Sings* in 1970.

One of the great voices in African American literature, Angelou struggled long against adversity, as is evocatively described in her reminiscences. "Her work reads like a novel because of her ability to craft language in prose that reads easily in paragraph form yet often sounds like poetry," in the view of Joyce L. Graham. "For example, early in *I Know Why the Caged Bird Sings*, Angelou confronts her own realization that only blond-haired, blue-eyed white girls are regarded as beautiful and that being black brings many apparent limitations to her life."

Graham gives as an example of Angelou's rich language this sentence from *I Know Why the Caged Bird Sings*: "If growing up is painful for the Southern Black girl, being aware of her displacement is the rust on the razor that threatens the throat."

5

The author was born Marguerite Annie Johnson in St. Louis, Missouri, in 1928. Her father was a U.S. Navy cook, her mother a nurse and real estate agent. Her parents divorced when she was three, and she and a brother were raised by a grandmother in Stamps, Arkansas. Maya attended public schools in Arkansas and California and later went back to live with her mother in St. Louis. After being raped by her mother's boyfriend, the author was incommunicative for several years. She returned to her grandmother's home and, with the help of a woman named Mrs. Flowers, gradually regained her speech, her dignity, and her self-confidence. Finding life with her mother one of turmoil, she ran away to stay with her father and his girlfriend. But his trailer-park life was one of destitution, so she went back to living at times with her mother and at times with her grandmother.

These years of overcoming her dysfunctional upbringing and breaking through the walls of white oppression are documented in her autobiographical books. The first, *I Know Why the Caged Bird Sings,* takes its title from a poem by poet Paul Laurence Dunbar and looks at her earliest years. The second, *Gather Together in My Name*, follows the author as she and her brother move from their grandmother's home in her late teen years when she served cocktails, tap danced, cooked Creole, worked as a prostitute, and at age sixteen had a son out of wedlock.

Singin' and Swingin' and Gettin' Merry Like Christmas is about the years when Angelou, in her early twenties, was married to a white man and former sailor, Tosh Angelou. There were a few years of stability for the author and her child. But the Angelous divorced after five years and she again became a dancer, joining a production of *Porgy and Bess* that was touring Europe and Africa. Angelou felt great guilt at neglecting her son. *The Heart of a Woman* finds Angelou active in the civil rights movement, married again (to Paul Du Feu, whom she eventually also divorced), and still feeling guilty about her son.

All God's Children Need Traveling Shoes, the fifth book, expresses Angelou's enthusiasm for the African country of Ghana, which she adopted as her homeland. By now Angelou had traveled widely, worked as a journalist and writer as well as entertainer, and attained a degree of success.

"The life and work of Maya Angelou are fully intertwined," according to a Women Writers of Color essay. "Angelou's poetry and personal narratives form a larger picture wherein the symbolic Maya Angelou rises to become a point of consciousness for African American people, and especially for black women seeking to survive masculine prejudice, white illogical hate, and Black lack of power."

"Maya Angelou's stories are aptly called testimonials. She 'testifies' not only for herself but also for her community," said Lyman B. Hagen in *Twentieth-Century Young Adult Writers*. "Her voice as a writer is the voice of her people. What her community endures, she endures. She writes about what she knows: the black experience. The universals contained in her work serve to underscore her frequently expressed thesis: that as people, we are more alike than unalike."

Angelou's 2002 work *A Song Flung Up to Heaven* brings the author's life story up to the 1960s and her experiences of racism and her discovery and loss of close friends Malcolm X and Martin Luther King Jr. As she has aged, she has come to believe that there are evil people in the world. But, the author told John Holden for *Pages* that she is optimistic "the majority of human beings have within us—and I put myself in that majority—the ability and the desire to do the right thing."

Works by the Author

Poetry

Just Give Me a Cool Drink of Water 'fore I Diiie (1971)
Oh Pray My Wings Are Gonna Fit Me Well (1975)
And Still I Rise (1978)
Shaker, Why Don't You Sing? (1983)
Poems: Maya Angelou (1986)
Life Doesn't Frighten Me (1993)
On the Pulse of Morning (1993)
Soul Looks Back in Wonder (1994)
Complete Collected Poems of Maya Angelou (1994)
Phenomenal Woman: Four Poems Celebrating Women (1994)
Amazing Peace: A Christmas Poem (2005)
Mother: A Cradle to Hold Me (2006)

Memoir

I Know Why the Caged Bird Sings (1970)
Gather Together in My Name (1974)
Singin' and Swingin' and Gettin' Merry Like Christmas (1976)
The Heart of a Woman (1981)
All God's Children Need Traveling Shoes (1986)
A Song Flung Up to Heaven (2002)
The Collected Autobiographies of Maya Angelou (2004), omnibus
Hallelujah! The Welcome Table: A Lifetime of Memories with Recipes (2004)

Drama

Cabaret for Freedom (1960), musical revue written with Godfrey Cambridge
The Least of These (1966)
The Clawing Within (1966)
Adjoa Amissah (1967)
Encounters (1973)
Sophocles, Ajax (1974), adaptation
And Still I Rise (1976)

Screenplays and Teleplays

Blacks, Blues, Black (1968)
Georgia, Georgia (1972)
All Day Long (1974)
I Know Why the Caged Bird Sings (1979), adaptation of autobiography, written
    with Leona Thuna and Ralph B. Woolsey
Sister, Sister (1982)
Brewster Place (1990)

Children's Fiction

Mrs. Flowers: A Moment of Friendship (1986)
Now Sheba Sings the Song (1987)
I Shall Not Be Moved (1990)
Lessons in Living (1993)
Wouldn't Take Nothing for My Journey Now (1993)
My Painted House, My Friendly Chicken, and Me (1994)
A Brave and Startling Truth (1995)
Kofi and His Magic (1996)
Even the Stars Look Lonesome (1997)
Maya's World: Angelina of Italy (2004)
Maya's World: Mikale of Hawaii (2004)
Maya's World: Renee Marie of France (2004)
Maya's World: Izak of Lapland (2004)

For Further Information

Angaza, Maitefa, "A Precious Prism: Maya," *Black Issues Book Review* (March-April 2001).

Baum, Joan, "An Interview with Poet Maya Angelou," *Education Update* (Feb. 2005).

Frost, David, "An Interview with Maya Angelou," *The Most Amazing Thing.* *http://www.newsun.com/angelou.html* (viewed Sept. 14, 2006).

Garcia-Johnson, Ronie-Richele, Maya Angelou entry, *Authors & Artists for Young Adults*, Vol. 20, Thomas McMahon, ed. Detroit: Gale, 1997.

Graham, Joyce L., Maya Angelou entry, *Writers for Young Adults,* Ted Hipple, ed. New York: Scribner's, 1997.

Hagen, Lyman B., Maya Angelou entry, *Twentieth-Century Young Adult Writers*, 1st ed., Laura Standley Berger, ed. Detroit: St. James Press, 1994.

Hogan, John, "A Conversation with Maya Angelou," *Pages* (March/April 2002).

Lim, Grace, "Spotlight on . . . Maya Angelou," *People Weekly* (Jan. 25, 1999).

"Maya Angelou," *Current Biography* (Feb. 1994).

Maya Angelou biography, *Voices from the Gaps.* http://voices.cla.umn.edu/vg/Bios/entries/angelou_maya.html (viewed July 3, 2006).

Maya Angelou entry, *Contemporary Authors, New Revision Series*, Vol. 65. Detroit: Gale, 1998.

Maya Angelou: The Official Web site. *http://www.mayaangelou.com/* (viewed July 3, 2006).

Meroney, Maya, "The Real Maya Angelou," *American Spectator* (March 1993).

Sylvester, William, Maya Angelou entry, *Contemporary Women Poets,* Pamela L. Shelton, ed. Detroit: St. James Press, 1998.

Tina McElroy Ansa

Romance, Contemporary Mainstream Literature

Benchmark Title: *The Hand I Fan With*

Macon, Georgia
1949

Photo credit: Joneé Ansa

About the Author and the Author's Writing

Tina McElroy Ansa considers herself a fixture of the region in which she lives. "I'm one of those black folks who identifies herself, along with African-American, female, author, womanist, and feminist, a 'southerner,' " she writes in *Callaloo*.

Born in Macon, Georgia, in 1949, the youngest of five children, Tina McElroy grew up listening to her mother read books and to her grandfather tell stories. She earned an English degree from Spelman College in Atlanta in 1971. After graduating, she joined the *Atlanta Constitution*'s copy desk—the first black woman on the newspaper's staff. In nearly two decades with the daily, she supervised layout, wrote entertainment features, and reported news. She also worked as an editor and copy editor for the *Charlotte Observer* in North Carolina. In 1982, she began writing freelance articles and newspaper columns. She instructed at writing workshops at Brunswick College, Spelman College, and Emory University. She contributed to the CBS *Sunday Morning* program her "Postcards from Georgia."

Ansa has won numerous awards for her writing, including the Georgia Authors Series Awards for her first and third novels and the American Library Association Best Book for Young Adults Award in 1990 for *Baby of the Family*. That book is about Lena McPherson, who at birth has the ability to see into the spiritual world. As she matures, she learns what it truly means to be different and to become comfortable with herself and her knack. *The Hand I Fan With,* a sequel, describes Lena's love affair with a ghost named Herman.

Ugly Ways, for which Ansa was nominated for an NAACP Image Award, follows the three very different Lovejoy sisters as they return to their hometown to bury their mother—a task not easily accomplished because the mother's presence is everywhere.

"I try to expand the canvas of American literature to include a mother, a black mother, who challenges, the 'conventional wisdom,' the accepted line on what 'mother' is and means in African culture," the author told *Contemporary Authors*. "To record, examine, and push the parameters of our lives is, I believe, the job and duty of literature."

The novel does not offer the typical depiction of a mother figure, observed *Notable Black American Women*. "*Ugly Ways* is a stark look at the antithesis of the strong, determined, protective, and loving African American mother. Although the sisters almost seem to hold some sense of admiration for their mother's ability to sustain such a singularly independent existence, Mudear is given no redeeming qualities."

The author's recent *You Know Better* continues the spiritual vein by introducing ghosts—an educator, a nurse, and a prostitute—who guide three generations of women, a rebellious teenager, her mother, and her grandmother, as they struggle to make something of their lives. "*You Know Better* is about turning generational 'curses' into blessings," noted reviewer Sara Webb Quest. "More importantly, it is about how people can change."

Ansa sets her novels in the imaginary Georgia town of Mulberry. She explained to *Essence* magazine her desire to recreate a 1950s feel: "I wanted to capture the sweetest memories of my girlhood—the sound of the juke joints my father owned; the rush of people on Saturday afternoons when you couldn't get from one end of the street to the next because everyone was out, on their way to the fish fry or to get their hair done." She and her husband, filmmaker Joneé Ansa, live on St. Simon's Island off the Georgia coast.

Works by the Author

Baby of the Family (1989)
Ugly Ways (1993)
The Hand I Fan With (1996), sequel to *Baby of the Family*
You Know Better (2002)

Anthologies

Breaking Ice: An Anthology of Contemporary African-American Fiction (1990), edited by Terry Macmillan
Calling the Wind (1993)

Screenplay

Baby of the Family (2003), with Joneé Ansa

Films Based on the Author's Works

Baby of the Family (2003)

For Further Information

Ansa, Tina McElroy, "What's the Confederate Flag Got to Do with It?" *Callaloo* (winter 2001).

Osborne, Gwendolyn, *The Hand I Fan With* review, *Romance Reader. http://www.theromancereader.com/ansa-fan.html* (viewed July 3, 2006).

Tina McElroy Ansa biography, African American Literature Book Club. *http://authors.aalbc.com/tina.htm* (viewed Feb. 17, 2005).

Tina McElroy Ansa biography, *Voices from the Gaps. http://voices.cla.umn.edu/vg/Bios/entries/ansa_tina_mcelroy.html* (viewed July 3, 2006).

Tina McElroy Ansa entry, Contemporary Authors Online. Gale Group, 2005. Reproduced in Biography Resource Center; Farmington Hills, MI: Thomson Gale, 2005 *http://galenet.galegroup.com/servlet/.BioRC* (viewed Feb. 17, 2005).

Tina McElroy Ansa entry, *Notable Black American Women,* Vol. 3. Detroit: Gale Group, 2002.

Tina McElroy Ansa Web site. *http://www.tinamcelroyansa.com* (viewed April 2, 2005).

James Baldwin

Mainstream Contemporary Literature, Poetry, Drama, Essays

Benchmark Title: *Go Tell It on the Mountain*

New York City

1924–1987

About the Author and the Author's Writing

James Baldwin was one of the leading African American authors of the past century. Novelist, essayist, poet, dramatist—as a writer, he knew no limits.

Critic Trudier Harris in *Oxford Companion to African American Literature* identified Baldwin's primary themes as "the failure of the promise of American democracy, questions of racial and sexual identity, the failures of the Christian church, difficult family relationships, and the political and social worlds that shaped the American 'Negro' and then despised him for that shaping." In other words, Baldwin pretty much covered the entire ground of African American literature.

Born in Harlem in 1924 to an unwed domestic worker from Maryland, Baldwin knew a father only after Emma Berdis Jones married a laborer and Louisiana clergyman, David Baldwin. James Arthur Jones took his father's surname. But he had an uncomfortable relationship with the pastor, as emerges in the author's autobiographical first novel, *Go Tell It on the Mountain*. The main character, John Grimes, is praised by his white teachers but despised by his stepfather because he is more accomplished than the man's legitimate son. Grimes (like Baldwin?) eventually becomes disillusioned with family, with church, with society.

Baldwin shouldered a good deal of household responsibility in helping raise his eight siblings. He read frequently to his brothers and sisters. While one of the books he read was Harriet Beecher Stowe's *Uncle Tom's Cabin*, he later criticized the novel for its pedanticism.

Baldwin found an early outlet in writing. He edited the junior high school newspaper. He joined a Pentacostal church and preached on the streets as a young teen. He graduated from DeWitt Clinton High School and worked in construction in New Jersey until he moved to Greenwich Village in 1944 to attempt to make a professional go of writing. He came to know writer Richard Wright and garnered a Eugene Saxton Fellowship in 1945. His first sale was a book review to *The Nation* in 1946.

Baldwin had heterosexual relationships until he went to France in 1948 to escape personal turmoil. From then on, he considered himself homosexual or bisexual. He again would use the novel form in *Giovanni's Room* to wrestle with the issue not only of sexual orientation, but of the cultural expectations of the black male.

As his work found its way into print, his reputation grew.

"Whether or not one agreed with what he was saying at any particular moment, his intelligence was luminous, too obvious to be questioned or doubted," wrote Don Wycliff in *Commonweal*. "His prose projected a ferocious self-assurance that I could only wish I possessed." But above all else, Wycliff said, Baldwin proved a black man could write with as much style and verve as a white man.

Baldwin ultimately found that France, while different from the United States, nevertheless harbored its own form of racism. "Any writer, I suppose, feels that the world into which he was born is nothing less than a conspiracy against the cultivation of his talent," Baldwin wrote in *Notes of a Native Son*. Although he visited other countries and several times returned to the United States, he remained in France the rest of his life.

By the 1960s, Baldwin's themes had changed. His writings became more secular, deriving from the blues instead of the spirituals, as Josef Jarab observed in *Scribner Encyclopedia of American Lives*. "His essays showed growing anger and heat, and his collection *Nobody Knows My Name: More Notes of a Native Son*, which became a best-seller, includes strong pieces about his trips to the American South. Race and sex were dramatically linked in his third novel, *Another Country*, in which black and white characters, mostly artists, grope through the chaos of their lives in search of love."

Baldwin came to know civil rights activists Martin Luther King Jr. and Malcolm X, and he turned to the essay form in *The Fire Next Time* to confront issues of race.

He also wrote for the stage. *Blues for Mr. Charlie,* produced in New York City in 1964 was based on his excursions to the South with Medgar Evers and on the murder of a young black man in Mississippi—the accused killer set free. In reviewing the play, Howard Taubman in the *New York Times* said Baldwin's dialogue "lay bare the heart of the Negro's suffering and explain the iron of his determination."

Baldwin earned a number of awards, including a Guggenheim Fellowship. Later in life he honored a number of speaking engagements in the United States and taught for the University of Massachusetts at Amherst, Bowling Green State University, and the University of California at Berkeley.

In 1987, the author died of cancer, leaving unfinished a biography of Martin Luther King Jr.

"As novelist, essayist, dramatist, and social critic," critic Fred Standley summed up, Baldwin's "corpus demonstrates unequivocally both a sustained productivity and a consistent and sensitive human perspective. At times alternately praised and damned by blacks and whites alike, he never lacked an audience."

Baldwin appeared on a commemorative U.S. postage stamp in 2004—emblematic of his enduring power for the next generations.

Works by the Author

Go Tell It on the Mountain (1953)
Giovanni's Room (1956)
Another Country (1962)
Going to Meet the Man (1965), short stories

Tell Me How Long the Train's Been Gone (1968)
If Beal Street Could Talk (1974)
Just above My Head (1979)
Early Novels and Stories (1998)
Vintage Baldwin (2004)

Drama

The Amen Corner (1955)
Giovanni's Room (1957), based on his novel
Blues for Mister Charlie (1964)
A Deed for the King of Spain (1974)
The Welcome Table (1987)

Screenplay

One Day, When I Was Lost: A Scenario (1972), based on *The Autobiography of Malcolm X* by Alex Haley and Malcolm X

Poetry

Jimmy's Blues: Selected Poems (1983)

Young Adult Fiction

Little Man, Little Man: A Story of Childhood (1976)

Contributor

American Negro Short Stories (1966)
Daddy Was a Number Runner (1970)

Nonfiction

Autobiographical Notes (1953)
Notes of a Native Son (1955)
Nobody Knows My Name: More Notes of a Native Son (1961)
The Fire Next Time (1983)
A Rap on Race with Margaret Mead (1971)
No Name in the Street (1972)
Cesar: Compressions d'Or with Francoise Giroud (1973)
A Dialogue with Nikki Giovanni (1973)
The Devil Finds Work (1976)
Harlem, U.S.A.: The Story of a City Within a City (1976), edited by John Henrik Clarke
The Evidence of Things Not Seen (1985)
The Price of the Ticket: Collected Nonfiction 1948–1985 (1985)

Perspectives: Angles on African Art (1987), edited by Michael J. Weber
Collected Essays (1998)

Contributor

Nothing Personal (1964), by Richard Avedon
Black Anti-Semitism and Jewish Racism (1969)
Menschenwuerde und Gerechtigkeit (1969), edited by Carl Ordung

Television and Stage Works Based on the Author's Works

The Amen Corner (1983), stage musical
Go Tell It on the Mountain (1985), adapted for Public Broadcasting System's *American Playhouse*

For Further Information

Harris, Trudier, James Baldwin entry, *The Oxford Companion to African American Literature*, William L. Andrews, Frances Smith Foster, and Trudier Harris, eds. New York: Oxford University Press, 1999.

James Baldwin entry, *Authors and Artists for Young Adults*, Vol. 34. Detroit: Gale Group, 2000.

"James Baldwin Stamp Unveiled," *Jet* (Aug. 16, 2004).

James Baldwin Web page, African American Literature Book Club. *http://authors.aalbc.com/james.htm* (viewed Feb. 17, 2005).

JaRab, Josef, James Arthur Baldwin entry, *Scribner Encyclopedia of American Lives, Volume 2: 1986–1990*. New York: Charles Scribner's Sons, 1999.

Shin, Andrew, and Barbara Hudson, "Beneath the Black Aesthetic: James Baldwin's Primer of Black American Masculinity," *African American Review* (summer 1998).

Standley, Fred, James Baldwin entry, *Dictionary of Literary Biography Yearbook, 1987*. Detroit: Gale, 1988.

Taubman, Howard, "Common Burden; Baldwin Points Duty of Negro and White," *New York Times* (May 3, 1964).

Wycliff, Don, "A preacher's son," *Commonwealth* (Oct. 9, 1998).

Toni Cade Bambara

Mainstream Contemporary Literature, Poetry

Benchmark Title: *The Salt Eaters*

New York, New York

1939–1995

About the Author and the Author's Writing

Toni Cade Bambara's best-known novel, *The Salt Eaters,* as with most of her work, uses rich language to weave social conscience into a nonlinear story. "With a dizzying array of characters and settings, the novel employs nearly seamless shifts of time and place to trace the journey of the main character, Velma Henry—and in fact her entire community—toward healing and wholeness," notes Ann Folwell Stanford in *Oxford Companion to African American Literature.*

Reviewer Alice A. Deck, in discussing a posthumous collection, *Deep Sightings and Rescue Missions,* put it this way: "There is a strong undercurrent of mutual love and respect in the black community in Bambara's world; children can talk to strangers without fear of harm, older black women are grandmothers to everyone, and men and women are spiritual healers who assist the people in their recovery from dealing with racism and economic exploitation."

Bambara could not fathom prose without politics.

Her longtime editor and friend Toni Morrison described the author on a BookRags.com profile: "Any hint that art was over there and politics was over here would break her up into tears of laughter, or elicit a look so withering it made silence the only intelligent response."

The author was born Miltona Mirkin Cade in 1939 in New York City—Toni was a nickname, and she later gave herself the name Bambara. She has said that her decade growing up in Harlem helped bring voice to her vision. She published her first short story while in high school.

She graduated from Queen's College in 1959 with a bachelor of arts degree in theater arts and English. Always active in social and community issues, she then worked for the New York state welfare department for two years. During the rise of the civil rights and feminist movements, she compiled the anthology *The Black Woman,* following it with a second collection that focused on black folktales.

In the early 1960s, Bambara went to Europe to study at the Commedia dell'Arte at the University of Florence and at the Ecole de Mime Etienne Decroux in Paris. Returning to the United States, she held a position in the psychiatry section at Metropolitan Hospital. While directing programs at Colony Settlement House in Brooklyn, she completed requirements at City College of the City University of New York for a master's degree in 1964. She taught for a time at that school and continued her studies, also becoming active in the theater. In 1969, she joined the faculty at Livingston College and continued writing and editing. Her first collection of short stories about blacks, *Gorilla My Love*, often featuring women or children in everyday life, appeared in 1972.

In the 1970s during the Vietnam War, she taught at several institutions, including Stephens College in Missouri, all the while involved as a political activist.

The Salt Eaters, the author's first novel, is set in rural Georgia. While some found the myriad characters and prose-poem writing difficult, it earned the American Book Award in 1981. By this time, Bambara and her daughter from a failed marriage had moved to Philadelphia where she scripted television documentaries.

While she published no fiction in her last years, a collection compiled by Toni Morrison showed Bambara still pursuing the same goals at life's end. "Bambara uses a wide range of literary devices in *Those Bones Are Not My Child*," wrote Shanna Greene Benjamin, "both traditional and experimental, which enhance the reader's aural and visual experience with the text. The most striking of these is her handling of narrative voice and her camera-like use of narrative perspective."

"When I look back at my work with any little distance," she once reflected to an interviewer, as described on the *Voices from the Gaps* Web page, "the two characteristics that jump out at me are one, the tremendous capacity for laughter, but also a tremendous capacity for rage." The author died of colon cancer in Philadelphia in 1995.

Works by the Author

Gorilla, My Love (1972), short stories
The Sea Birds Are Still Alive (1977), short stories
The Salt Eaters (1980)
If Blessing Comes (1987)
Those Bones Are Not My Child (1999)

Collection

Deep Sightings and Rescue Missions: Fiction, Essays, and Conversations (1996), edited by Toni Morrison

Editor

The Black Woman: An Anthology (1970), with Eleanor W. Taylor
Tales and Stories for Black Folks (1971)
Southern Black Utterances Today (1975), with Leah Wise

Young Adult Fiction

Raymond's Run (1990)

Screenplays

Zora (1971)
The Johnson Girls (1972)
Transactions (1979)
The Long Night (1981)
Epitaph for Willie (1982)
Tar Baby (1984), based on Toni Morrison novel
Raymond's Run (1985)
The Bombing of Osage (1986)
Cecil B. Moore: Master Tactician of Direct Action (1987)
W.E.B. Du Bois: A Biography in Four Voices (1997), cowriter

For Further Information

Benjamin, Shanna Greene, *Those Bones Are Not My Child* review, *African American Review* (summer 2001).

Deck, Alice A., *Deep Sightings and Rescue Missions* review, *African American Review* (spring 1999).

Stanford, Ann Folwell, Toni Cade Bambara entry, *Oxford Companion to African American Literature*, William L. Andrews, Frances Smith Foster, and Trudier Harris, eds. New York: Oxford University Press, 1997.

Toni Cade Bambara biography, BookRags.com. *http://www.bookrags.com/biography-toni-cade-bambara/* (viewed July 3, 2006).

Toni Cade Bambara biography, Voices from the Gaps. *http://voices.cla.umn.edu/vg/Bios/entries/bambara_toni_cade.html* (viewed July 3, 2006).

Toni Cade Bambara entry, *Authors and Artists for Young Adults,* Vol. 49. Detroit: Gale Group, 2003.

Toni Cade Bambara entry, *Notable Black American Women,* Vol. 3. Detroit: Gale Group, 2002.

Traylor, Eleanor W., Toni Cade Bambara entry, Heath Anthology of American Literature. *http://college.hmco.com/english/lauter/heath/4e/students/author_pages/contemporary/bambara_to.html* (viewed July 3, 2006).

Leslie Esdaile Banks

Horror, Romance, Romantic Suspense

Benchmark Titles:
Vampire Huntress Legend Series

Philadelphia, Pennsylvania

ca. 1960

Photo credit: Courtesy of the author

About the Author and the Author's Writing

Leslie Esdaile Banks is on her third career. She was a corporate marketing and sales executive. Then she was an independent small-business consultant. Now, as unlikely as that background might suggest, she's a writer of fiction and screenplays. And she's so busy, she uses four pennames!

Born Leslie Ann Peterson in West Philadelphia, she graduated from Girls' High School. She almost didn't apply to nearby University of Pennsylvania because of the high tuition. But she did apply and ultimately graduated from the Wharton business program in 1980. For several years she worked for Fortune 100 companies including Xerox, Hewlett Packard, and Digital Equipment. She had a home in Delaware, drove a Volvo, and declared six-figure earnings on her income tax return. "I was the quintessential black yuppie," she told the *Philadelphia Inquirer*'s Michael Vitez. "I was a Buppie."

Circumstances forced a sudden change. Her daughter was seriously burned in an accident at a day-care facility and required seventeen operations that used up insurance and savings. She was laid off. Her husband, Michael Esdaile, left. Leslie was down but not out.

She established a private consulting business specializing in developing marketing strategies, writing grant applications, and facilitating workshops. "Meanwhile, always a 'serial entrepreneur'—I kept plugging away at my 'hobby' of writing fiction . . . the hobby paid off better than any job or other venture," she said in an interview for a Wharton School newsletter, "Get It Started." While she misses the paid vacations and other benefits of working for someone else, "I now write at home, full-time, and love it," she said.

By 1998, Banks had completed requirements for a master of fine arts degree from Temple University in film and media arts. Still doing her consulting work, she wanted to develop professional tools for an eventual permanent move to a literary career. In 2001, she took home the U.S. Small Business Administration Minority Advocate of the Year Award for the Eastern Region. That same year, with two romance novels in print, she was nominated for a Golden Pen Award by the Black Writers Alliance for best anthology.

She not only wrote romances—the first was inspired by an Essence magazine contest—she lived a romance. A high school sweetheart, Al Banks, came back into her life, newly divorced and with children. Old love sparked. They married in 2000.

"I definitely believe in the transformative power of love and second chances," Banks explained of her writing to Gwendolyn Osborne. She said she had just about decided to quit writing romances when she found her own new romance, Banks. "He came back as a force to be reckoned with and loved me, warts and all.. . . It was indeed transformative."

Straddling genres, *Love Notes* is a suspense-relationship novel that makes good use of the author's business background. It is about a couple who own and operate their own business. But that endeavor is teetering on the edge. As they struggle to hold their marriage together, "they begin peeling away unknown information about their parents' marriages, and they start to see their friends and siblings for who they really are," the author told Romanceincolor.com. "All of this is going on at the same time the couple is also coping with significant fertility issues." Plus, they are in the center of an intricate robbery scheme.

Banks's *Rivers of the Soul* and its sequel are nontraditional books—they look at the impact of divorce on relationships and children. Although she is aware the books push the limits of women's fiction, the author assures readers they end positively.

She has said her favorite writers include Alice Walker, Toni Morrison, Zora Neal Hurston, Sonia Sanchez and bell hooks, Diane McKinney-Whetstone, Donna Hill, and Lorene Cary.

Banks contracted to write novels based on the popular network television series *Soul Food*. And she crafted a half dozen dark horror adventures of the Vampire Huntress books.

"I wanted to tackle the issues of good versus evil and have the romance genre constraints removed so that I could build my story," she told Bernadette Adams Davis.

To hear Banks explain it, switching from sweet romance heroines to blood-lusting vampires is easy. "Develop your characters based on realistic human emotions and reactions to stimuli in your novel plot. Within every good book, what makes for reality-suspending reading is ironically reality. If your characters are credible, the way they see the world is identifiable as true to life, because you can empathize with their thoughts and feelings" she wrote for *Fiction Factor*.

Banks maintains a strong fan base—particularly for the Damali Richards dark fantasies. She acknowledges there are "certain signature elements to my work. For example," she told thesistacircle.com, "I will always have a little Divine Intervention thrown in to help the characters along, as well as mother-wisdom from an elderly secondary character—because I have so strongly leaned on those 'old wisdoms' to get me through tough times."

Banks in an e-mail message said that underlying her prose is what she sees as powerful political forces manipulating inner-city youth, nurturing violent predators of both genders who sap the community of its life blood. She believes the solution is not in imprisoning these people but in getting to the roots of the crisis and finding and offering more human-level solutions.

Works by the Author

Fiction

Written as L. A. Banks

Vampire Huntress Legend Series

Minion (2003)
The Awakening (2004)
The Hunted (2004)
The Bitten (2005)
The Forbidden (2005)
The Damned (2006)
The Forsaken (2006)
The Wicked (2007)

Collection

Stroke of Midnight (2004), with Amanda Ashley, Lori Handleland, and Sherrilyn Kenyon

Written as L. E. Banks

***Soul Food,* series based on television show**

For Better, for Worse (2002)
Through Thick and Thin (2003)
No Mountain High Enough (2003)

Collections

Dark Dreams (2004)
Dark Dreams II (2005)

Written as Leslie Banks

Collection

Chicken Soup for the African American Soul (2004)

Written as Leslie Esdaile Banks

Betrayal of the Trust (2004)
Blind Trust (2005)
Shattered Trust (2006)

Written as Leslie Esdaile

Sundance (1996)
Slow Burn (1997)

Love Lessons (2001)
Rivers of the Soul (2001)
Love Potions (2002)
Still Waters Run Deep (2002), sequel to *Rivers of the Soul*
Through the Storm (2002)
Valentine's Love (2003)
Sister Got Game (2004)
Keepin' It Real (2005)

Heroes and Heroines Series
Tomorrow's Promise (2002)

Collections

Midnight Clear (2000), with Gwynne Forster, Carmen Green, Donna Hill, and Monica Jackson
After the Vows (2001)
Candlelight and You (2003), with Melanie Schuster and Linda Walters
The Sistahood of Shopaholics (2003), with Monica Jackson, Reon Laudat, and Niqui Stanhope
Stroke of Midnight (2004), with Amanda Ashley, Lori Handeland, and Sherilyn Kenyon

For Further Information

"Author of the Month—Leslie Esdaile," Romance in Color, February 2001. *http://www. romanceincolor.com/authormthesdaile.htm* (viewed Feb. 26, 2005).

Banks, Leslie Esdaile, "Building Realism through Characters," *Fiction Factor. http://www.fictionfactor.comguests/realism.html* (viewed Feb. 13, 2005).

Banks, Leslie Esdaile, e-mail to the author, June 7, 2005.

Banks, Leslie Esdaile, Newsletter, Official Fan Club of Leslie Esdaile Banks. *http://home.comcast.net/~zulma822.wsb/html/view.cgi-image.html— SiteID-205939. html* (viewed Feb. 26, 2005).

Davis, Bernadette Adams, "To Each, His or Her Own Genre," *Black Issues Book Review* (Jan.-Feb. 2004).

Leslie E. Banks interview, *Get It Started. http://www.wep.wharton.upenn.edu/newsletter/ winter03/banks.html* (viewed Feb. 13, 2005).

Leslie Esdaile Banks biography, Official Fan Club of Leslie Esdaile Banks. *http://home.comcast.net/~zulma822/wsb/html/view.cgi-photo.html—delay- 20- SiteID-1861243.html* (viewed July 18, 2006).

Leslie Esdaile Banks interview, Sistah Circle Book Club. *http://www. thesistahcircle.com/interview-lebanks.htm+Leslie+E.+Banks+interview& hl=en&ie=UTF-8* (viewed March 5, 2005).

Osborne, Gwendolyn, "Meet Leslie Esdaile," *Romance Reader. http://www. theromancereader.com/esdaile.html* (viewed March 5, 2005).

Vitez, Michael, "Romance Writer Pencils a New Chapter in Life," *Philadelphia Inquirer* (Feb. 9, 2003).

Steven Barnes

Science Fiction, Fantasy, Horror, Historical Literature

Benchmark Title: *Lion's Blood*

Los Angeles, California

1952

Photo credit: Courtesy of the author

About the Author and the Author's Writing

Steven Barnes turned history askew in his alternate-world novel *Lion's Blood*. His premise is that Socrates did not drink the hemlock and did not die. He instead fled to Egypt. As a consequence, Carthage and Egypt flourished and rose to challenge Alexander the Great, who had become pharaoh. America was colonized by Africans, instead of Europeans.

The story takes place in the 1860s and is told through the experiences of Aidan O'Dere, an Irish slave boy who had been kidnapped and sold to the Moors, and Iai ibi Jallaledin ibn Rashid, the slaveholder. These characters, one Christian, one Islamic, become friends.

"Friendship has to do with seeing yourself in another person," Barnes said in a *Publishers Weekly* interview, "and when you begin to see that, friendship tends to cut across lines of income, race, social status. That's what friendship is, what human decency is—the ability to see yourself walking in another man's shoes."

Barnes said he came up with the story concept as he searched for a hook to reach black male readers while holding on to a core readership of alternate-history buffs. "I was looking for a way to relate my experience and feelings about being a black American male," he told GRITS. "I was also interested in creating adventure stories for black men. The black male reading audience isn't nearly as developed as the black female readership."

Barnes was born in Los Angeles, California, in 1952. He attended Los Angeles High School and studied communication arts at Pepperdine University. He is a certified hypnotherapist and holds a black belt in Kenpo karate (Aikka style) and Kodokan judo and has studied in a variety of other martial arts and in yoga. He lives in Longview, Washington, with his wife, the science fiction writer Tananarive Due, and their daughter.

Barnes leapt from guiding tours at the CBS studios to scripting television shows such as *The Twilight Zone*. He has written a screenplay, *The Soulstar Commission*, and was a creative consultant on *The Secret of NIMH*. Most of his scripting work has been in television programs ranging from *Baywatch* to *Stargate SG-1*.

The author teamed with science fiction writer Larry Niven to produce books in two series before writing three novels in his own series featuring futuristic gang drop-out and martial arts assassin Aubry Knight. *Streetlethal* takes place in a lawless Los Angeles as a professional fighter breaks up a gang that is harvesting human organs and selling them. "Barnes draws on his own knowledge of martial arts to add credulity to this often depressing and quite violent novel of the underside of human society," said *St. James Guide to Science Fiction Writers*. Although some of his books have been violent, critics have noted a devotion to plot development, pacing, and characterization.

"My primary area of interest is human mental and physical development," Barnes told Contemporary Authors Online. "To this end I research psychology, parapsychology, and kinesiology, practice and teach martial arts, and meditate and study comparative religious philosophy. My major viewpoint is that all human beings are perfect, but that we allow ourselves to dwell in our illusions of imperfection, creating fear, hate, and all negativity in human experience."

Barnes has written entries in the Star Wars and Star Trek franchises. But he has also continued his independent work. *Zulu Heart* takes the character of Kai from *Lion's Blood* into a new story line. He plans to take a second wife, a Zulu of high rank, but a social gaff threatens war. Aidean, the hero in *Zulu Heart*, is now free in a slave society but lives a perilous and uncertain life. He has his eyes on, of all people, the caliph's wife.

As one of the few African Americans writing science fiction, Barnes has found himself increasingly dealing with race issues. "I had to find a way to make my black characters accessible to everyone, and to assure white readers they weren't going to get bashed if they read my work," he told Strange Horizons.

Science fiction, which concerns itself with myth, is a critical genre. "When you exclude one group of people from your culture's dramatic iconography, you're saying, 'We're gonna keep our secrets to ourselves. We're not gonna let you be the heroes, let you empathize with the heroes fully, so you're not gonna learn how to be victorious,' " he said in a *Locus* interview, elaborating that black mythology is unique in that it was largely crafted by others, with little room for hope. He's changing that.

◣ Works by the Author

The Descent of Anansi (1982), with Larry Niven
The Kundalini Equation (1986)
The Legacy of Heorot (1987), with Larry Niven and Jerry Pournelle
Fusion (1987), graphic novel
Achilles' Choice (1991), with Larry Niven
Game (1991)

Beowulf's Children (1995), sequel to *The Legacy of Heorot,* with Larry Niven
   and Jerry Pournelle (in Britain as *The Dragons of Heorot*)
Blood Brothers (1996)
Iron Shadows (1998)
Saturn's Race with Larry Niven (2000)
Charisma (2002)
Lion's Blood: A Novel of Slavery and Freedom in an Alternate America (2002)
Zulu Heart (2003), sequel to *Lion's Blood*
Great Sky Woman (2006)

Aubrey Knight Series

Streetlethal (1982)
Gorgon Child (1989)
Firedance (1993)

Dream Park Series with Larry Niven

Dream Park (1981)
The Barsoom Project (1989)
The California Voodoo Game (1992) (in Britain as *Dream Park: The Voodoo*)

Star Trek: Deep Space Nine Series

Far Beyond the Stars (1998)

Star Wars: Clone Wars Series

The Cestus Deception (2004)

Contributor

Horseclans (1987 and 1988), edited by Robert Adams
Warriors of Mist and Dreams (1995), edited by Roger Zelazny

Screenplays and Teleplays

Little Fuzzy (1979), adapting novel by H. Beam Piper
The Test (1982), adapting Stanislaw Lem short story
The Secret of NIMH (1982)
Twilight Zone (1985–86), scripts
Real Ghostbusters (1987), scripts
The Wizard (1986), scripts
The Soulstar Commission (1987), screenplay
Baywatch (1989), scripts
The Outer Limits (1995), scripts
Stargate SG-1 (1997), scripts
Andromeda (2000), scripts

Nonfiction

Ki: How to Generate the Dragon Spirit (1976)

For Further Information

Barnes, Steven, e-mail to author, June 6, 2005.

Beatty, Greg, "Interview: Steven Barnes," *Strange Horizons. http://www. strangehorizons.com/2002/20020729/interview.shtml* (viewed July 3, 2006).

Cestus Deception review, *Library Journal* (June 15, 2004).

Charisma review, *Library Journal* (July 2002).

Hall, M. M., "PW Talks with Steven Barnes," *Publishers Weekly* (Jan. 21, 2002).

"Interview with Steven Barnes," *Futurist.com. http://www.futurist.com/portal/ science_fiction/interview_steve_barnes.htm* (viewed July 3, 2006).

Lion's Blood review, *Publishers Weekly* (Jan. 21, 2002).

Stephen [sic] Emory Barnes entry, Contemporary Authors Online. Gale, 2005. Reproduced in Biography Resource Center. Farmington Hills, MI: Thomson Gale, 2005. *http://galenet.galegroup.com/servlet/BioRC* (viewed Feb. 21, 2005).

Steven (Emory) Barnes entry, *St. James Guide to Science Fiction Writers,* 4th ed. Detroit: St. James Press, 1996.

Steven Barnes interview, GRITS. *http://www.thegritsbookclub.com/Interviews/ StevenBarnes.html* (viewed July 3, 2006).

Steven Barnes interview, *SciFi.Com. http://www.scifi.com/transcripts/2002/ barnes_chat.html* (viewed July 3, 2006).

Steven Barnes Web site. *http://www.lionsblood.com/html/aboutsteve/bio.htm* (viewed July 3, 2006).

"Steven Barnes: Black & White," *Locus* online. *http://www.locusmag.com/2003/ Issue03/Barnes.html* (viewed July 3, 2006).

Zulu Heart review, *Publishers Weekly* (Feb. 24, 2003).

Angela Benson

Inspirational Literature, Romance, Contemporary Mainstream Literature

Benchmark Title: *Abiding Hope*

Alabama

Date of birth not revealed

Photo credit: Glamour Shots

About the Author and the Author's Writing

Angela Benson wrote the book on writing African American fiction—literally. A veteran inspirational romance novelist, she decided she wanted to inspire budding writers and produced an instructive guide for beginners. Her book *Telling the Tale: The African-American Fiction Writer's Guide* was published in 2000.

"I find joy in the writing process," she explained in *Telling the Tale,* adding that there certainly "are times when the process is a struggle. Sometimes it's torture. But even during the toughest times I still find enjoyment."

That she could clearly see and explain the structure of a good novel is no surprise, given the author's background. Alabama-born Benson showed an early flare for writing when, in fifth grade, she penned several short stories. But she ultimately followed a different course. She became a math major at Spelman College and then pursued a degree in industrial engineering at Georgia Institute of Technology. She worked from 1980 until 1995 as an engineer specializing in telecommunications. She furthered her education with two master's degrees—in operations research and in human resources development. She completed requirements for a doctoral degree in instructional technology at the University of Georgia and shifted into a new career as an assistant professor.

Meanwhile, she sat at the keyboard to begin a side career as a novelist. *A Family Wedding,* for example, is a contemporary mainstream novel about relationships, and *The Way Home* works issues of class and social standing into a touching love story. Josh's sudden loss of his job jeopardizes his life with Gloria in *For All Time.* And the

27

author's own background works into *Bands of Gold* as the heroine, Christina Marshall, manager of a successful engineering firm, yearns to meet Mr. Right.

Benson's works garnered several writing awards, and she was a finalist for the 2000 Romantic Times Lifetime Achievement Award in Multicultural Romance.

After seven traditional Silhouette and Arabesque romances, the author began the Genesis House series for Tyndale and took a new direction. "I consider it an honor to write for the Christian market," she said on her Web site, adding, "in many ways, CeCe's story—about living with the consequences of our bad choices, and finding forgiveness—is my story, too." That first book, *Awakening Mercy,* was a finalist for a Romance Writers of America RITA Award and a Christian Booksellers Association Christy Award. The second in the trilogy, *Abiding Hope,* earned an Emma Award from Romance Slam Jam. Reviewer Melanie C. Duncan said of the story, which is about the near destruction of a marriage after the death of a child, that Benson's "insight into God's impact on our lives makes her work a requirement for growing collections."

The author has a simple definition of Christian fiction: The main characters, all of whom are affiliated with a community-based, spiritual organization in the heart of Atlanta, are Christians who face challenges in their lives. The second novel, for example, follows the joint ministry and family tribulations of Shay and Marvin, a couple introduced in the first book.

In an interview with GRITS, Benson said inspirational novels are much akin to romances: "They're the same in that as romances, the stories 'turn' on the romance. That is, the force behind the major events in the stories is the growing romantic relationship between the hero and heroine. They're different in that in the Christian romance the hero and heroine's relationship with Christ is pivotal in their lives, and thus in their romance."

Although she brought many of her original romance fans with her in her new exploration of spiritual themes, Benson isn't surprised if fans of one style aren't fans of the other.

Benson said she often becomes emotionally linked with her characters. In a Good Girls Book Club interview, she said she thinks "that people read looking for themselves and their situations so I try to create honest characters in honest situations. I don't go for the 'good' character versus the 'bad' character scenario, because I see that as an easy out. I go for characters that are complex, characters that are challenged to live their faith, not just talk about it."

Continuing her steady rise in the publishing field—the Genesis House books were brought out in mass market editions by BET Books—the Decatur, Georgia, resident's first hardcover came out in 2005.

Works by the Author

Bands of Gold (1994)

For All Time (1995)

Between the Lines (1996)

A Family Wedding (1997)

The Nicest Guy in America (1997)

The Way Home (1997)

Second Chance Dad (1997)

The Pastor's Wife (2005)
The Amen Sisters (2005)
A Family Wedding (2006)

Genesis House Series

Awakening Mercy (2000)
Abiding Hope (2001)
Enduring Love (announced)

Anthologies

Holiday Cheer (1995)
Sweet Passion: Bonds of Gold/For All Time/Between the Lines (2006)

Nonfiction

Telling the Tale: The African-American Fiction Writer's Guide (2000)

For Further Information

Angela Benson entry, *Contemporary Black Biography*, Vol. 34, Ashyla Henderson, ed. Gale Group, 2002. Reproduced in Biography Resource Center. Farmington Hills, MI: Thomson Gale, 2005. *http://galenet. galegroup.com.servlet/BioRC.*

Angela Benson Web page. *http://www.bensonink.com/angela_bio.htm* (viewed July 3, 2006).

Duncan, Melanie C., *Abiding Hope* review, *Library Journal* (Nov. 1, 2001).

"Interview with Angela Benson," *Good Girl Magazine. http://www. goodgirlbookclubonline.com/magazine/interviews/content/abenson.html* (viewed July 3, 2006).

"Interview with author Angela Benson," GRITS. *http://www.thegritsbookclub. com/Interviews/AngelaBenson.html* (viewed July 3, 2006).

Roberts, Lee B., "Learn to Write by Writing," *The Writer* (Feb. 2001).

Eleanor Taylor Bland

Mystery

Benchmark Title: *Dead Time*

Boston, Massachusetts

1944

About the Author and the Author's Writing

Eleanor Taylor Bland sees the role she and other African American writers of mystery fiction play as going beyond just the introduction of ethnic faces to an established genre: "The most significant contribution we have made, collectively, to mystery fiction is the development of the extended family; the permanence of spouses and significant others, most of whom don't die in the first three chapters or by the end of the novel; children who are complex, wanted, and loved; and even pets," she said in a *Publishers Weekly* review of her anthology, *Shades of Black*.

Bland is best known for the dozen books in her popular Marti MacAlister crime series, which began with *Dead Time* in 1992. The main character, a detective in Lincoln Prairie, Illinois, investigates the murder of Lauretta Dorsey, a schizophrenic who has fled her wealthy family to live in a flophouse. Marti, who has left Chicago with her son Theo to try to get over her husband's recent death, tackles both the complex case and the uncertainties of a new male partner, "Vik" Jessonovik.

"I wanted a strong, Black woman who plays it by the book with integrity, morals and values," the author said to journalist Paula L. Woods. "A woman who raised a family, did a job, was tough, compassionate, and caring. A woman in a 'man's' job who remains a woman, and 'hangs out with the boys' without compromising who she is."

As the series progressed, Marti and Vik have come to an understanding—his issue is gender, not race—and at times tackle issues of discrimination together. Bland insists she will not kill off Marti's new husband, Ben. She said in a Mystery One interview she frequently discusses story ideas with fans. Such conversations led to a stronger role for the character Denise Stevens, a juvenile probation officer.

Bland was born in Boston, Massachusetts, in 1944. She married a sailor in 1958 and relocated to the Great Lakes area, where he was stationed. They raised two children and later divorced. She received a bachelor of arts degree in accounting and education from Southern Illinois University in 1981. She worked as an accountant for Abbot Laboratories from 1981 to 1999. She is a cancer survivor. In 1992, she began writing. She now lives in Waukegan, Illinois.

Bland examines a range of social issues in her novels, from homelessness and spousal abuse to mental illness and sexual predation. "You can do anything that interests you in the mystery," she said in an interview with Andrew S. Hughes. "You really get to say something. We also get to comment on a variety of slices of life within the black culture. There's a tremendous amount of diversity and this is the one genre where you can talk about it and have a little fun with it."

Further discussing ethnic fiction, Bland told reporter Rosalind Bently, "I truly believe minorities are underrepresented in most things and where we are [represented], we're some auxiliary to someone else. I want us to be center stage."

Works by the Author

Marti MacAlister Mystery Series

Dead Time (1992)
Slow Burn (1993)
Gone Quiet (1994)
Done Wrong (1995)
Keep Still (1996)
See No Evil (1998)
Tell No Tales (1999)
Scream in Silence (2000)
Whispers in the Dark (2001)
Windy City Dying (2002)
Fatal Remains (2003)
A Cold and Silent Dying (2004)
A Dark and Deadly Deception (2005)

Editor

Shades of Black: Crime and Mystery Stories by African American Authors (2004)

For Further Information

Bently, Rosalind, "Magical Mystery Tour; Black Writers Provide Clues to an Emerging Fiction Trend," *Star Tribune* (Minneapolis, Minn.) (July 21, 1992).

Dead Time review, *Publishers Weekly* (Feb. 3, 1992).

Eleanor Taylor Bland entry, *Contemporary Black Biography*, Vol. 39, Ashyla Henderson, ed. Detroit: Gale Group, 2003.

Eleanor Taylor Bland interview, Mystery One Bookstore. *http://www.mysteryone.com/EleanorTaylorBlandInterview.htm* (viewed July 3, 2006).

Eleanor Taylor Bland Web page, African American Literature Book Club. *http://authors.aalbc.com/eleanorbland.htm* (viewed July 3, 2006).

Eleanor Taylor Bland Web page, *Voices from the Gap*. *http://voices.cla.umn.edu/vg/Bios/entries/bland_eleanor_taylor.html* (viewed July 3, 2006).

Hughes, Andrew S., "Golden Age for Mysteries; African Americans Make Their Mark in Writing Whodunits," *South Bend* (Indiana) *Tribune* (Feb. 22, 1998).

Klett, Rex E., *Cold and Silent Dying* review, *Library Journal* (Dec. 1, 2004).

Shades of Black review, *Publishers Weekly* (Jan. 19, 2004).

Woods, Paula L., "Decoding the History of Black Mysteries," *New Crisis* (September/October 2001).

Arna Bontemps

Historical Literature, Poetry, Young Adult Literature

Benchmark Title: *Black Thunder*

Alexandria, Louisiana

1902–1973

About the Author and the Author's Writing

Arnaud "Arna" Wendell Bontemps was one of the shining lights of the Harlem Renaissance.

Born in 1902 in Alexandra, Louisiana, of Creole parents, he moved with his family to the Watts section of Los Angeles when he was three. When he refused to apprentice to his father's trade as a brick mason, he was sent to a white boarding school in Fernando. Bontemps eventually graduated from Pacific Union College in 1923 and within a year was actively marketing his poetry. *The Crisis,* edited by W. E. B. Du Bois, was an early and receptive market. It published his first verse, "Hope," in 1917.

Bontemps roved among literary genres. "The impact of his work as poet, novelist, historian, children's writer, editor, and librarian is far greater than the sum of its parts," observed Afropoets.net. "He played a major role in shaping modern African-American literature and had a wide-ranging influence on African American culture of the latter half of the twentieth century."

Bontemps married Alberta Johnson in 1926 and they raised six children. He taught at Harlem Academy in New York City for five years and entered the community's artistic network. His first book, *God Sends Sunday,* was about a St. Louis jockey named Little Augie whose luck turned bad, and he fell into a drifting life. The year it was published, 1931, Bontemps accepted a teaching assignment at Oakwood Junior College in Huntsville, Alabama. He later taught at Shiloh Academy in Chicago and worked for the WPA Writers Project in Illinois.

Eventually frustrated with his lack of a strong audience, he redirected himself toward younger readers and for four decades produced a steady stream of biographies, histories, and fiction for children. His *Story of the Negro* was designated a 1949 Newbery Honor Book. His novel *Black Thunder: Gabriel's Revolt* was about Gabriel Potter's real-life slave rebellion. The work, which was well received critically, is typical of Bontemps's freedom theme and brought him welcome in the black writing fraternity.

With his friends Langston Hughes and Jack Conroy, Bontemps collaborated on several literary anthologies. He completed requirements for a master's degree in library science from the University of Chicago's graduate school and became head librarian at Fisk University in Nashville, Tennessee, where he developed an African American archive. In 1966, he retired.

Bontemps died in 1973 of a heart attack. His birth home in Alexandria is the Arna Bontemps African American Museum and Cultural Arts Center today.

"Bontemps' most distinctive works are ringing affirmations of the human passion for freedom and the desire for social justice inherent in us all," observed critic Charles L. James.

Works by the Author

God Sends Sunday (1931)
Black Thunder (1936)
Drums at Dusk (1939)

Contributor

Grandma Moses' Story Book (1961)
Black Voices (2001), with James Baldwin, Gwendolyn Brooks, and W. E. B. Du Bois

Fiction for Young Adults

Popo and Fifinia: Children of Haiti (1932), with Langston Hughes
You Can't Pet a Possum (1934)
Sad Faced Boy (1937)
The Fast Sooner Hound (1942), with Jack Conroy
Slappy Hooper, the Wonderful Sign Painter (1946)
Sam Patch, the High, Wide and Handsome Jumper (1951)
Mr. Kelso's Lion (1970)
The Pasteboard Bandit (1997), with Langston Hughes
Bubber Goes to Heaven (1998), with James Haskins

Nonfiction for Young Adults

Chariot in the Sky: A Story of the Jubilee Singers (1951)
Famous Negro Athletes (1964)
Young Booker: Booker T. Washington's Early Days (1972)

Drama

St. Louis Woman (1946), with Countee Cullen, based on *God Sends Sunday*
Free and Easy (1949)
Creole
Careless Love

Poetry

Personals (1963)

Editor

Golden Slippers: An Anthology of Negro Poetry for Young Readers (1941)
The Poetry of the Negro: 1746–1949 (1949), revised as *The Poetry of the Negro: 1746–1970* (1970)
Anthology of Negro Poetry for Young People (1955), sound recording
American Negro Poetry (1963), revised (1973)
Hold Fast to Dreams: Poems Old and New (1969)

Nonfiction for Adults

We Have Tomorrow (1945)
They Seek a City, with Jack Conroy (1945), revised as *Anyplace but Here* (1966)
Story of the Negro (1948)
George Washington Carver (1950)
Frederick Douglass: Slave, Fighter, Freeman (1958)
One Hundred Years of Negro Freedom (1961)
I Too Sing America (1964), with Langston Hughes
Free at Last: The Life of Frederick Douglass (1971)
The Old South: "A Summer Tragedy" and Other Stories of the Thirties (1973)
Arna Bontemps–Langston Hughes Letters, 1925–1967 (1980), edited by Charles H. Nichols

Editor

Father of the Blues: An Autobiography, by W. C. Handy (1941)
The Book of Negro Folklore (1958), with Langston Hughes
American Negro Heritage (1965), coeditor
Great Slave Narratives (1969)
Five Black Lives: The Autobiographies of Venture Smith, James Mars, William Grimes, G.W. Offley, and James L. Smith (1971), coeditor
The Harlem Renaissance Remembered: Essays Edited with a Commentary by Arna Bontemps (1972)

For Further Information

Arna Bontemps African American Museum Web site. *http://www. arnabontempsmuseum.com/* (viewed July 3, 2006).

Arna Bontemps entry, *The Essential Black Literature Guide,* Roger M. Volade III, ed. Detroit: Visible Ink, 1996.

Arna Bontemps Web page, AfroPoets.Net. *http://www.afropoets.net/ arnabontemps.html* (viewed July 3, 2006).

Arna Bontemps Web page, AmericanPoems.com. *http://www.americanpoems. com/poets/bontemps/* (viewed July 3, 2006).

Arna Wendell Bontemps (1902–73), Teacher Resource File. *http://falcon. jmu.edu/~ramseyil/bontemps.htm* (viewed July 3, 2006).

Arnaud (Wendell) Bontemps entry, Contemporary Authors Online, Gale, 2005. Reproduced in Biography Resource Center. Farmington Hills, MI: Thomson Gale, 2005. *http:/galenet.galegroup.com/servlet/BioRC* (viewed Feb. 27, 2005).

James, Charles L., Arna Bontemps entry, *Oxford Companion to African American Literature,* William L. Andrews, Frances Smith Foster, and Trudier Harris, eds. New York: Oxford University Press, 1997.

Michele Andrea Bowen

Inspirational Literature

Benchmark Title: *Church Folk*

St. Louis, Missouri

Date of birth not revealed

Photo credit: Valerie Ann Kaalund

About the Author and the Author's Writing

Michele Andrea Bowen brings humor and an anecdotal touch to her novels of rural Southern life.

Born in St. Louis, Missouri, and now a resident of Durham, North Carolina, the author graduated from University of North Carolina at Chapel Hill with master's degrees in history and public health.

She long yearned to write. "Her subject is near and dear to her heart," explained Hickory Public Library, "as she is the niece of an Apostolic Bishop and the granddaughter of an evangelist. She chose to write about the church because it has been a vital part of her life since she was a child."

While her fictional characters are parish faithful, they have their share of issues to deal with. The honeymoon is over quickly for newlyweds Essie Lee and Theophilus Henry Simmons, the main characters in *Church Folk,* for example. He is pastor of Greater Hope Gospel United Church in Charleston, Mississippi. She is a short-order cook and not your everyday minister's wife. Both get a quick lesson from the congregation on proper behavior. Although her work is rooted in experience, the author does embellish. Don't take it all as gospel—Bowen is, after all, a storyteller—as things become uneasy behind the pulpit. There are, as a *Bookreporter* reviewer described them, some "rather steamy love scenes," tempered with matters of tribulation. An old flame, Glodean Benson, is thoroughly irked at Theophilus' marriage. Parish women seem to have it in for Essie. And church leadership is apparently fronting a call-girl service.

But Bowen's message is a powerful one. "*Church Folk* affirms that love, passion, and desire, when properly focused, are acceptable feelings/behaviors for God's people and are part of His blessings to His people," according to a reviewer for *A Place of Our Own*.

In Bowen's next novel, *Second Sunday*, a prominent member of Gethsemane Missionary Baptist Church in North St. Louis is plotting to put one of his minions in the pulpit and Nettie, Sylvia, Louisie and other women of the church take counter measures, in the form of street-savvy Sheba Cochran. A reviewer for *Romance in Color* noted the novel's "wealth of rich characters," including "the conniving, wicked and underhanded ways of Cleavon Johnson."

Works by the Author

Church Folk (2001)
Second Sunday (2003)
Holy Ghost Corner (2006)

Contributor

Gumbo: A Literary Rent Party to Benefit the Hurston/Wright Foundation (2002), edited by Marita Golden and E. Lynn Harris

For Further Information

Church Folk review, *A Place of Our Own*. *http://apooo.org/Library/dynamic/ DiscussionGuides/discussionGuide.cfm?Dis_Guide_ID=29&Title=Church% 20Folk* (viewed Feb. 28, 2005).

Dawson, Alma, and Connie Van Fleet, eds. *African American Literature: A Guide to Reading Interests*. Westport, CT: Libraries Unlimited, 2004.

Michele Andrea Bowen biography, Hickory Public Library. *http://www. hickorygov.com/library/press/2004/1015bowen.htm* (viewed March 12, 2005).

Second Sunday review, *Romance in Color*. *http://www.romancincolor.com/ REVIEW_Second_Sunday_Bowen_TB_.htm* (viewed Feb. 14, 2005).

Second Sunday review, Romantic Times Book Club. *http://www.romantictimes. com/bookpage.php?bookid=20193* (Viewed Feb. 28, 2005).

Siciliano, Jana, *Church Folk* review, *Bookreporter*. *http://www.bookreporter. com/reviews/0446527998.asp* (viewed March 12, 2005).

Dionne Brand

Mainstream Contemporary Literature, Poetry

Benchmark Title: *Land to Light On*

Guayaguayare, Trinidad

1953

Photo credit: Stephanie Martin

About the Author and the Author's Writing

There's something about being a Dionne and Canadian. From the Dionne Quintuplets to hockey Hall of Famer Marcel Dionne to Olympic freestyle ski medalist Deidra Dionne, the name is seemingly magical. (And we're not even considering the shorter spelling of Céline Dion.)

That's an untraditional introduction to an untraditional wordsmith named, obviously, Dionne—Dionne Brand. She was born in Guayaguayare, Trinidad, in 1953. After graduating from Naparima Girls' High School in 1970, she moved to Canada where she earned a bachelor of arts degree in English and philosophy from the University of Toronto in 1975 and a master's in philosophy of education from the same school in 1989. Then she began work on a doctorate in women's history.

But another interest intruded—writing. Her essays for several journals caught immediate attention. Her first book of fiction, *Sans Souci and Other Stories,* depicts the lives of Caribbean women who have left their native countries to live in Canada. "I count myself in the tradition of writers who take up the hard questions," she told Athabasca University's Canadian Writers Web site, "who want to see equality in the world and who will push their ideas and their language and their minds to embrace it." She dealt with many of her major themes in *Bread Out of Stone*, which collects her writings on race, gender, and politics in Canada today.

This 1997 Governor General's Literary Award recipient has taught English literature and creative writing at Guelph, York, and Toronto Universities. She has been writer-in-residence at the University of Toronto and at Halifax City Regional Library.

She has taught poetry writing at West Coast Women and Words Summer School in Vancouver, British Columbia, and at Humber School of Writing in Toronto.

All the while, she has produced a steady stream of poetry, prose, and nonfiction, works that often express her strong political views. She has been a member of the Communist Party of Canada and has worked as an activist in black, feminist, labor, and other causes. Themes in her verse range from colonialism to the Caribbean diaspora to lesbianism to multicultural identity.

But what shines in her work, critics have noted, is her deftness in the use of detail to bring alive small bits of history, to enliven and make all the more real broad themes of history.

"In the Sixties when I was in elementary and high schools, none of the books we studied were about Black people's lives; they were about Europeans, mostly the British," Brand told the Northwest Passages Canadian Literature Online Web site. "But I felt that Black people's experiences were as important and as valuable and needed to be written down and read about. That is why I became a writer."

Her radicalism, the author said in a Ciber Kiosk interview, came from the Black Power and other movements in Canada and the United States in the 1970s. "It was an important historical moment, teeming with philosophy and poetry. I was lucky enough to be there. I felt that those ideas and that political engagement would also free me from the bonds to the ideology that racism contains."

History is an important element of cultural identity and Brand in *At the Full and Change of the Moon* takes a multigenerational look at the impact of slavery. The story begins in the nineteenth century with Marie Ursule, a Trinidadan estate slave who persuades others to participate in a group suicide. Her daughter Bola survives, however, although all is not destined to have a happy ending. "The narrative gains momentum as Brand moves to the present-day lives of Bola's grandchildren." In the opinion of reviewer Maureen Garvie, Brand's work is "textured with vivid interior reportage. The characters become solid and take up residence in us."

The author, who lives north of Toronto, recently wrote a contemporary novel, *What We All Long For,* which is also grounded in the past but extends beyond the African American experience. The main characters are Vietnamese who fled that country to Canada in the 1970s. Quy, separated from his family, does not reach Toronto until twenty years later, by now a criminal looking to find at last his lost family. Reviewers commented on the insightful portrayal of young characters, of the well-captured rhythms of the streets, of rage and sweetness and gritty reality. It is a paean to urban life: "She loved the city," we read of the main character. "She loved riding through the neck of it.. . . . She loved the feeling of weight and balance it gave her."

Works by the Author

Sans Souci and Other Stories (1988)
Another Place, Not Here (1996)
At the Full and Change of the Moon (1999)
What We All Long For (2005)

Poetry

'Fore Day Morning: Poems (1978)

Earth Magic (1979)

Primitive Offensive (1982)

Winter Epigrams and Epigrams to Ernesto Cardenal in Defense of Claudia (1983)

Chronicles of the Hostile Sun (1984)

No Language Is Neutral (1990)

Land to Light On (1997)

Thirsty (2002)

Nonfiction

Rivers Have Sources, Trees Have Roots: Speaking of Racism (1986)

A Conceptual Analysis of How Gender Roles Are Racially Constructed: Black Women (1988)

Sight Specific: Lesbians & Representation (1988)

No Burden to Carry: Narratives of Black Working Women in Ontario 1920s–1930s (1991), with Lois De Shield

Bread Out of Stone: Recollections Sex, Recognitions Race, Dreaming Politics (1994)

A Map to the Door of No Return: Notes to Belonging (2001)

Contributor

Other Voices, Other Places: An Anthology of Third World Poetry (1972), edited by Cecil Rajendre

Anthology of Canadian Literature (1973), edited by Robert Leigh

Penguin Book of Caribbean Verse in English (1986)

Finding Courage: Writings by Women (1989) edited by Irene Zahava

Poetry by Canadian Women (1989) edited by Rosemary Sullivan

Her True-True Name: An Anthology of Women's Writing from the Caribbean (1990), edited by Pamela Mordecai and Betty Wilson

Other Solitudes: Canadian Multicultural Fiction and Interviews (1991), edited by Linda Hutcheon

From Ink Lake: Canadian Stories Selected (1992), edited by Michael Ondaatje

Twist and Shout: A Decade of Feminist Writing in This Magazine (1992), edited by Susan Crean

Grammar of Dissent: Poetry and Prose by Claire Harris, M. Nourbese Philip and Dionne Brand (1994), edited by Carol Morrell

Eyeing the North Star: Directions in African-Canadian Literature (1997), edited by George Eliot Clarke

Oxford Book of Stories by Canadian Women (1999), edited by Rosemary Sullivan

No Pain Like This Body (2003), by Harold Sonny Ladoo

Film

Older, Stronger, Wiser (1989), associate director and writer
Long Time Comin' (1991), director
Sisters in the Struggle (1991), codirector
Listening for Something—Adrienne Rich and Dionne Brand in Conversation (1996), director

For Further Information

Dion Brand biography, Canadian Writers. *http://www.athabascau.ca/writers/dionnebrand.htm* (viewed July 18, 2006).

Dionne Brand biography, Canadian Poets. *http://www.library.utoronto.ca/canpoetry/brand/bio.html* (viewed July 18, 2006).

Dionne Brand biography, Random House of Canada. *http://www.randomhouse.ca/catalog/author.pperl?authorid=3068* (viewed July 18, 2006).

Dionne Brand biography, *Voices from the Gaps. http://voices.cla.umn.edu/vg/Bios/entries/brand_dionne.html* (viewed March 12, 2005).

Dionne Brand biography, Women Make Movies. *http://www.wmm.com/filmCatalog/makers/fm25.shtml* (viewed July 18, 2006).

Dionne Brand entry, Canadian Encyclopedia. *http://www.thecanadianencyclopedia.com/index.cfm?PgNm=TCE&Params=A1ARTA0010878* (viewed July 18, 2006).

Garvie, Maureen, *At the Full and Change of the Moon* review, *Quill & Quire* (April 1999).

"Interview with Dionne Brand," Ciber Kiosk. *http://www.ciberkiosk.pt/entrevista/brand.html* (viewed March 12, 2005).

Lasotta, Carmen, Dionne Brand biography, *Northwest Passages: Canadian Literature Online. http://www.nwpassages.com/bios/brand.asp* (viewed March 12, 2005).

Mavjee, Maya, "Opening the Door: An Interview with Dionne Brand," *Read* magazine. *http://www.randomhouse.ca/readmag/page28.htm* (viewed March 12, 2005).

"1997 Governor General's Literary Award Winner: Dionne Brand," Library and Archives Canada. *http://www.collectionscanada.ca/3/8/t8-5002-e.html* (viewed March 12, 2005).

Connie Briscoe

Romance, Historical Literature

Benchmark Title: *Sisters and Lovers*

Washington, D.C.

1952

Photo credit: Welton Doby

About the Author and the Author's Writing

Connie Briscoe looks back fondly on her childhood. "I was blessed with a wonderful upbringing," she said on her Web site, "sort of like that portrayed on the Bill Cosby show. Although my family is smaller and we were not as well-to-do as the Cosby family, we are very close and supportive of each other."

Of course, popular fiction is not driven by happy times, but by conflict and tensions. So when she crafted her first novel, *Sisters and Lovers,* she depicted three sisters personally stretched to their limits. Beverly, Charmaine, and Evelyn share ancestry and location (all live in Washington, D.C.) but otherwise have taken different career and family paths. Editor Beverly is successful with books but not with finding a faithful partner. Therapist Evelyn has a husband and two children and a suburban world teetering on the edge of debt. And secretary Charmaine is afraid that her husband's plans to establish his own law practice will bring failure. Where the three women find strength is with each other in a novel hailed for its fresh voice. "The message sent is affirming, the characters believable, the style upbeat and lively," said *Library Journal* reviewer Nancy Pearl. Eventually the novel became the basis for a television miniseries.

Born in 1952 in Washington, D.C., Briscoe attended Hampton University, where she received a bachelor of science degree in 1974, and American University, for an MPA in 1978. She has worked as a financial analyst for Analytic Services, an associate editor for Joint Center for Political and Economic Studies, and managing editor (1990–94) for *American Annals of the Deaf* at Gallaudet University. Briscoe has experienced increased hearing loss—something she inherited from her father's side of the family—but reads lips and American Sign Language. She and her second husband live in Maryland.

Briscoe—who became a full-time writer with the 100,000-hardcover-sales success of that first novel—followed up with another contemporary story, *Big Sisters Don't Cry.* For her third work, *A Long Way from Home,* she did considerable research for a multigenerational story based on her own family. Susie, her daughter Clara, and Clara's daughter Susan are house slaves for the Virginia Madisons. They live a life of comfort compared with the ill conditions of the field hands. Susie is content. Clara yearns for the North. Death and breakup of the plantation household forces Susan into an entirely new experience. The novel was nominee for a NAACP Image Award in 2000.

Briscoe explained that her forebears were offspring of a black slave and a white master and worked in the house, not the fields. "They are not the typical stories about slaves most people see," she said in an interview with Sarah Skidmore. "People have certain images of slavery they want you to remember and think is true."

Briscoe returned to a modern setting, and an opportunity for lighter fare, in a complex relationship novel set in Prince George County. The novel among other things looks at interracial dating and racially mixed ancestries. "Most African Americans have non-black ancestors in their family line and we grow up knowing it," the author told Robin Green-Cary. "So it's not a huge shock to us to learn that our great-great granddaddy was a white slave owner. I can remember when my mother told me. It can be disappointing, perhaps, but it doesn't change who we are or how we're labeled or seen in America."

The book also looks at middle class social pressures on women. "How many men do you know who won't step outside without putting their makeup on?" she asked in a Black Ink Online interview. "Unfortunately, many women are like that. I was at one time, too, so I can understand someone like Jolene [another character in *P. G. County*]. But I grew out of it."

Although the author finds it easiest to write about the modern day, she admitted to reporter Skidmore that her family was delighted with her telling of her mother's side of the family in *A Long Way from Home* and is now anxious for her to give the same treatment to her father's ancestors.

◣ Works by the Author

Sisters and Lovers (1994)
Big Girls Don't Cry (1996)
A Long Way from Home (1999)
P. G. County (2002)
Can't Get Enough (2004)

Contributor

Gumbo: A Literary Rent Party to Benefit the Hurston/Wright Foundation (2002), edited by Marita Golden and E. Lynn Harris

Television Miniseries Based on the Author's Work

Three Lives (1994, CBS), based on *Sisters and Lovers*

For Further Information

Connie Briscoe entry, Contemporary Authors Online. Gale, 2005. Reproduced in Biography Resource Center, Farmington Hills, MI: Thomson Gale, 2005. *http://galenet.galegroup.com/servlet/BioRC*.

Connie Briscoe interview, *Black Ink Online*. *http://www.randomhouse. com/broadway/blackink/qa_connie.html* (viewed March 12, 2005).

Connie Briscoe interview, *World around You*. http://clerccenter.gallaudet.edu/ WorldAroundYou/mar-apr97/connie.html (viewed March 12, 2005).

Connie Briscoe Web page, African American Literature Book Club. *http:// authors.aalbc.com/connie.htm* (viewed Feb. 17, 2005).

Connie Briscoe Web site, *http://www.conniebriscoe.com*.

Dawson, Alma, and Connie Van Fleet, editors. *African American Literature: A Guide to Reading Interests.* Westport, CT: Libraries Unlimited, 2004.

"Deaf Novelist Pens Hit Book on Black Women and Dating Titled 'Sisters & Lovers,' " *Jet* (Sept. 5, 1994).

Green-Cary, Robin, Connie Briscoe interview, *Black Issues Book Review* (Sept.–Oct. 2002).

Pearl, Nancy, "Waiting for Terry: African American Novels," *Library Journal* (Jan. 1, 2001).

Skidmore, Sarah, "Writer Polishes a Family Heirloom as She Brings Slave Ancestors to Life," *Seattle Post-Intelligencer* (July 14, 1999).

Anita Richmond Bunkley

Romance, Historical Literature

Benchmark Title: *Black Gold*

Columbus, Ohio

Date of birth not revealed

Photo credit: Barfield Studios

About the Author and the Author's Writing

Anita Richmond Bunkley is one busy woman. She's an inventor, motivational speaker, writing coach, and writer of historical fiction.

The Columbus, Ohio, native holds patents on two inventions: the "Bathroom Valet," a utilitarian accessory for the guest bathroom that dispenses paper hand towels, and "Read-Up," a flexible device that holds a book in position while the reader is in a chair, car, or bed.

Bunkley also mentors aspiring writers—of fiction or nonfiction—and offers personal manuscript evaluation and editing services through her Web site.

She presents programs on shaping attitude, organizing, prioritizing and energizing. Her nonfiction book *Steppin' Out with Attitude: Sister Sell Your Dream* tells Bunkley's own story and gives tips toward personal success.

Bunkley, who earned a bachelor of arts degree from Mount Union College in Ohio, is recipient of the United Negro College Fund's Excellence in Achievement Award.

But Bunkley is perhaps best known nationally for her richly textured historical novels. Her other activities show Bunkley is an energetic self-starter, and that's how she entered the fiction field. She self-published her first book, *Emily, the Yellow Rose,* based on the words to the traditional folk song "The Yellow Rose of Texas." Taking place in the mid-1830s, during the turmoil of the Texas revolution, Bunkley's book follows the mulatto serving girl Emily D. West and her mysterious lover.

Thirty-two publishers rejected *Emily* before Bunkley paid to print it herself. Once it was out, the book caught the attention of the publisher Dutton, which contracted for her next two novels (and two more after that, until the author switched to Kensington). *Publishers Weekly* singled out *Wild Embers* as one of the ten best romances of 1995.

As part of her research for her ambitious historical books, Bunkley reads widely in Texas history and in biography. Among fiction writers she reads regularly are Walter Mosely, Valerie Wilson Wesley, and Tananarive Due.

"I have always loved to read books by and about women," the author told Paula L. Woods for *Essence*, "but in the 1980s I was appalled at the lack of popular fiction about Black women and strong male characters. I remember thinking at one point, if I can't find the kind of books I want to read, then maybe I'll have to write them myself."

So she did. She wrote the draft of her first novel while juggling responsibilities of teaching language in middle school and, with her husband, raising two daughters. She is an early-morning writer and typically sticks to her word processor for six hours a day when under deadline.

Her writing caroms her from present to past to present again. In *Starlight Passage,* for example, the heroine Kiana Sheridan, who is researching her family tree as part of a doctoral dissertation, realizes the great family legacy in her great-great-grandfather's gift as an artisan in decorative glass on a Tennessee plantation. Thus, she and the reader are transported to another time.

Bunkley also writes contemporary novels, such as *Balancing Act,* which is about a corporate spokeswoman. Elise Jeffries never anticipated she would one day be squarely between her company and the national media when there's a chemical plant explosion in a small town in Texas.

The author resents those who take romance writers for granted. "When critics argued how boring the 'predictable' happy ending was I always countered that mystery readers knew that there would be a death at the beginning of the story and the murderer would be discovered at the end. No one complained about their literary quality," Bunkley said on the *Voices from the Gaps* Web page. Within the conventions of romances and historicals, Bunkley feels quite comfortable pushing at the boundaries—as her fans know.

Works by the Author

Emily, the Yellow Rose (1989)
Black Gold (1994)
Wild Embers (1995)
Starlight Passage (1996)
Balancing Act (1997)
Mirrored Life (2002)
Relative Interest (2003)

Anthologies

Sisters (1996), with Sandra Kitt and Eva Rutland
Girlfriends (1999), with Sandra Kitt and Eva Rutland

Nonfiction

Steppin' Out with Attitude: Sister Sell Your Dream (1998)

For Further Information

Anita Bunkley Web page, African American Literature Book Club. *http://authors.aalbc.com/anita.htm* (viewed March 12, 2005).

Anita Bunkley Web site. *http://www.anitabunkley.com/page/page/178942.htm* (viewed July 3, 2006).

Anita Richmond Bunkley profile, Voices from the Gaps. *http://voices.cla.umn.edu/vg/Bios/entries/bunkley_anita_richmond.html* (viewed July 3, 2006).

Woods, Paula L., "Isn't It Romantic? Romance Novels These Days Are Sensitive, Affirming and Hotter than July," *Essence* (July 1997)

Octavia E. Butler

Science Fiction

Benchmark Title: *Kindred*

Pasadena, California

1947–2006

About the Author and the Author's Writing

Octavia E. Butler began writing science fiction at age twelve, after seeing the motion picture *Devil Girl from Mars*. She declared she could write something better.

Since publication of her first story, "Crossover," in the 1971 Clarion anthology, Butler proved herself to be a powerful, if not prolific, writer of science fiction. As with many of her later works, "Crossover" deftly quilts African American history and futuristic social themes.

Hugo- and Nebula-award-winning Octavia Estelle Butler was born in Pasadena, California, in 1947. Her father died when she was a baby, and her mother went to work as a domestic. As a girl, she heard family stories from her mother and grandmother.

In 1968, she received an associate's degree from Pasadena City College. She subsequently attended California State University and the University of California in Los Angeles as part of the Screen Writers' Guild Open Door Program, where one of her instructors was science fiction writer Harlan Ellison. She also attended the Clarion Science Fiction Writers Workshop.

The author was drawn to science fiction, she said, because it allowed her the most creative freedom.

Butler's first novel, *Patternmaster,* began a five-book series about elite telepaths ruled by a four-thousand-year-old immortal African named Doro, who seeks to establish a super race.

"The series' strength," in the view of critic John Clute in *The Encyclopedia of Science Fiction,* "is in the author's capacity to inhabit her venues with characters whose often anguished lives strike the reader as anything but frivolous."

Another novel, *Kindred,* is about a black woman who time travels to a Southern slave plantation where she ends up rescuing her white, slave-owning ancestor. She must grapple with torn emotions as she owes her being to a man who was an oppressor of her race.

This story creates "a dialectic between two specific historical moments in American history: the period of chattel slavery and the richly symbolic bicentennial year of 1976" explains Angelyn Mitchell in a critical piece in the periodical *Melus.*

Butler is known for her richly depicted, strong female characters and her tight but swift prose style. According to critic Rosemary Stevenson, her "work is both fascinating and highly unusual; character development, human relationships, and social concerns predominate over intergalactic hardware."

"Her stories do not insist upon particular solutions," observed John Pfeiffer in *Twentieth-Century Science Fiction Writers*. "They do encourage hope that some kind of enlightened species, related to humanity, can survive."

Butler's Xenogenesis stories focus on the Oankali, a genetically impoverished alien race that wants to interbreed with humans to survive in the postnuclear era. Selected humans, who have pretty much destroyed Earth, are held in suspended animation. The Oankali abhor human class divisions and conflict, and hope to breed those qualities out of their future offspring. The heroine, Lilith, is chosen to be the first human to start this new race.

The Parable books are a psychological exploration of people in a world now gone mad. Butler uses her prose to look at the use and abuse of power and the appropriateness of religion in political power.

"As one of the few African-American writers in the science-fiction field, and the only black woman, Butler's racial and sexual perspective is unique," *Contemporary Authors* noted.

Butler has wrote short stories for Isaac Asimov's *Science Fiction* magazine, *Omni* and *Future Life*. Her "Bloodchild" novella won both the Hugo and Nebula awards. It is about men who bear children of an alien race—putting a twist on issues of power and gender. In 1995, Butler received a MacArthur Foundation five-year, $295,000 "genius grant" fellowship for her unusual synthesis of science fiction with mysticism, mythology and African-American spiritualism. But Butler remained modest in the wake of her achievements.

"I'm not writing for some noble purpose, I just like telling a good story," she told Robert McTyre of *Michigan Chronicle*. "If what I write about helps others understand this world we live in, so much the better for all of us." Butler died in 2006 at age fifty-eight in her home near Seattle, where she had lived since 1999.

Works by the Author

Fiction

Kindred (1979)
Fledgling (2005)

Parable Books

Parable of the Sower (1994)
Parable of the Talents (1998)

Patternist Series

Patternmaster (1976)
Mind of My Mind (1977)
Survivor (1978)
Wild Seed (1980)
Clay's Ark (1984)

Seed to Harvest (2007), contains *Pattermaster, Mind of My Mind, Wild Seed*, and *Clay's Ark*

Xenogenesis Trilogy

Dawn (1987)
Adulthood Rites (1988)
Imago (1989)

Short Stories

Bloodchild and Other Stories (1995)

Anthologies

Dark Matter: A Century of Speculative Fiction from the African Diaspora (2000), edited by Sheree R. Thomas

For Further Information

Clute, John, Octavia E(stelle) Butler entry, *The Encyclopedia of Science Fiction*, Clute and Peter Nicholls, eds. New York: St. Martin's Press, 1993.

"Four Blacks among 24 MacArthur Foundation Fellowship winners," *Jet* (July 3, 1995).

Jones, Daniel, and John D. Jorgenson, eds., Octavia E(stelle) Butler entry, *Contemporary Authors New Revision Series*, Vol. 73. Detroit: Gale Research, 1999.

McTyre, Robert E., "Octavia Butler: Black America's First Lady of Science Fiction," *Michigan Chronicle* (April 26, 1994).

Mitchell, Angelyn, "Not Enough of the Past: Feminist Revisions of Slavery in Octavia E. Butler's Kindred," *Melus* (fall 2001).

Octavia Butler biography, *Voices from the Gaps. http://voices.cla.umn.edu/vg/Bios/entries/butler_octavia_estelle.html* (viewed July 3, 2006).

Octavia Butler biography. *http://www.math.buffalo.edu/~sww/butler_octavia_bio.html* (viewed April 7, 2003).

Octavia Butler interview, National Public Radio (Sept. 1, 2001). *http:www.npr.org/programs/specials/racism/010830.octaviabutler.html* (viewed July 3, 2006).

"Octavia E. Butler: Persistence," *Locus Magazine* (June 2000).

Pfeiffer, John, Octavia Butler entry, *Twentieth-Century Science-Fiction Writers,* 3rd ed., Noelle Watson and Paul E. Schellinger, eds. Chicago: St. James Press, 1991.

Stevenson, Rosemary. *Black Women in America: An Historical Encyclopedia.* Brooklyn, NY: Carlson, 1993.

Xenogenesis and other reviews, *Ravens Reviews. http://tatooine.fortunecity.com/leguin/405/ko/octaviab.html* (viewed July 6, 2006).

Yaszek, Lisa," 'A Grim Fantasy': Remaking American History in Octavia Butler's *Kindred*," *Signs* (summer 2003).

Bebe Moore Campbell

Women's Literature, Mainstream Contemporary Literature, Memoir

Benchmark Title: *Brothers and Sisters*

Philadelphia, Pennsylvania

1950

About the Author and the Author's Writing

A leading African American voice in the blossoming genre of women's fiction, Bebe Campbell Moore wrote a well-received memoir, *Sweet Summer: Growing Up with and without My Dad,* before penning four *New York Times* best-seller list novels. Among the best sellers was *Your Blues Ain't Like Mine,* which garnered the author a NAACP Image Award for outstanding literary work (fiction).

Bebe Moore was born in Philadelphia in 1950. By the time she reached school age, she was spending nine months of the year in a multiethnic neighborhood in Philadelphia with her mother and maternal grandmother and summers in North Carolina with her father and paternal grandmother—the split home she wrote of in *Sweet Summer.* She credits both parents with helping shape her writing career. Her mother set aside Sundays for church and for going to the library. George Moore, who had been left a paraplegic following a car accident, listened attentively to the stories his daughter wrote to entertain him and draw his reaction. (The experience of living in two places also provided the author with differing views of subtle inequities and racism in the two sections of the country.)

After earning a bachelor of science degree (summa cum laude) in elementary education from the University of Pittsburgh, Moore taught for five years. Her marriage to Tiko F. Campbell ended in divorce. She and her second husband, Ellis Gordon Jr., live in Los Angeles. She has two children.

The author gave up teaching to become a writer. After taking a class with author Toni Cade Bambara, she began freelance writing for the *New York Times, Washington Post, Ebony, Essence,* and other publications. She eventually became a commentator on National Public Radio's *Morning Edition.*

Her first book, *Successful Women, Angry Men,* examines marital relationships as women rise higher on the success ladder than their husbands. She followed that with *Sweet Summer: Growing Up with and without My Dad*, a remembrance of coming to grips with being a child of divorce. Her novel *Your Blues Ain't Like Mine* looks at the impact on families, black and white, of a racially motivated killing in the 1950s.

On her Web page the author said ideas usually take time to gestate in her mind; in the case of *Your Blues Ain't Like Mine,* the gestation lasted for three years. It drew inspiration from the 1955 murder of Chicago teen Emmett Till, slain because he spoke to a white woman.

"When an idea for a book hits me I sit on it for a while to see if it will go away," she said. "If it doesn't, I begin to play with it in my mind. I shuffle beginnings, endings and the so-elusive middle. Characters begin to emerge, usually the main ones. That's all I need to begin. After some time it will take on a life of its own."

Brothers and Sisters uses the backdrop of unrest and rioting in Los Angeles in 1992 after the Rodney King verdict to explore the friendship between two women—one black, the other white—as they each face sexual discrimination, failed relationships, and "glass ceilings."

"As in *Blues*, Campbell demonstrates [in *Brothers and Sisters*] an uncanny ability to write from many different perspectives, black and white, male and female," observed the Voices from the Gaps Web site.

In a *Washington Post*–sponsored Internet chat, Campbell said she hoped the book would stir dialogue about race, class, and other issues. "I certainly hoped people would think about the issue of race and I wanted people to realize that subtle discrimination—a la the waitress who pays no attention to the diner of color—is as emotionally and psychologically damaging as being restricted to the back of the bus."

The book features a range of characters, and Campbell has commented that her years as a journalist writing for *Essence* particularly exposed her to the many facets of human personalities.

Singing in the Comeback Choir is about a television producer seeking to boost the spirits of her now-past-prime jazz-singer grandmother, the grandmother who raised her but has now suffered a stroke. It is a book about second chances.

Singing, and particularly the loss of one's voice, is a natural background for the novel as Campbell grew up in a household of women who sang a lot and she belonged to a youth choir in the Baptist Church.

It further examines the importance of roots, particularly to that segment of the population that has had to take a backseat to the rest, including African Americans, Asians, Native Americans, and Hispanics. To go beyond the success level of the community in which they live, in other words, people often must move to another community.

"I think that a lot of people who have achieved success have to struggle with the duality and don't give up the good part of the community that has molded us," she said in a *Bookreporter* interview. "But I do think that it is a struggle to remember where you came from and see where you are going."

Three other books withered in the trying before the author completed *What You Owe Me,* which looks at the unraveling of a business partnership between Hosanna Clark, now a maid after working in the Texas farm fields, and Gilda Rosenstein, a Holocaust survivor who is working at the same hotel. The book is an examination of betrayal and of healing.

72 Hour Hold takes a look at mental health in the African American community. The heroine, divorcee Keri, grew up with an alcoholic mother, lost a son at an early age, and struggles with her teenage daughter's bipolar disorder. The author told Amy Alexander of *Black Issues Book Review* that readers "should realize that there are at least two victims involved—the person who has it and their loved ones. What I've learned is that there is an enormous emotional toll on the caregiver." The novelist tackles not only personal issues relating to mental health, but social ones as well, delving into the history of a knotty relationship between black Americans and the health care establishment.

As a child, the author read the works of the Brönte sisters, Mark Twain and Charles Dickens. Toni Morrison influenced her as a young adult. Then and now, she reads classics and fairy tales, the latter for their liveliness and moral instruction.

Campbell obviously delights in black culture. On her Web page, she answered her own question: What is your idea of the ultimate dinner party? Her response was that it would be one with guests Harriet Tubman, emancipator of slaves; Mary McLeod Bethune, founder of a college for African Americans; C. J. Walker, beauty industry entrepreneur; Billie Holiday, jazz singer; and Katherine Dunham, a dancer who espoused African and Caribbean movement.

Works by the Author

Fiction

Your Blues Ain't Like Mine (1992)
Brothers and Sisters (1994)
Singing in the Comeback Choir (1998)
What You Owe Me (2001)
72 Hour Hold (2005)

Radio Plays

Old Lady Shoes
Sugar on the Floor

Children's Books

Sometimes My Mommy Gets Angry (2003)

Nonfiction

Successful Women, Angry Men (1986)
Backlash Marriage: The Two Career Family under Siege (1987)
Sweet Summer: Growing Up with and without My Dad (1989)

For Further Information

Alexander, Amy, "Troubled Minds," *Black Issues Book Review* (Sept.–Oct. 2005).

"Author Bebe Moore Campbell Says Publishers Now Recognize the Importance of Black Authors, Readers," *Jet* (March 30, 1998).

Bebe Moore Campbell biography, *Voices from the Gaps. http://voices.cla. umn.edu/vg/Bios/entries/campbell_bebe_moore.html* (viewed July 12, 2006).

Bebe Moore Campbell entry, *Contemporary Authors, New Revision Series*, Vol. 81, Peacock, Scot, ed. Detroit: Gale Research, 1999.

Bebe Moore Campbell interview, *Bookreporter* (April 14, 1998). *http://www.bookreporter.com/authors/au-campbell-bebe-moore.asp* (viewed July 12, 2006).

Bebe Moore Campbell Web site. *http://www.bebemoorecampbell.com/* (viewed July 12, 2006).

Benton, Jacquelyn, Bebe Moore Campbell entry, *American Ethnic Writers*, Vol. 1, David Peck, ed. Pasadena, CA: Salem Press, 2000.

Brown, DeNeen L., "Transcript of Bebe Moore Campbell's live chat," *Washington Post* (Nov. 25, 1997). *http://www.washingtonpost.com/wp-srv/zforum/97/campbell.htm* (viewed July 12, 2006).

See, Lisa, "Bebe Moore Campbell: Her Memoir of 'A Special Childhood' Celebrates the Different Styles of Her Upbringing in a Divided Black Family," *Publishers Weekly* (June 30, 1989).

What You Owe Me review, *Publishers Weekly* (July 9, 2001).

Charlotte Carter

Mystery

Benchmark Title: *Coq au Vin*

Chicago

1943

About the Author and the Author's Writing

Charlotte Carter's background as a wordsmith—she works as a freelance editor and proofreader—prepared her well for a career as a writer. Born in 1943, Carter grew up in Chicago, which is the setting for her Cook County Mystery series. She has also lived in Paris, Montreal, and Tangier, where she studied for a time with composer Paul Bowles. She now resides in New York City.

Rhode Island Red, her first murder mystery, features Nanette Hayes, whose life-long passions are men, jazz, and traveling in France, and not necessarily in that order. In this novel, Nanette is picking up living expenses by playing the saxophone on the streets; her boyfriend Walter takes care of most of her other financial needs. When the romance cools, she takes in a fellow street performer. The next morning, she discovers the man—an undercover police officer—has been murdered on her living room sofa.

Critic Anthony D. Langford found the heroine Hayes "an engaging, no-nonsense and very sexy woman. Her deep, almost obsessive, love of jazz music and her unique outlook on life make her charming and likable." Willetta L. Heising observed that Hayes is "A Spike Lee heroine in a Woody Allen world."

"It's not hard to fall in love with Nanette Hayes," opined Chris Wiegand, crediting Carter both for her noir writing and her inclusion of jazz-inspired riffs. "Growing up a 'bookish, neurotic, paranoid, unhappy kid,' the author admits that 'bebop and film noir saved my life' and cites a host of classic crime movies when recalling early influences."

A second series follows Chicago college student Cassandra and her guardians, great aunt and uncle, Ivy and Woody. A *Publishers Weekly* reviewer of one of the titles in the series, *Jackson Park,* quibbled about the resolution but noted, "readers will appreciate the author's incisive portrait of a black family's struggle with racism, power-lessness and their individual responsibilities to society."

The story in *Trip Wire* takes place in 1968. There are riots at the Democratic convention, and Martin Luther King Jr. is assassinated. Cassandra decides to move into a commune. When her hippie friend, Will Mobley, is murdered and the police will only consider African American suspects, she follows the clues herself. Rex E. Klett remarked on its "focused prose, frigid atmosphere, fanciful plot."

A stand-alone book, *Walking Bones*, reviewer Eugene Wildman likened to one of Chester Himes's darker works. He said, "Written in a spare, telegraphic style, it is in a way a classic noir novel. But it is also thoroughly contemporary." A black former fashion model has two loves, a white businessman and a gay black man. "This is a wrenching and beautiful novel," said Eugene Wildman, "and an unflinching look at the human soul."

Carter has found in the mystery genre a comfortable anchor from which to explore many aspects of black life and experience.

Works by the Author

Personal Effects (1991)
Walking Bones (2002)

Nanette Hayes Mysteries

Rhode Island Red (1997)
Coq au Vin (1999)
Drumsticks (2000)
Rooster's Riff (2001)

Cook County Mysteries

Jackson Park (2003)
Trip Wire (2005)

For Further Information

Charlotte Carter entry, Contemporary Authors Online, Gale, 2005. Reproduced in Biography Resource Center. Farmington Hills, MI: Thomson Gale, 2005. *http://galenet.galegroup.com/servlet/BioRC* (viewed Feb. 21,2005).

Charlotte Carter Web page. *http://www.twbookmark.com/authors/45/1530/* (viewed July 12, 2006).

Heising, Willetta L. *Detecting Women*, 3d ed. Dearborn, MI: Purple Moon Press, 2000.

Jackson Park review, *Publishers Weekly* (July 14, 2003).

Klett, Rex E., *Trip Wire* review, *Library Journal* (Feb. 1, 2005).

Langford, Anthony D., *Rhode Island Red* review, *Mystery Reader. http://www.themysteryreader.com/carter-red.html* (viewed July 12, 2006).

Wiegand, Chris, "Chris Wiegand Falls for Charlotte Carter's Trio of Musical Mysteries," *Spike* magazine. *http://www.spikemagazine.com/0602carter.php* (viewed March 4, 2005).

Wildman, Eugene, *Walking Bones* review, *Other Voices Bookshelf. http://www.webdelsol.com/Other_Voices/Reviews38.htm* (viewed July 12, 2006).

Winberry, Jennifer Monahan, Jackson Park review, *Mystery Reader. http://www.themysteryreader.com/carter-jackson.html* (viewed July 12, 2006).

Lorene Cary

Photo credit: Lonnie Graham

Memoir, Historical Literature, Women's Literature

Benchmark Title: *Black Ice*

Philadelphia, Pennsylvania

1956

About the Author and the Author's Writing

Although they all show a freshness of approach, Lorene Cary's first three books are as different as morning, noon, and night when it comes to genres. One is a memoir, one is a historical novel, and one is a novel dealing with contemporary women's issues.

Lorene Cary was born in 1956 in Philadelphia and grew up in suburban Yeadon. She attended newly coed and integrated St. Paul's preparatory school in New Hampshire, the experience enriching *Black Ice,* her prose recreation of the time. She received bachelor's and master's degrees in arts from the University of Pennsylvania, and a second master's in Victorian literature, from the University of Sussex in England, which she attended on a fellowship. She received honorary doctor of letters degrees from Colby College in Maine, Keene State College in New Hampshire, and Chestnut Hill College in Philadelphia.

Cary worked as a writer for *Time* magazine and as an associate editor for *TV Guide* as well as a contributing editor to *Newsweek*. As a freelance writer, she contributed pieces to *Mirabella* and *Essence* and the *Philadelphia Inquirer* Sunday magazine. In 1983, she married the Reverend Robert C. Smith; they live in Philadelphia with their two daughters. She is senior lecturer in creative writing at the University of Pennsylvania and also guest lectures at other schools.

The American Library Association singled out *Black Ice*, which the author expanded from an article for *American Visions,* as a notable book for 1992. "I learned to hold myself to standards that were always just beyond my reach," she writes in the

58

book, which describes not only her experiences as a student in an enclosed white environment, but also for a time as a teacher.

The Price of a Child is about a figure from history, Ginnie Pryor, who is forced to leave her baby behind when she escapes from slavery on a southern plantation. She encounters rude racism in what she'd hoped would be a freer world in the North. Oppressed by guilt, she transforms herself into an abolitionist speaker and calls herself Mercer Gray—thereby repaying her unwritten obligation to her child.

"Cary's novel, in evoking memories of ante-bellum black life, also pays homage to the African-American literary tradition," observed *Notable Black American Women*. "As the first extended prose written by blacks in America, the slave narratives are the progenitors of all subsequent African-American novels."

Cary further explores women's self-discovery in *Pride,* which follows four female characters who have been best friends since high school. "With a warm, saucy style and surprisingly complex characterization and plot lines, this is a jewel of a book," said Nancy Pearl in *Library Journal*.

Cary has become active in the Art Sanctuary, an organization that she established in 1998 that brings prominent artists and writers to a general public at the Church of the Advocate in Philadelphia. "I really love the idea of an arts and lecture series whose critical mass was formed around African-American arts—particularly since I was a writer, since I had done lots of book tours, workshops and readings and that sort of stuff all over the country," she told interviewer Michael Feagans. "It was clear to me that these things almost never happened in a venue in the middle of the inner city."

Works by the Author

The Price of a Child (1995)
Pride (1998)

Memoir

Black Ice (1991)

Contributor

Gumbo: A Literary Rent Party to Benefit the Hurston/Wright Foundation (2002), edited by Marita Golden and E. Lynn Harris

Young Adult Fiction

Free! Escape from Slavery on the Underground Railroad (2006)

For Further Information

"Acclaimed Writer Lorene Cary to Be Keynote Speaker at La Salle University Panel on 'The African-American Family,' " La Salle University Web site. *http://www.lasalle.edu/univcomm/2003/cary.htm* (viewed July 12, 2006).

Feagans, Michael, Lorene Cary interview, *Human Capital. http://www.4npo.org/lorene_cary.html* (viewed July 12, 2006).

Lorene Cary biography, altrue.net. *http://www.altrue.net/site/lorenecary/section.php?id=7002* (viewed July 12, 2006).

Lorene Cary biography, *Notable Black American Women*, Vol. 3. Detroit: Gale Group, 2002.

Lorene Cary biography, *Voices from the Gaps. http://voices.cla.umn.edu/vg/Bios/entries/cary_lorene.html* (viewed July 12, 2006).

Pearl, Nancy, "Waiting for Terry: African American Novels," *Library Journal* (Jan. 1, 2001).

Barbara Chase-Riboud

Historical Literature

Benchmark Title: *Sally Hemings*

Philadelphia, Pennsylvania

1949

About the Author and the Author's Writing

Barbara Chase-Riboud is adept at blending history and fiction. She has stirred controversy since publication of her first novel, which recreated the life of Sally Hemings, slave and consort of Thomas Jefferson.

Born in Philadelphia in 1939, Barbara Chase exhibited artistic talent as a child. She played piano, sculpted, and wrote poetry. When Barbara was ten, her mother withdrew her from school over an accusation of plagiarism and home-taught her daughter for several years. Barbara received a bachelor of fine arts degree from Temple University's Tyler Art School, studied for a time in Rome and earned a master of fine arts degree from Yale University's Graduate School of Art in 1960. After settling in Paris, Chase launched a successful career as a sculptor. She married photojournalist Marc Edward Riboud, and they raised two children. She later divorced and married Sergio Tosi. She alternates between homes in Paris, Rome, and Capri.

Her first venture into professional writing was a 1974 book of poetry, edited by Toni Morrison. Although it stretched her—"I'm a poet, which means I'm a sprinter not a long-distance runner," she said on her Voices from the Gaps Web page—she researched and wrote of Hemings at the urging of her editor, Jacqueline Kennedy Onassis. The book inspired ire among many white readers for its depiction of Jefferson's relationship with a black woman but brought her a Janet Heidinger Kafka Prize.

The novel proved popular in an unexpected way. The playwright Granville Burgess in 1987 wrote a stage drama, *Dusky Sally,* which Chase-Riboud successfully proved in court infringed on her copyright. Another round of controversy came with Chase-Riboud's belief that Steven Spielberg's 1997 film *Amistad,* about the 1839 slave ship revolt, was based, without attribution or compensation, on another of her novels, *Echo of Lions.* She brought a $10 million copyright infringement suit against the filmmaker and his DreamWorks studio, asserting it had taken her idea, the manuscript for *Echo of Lions,* which she had pitched to Spielberg's earlier Amblin' Entertainment studio, in 1988. The manuscript, then titled "Summer of Triangles," carried with it an endorsement from Chase-Riboud's Doubleday editor, Onassis. *Amistad* the film carried one character and situations and dialogue that appeared in her book, Chase-Riboud asserted. Scriptwriter David Franzoni denied having read *Echo of*

Lions. DreamWorks countered that Chase-Riboud's work contained passages that were very similar to ones in William A. Owens's nonfiction *Black Mutiny* (1953). Chase-Riboud claimed she and Owens both drew from the same historical sources; but the matter took a strange twist when a *New York Times* reporter asserted that Chase-Riboud herself had used extended unattributed quotes from a nonfiction work about harems in her novel *Valide: A Novel of the Harem*. That book had been optioned by Debbie Allen in 1984 and was the concept that eventually had caught Spielberg's interest. In spite of the complexities of the case, Chase-Riboud settled DreamWorks suit within a year.

The author's recent *Hottentot Venus* is about Sarah Baartman, a woman with unusually large posterior and genitalia who was exhibited widely in European freak shows in the early 1800s and whose skeleton and brain were held in various national collections in France until returned to her native South Africa at Nelson Mandela's request in 2001. The novel, Chase-Riboud told Black Ink Online, "is a re-creation of Baartman's short, brutal and tumultuous life in the same blend of history and fiction I used for my *Sally Hemings: A Novel*—and for the same reasons—to walk her through the front door of history." The writer asserted that the herdswoman Baartman, widely examined by the medical profession, became "a kind of Rosetta Stone of race as science literally invented racism before her very eyes. One could say that in that short life, Baartman actually became the mother of scientific racism."

Chase-Riboud said she learned of Baartman through material sent to her by a French historian. "She haunted me," she told *Essence*. "The more I read, the more I wept. I wanted to memorialize her."

In her parallel career, meanwhile, Chase-Riboud in 1999 was the first African American with a one-woman show (of her drawings) at the Metropolitan Museum of Art.

Although the author's career has certainly had its twists and turns, nothing has detracted from the strength of her prose.

Works by the Author

Sally Hemings: A Novel (1979)
Valide: A Novel of the Harem (1986)
Echo of Lions (1989)
The President's Daughter (1994), sequel to *Sally Hemings*
Hottentot Venus (2003)

Poetry

From Memphis and Peking (1974)
Portrait of a Nude Woman as Cleopatra (1987)
Egypt's Nights (1994)

For Further Information

"Author Barbara Chase-Riboud Sues Steven Spielberg for $10 Mil. Charging Film 'Amistad' Was Based on Her Book," *Jet* (Dec. 8, 1997).

Barbara Chase-Riboud entry, *Contemporary Black Biography*, Vol. 46. Detroit: Thomson Gale, 2005.

Barbara Chase-Riboud interview, *Black Ink. http://www.randomhouse.com/broadway/blackink/essay_barbara.html* (viewed March 12, 2005).

Barbara Chase-Riboud interview, *Virago. http://www.virago.co.uk/meet/chase-riboud profile.asp?TAG=&CID=virago* (viewed Aug. 4, 2006).

Barbara Chase-Riboud Web page, Voices from the Gap. *http://voices.cla.umn.edu/vg/Bios/entries/chaseribaud_barbara.html* (viewed July 12, 2006).

"First Person Singular," *Essence* (Dec. 2003).

Giddings, Paula, "Echo of Lions," *Essence* (Feb. 1989).

Gordinier, Jeff, "Mutiny and the Bounty," *Entertainment Weekly* (Dec. 12, 1997).

Handy, Bruce, "Steven Stealberg? The Director's New Film Is Hit with a $10 million Plagiarism Suit. But Isn't History Free to All?," *Time* (Nov. 24, 1997).

"Repeating History," *Time* (Dec. 29. 1997).

Sandler, Adam, "WGA Opens New Chapter in 'Amistad' Book Battle," *Variety* (Dec. 8, 1997).

Wells, Monique Y., "Barbara Chase-Riboud, Visionary Woman: In Words and Art the Renowned Author and Sculptor Breathes Life into the History of the Forgotten Female," *Black Issues Book Review* (March–April 2005).

Zeitchik, Steven M., "Chase-Riboud Drops 'Amistad' Copyright Suit," *Publishers Weekly* (Feb. 16, 1998).

Austin Clarke

Mainstream Contemporary Literature, Historical Literature

Benchmark Title: *The Polished Hoe*

Barbados

1934

Photo credit: Thomas Allen Publishers

About the Author and the Author's Writing

> I have to laugh, why, all-of-sudden, I went back to a hoe, I had-first-used when I was a girl, working in the cane fields, not quite eight years of age. The same hoe, weeding young canes, sweet potato slips, "eight-weeks" yams, eddoes, all those ground provisions.
>
> This hoe that I used all those years, in the North Field, is the same hoe I used this Sunday night.
>
> —from *The Polished Hoe*

Austin Clarke's *The Polished Hoe* won the Commonwealth Writers Prize for Best Book in 2003. Set in the West Indies in the 1940s, the book reveals in a twenty-four-hour confession one woman's life and one nation's plantation experience. The committee that awarded Clarke the Giller Prize for the same novel, despite its use of dialect and under stiff competition from other works that year, commented, "Austin Clarke's *The Polished Hoe* is a symphony of Caribbean life and history that arranges the jangle of race and class, rage and passion into an eloquent composition, part slave narrative, part love ballad, part Shakespearean opera, sun against the backdrop of one woman's life."

Although he had computer problems while writing the story, and he didn't realize until it was in print that the title is a double entendre to Americans, the author said he believes the book represents his apex. "I felt the freedom and the liberation from all of the things that could influence the writing of a book negatively," he told *January Magazine*'s Linda Richards. "I was not anxious for anything. I was in a very good mood. I was healthy. I was cheerful. And I had retained my sense of humor."

Mary Mathilda's voice is that of Clarke's mother, he said in an interview with the Canadian Broadcasting Corp.'s Evan Solomon. "The strong female presence was the presence of my mother. Which was a ubiquitous presence. Hearing the narratives spoken in the kitchen of my house at night by my mother and other women, and when I visited friends, hearing the same narrative spoken."

Austin Ardinel Chesterfield Clarke was born in Barbados in 1934 and grew up there in poverty. He was able to attend a middle-class secondary school and discovered the joy of reading English literature. Graduating from Harrison College, he studied politics and economics at Trinity College, University of Toronto. He married Betty Reynolds in 1957, and they raised three children. Prosperity was slow in coming. Clarke took a series of menial jobs. He wrote his first novel on colorful tablets he swiped from the CBC—he couldn't afford to purchase paper. He found employment as a journalist. He began to write short stories and his first novel, *The Survivors of the Crossing,* came out in 1964. At the CBC, he recorded radio interviews and assembled documentaries on black issues.

By the early 1970s, he was a regular lecturer in creative writing and African American literature at universities including Yale, Duke, and Brandeis. Living in the United States, he received appointment as cultural attaché to the Barbadian Embassy in Washington in 1974 to 1975, when he returned to Barbados to take an assignment as general manager of the Caribbean Broadcasting Corporation. When political waters became too warm, he returned to Canada and to his prose writing career. The novel *The Prime Minister* contains many autobiographical elements fresh in the author's mind. He compiled three books of memoirs. In addition to writing, he ran unsuccessfully for political office as a Progressive Conservative. He served from 1988 to 1993 as a member of the Immigration and Refugee Board of Canada.

After a decade in nonfiction, Clarke returned to the novel form with *The Origin of Waves* in 1997, a book that won the Rogers Communications Writers' Trust Fiction Prize and prompted reissue of earlier books.

Austin Clarke continues to explore with power and grace aspects of cultural clashes and the struggle of blacks in a predominantly white society.

Works by the Author

The Survivors of the Crossing (1964)
The Meeting Point (1967)
Storm of Fortune (1973)
The Bigger Light (1975)
The Prime Minister (1977)
Proud Empires (1988)
The Origin of Waves (1997)
The Question (1999)
The Polished Hoe (2002)

Short Stories

Amongst Thistles and Thorns (1965)
When He Was Free and He Used to Wear Silks (1971)
When Women Rule (1985)
Nine Men Who Laughed (1986)
In This City (1992)
There Are No Elders (1993)
The Austin Clarke Reader (1996), edited by Barry Callaghan

Memoirs

Growing Up Stupid under the Union Jack: A Memoir (1980)
Public Enemies: Police Violence and Black Youth (1992)
A Passage Back Home: A Personal Reminiscence of Samuel Selvon (1994)
Pigtails 'n' Breadfruit: The Rituals of Slave Food, A Barbadian Memoir (1999)

For Further Information

Austin C(hesterfield) Clarke entry, Contemporary Authors Online, Gale, 2005. Reproduced in Biography Resource Center. Farmington Hills, MI: Thomson Gale, 2005. *http://galenet.galegroup.com/servlet/BioRC* (viewed Feb. 26, 2005).

Austin Clarke biography, Canadian Writers, Athabasca University. *http://www.athabascau.ca/writers/aclarke.html* (viewed July 12, 2006).

Austin Clarke biography, Northwest Passages Author Profiles. *http://www.nwpassages.com/bios/clarke.asp* (viewed July 12, 2006).

Austin Clarke Interview, Canadian Broadcasting Corp. *http://www.cbc.ca/hottype/season02-03/02-11-22.html* (viewed July 12, 2006).

Austin Clarke interview, CBC Newsworld Online. http://www.cbc.ca/hottype/season02-03/02-11-22.html (viewed Sept. 14, 2006).

Austin Clarke Web page, Bukowski Agency. *http://www.thebukowskiagency.com/PolishedHoe.htm* (viewed July 12, 2006).

"Austin Clarke wins Giller Prize," CBC News (Nov. 6, 2002). *http://www.cbc.ca/story/canada/national/2002/11/06/giller_clark021106.html* (viewed July 12, 2006).

Richards, Linda, Austin Clarke interview, *January* magazine. *http://www.januarymagazine.com/profiles/aclarke.html* (viewed July 12, 2006).

Robinson, Marcus, and Jason Gileno, Austin Clarke interview, *Pagitica*. *http://www.pagitica.com/extras.austindialog.html* (viewed July 12, 2006).

Pearl Cleage

Women's Literature, Young Adult Literature, Drama, Poetry

Benchmark Title: *What Looks Like Crazy on an Ordinary Day*

Springfield, Massachusetts

1948

About the Author and the Author's Writing

Oprah's Book Club featured Pearl Cleage's first novel, *What Looks Like Crazy on an Ordinary Day,* in 1998, bringing the author an instant audience of readers who might otherwise have taken several years to discover her. She didn't let the sudden fame change her writing—and after all, it's not as if she was a newcomer.

"I've been writing professionally for all of my adult life," she told Jana Siciliano of *Bookreporter.* "My style and my habits are pretty much set by now. I'm always trying to figure out what I know and then find a story that will help me pass that information on. That hasn't changed at all."

Cleage was born in 1948 in Springfield, Massachusetts, the daughter of a minister and an elementary school teacher. She grew up in Detroit, Michigan. She attended Howard University, Yale University, and the University of the West Indies. She received a bachelor of arts degree from Spelman College in 1971 and did graduate studies at Atlanta University the same year. She married and divorced Michael Lomax; they had one child. She lives in Atlanta, Georgia, with her second husband, novelist Zaron W. Burnett Jr.

From 1969 to 1970, Cleage served on the field collection staff for Martin Luther King Jr. Archival Library, and in 1970 and 1971, she was an assistant director for Southern Education Program. She was hostess and interviewer for *Black Viewpoints,* produced for WETV in Atlanta by Clark College (1970 and 1971) then worked variously as a staff writer, interviewer, and producer for WCZI and WXIA. Beginning in 1973, she was director of communications for Atlanta's first black mayor, Maynard Jackson. She was a writer for Brown/Gray Ltd. beginning in 1976. From 1983 to 1987, she was playwright-in-residence for the Just Us Theater Company in Atlanta and then became its artistic director. She taught creative writing at Spelman College from 1986 to 1991 before becoming playwright-in-residence there. She has been a columnist for the *Atlanta Tribune* and other newspapers and a contributing editor to *Essence* magazine.

By the time *What Looks Like Crazy on an Ordinary Day* came out, she had published poetry, essays and performance pieces and ten of her plays had been performed nationally and internationally—the best known being *Flyin' West*, the story of a pioneer black woman at the turn of the century, *Bourbon at the Border* and *Blues for an Alabama Sky*. The book is a love story with a bit of a twist: The woman, Ava Johnson, is HIV-positive and the man, Wild Eddie, is a New-Ager.

"I longed to write a love story," she told Tara Roberts for *Essence*, "a story where the man is like my husband, soothing to me. I wanted a book with love scenes that don't require brothers to act a certain way. Men have learned so many repressive things being in control. It's hard to find space to be vulnerable, but HIV requires that different attention."

Cleage followed that novel with *I Wish I Had a Red Dress,* the story of Ava's sister, Joyce, a hardworking woman who has lived a passionless life for many years, and *Some Things I Never Thought I'd Do*, about Regina Burns's struggle to overcome drug addiction and a nervous breakdown.

"The contradictions I write about in my novels are here every day," Cleage told interviewer Gwendolyn Glenn, describing her home environs in Southwest Atlanta. "Some writers write about blacks, but they never see blacks."

Although the author does not intend to abandon drama, she finds novels offer a wider audience. She says she writes her novels in the first person because it closely resembles the writing of dialogue for stage productions.

"I think voice is a critical element in all forms of creative writing," she said in an interview on the Spelman College Web site. "In fiction, the voice of the narrator is critical. With poetry, we are drawn into the experience by the poet's voice. I think with plays the voice of the writer is augmented by the voice and expression of the actor, but in the end, it is the writer's words that shape the piece and the writer's voice that brings it to life."

Cleage admitted to *Pages'* Leslie Stainton that she sometimes struggles with her prose. "There's a point when I take all these pages in my hysteria and say to my husband, '*What* am I talking about? *What* is the story? And he can reach in there and find that thread."

Thematically, novels offer the same opportunities as plays for Cleage. Whatever the genre, the author holds back on the politics and message, and emphasizes the character and story.

"I'm always talking in some sense about questions of race and gender," she told *Black Issues Book Review*'s Samiya A. Bashir. "But in a wider sense I'm trying to tell stories about interesting, complicated, black women characters who've been defeated by their lives. I'm interested in people who have been engaged and do interesting things and have powerful lovers. I want to write about people I want to read about. I'm not interested in hearing about people."

Works by the Author

What Looks Like Crazy on an Ordinary Day (1997)
I Wish I Had a Red Dress (2001)
Some Things I Never Thought I'd Do (2003)

Babylon Sisters (2005)
Baby Brother Blues (2006)

Contributor

Gumbo: A Literary Rent Party to Benefit the Hurston/Wright Foundation (2002), edited by Marita Golden and E. Lynn Harris

Young Adult

The Brass Bed and Other Stories (1991)

Drama

Hymn for the Rebels (1968)
Duet for Three Voices (1969)
The Sale (1972)
Puppetplay (1983)
Hospice (1983); published in *New Plays for the Black Theater* (1989), edited by Woodie King Jr.
Good News (1984)
Essentials (1985)
Banana Bread (1985)
PR: A Political Romance (1985), with Walter J. Huntley
Porch Songs (1985)
Come and Get These Memories (1988)
Chain (1992), published in *Playwrighting Women: Seven Plays from the Women's Project*, edited by Julia Miles (1993)
Late Bus to Mecca (1992)
Flyin' West (1992)
Blues for an Alabama Sky (1994)
Bourbon at the Border (1997)

Poetry

We Don't Need No Music (1971)
Dear Dark Faces: Portraits of a People (1980)
One for the Brothers (1983)
We Speak Your Name: A Celebration (2006), with Zaron W. Burnett Jr.

Contributor

The Insistent Present (1970), edited by John Mahoney and John Schmittroth
We Speak as Liberators: Young Black Poets (1970), edited by Orde Coombs
A Rock against the Wind (1973), edited by Lindsay Patterson
The Poetry of Black America (1973), edited by Arnold Adoff and Gwendolyn Brooks

Nonfiction

Mad at Miles: A Blackwoman's Guide to Truth (1990)
Deals with the Devil: And Other Reasons to Riot (1993)
Live at Club Zebra: The Book, Volume 1, Just Us Theater Press (1981), with
Zaron Burnett

For Further Information

Baker, John F., "African-American Author/Dramatist Pearl Cleage Has Signed
for Another Two Novels with Ballantine's Nancy Miller, for the House's
One World imprint," *Publishers Weekly* (July 5, 2004).

Bashir, Samiya A., "Pearl Cleage's Idlewild Idylls—Interview," *Black Issues
Book Review* (July 2001).

Gelsomino, Tara, *Babylon Sisters* review, *Romantic Times Bookclub Magazine*
(April 2005).

Glenn, Gwendolyn, "Home Time and Island Time," *Black Issues Book Review*
(March–April 2004).

Pearl Cleage biography, ArtMakers. *http://www.thehistorymakers.com/biography/
biography.asp?bioindex=834&category=artMakers* (viewed March 11,
2005).

Pearl Cleage biography, BookBrowse.Com. *http://www.bookbrowse.com/
biographies/index.cfm?author_number=665* (viewed July 13, 2006).

Pearl Cleage biography, Ingrid Kerkhoff, Contemporary American Drama.
http://www.fb10.uni-bremen.de/anglistik/kerkhoff/ContempDrama/Cleage.htm
(viewed July 13, 2006).

Pearl (Michelle) Cleage entry, Contemporary Authors Online, Gale, 2005. Reproduced in Biography Resource Center, Farmington Hills, MI: Thomson
Gale, 2005. *http://galenet.galegroup.com/servlet/BioRC* (viewed Feb. 26,
2005).

Pearl Cleage Web page, African American Literature Book Club. *http://authors.
aalbc.com/cleagepearl.htm* (viewed July 13, 2006).

Pearl Cleage, Women of Color, Women of Words. *http://www.scils.rutgers.
edu/~cybers/cleage.html* (viewed July 13, 2006).

Pearl Michelle Cleage interview, Spelman College Web site. *http:www.
spelman.edu/bush-hewlett/linked/Interviews/pearl_cleage_interview.html*
(viewed July 13, 2006).

Roberts, Tara, "Pearls of Wisdom," *Essence* (December 1997).

Siciliano, Jana, Pearl Cleage interview, *Bookreporter. http://www.bookreporter.
com/authors/au-cleage-pearl.asp* (viewed July 13, 2006).

Stainton, Leslie, "Born a Storyteller," *Pages* (March/April 2005).

J. California Cooper

Mainstream Contemporary Literature, Drama, Historical Literature, Young Adult Literature

Benchmark Title: *A Place of Mine*

Berkeley, California

Date of birth not revealed

About the Author and the Author's Writing

J. California Cooper played with paper dolls, manipulating them to act out stories, until her mother took them away from her when she was seventeen. She substituted words for dolls and continued to craft situations for her characters in stage dramas, short stories, and novels that have a wide audience among young adults as well as older readers.

The author gave herself the name California—she was born in Berkeley, California—and reveals her true first name only during personal conversation. She is equally withholding of information about her year of birth, her childhood, her education, her marriage and divorce, and her daughter. She lived in Texas for a time but now resides again in her native state.

Cooper wrote seventeen plays that were brought to the stage. She was named Black Playwright of the Year in 1978. Novelist Alice Walker encouraged her to write short stories. The author's first collection, *A Place of Mine,* "introduced Cooper's trademark style: her intimate and energetic narration, sympathetic yet sometimes troubled characters, and the profound moral messages that underline seemingly simple stories," according to *PageTurner*. Her next book, *Homemade Love,* won an American Book Award.

Cooper's first novel, *Family*, is a multigenerational family story narrated by a Southern slave who in despair takes her own life rather than continue in unrelenting subjugation. Her spirit continues to watch over her descendants. "While it details the tragedy of slavery, the novel is ultimately a tale of triumph over adversity, for it expresses optimism that racial distinctions will become irrelevant and that all people will consider themselves part of the same family," suggests Contemporary Authors Online.

"I know all these people still live in me," Cooper said of her characters in an interview with Demolyn Carroll of *Essence*. "I haven't left anything behind. I've got them all, and I'm full of their stories, their feelings. I can understand. I'm listening to them, and I'm seeing them, and I'm feeling them. Sometimes I cry and sometimes I laugh. I live it."

Cooper's stories are noted for being moralistic. They offer distinctions between good and evil, optimism and frustration. They are often intentionally biblical, although they do not shy from the controversial, and they don't necessarily take stands on issues such as homosexuality.

Cooper's straightforward style, with her own, often folksy prose have drawn comparisons to Langston Hughes and Zora Neale Hurston. Of note is the fact that she likes exclamation points.

"The people in my short stories live in exclamation points," Cooper said in an interview with Stephanie Stokes Oliver.

The author's recent *Some People, Some Other Place* is another, ambitious saga which looks at multiethnic families who live on "Dream Street" in "Place." The narrator's great-grandparents had fled poverty in the South in 1895, migrating to Oklahoma to farm independently. Their children moved on to the industrialized Midwest. The next generation came to Dream Street, with the hope that name suggests, to encounter a new set of challenges to their aspirations.

"In my books I want to explore characters who bring me problems," the author said in a 2004 *Essence* conversation. "I want to solve them. Through my stories I'm trying to say something that may help…. Through my work, I want to show that you can stand up and take care of yourself and change your life."

Works by the Author

A Place of Mine (1984), short stories
Homemade Love (1986), short stories
Some Soul to Keep (1987), short stories
The Matter Is Life (1991), short stories
Family: A Novel (1991)
In Search of Satisfaction (1994)
Some Love, Some Pain, Some Time: Stories (1995)
The Wake of Wind (1998)
The Future Has a Past (2000), short stories
Some People, Some Other Place (2004)
Wild Stars Seeking Midnight Suns (2005), short stories

Drama (Partial List)

Strangers (1978)
Loners

Contributor

Center Stage: An Anthology of Twenty-One Contemporary Black-American Plays (1991), edited by Eileen Joyce Ostrow

For Further Information

Carroll, Denolyn, "Sometimes I Cry, Sometimes I Laugh," *Black Issues Book Review* (Nov.-Dec. 2004).

J(oan) California Cooper entry, Contemporary Authors Online. Gale, 2005. Reproduced in Biography Resource Center, Farmington Hills, MI: Thomson Gale, 2005. *http://galenet.galegroup.com/servlet.BioRC* (viewed Feb. 25, 2005).

J. California Cooper entry, *Authors and Artists for Young Adults*, Vol. 12. Detroit: Gale Research, 1994.

J. California Cooper Reader's Companion, *PageTurner. http://*www.randomhouse.com/resources/*bookgroup/jcalifornia_bgc.html* (viewed Aug. 4, 2006).

J. California Cooper Web page, African American Literature Book Club. *http://authors.aalbc.com/j.htm* (viewed Feb. 17, 2005).

Oliver, Stephanie Stokes, "J. California Cooper: from Paper Dolls to Paperbacks," *Essence* (May 1991).

Stone, Robin D., "First Person Singular: J. California Cooper," *Essence* (Nov. 2004).

Edwidge Danticat

Mainstream Contemporary Literature

Benchmark Title: *The Farming of Bones*

Port-au-Prince, Haiti

1969

Photo credit: Jill Krementz

About the Author and the Author's Writing

Edwidge Danticat began writing at about age eight as a way to work out anxieties over an abrupt transition from a happy childhood in poor circumstances in Haiti to the bustling world of Brooklyn, New York. She was born in Port-au-Prince in 1969. Two years later, her father left for the United States and a new beginning as a cab driver. Her mother followed two years after that, getting a job as a textile worker. Until age twelve, Edwidge and her brother Andre lived with an aunt and uncle in Haiti. Then the two siblings immigrated as well. Because she grew up speaking French and Creole, she was quite conspicuous when she attended public school in Crown Heights. So she began to write for herself and for a school newspaper.

"It was during these early years that Danticat was influenced by the Haitian practice of story telling which developed because much of the population was illiterate at the time," according to a biography on the author's Voices from the Gap Web page. "Danticat says that the memories of Haiti are still extremely vivid in her mind, and that her love of Haiti and things Haitian deeply influences her writing."

The author received a bachelor of arts degree in French literature from Barnard College, and, although her parents hoped she would pursue a degree in medicine, she accepted a scholarship to Brown University and earned a master of fine arts degree in 1993. Her master's thesis became the novel *Breath, Eyes, Memory,* which describes four generations of Haitian women and their struggle in poverty. Said to be the first novel by a Haitian woman written in English, its selection as a feature novel in the Oprah Winfrey Book Club brought it to the attention of a wide audience. And that was yet another first for a Haitian writer.

In an interview with alcoholreview.com Danticat said Haitian literature was sparse when she was growing up. "I think that [Jacques] Roumain was one of the first [Haitian] writers to look at what was going on in Africa and his own environment, rather than relying on abstract models of the Symbolists. There was a whole moment happening at the same time as the Harlem Renaissance. That was the first time I read about people I knew. That made a strong impression on me."

Her mountain childhood may have been comfortable, but Haitian society was in turmoil, as Danticat depicted in her first book. Rape was a routine tool of dominance over the country's women. "Focusing on rape as a crime against women which violates women's rights to protection and due process as citizens, Danticat highlights the ideological sexism operative in Haitian political culture, which systematically silences—through concealment, deferral, or dismissal—women's testimonies of sexual violations," explained Donette A. Francis in *Research in African Literature*.

Danticat verified the legitimacy of her young writings when she won a Pushcart Prize for short fiction and became a National Book Award finalist for her collection of short stories, *Krik? Krak!* in 1996. She was twenty-six. As influences on her writing, she has acknowledged the "kitchen poets," which is the oral tradition of women in her native country.

"Concentrating her focus on the life that she left behind in Haiti and her personal experiences as an immigrant to the United States, Danticat writes from the point of view of a young woman of color who realizes all too quickly that the attributes she possesses are of little value in either culture," according to *Authors and Artists for Young Adults*.

Danticat's *Behind the Mountains* is about Celiane Esperance, a Haitian teenager, who experiences a long struggle as her family attempts to reunite with her father, who has gone to the United States for better economic opportunity. "Danticat brings her formidable skill as a writer and her own firsthand knowledge of Haiti and immigrating to America to this heartfelt story told in the intimate diary format," observed Claire Rosser in *Kliatt*.

The author has by no means exhausted the literary possibilities of her native country. Her recent *The Dew Breaker* looks at the deceit woven by a dew breaker, a torturer, who has hidden his past in a new life in America with a family, neighbors, and business associates.

Works by the Author

Breath, Eyes, Memory (1994)
Krik? Krak! (1995), short stories
The Farming of Bones (1998)
Behind the Mountains (2002)
The Dew Breaker (2004)
Vale of Tears: A Novel from Haiti (2006), with Paulette Poujol Oriol and Dolores A. Schaefer

Editor

Beacon Best of 2000: Great Writing by Women and Men of All Colors and Cultures (2000)
Butterfly's Way: Voices from the Haitian Dyaspora in the United States (2001)

Translator

In the Flicker of an Eyelid (by Jackes Stephen Alexis) (2002)

Drama

Creation of Adam (1992)
Dreams Like Me (1993)
Children of the Sea (1997)

Fiction for Juvenile Readers

Anacaona: Golden Flower, Haiti, 1940 (2006)

Nonfiction

Odillon Pierre, Artist of Haiti (1999), with Jonathan Demme
After the Dance: A Walk through Carnival in Haiti (2002)

For Further Information

Edwidge Danticat biography, *Voices from the Gap. http://voices.cla.umn. edu/vg/Bios/entries/danticat_edwidge.html* (viewed April 23, 2005).

Edwidge Danticat entry, *Authors and Artists for Young Adults*, Vol. 29. Detroit: Gale, 1999.

Edwidge Danticat entry, Contemporary Authors Online. Gale, 2005. Reproduced in Biography Resource Center. Farmington Hills, MI: Thomson Gale, 2005. *http:galenet.galegroup.com/servlet/BioRC* (viewed Feb. 26, 2005).

Edwidge Danticat entry, *KidsReads.com. http://www.kidsreads.com/series/ series-first-person-author.asp* (viewed July 13, 2006).

Edwidge Danticat Web page, African American Literature Book Club. *http://authors.aalbc.com/edwidge.htm* (viewed July 13, 2006).

Edwidge Danticat Web page, American Immigration Law Foundation Immigrant. *http://www.ailf.org/notable/iaa/ny2000/danticat.htm* (viewed July 13, 2006).

Edwidge Danticat Web page, Emory College Web site. *http://www.english. emory.edu/Bahri/Danticat.html* (viewed July 13, 2006).

Francis, Donette A., "Silences Too Horrific to Disturb: Writing Sexual Histories in Edwidge Danticat's Breath, Eyes, Memory," *Research in African Literature* (summer 2004).

Laurence, Alexander, Edwidge Danticat interview, *alcoholreviews.com. http://www.freewilliamsburg.com/still_fresh/edwidge.html* (viewed Feb. 19, 2005).

Mathurin, Ginau, "Edwidge Danticat: Kitchen Poet," Echodhaiti.com. *http://www. echodhaiti.com/culture/danticat/html* (viewed April 23, 2005).

Rosser, Claire, *Behind the Mountains* review, *Kliatt* (November 2002).

Samuel R. Delany

Science Fiction, Fantasy

Benchmark Titles: Nevèryon Series

New York, New York

1942

About the Author and the Author's Writing

Samuel R. Delany has always pushed the boundaries—thematically, linguistically, stylistically. Early in his writing career, he took the science fiction world by storm. He garnered four Nebula Awards—the first for his debut novel *The Jewels of Aptor* in 1962—by age twenty-six and over the next decades he has made further marks on the genre. He has brought an atypical perspective to futuristic writing; as a gay man and an African American, he is an outsider. He has embraced touchy topics. His apocalyptic 1975 novel *Dhalgren,* for example, explores bisexual themes, and his Nevèryon series touches on the AIDS crisis.

"Samuel R. Delany is one of today's most innovative and imaginative writers of science-fiction," in the view of biographer Jane Branham Weedman.

Samuel Ray "Chip" Delany was born in 1942 in Harlem. His father ran a funeral home, and his mother was a library clerk. As a child, he was drawn to both math and the sciences, and to literature, music, and drama. He undertook psychotherapy at age ten, after his mother discovered his homosexual preference. At age thirteen, he began to write imaginative fiction and compose music. He attended Dalton School, Bronx High School of Science and City College (later City University of New York) in the early 1960s and was editor of its poetry publication, *Promethean.* He married poet Marilyn Hacker in 1961. They divorced nineteen years later. They had one child.

In *The Motion of Light in Water: Sex and Science Fiction Writing in the East Village, 1957–1965*, the author's 1988 memoir, Delany writes of his life cruising the nighttime sexual underground of New York. "His curiosity about his experience as a gay black man is utterly scrupulous in its quest for honest expression and true explanation," said Brian Stableford, "and his attempts to understand and explain the different experiences of others are marked by great generosity of spirit and critical insight."

In 1967, Delany performed music with the jazz group Heavenly Breakfast. He lived in a commune in 1967–68. All the while, he wrote. "The core fiction of the 1960's, from *The Jewels of Aptor* up to *Nova*, is astonishing both for its inventiveness and its story-telling verve," asserts critic Paul Brazier. "Quasi-medieval societies, beggars, mutants, spaceships, and quests mingle in pyrotechnic story-telling. Along with the wonder and adventure, however, there are more serious themes." These themes include the power of linguistics and eroticism (*The Tides of Lust*).

Delany has been Butler Professor of English at State University of New York at Buffalo (1975), a senior fellow at the Center for Twentieth Century Studies at the University of Wisconsin in Milwaukee (1977) and at the Society for the Humanities at Cornell University (1987), and a professor of comparative literature at the University of Massachusetts in Amherst (1988).

The author's well-delineated futuristic novels of the 1970s gave way in the next decade to the Nevèryon stories, sword-and-sorcery fantasy in the Robert E. Howard and Fritz Leiber vein, following the adventures of Gorgik from slavery to power in a raw world.

These complex stories, suggests critic Sandra Y. Govan, "unveil sophisticated examinations of the movement of a barbarian, preindustrial society as it slowly evolves to a market economy and moves from barter to a cash system. Along with this development, Delany investigates slavery, political intrigues, the power of signs, and an emphasis which could be called 'womanist mythologies.' "

"Delany is as much concerned with showing how fact turns into legend as with narrative; one of the many threads that weave the series together is the gradual revelation of the true story of particularly bloody political intrigue among the ruling family of Nevèryon—on which is based a rhyme chanted by children as they bounce rubber balls," explains *St. James Guide to Fantasy Fiction*.

Delany disdains face-to-face interviews, preferring, as a writer, to compose written responses to questions. "My thoughts are formed by writing. When I want to think with any seriousness about a topic, I write about it. Writing slows the thought processes down to where one can follow them—and elaborate on them—more efficiently," he told interviewer K. Leslie Steiner. "Writing is how I do my thinking. Thus, if you want to understand what I think, ask me to write—not to speak."

Delany thus wrote of his place in the American literary scene in *Silent Interviews*: "The constant and insistent experience I have as a black man, as a gay man, as a science fiction writer in racist, sexist, homophobic America, with its carefully maintained tradition of high art and low, colors and contours every sentence I write. But it does not delimit and demarcate those sentences, either in their compass, meaning, or style. It does not reduce them in any way."

Works by the Author

Fiction

The Jewels of Aptor (1962)
The Ballad of Beta-2 (1965)
Babel-17 (1966)
Empire Star (1966)
The Einstein Intersection (1967)
Nova (1968)
The Tides of Lust (1973), revised as *Equinox* (1994)
Dhalgren (1975)
Triton (1976)

Trouble on Triton: An Ambiguous Heterotopia (1976), with Kathy Acker
Empire: A Visual Novel (1978)
Stars in My Pocket Like Grains of Sand (1984)
The Star Pit (1989)
We, in Some Strange Power's Employ, Move on a Rigorous Line (1990)
Hogg (1994)
The Mad Man (1994)
Bread and Wine: An Erotic Tale of New York (1998)
1984 (2000)
Stars in My Pocket Like Grains of Sand (2005), with Carl Friedman

Fall of the Towers Series

Captives of the Flame (1963), revised as *Out of the Dead City* (1968)
The Towers of Toron (1964)
City of a Thousand Suns (1965)
Out of the Dead City (1968)
The Fall of the Towers (1971), includes revised *Out of the Dead City, The Towers of Toron,* and *City of a Thousand Suns*

Nevèryon Series

Tales of Nevèryon (1975), stories
Flight from Nevèryon (1978), stories
Nevèryona: or The Tale of Signs and Cities (1983), stories
The Bridge of Lost Desire (1987), retitled *Return to Nevèryon* (1989), stories
They Fly at Ciron (1992)

Collections

Driftglass: Ten Tales of Speculative Fiction (1971)
Distant Stars (1981)
The Complete Nebula Award-Winning Fiction (1986)
Atlantis: Model 1924 (1995)
Aye and Gomorrah: And Other Stories (2003)

Anthologies

Nebula Award Stories 3 (1967)
Nebula Award Stories 5 (1969)
Partners in Wonder (1971)
Modern Science Fiction (1974)
Modern Classic Short Novels of Science Fiction (1993)
The Norton Book of Science Fiction (1993)
Off Limits: Tales of Alien Sex (1996)
Dark Matter: A Century of Speculative Fiction from the African Diaspora (2000), edited by Sheree R. Thomas
Dark Matter II: Reading the Bones (2004), edited by Sheree R. Thomas

Editor

Quark 1 (1970), with Marilyn Hacker
Quark 2 (1971), with Marilyn Hacker
Quark 3 (1971), with Marilyn Hacker
Quark 4 (1971), with Marilyn Hacker
Nebula Award Stories 13 (1979)

Drama

Wagner/Artaud (1988)

Nonfiction

The Jewel-Hinged Jaw: Notes on the Language of Science Fiction (1977)
The American Shore: Meditations on a Tale of Science-Fiction by Thomas M. Disch-Angoulene (1978)
Heavenly Breakfast: An Essay on the Winter of Love (1979)
Times Square Red, Times Square Blue (1983)
Starboard Wine (1984)
The Straits of Messina (1986)
The Motion of Light in Water: Sex and Science Fiction Writing in the East Village, 1957–1965 (1988)
Silent Interviews: On Language, Race, Sex, Science Fiction, and Some Comics: A Collection of Written Interviews (1994)
Longer Views (1996)
Shorter Views (1999)
Black Gay Man (2001), with Robert Reid-Pharr
About Writing: Seven Essays, Four Letters, and Five Interviews (2005)

For Further Information

Aye and Gomorrah review, *Library Journal* (March 15, 2003).

Barbour, Douglas. *Worlds out of Words: The SF Novels of Samuel R. Delany.* Frome, England: Bran's Head, 1979.

Brazier, Paul, Samuel R. Delany entry, *Twentieth-Century Science-Fiction Writers*, 3d ed., Noelle Watson and Paul E. Schellinger, eds. Chicago: St. James Press, 1991.

Govan, Sandra Y., "Silent Interviews: On Language, Race, Sex, Science Fiction, and Some Comics," *African American Review* (spring 1997).

McAuley, Paul J., Samuel R. Delany entry, *St. James Guide to Fantasy Writers*, David Pringle, ed. Detroit: St. James Press, 1996.

McEvoy, Seth. *Samuel R. Delany.* New York: Ungar, 1984.

Peplow, Michael W., and Robert S. Bravard. *Samuel R. Delany: A Primary and Secondary Bibliography, 1962–1979.* Boston: G. K. Hall, 1980.

Samuel R. Delany biography. *http://www.uic.edu/depts/quic/history/samuel_delaney.html* (viewed July 14, 2006).

Samuel R. Delany entry, *Contemporary Authors New Revision Series,* Vol. 43, Trosky, Susan M., ed. Detroit: Gale Research, 1994.

Samuel R. Delany entry, *Gay & Lesbian Biography.* Detroit: St. James Press, 1997.

Slusser, George. Samuel R. Delany entry, *St. James Guide to Science Fiction Writers,* Jay P. Pederson, ed. Detroit: St. James Press.

Slusser, George Edgar. *The Delany Intersection: Samuel R. Delany Considered as a Writer of Semi-Precious Words.* San Bernardino, CA: Borgo, 1977.

Stableford, Brian, Samuel R. Delany entry, *American Ethnic Writers*, Vol. 1, David Peck, ed. Pasadena, CA: Salem Press, 2000.

Steiner, K. Leslie, "An Interview with Samuel R. Delany," *Review of Contemporary Fiction* (fall 1996).

Weedman, Jane Branham. *Samuel R. Delany.* Mercer Island, WA: Starmont House, 1982.

Nora DeLoach

Mystery

Benchmark Titles: Mama Mystery Series

Orlando, Florida
1940–2001

About the Author and the Author's Writing

Mama is a social worker (she wears her heart on her sleeve). She's a kitchen wonder (you wouldn't pass up her sweet-potato pie). And she's an experienced, if amateur, crime solver (nothing stands between her and a valuable clue) in Nora DeLoach's mystery series.

Mama Pursues Murderous Shadows, typically, finds the South Carolina heroine looking into the apparent suicide of Ruby Spikes in a motel room. Mama's friend Sarah had taken out an insurance policy on Ruby and stands to make some much-needed money. With the help of paralegal daughter Simone, who is in town to prepare a gala thirty-fifth wedding anniversary party for her mother, Mama of course solves the crime in a novel that *Publishers Weekly* said "charms with its descriptions of delicious food, realistic family dynamics and smart dialogue."

The author was born Nora Frazier in Orlando, Florida, in 1940. She worked as a social worker in the South Carolina community of Hampton (which provides the backdrop to the mystery novels), and also lived in Georgia and Florida. She married William DeLoach in about 1963, and they had three children. She began writing in the early 1990s. Her second novel, *Mama Solves a Murder,* began her popular mystery series, first for Holloway House, later Bantam.

DeLoach began writing at a low time in her life. "I was going through menopause, and my daughter was doing her best to be a typical teenager," she told Carolyn Tillery. "My husband was trying to mediate and trying to keep us from killing each other. I decided I needed time by myself and turned a room in our home into a study and started writing."

The books were proclaimed the African American version of cozy, Miss Marple–type puzzlers and were singled out for their depiction of small-town life and their evolving relationship between Mama and Simone.

Jocelyn Singleton and cowriters on the Voices of the Gap Web page for DeLoach remarked, "This relationship is founded on the idea that each character depends on the other in order to get the job done. Their relationship resolves around mutual respect and participation . . . Simone and Mama are rarely separated when searching for clues or sleuthing. The powerful mother–daughter bond, their ties within the community, and the development of the other types of interpersonal relationships are several of the strongest themes in DeLoach's series."

DeLoach said she used the mystery form "to introduce people to real African American characters."

The two-time recipient of the George Author of the Year award died in 2001 of leukemia.

 **Works by the Author**

Silas (1993)

Mama Mystery Series

Mama Solves a Murder (1994)
Mama Traps a Killer (1995)
Mama Saves a Victim (1997)
Mama Stands Accused (1997)
Mama Stalks the Past (1998)
Mama Rocks the Empty Cradle (1999)
Mama Pursues Murderous Shadows (2000)
Mama Cracks a Mask of Innocence (2001)

Nonfiction

How to Write and Sell Genre Fiction (1994)

For Further Information

Mama Pursues Murderous Shadows review, *Publishers Weekly* (May 15, 2000).

Nora DeLoach entry, *Contemporary Black Biography*, Vol. 30, Ashley Henderson, ed. Detroit: Gale, 2001.

Nora DeLoach profile, *Pittsburgh Post-Gazette* (April 24, 1998).

Nora DeLoach Web page, *Voices from the Gaps. http://voices.cla.umn.edu/ vg/Bios/entries/deloach_nora.html*(viewed July 14, 2006).

Singleton, Jocelyn, Bao Vang, and Sarah Myseth, Nora DeLoach Web page, African American Literature Book Club. *http://authors.aalbc.com/ themama.htm* (viewed July 14, 2006).

Tillery, Carolyn, "The Fiction of Black Crime: It's No Mystery," *American Visions* (April–May 1997).

Eric Jerome Dickey

Mainstream Contemporary Literature, Romance

Benchmark Title: *Liar's Game*

Memphis, Tennessee
1961

Photo credit: Ken Coleman

About the Author and the Author's Writing

Eric Jerome Dickey's relationship novels are boiled with emotion, seasoned with humor and served with rich characterization.

The author was born in 1961 in Memphis, Tennessee. He attended Memphis State University (now the University of Memphis) and earned a bachelor of science degree in computer systems technology. He worked at jobs ranging from bill collector to stand-up comic to substitute teacher. When he was laid off as a computer systems technician with Rockwell aerospace, he began writing.

"I've always had another, creative side," he said in a *Chance22* interview. "A silly side that didn't match my former occupation. I'd written a few shorts in high school, nothing great, but during the time I was about to get laid off, I sat back and recaptured that. Remembered how much fun it was to make something out of nothing, and get ALL of the credit for it."

Dickey was trained for a black belt in karate, and he runs. He has taken no writing classes, but he does read widely, including books by Walter Moseley, Maya Angelou, Lolita Files, Franklin White, and Sharon Mitchell, and has expressed a desire to put an African American angle on the thriller/Stephen King genre.

His first novel, *Sister, Sister,* took a bemused look at a mixed-race trio of siblings in Los Angeles. Red has stood by her husband, Walter, even as his pro football career has floundered and he's parked himself permanently in front of the TV. That doesn't mean she hasn't been tempted by a flirt named Daniel. Red's sister Inda, a social worker, has the opposite problem: her hunk, Raymond, has a girl on the side. And that girl, flight attendant Chiquita, has just shone her eyes on Red and Inda's brother,

Thaddeus. *Publishers Weekly* found the novel "a high-spirited celebration of black sisterhood."

Dickey puts another twist on an old story with *Drive Me Crazy*. An ex-con named Driver reneges on an agreement with Lisa to kill her husband. Driver used the $15,000 she paid him to pay for his mother's burial. And now Lisa wants revenge.

In an interview with Black Book Network, Dickey said he has no particular agenda in his writing. He just enjoys writing and juggling characters. "I know White people. I know Black people. Aside from the external, I think people are basically the same, we have the same fears, the same wants. As a writer, you mix things up, you don't give people the same reaction to conflict, you tap into their belief systems. You put three people on a page, you throw out some conflict, and work three different reactions."

Dickey is frustrated when editors don't understand what he's trying to accomplish in his prose or question his characters. "Someone e-mailed me that she would read mainstream writers who are either too politically correct or who just don't write with that edge that you get when you're being honest. Not that my stories are gritty or filthy, but they just seem more real to these readers," he said in a *BookPage* interview. "I'm trying to be honest and real."

The author says he varies his approach from book to book. In fact, he took a cue from Judy Blume and made *Liar's Game* more explicit than earlier works. It is the story of two people who find each other in Los Angeles but aren't ready to reveal their pasts, which contain some episodes that they are ashamed of.

Give him a good character to write about, and Dickey soars, he said in an interview for Penguin Group (Canada). "For me, once you say the character is African-American you're done—you don't have to go through every page reminding people how black I am. Can we get on with the story? Can we move on?"

Works by the Author

Sister, Sister (1996)
Friends and Lovers (1997)
Milk in My Coffee (1998)
Cheaters: Caught Up in the Game (199)
Liar's Game (2000)
Mothers and Sons (2001)
Between Lovers (2001)
Black Silk (2002)
Thieves' Paradise (2002)
The Other Woman (2003)
Naughty or Nice (2003)
Drive Me Crazy (2004), sequel to *Thieves' Paradise*
Genevieve (2005)
Chasing Destiny (2006)
Sleeping with Strangers (2007)

Screenplay

Cappuccino (1998)

Contributor

Got To Be Real (2000), with E. Lynn Harris, Colin Channer and Marcus Major
Gumbo: A Literary Rent Party to Benefit the Hurston/Wright Foundation (2002),
    edited by Marita Golden and E. Lynn Harris
Griots Beneath the Baobab: Tales from Los Angeles (2002)

For Further Information

Eric Dickey interview, BookPage. *http://www.bookpage.com/0007bp/eric_
    dickey.html* (viewed July 14, 2006).

Eric Jerome Dickey entry, Contemporary Authors Online, Gale, 2005. Repro-
    duced in Biography Resource Center. Farmington Hills, MI: Thomson Gale.
    2005. *http://galenet/galegroup.com/servlet/BioRC* (viewed Feb. 26, 2005).

Eric Jerome Dickey interview, *Black Book Network*. *http://www.
    blackbooknetwork.com/interview-dickey.htm* (viewed March 31, 2005).

Eric Jerome Dickey interview, *Chance22*. *http://www.chance22.com/* (viewed
    Feb. 17, 2005).

Eric Jerome Dickey interview, Penguin Group (Canada). *http://www.penguin.
    ca/nf/shared/SharedDisplay/0,,96743,00.html* (viewed July 14, 2006).

Eric Jerome Dickey Web page, African American Literature Book Club.
    http://authors.aalbc.com/eric.htm (viewed July 14, 2006).

Eric Jerome Dickey Web site. *http://www.ericjeromedickey.com/* (viewed July
    14, 2006).

Sister, Sister review, *Publishers Weekly* (Aug. 5, 1996).

Rita Dove

Mainstream Contemporary Literature, Poetry

Benchmark Title: *Thomas and Beulah*

Akron, Ohio

1952

Photo credit: Fred Viebahn

About the Author and the Author's Writing

Pulitzer Prize winner at age thirty-five. United States Poet Laureate at forty. Rita Dove was twice caught by pleasant surprise, twice precipitously tipped by the acclaim, twice capably swam with the swift currents to bring poetry to a broader audience.

Born in 1952 in the center of tire production country—Akron, Ohio—where her father had broken the color barrier to become a chemist with a leading manufacturer, Rita Dove grew up in a house full of books. She also delighted in going to the library where she could be the first to discover a particular author. She excelled in school, became a National Merit Scholar and attended Miami University in Ohio, graduating summa cum laude in 1973. A Fulbright Scholarship took her to the Universeat Tuebinger in West Germany for two years. In 1977, she graduated with a master's in fine arts degree from University of Iowa Writers' Workshop.

In Iowa, Dove met German-born novelist Fred Viebahn, who became her husband in 1979. They have one grown daughter.

Dove taught at Arizona State University in Tempe, then at the University of Virginia in Charlottesville, Virginia, where in 1993 she was named Commonwealth Professor of English. For several years, Dove quietly and regularly wrote and published poetry until the Pulitzer and the poet laureate designations yanked her into the public spotlight.

The honors afforded "a platform from which to talk about something that's very near to me, about a very intimate art. It's the combination of the intimate and the public that I find so exciting being poet laureate," she said in a 1994 interview found on the Modern American Poetry Web site.

She embraced the notoriety yet found it took a toll on private time, she later explained. Her solution was to build a small cabin on her property as a writing sanctuary where she could do her composition, usually late at night. She has garnered many other honors over the years, including Guggenheim and Melon awards, a New York Public Library Literary Lion citation, and the Heinz Award in the Arts and Humanities. She has socialized with such luminaries as Bill Clinton, Oprah Winfrey, and Nelson Mandela.

Thomas and Beulah, which earned the Pulitzer, was inspired by the lives of her maternal grandparents. Dove pushed herself to explore new territory and found, as she told interviewer Grace Cavalieri for *American Poetry Review,* that what she was writing was atypical narrative. "I began to think, how do we remember our lives? How do we think of our lives or shape our lives in our own consciousnesses, and I realized that we don't actually think of our lives in very cohesive strands but we remember as beads on a necklace, moments that matter to us, come to us in flashes, and the connections are submerged."

In her Library of Congress assignment, Dove strove to bring poetry to the people and vice versa. She arranged for Crow schoolchildren from Montana to read their verses before Congress, and she worked with Lifetime cable television network to promote poetry—to make it more comfortable to the general public.

Dove lives in Virginia, a state of dichotomy, of slave owner and champion of liberty Thomas Jefferson, where Confederate generals are celebrated on Martin Luther King Jr. Day. "It's astonishing, but that's really who we are as Americans; we contain all these contradictions, and our concepts of what this country is and our great myths about America are riddled with contradictions," she said in a conversation with Malin Pereira. "So I like being at this kind of place. I can't tell you what it's doing to my writing yet. It generally takes me a good many years before I start writing about wherever I'm at."

While race is certainly part of her work, Dove said in an interview for Modern American Poetry that she thinks of herself first of all as a poet. "My own reluctance at being labeled an African-American poet comes from battling the assumption that this means writing in a racially programmatic way. As far as I'm concerned no programmatic poetry, no matter how well meant the ideology, can truly be as free."

In addition to poetry, Dove has written short stories (collected in *Fifth Sunday*) and a novel (*Through the Ivory Gate,* which alternates present and past in the telling of the experiences of a gifted black women who becomes artist-in-residence at an elementary school in Akron). She extended herself into drama with *The Darker Face of the Earth,* which was produced at the Kennedy Center for the Performing Arts in Washington, D.C.

"Dove is a master at transforming a public or historic element, re-envisioning a spectacle and unearthing the heartfelt, wildly original private thoughts such as historic moments always contain," suggested Brenda Shaughnessy in *Publishers Weekly.*

Her recent volume of poetry, *American Smooth,* finds Dove revisiting favorite themes such as race and war (especially the exploits of the 369th African-American regiment, which actually served under the French) but in technically different ways. Music has long permeated the author's writing, and now dance does as well. The title poem, "American Smooth," grows from Dove and her husband's newfound attachment to ballroom dancing.

Works by the Author

Fifth Sunday (1985), short stories
Through the Ivory Gate (1992)

Poetry

Ten Poems (1977)
The Only Dark Spot in the Sky (1980)
The Yellow House on the Corner (1980)
Mandolin (1982)
Museum (1983)
Thomas and Beulah (1986)
The Other Side of the House (1988)
Grace Notes (1989)
Selected Poems (1993), includes *The Yellow House on the Corner, Museum,* and
    Thomas and Beulah
Lady Freedom Among Us (1993)
The Poet's World (1995)
Evening Primrose (1998)
On the Bus with Rosa Parks: Poems (1999)
American Smooth (2004)

Editor

The Best American Poetry 2000 (2000)
Domestic Work: Poems (by Natasha Trethewey) (2000)

Drama

The Darker Face of the Earth: A Play (1996)

For Further Information

Cavalieri, Grace, "Rita Dove: an Interview," *American Poetry Review* (March–April 1995).
"First Black Woman Poet Laureate Seeks Respect for Poetry," *Jet* (Nov. 1, 1993).
Ingersoll, Earl G., ed. *Conversations with Rita Dove.* Jackson: University Press of Mississippi, 2003.
"An Online Interview with Rita Dove," Modern American Poetry. *http://www.english.uiuc.edu/maps/poets/a_f/dove/onlineinterview.htm* (viewed March 28, 2005).
Pereira, Malin, "An Interview with Rita Dove," *Contemporary* (summer 1999).
Rita Dove biography, *Women of Color, Women of Word. http://www.scils. rutgers.edu/~cybers/dove2.html* (viewed July 14, 2006).
Rita Dove entry, *Authors and Artists for Young Adults,* Vol. 46. Detroit: Gale Group, 2002.

Rita Dove entry, Contemporary Authors Online, Gale, 2005. Reproduced in Biography Resource Center. Farmington Hills, MI: Thomson Gale, 2005. *http://galenet.galegrou.com/servlet/BioRC* (viewed Feb. 26, 2005).

Rita Dove Web page, African American Literature Book Club. *http://authors. aalbc.com/ritadove.htm* (viewed July 14, 2006).

Rita Dove Web page. *http://www.people.virginia.edu/~rfd4b/* (viewed July 14, 2006).

Shaughnessy, Brenda, "Rita Dove: Taking the Heat," *Publishers Weekly* (April 12, 1999).

Shea, Reneé H., "American Smooth: A Profile of Rita Dove," *Poets & Writers* (Sept./Oct. 2004).

Thomas, M. Wynn, "An Interview with Rita Dove," *Modern American Poetry. http://www.english.uiuc.edu/maps/poets/a_dove/mwthomas.htm* (viewed March 28, 2005).

Sharon Mills Draper

Photo credit: Courtesy of the author

Young Adult and Middle Readers Literature, Poetry, Historical Literature, Biography

Benchmark Title: *Tears of a Tiger*

Cleveland, Ohio

1948

About the Author and the Author's Writing

The 1997 National Teacher of the Year, Sharon M. Draper is an award-winning author of fiction for young adults and children. "When I was selected as the National Teacher of the Year," she said in *Eighth Book of Junior Authors and Illustrators* (2000), "all of my dreams became a reality. To be honored and recognized as the representative for the three million teachers in this country is an awesome responsibility and a wonderful opportunity. I was privileged to travel all over the country speaking to students, educators, and learners."

Draper had aspired to become a teacher since she was a child. She came to believe that success in reading leads to success in writing. For a young adult audience, she makes sure a book's first chapter is a "grabber," something that can't be put down. She likes her stories to evolve from the characters, likewise themes and messages need to emerge naturally.

"I am a creator, an educator, a visionary . . . I approach the world with the eyes of an artist, the ears of a musician, and the soul of a writer. I see rainbows where others see only rain, and possibilities when others see only problems," Draper said on her Web page (www.sharondraper.com).

She was born Sharon Mills in Cleveland, Ohio, in 1948, the daughter of a hotel manager and a gardener. She received a bachelor of arts degree from Pepperdine University and a master's from Miami University in Ohio. She married fellow educator Larry E. Draper. They have four children.

The author received wide honor in her thirty years as a teacher. The Milken Family Foundation chose her for its National Educator Award in 1997, the same year she earned the YMCA Career Woman of Achievement honor and was named to the board of directors of The National Board for Professional Teaching Standards.

Her first fiction writing effort, "One Small Torch," was the result of a dare by one of her students. It won her $5,000 in *Ebony* magazine's literary contest in 1991. (That story now appears as the first chapter of *Forged by Fire,* the second book in the Hazelwood High Trilogy.) Her first young adult novel, *Tears of a Tiger,* was selected for the 1995 American Library Association/Coretta Scott King Genesis Award for outstanding new book. American Library Association also chose it as a Best Book for Young Adults.

The author's next book, *Forged by Fire,* looks at the themes of child sexual abuse and drug addiction. It also won the Coretta Scott King Award, as well as the ALA Best Book Award and the Parents' Choice Award.

Romiette and Julio is a takeoff on the familiar Shakespeare story. Romiette Capelle, who calls herself "Afroqueen" when on the Internet, meets Julio Montague, "Spanishlover," in a chat room, unaware they go to the same high school in Cincinnati. They meet, fall in love, and go through the same travails as the Shakespearean characters.

Using *The Battle of Jericho,* a novel that examines peer pressures and high school hazing, as an example, Draper said in an interview on the Simon & Schuster Web page, "Teenaged girls today need strong, positive role models that can show them how to be independent thinkers and confident decision makers." A main character, Dana, illustrates this, but her friends Jericho and Joshua make unwise decisions with tragic results. The topicality of all of her books, Draper said, is to appeal directly to her readers and perhaps help them make decisions should they be in similar circumstances.

Draper has broadened her writing with biography (*We Beat the Street*) and historical fiction (*Copper Sun*) and books for younger readers featuring Ziggy and his fellow Black Dinosaurs, who solve mysteries.

"I try to write powerful, meaningful, memorable stories for young people," Draper wrote on the Ohio Authors & Illustrators Web site. "I want to show them I understand the difficulties of growing up. And I want to let them know I care about their lives, their hopes and dreams, and their joys."

Works by the Author

Young Adult Fiction

Romiette and Julio (1999)
Shadows of Caesar's Creek (1997)
Jazzimagination: A Journal to Teach and Write (1999)
Double Dutch (2002)
The Battle of Jericho (2003)
Copper Sun (2006)

Hazelwood High Trilogy

Tears of a Tiger (1994)
Forged by Fire (1997)
Darkness before Dawn (2001)

Nonfiction for Young Adults

We Beat the Street (2000)

Fiction for Middle Readers

Ziggy Series

Ziggy and the Black Dinosaurs: The Buried Bones Mystery (1994)
Ziggy and the Black Dinosaurs: Lost in the Tunnel of Time (1995)
Ziggy and the Black Dinosaurs: Shadows of Caesar's Creek (1997)
Ziggy and the Black Dinosaurs: The Space Mission Adventure (1998)

Poetry

Let Our Circle Be Unbroken—Children's Poetry (1996)
Buttered Bones—Adult Poetry (1996)

Nonfiction

Teaching from the Heart (1999)
Not Quite Burned Out but Crispy around the Edges: Inspiration, Laughter, and Encouragement for Teachers (2001)

For Further Information

Draper, Sharon, e-mail from the author, Aug. 15, 2005.

Kiesewetter, Sue, "She Reaches Kids in Her Books," *Cincinnati Enquirer* (March 15, 2003).

Piehl, Norah, *Battle of Jericho* review, *Teen Reads*. http://www.teenreads.com/reviews/068984235.asp (viewed March 5, 2005).

Reynolds, Angela J., *Darkness before Dawn* review, *School Library Journal* (Feb. 2001).

Saari, Jon, Sharon M. Draper entry, *Authors & Artists for Young Adults*, Vol. 28, Thomas McMahon, ed. Detroit: Gale, 1999.

Sharon Draper interview, Ohio Authors & Illustrators for Young People. http://green.upper-arlington.k12.oh.us/ohioauthors/draper.sharon.htm (viewed March 5, 2005).

Sharon Draper interview, Simon & Schuster Web site. http://www.simonsays.com/content/content.cfm?sid=183&pid=413196&agid=8&p=1 (viewed July 14, 2006).

Sharon M. Draper entry, *Contemporary Authors*, Vol. 170. Detroit: Gale, 1999.

Sharon M. Draper entry, *Eighth Book of Junior Authors and Illustrators,* Connie C. Rockman, ed. New York: H. W. Wilson, 2000.

Sharon M. Draper Web page. http://www.sharondraper.com/ (viewed July 14, 2006).

Van Arsdale, Cassia, *Romiette and Julio* review, *Teen Reads*. http://www.teenreads.com/reviews/0689842090.asp (viewed August 5, 2006).

Tananarive Due

Horror, Fantasy, Romantic Suspense, Historical Literature

Benchmark Title: *The Between*

Tallahassee, Florida

1966

Photo credit: C. W. Griffin

About the Author and the Author's Writing

After initially establishing a niche writing supernatural suspense tales with a distinct African American flavor, author Tananarive Due has since crafted a historical novel and a family memoir of the civil rights era.

Born in Tallahasse, Florida, in 1966, Tananarive was one of three daughters of civil rights activists. (Her first name was taken from the capital city of Madagascar.) Born too late to experience much of the racial turmoil of the 1960s firsthand, she does recall at age three covering herself with baby powder to become white, as her mother had been unable to find a school in Florida that would enroll a black child. Tananarive grew up in an integrated neighborhood but never felt accepted in that or in the black community. When she was six, she watched the television mini-series *Roots* and immediately wrote her own family's history.

Due earned a bachelor of science degree in journalism from Northwestern University. She completed requirements for a master's in English literature from University of Leeds. At that English university, she was a Rotary Foundation Scholar and specialized in Nigerian literature.

The author has worked as a journalism intern for the *New York Times* and *Wall Street Journal* and as a feature writer and columnist for the *Miami Herald* for a decade. She has taught at the Clarion Science Fiction and Fantasy Writers' Workshop at Michigan State University and the University of Miami. Due has also taught creative writing at the Imagination conference at Cleveland State University.

Avocationally, she has been a keyboard player and vocalist with fellow writers Stephen King, Dave Barry, and Amy Tan in the music group Rockbottom Remainders.

She and her husband, novelist and television writer Steven Barnes (whom she met at a conference for writers), their son, Jason, and Due's stepdaughter, Niki, live in Southern California.

When working as a reporter and hoping to become a science fiction writer, Due once interviewed author Anne Rice. The famous author scoffed at those who were critical of her "wasting her talents" writing about vampires, and Due was heartened. She began her own first novel, *The Between,* writing chapters in the morning before going to work. *Essence* called the book "a major breakthrough in supernatural suspense writing."

The Between was nominated for the Bram Stoker Award for Superior Achievement in a First Novel by the Horror Writers Association. Another of her novels, *The Living Blood,* garnered a 2002 American Book Award.

In Due's second novel, *My Soul to Keep,* a woman reporter discovers her husband is really 500 years old and belongs to a secret group of immortal Ethiopians. The author wrote in the horror realm, she has said, because until then it had not seen an African American voice. Beyond that, Due, because of her own rich family experience, crafts characters in her books with dimension and feeling. As one small example, Jessica, the heroine in *My Soul to Keep,* is a practicing Christian—as is a large segment of the black community.

In 2001, Due told *Publishers Weekly*'s Stefan Dziemianowicz that she gravitated to the supernatural field to do something different from well-established African American fiction writers such as Toni Morrison, Gloria Naylor, or Alice Walker. "By looking at the world through a supernatural prism I can step back from my own real-life fears of loss and death, and make them feel a little bit safer when I write stories with characters who are facing things that I'll never have to face."

"Fear has actually propelled most of my writing," she elaborated for *Essence* that same year. "There is a misconception that I write about gore. For the most part, I don't have buckets of blood in my novels. My novels really are about ordinary people in the midst of extraordinary circumstances and how they deal with these situations."

Although she feels pretty much limited to an ethnic readership, Due in a Dark Echo Horror interview noted it has been in her favor that "the black community draws on so many belief systems that they take the supernatural for granted. I also find that a lot of black readers are willing to share their stories of prophetic dreams or ghost sightings, and to them, that isn't horror or dark fantasy, it's true life." She credits writers Terry McMillan, Samuel R. Delany, and Octavia Butler for opening the market for black genre writers.

The Alex Haley estate approached Due to use the late author's notes to complete the biographical novel *The Black Rose,* about millionaire makeup queen C. J. Walker. "I was incredibly flattered," she said in an interview found on her Web site, "just to be asked—and then Madam Walker's life is such a testament to vision and endurance. I found that it inspired me. I couldn't say no." Due's maternal grandmother had graduated from the Madam C. J. Walker School of Beauty Culture in Indianapolis, giving her a further personal connection. That book was nominated for an NAACP Image Award.

The author felt it her life's mission to, with her mother, write a family memoir of the 1960s struggle for civil rights, *Freedom in the Family.* She had long heard the stories of sit-ins, arrests, marches, and speeches. "In the Due house, Freedom songs were every bit as much of the family sing-a-long repertoire as nursery songs," she said in a

HorrorWorld interview. "We were raised attending NAACP national conventions, protests and speeches. Our exposure was very deep from the beginning.. . . I consider this book a tribute to my parents as well as all those other 'foot-soldiers' my mother taught us about." Although she had worked as a reporter and feature writer, she said she found it difficult to write the nonfiction work containing such emotion and memories.

"I hope one of the prime effects of *Freedom in the Family* will be to give people a sense of context," she said in an *Africana* interview. "For example, when you look at what happened in Florida during the 2000 elections, hearing complaints about discrimination and how the machines weren't working and were people being turned away, observers and outsiders tend to think that it was exaggeration. When you understand the history of Florida, it suddenly becomes a lot less farfetched."

◣ Works by the Author

Fiction

The Between (1995)
My Soul to Keep (1997)
The Black Rose (2000)
The Living Blood (2001), sequel to *My Soul to Keep*
The Good House (2003)
The Between (2005)
Joplin's Ghost (2005)

Contributor

Naked Came the Manatee (1997)
Year's Best SF 6 (2000), edited by David G. Hartwell
The Year's Best Science Fiction: 17th Annual Collection (2000), edited by Gardner R. Dozois
Dark Matter: A Century of Speculative Fiction from the African Diaspora (2000), edited by Sheree R. Thomas
Best Black Women's Erotica (2001), edited by Blanche Richardson
Gumbo: A Literary Rent Party to Benefit the Hurston/Wright Foundation (2002), edited by Marita Golden and E. Lynn Harris
Dark Dreams: A Collection of Horror and Suspense by Black Writers (2004), edtited by Brandon Massey
Dark Matter II: Reading the Bones (2004), edited by Sheree R. Thomas
Voices from the Other Side: Dark Dreams II (2006), edited by Brandon Massey

Nonfiction

Freedom in the Family: Mother-Daughter Memoir of the Fight for Civil Rights (2002), with Patricia Stephens Due

For Further Information

Baker, John F., "First Black Millionaire," *Publishers Weekly* (Nov. 8, 1999).

Bass, Patrick Henry, "The Living Blood," *Essence* (May 2001).

Dziemianowicz, Stefan, "PW Talks to Tananarive Due," *Publishers Weekly* (March 19, 2001).

Freedom in the Family review, *Publishers Weekly* (Dec. 23, 2002).

Good House review, *Entertainment Weekly* (Sept. 19, 2003).

Grant, Gavin J., Steven Barnes interview, BookSense.com. *http://www. booksense.com/people/archive/barnesteven.jsp* (viewed June 21, 2003).

Guran, Paula, "Tananarive Due: Unique Name for a New Dark Star," Dark Echo Horror. *http://www.darkecho.com/darkecho/archives/due.html* (viewed July 14, 2006).

Patricia Stephens, Due interview, Tananarive Due Web page. *http://www. tananarivedue.com/* (viewed July 14, 2006).

Peacock, Scot, ed., Tananarive Due entry, *Contemporary Authors*, Vol. 170. Detroit: Gale Research, 1999.

Sherwin, Elisabeth, " 'Black Rose' Describes Life of Madam C. J. Walker." *http://www.dcn.davis.ca/us/go/gizmo/2000/due.html* (viewed June 21, 2003).

Tananarive Due entry, *Contemporary Black Biography*, Vol. 20, Ashyia Henderson, ed. Detroit: Gape Research, 2001.

Tananarive Due interview, Africana.com. *http://www.africana.com/articles/qa/bk20030218due.asp* (viewed June 21, 2003).

Tananarive Due interview. *horrorworld.cjb.net* (viewed June 21, 2003).

Tananarive Due interview (March 17, 2002). *http://www.tananarivedue.com/* (viewed July 14, 2006).

Tananarive Due Web page. *http://www.tananarivedue.com/* (viewed July 14, 2006).

White, Evelyn C., *The Good House* review, *Washington Post Book World* (Oct. 19, 2003).

David Anthony Durham

Western, Historical Literature

Benchmark Title: *Gabriel's Story*

New York, New York

1969

About the Author and the Author's Writing

Facing obstacles that Laura Ingalls Wilder couldn't have imagined, David Anthony Durham's fifteen-year-old protagonist Gabriel Lynch fled the urban north in the 1870s hoping to find racial acceptance on the Kansas plains. Blacks in the Wild West? Of course. Although generally overlooked in histories, they were all over, during the Reconstruction era and later, as cattle herders, blacksmiths, hustlers, gamblers, outlaws. Gabriel encounters a sampling of these westerners all as he spurns his family's farm and searches for adventure—and affirmation.

The author "draws an impressive moral fable from the history and legends of the American West," observed a *Time* magazine reviewer. "What Gabriel learns quickly enough is that his new mentors are psychopaths embarked on a trail of revenge, rape and murder across the Southwest. When he escapes from their rampage, Gabriel must find his way not only back to Kansas but to a reckoning with his conscience."

A *Publishers Weekly* critic commented, "Durham is a born storyteller. Each step of Gabriel's descent into hell proceeds from the natural logic of the narrative itself, which manages to be inevitable even as it's totally surprising. Equally impressive is Durham's gift for describing the awful beauty of the American West."

Durham was born in New York City in 1969 but grew up in his parents' homeland, Trinidad. He earned a bachelor's degree from the University of Maryland, received the Zora Neale Hurston/Richard Wright Fiction Award in 1992, and went on to complete requirements for his master of fine arts degree in 1996, also from the University of Maryland. He accumulated many meaningful life experiences when he led Outward Bound treks and "worked as a substitute teacher in Maryland, sold expensive cheese in Portland, tended bar in Edinburgh, prepared sushi at a restaurant in Baltimore, and shoveled horse manure in Eugene," Durham told Contemporary Authors Online.

Durham's second novel, *A Walk through Darkness*, which takes place on the eve of the Civil War, is a dual examination of the harshness of slavery and the grim life of immigrants. The story follows escaped slave William as he seeks his pregnant wife Dover, who has been separated from him, so that they can flee to freedom. It also tells the story of Morrison, a Scotsman who is looking for new opportunity in a new land.

Durham's next work, *Pride of Carthage,* goes a great deal further back in history to delve into the life of the general Hannibal who nearly conquered the Roman Empire.

The author has said his novels are well grounded in research, yet he has been careful not to overindulge in his use of that research—to let the story dominate. Critics have found all of his novels to contain a strong element of violence—something Durham said is necessary to show the strength of his characters.

Today Durham and his wife, Gudrun Celia Johnston, and their children have homes in Scotland and Shrewsbury, Massachusetts. His offshore residency has given him a vital perspective, the author told Robert Fleming for *Publishers Weekly.* "America has so many things going for it.. . . . Issues of race and culture are still being worked out and aren't really fully understood. I'm interested in raising some interesting questions about race, racism and identity, both racial and national identity. The American experiment is still so new. We seem to lack the courage to fully explore and define it."

Works by the Author

Gabriel's Story (2001)
A Walk through Darkness (2002)
Pride of Carthage: *A Novel of Hannibal* (2004)
Aracia (2007)

Contributor

Gumbo: A Literary Rent Party to Benefit the Hurston/Wright Foundation (2002), edited by Marita Golden and E. Lynn Harris

For Further Information

Conroy, Robert, *Pride of Carthage* review, *Library Journal* (Nov. 1, 2004).

David Anthony Durham biography, Hurston/Wright Foundation. *http://www. hurston-wright.org/durhambio.html* (viewed Feb. 17, 2005).

David Anthony Durham entry, Contemporary Authors Online, Gale, 2005. Reproduced in Biography Resource Center. Farmington Hills, MI: Thomson Gale. 2005. *http://galenet.galegroup.com/servlet.BioRC* (viewed Feb. 21, 2005).

Fleming, Robert, "PW Talks to David Anthony Durham," *Publishers Weekly* (April 1, 2002).

Gabriel's Story review, *Publishers Weekly* (Dec. 4, 2000).

Gabriel's Story study guide, Anchor Books. *http://www.randomhouse.com/anchor/ catalog/display.pper?isbn=0385720335&view=rg* (viewed April 20, 2005).

Gray, Paul, and Walter Kirn, "Seven New Voices," *Time* (Feb. 12, 2001).

Grace F. Edwards

Mystery

Benchmark Title: Mali Anderson Series

New York City

ca. 1932

About the Author and the Author's Writing

It's a sweltering night in Harlem, and Mali Anderson is ready to help her friend Claudine celebrate her divorce from a cheating, abusive, deadbeat husband. But Claudine doesn't show up for dinner. She shows up dead. In Grace F. Edwards's mystery novel *No Time to Die,* Anderson won't be satisfied until she's found the killer.

In her creator's Anthony Award–winning series debut, *If I Should Die,* Anderson was once a New York City police officer but left the force under a cloud and a lawsuit. She enrolls in university to study for a master's degree in sociology, and she conducts her own sociology studies at her regular hangout, the Half-Moon Bar, where her father Jeffrey Anderson often plays jazz bass. Also in her household is an orphaned nephew.

A member of the Harlem Writer's Guild since 1974, Edwards began her writing career with a novel, *In the Shadow of the Peacock,* her graduate thesis for a writing program at CUNY.

Edwards was nearly finished with a romance novel, she explained to *Essence,* when an agent and editor suggested a Harlem-based mystery. "I was excited not only because I was born there but also because I thought it would be nice to write about a protagonist who is young, middle-class, well-educated and beautiful and has an independent Afrocentric spirit."

Edwards, who has taught creative writing, won a 1999 Honor Book citation from the black Caucus of the American Library Association for another mystery, *A Toast before Dying.*

After four mysteries, Edwards took a different direction with *The Viaduct,* which is about Vietnam War veteran Marin Taylor, who is assaulted and stabbed one night in a Harlem viaduct. He throws an assailant to his death, but the dead man's brother, who fled the scene, vows revenge by the most treacherous means he can think of—kidnapping Taylor's newborn child. Besides being a gritty suspense novel, the book examines the working-class life of Marin and his wife, Margaret, as they confront chilling adversity.

The novel was already in progress before Edwards wrote the Anderson series, the author said in a Black Ink Online interview. It is written from a male perspective—which the author found easy, having grown up in a household with five brothers and having two ex-husbands. "I was always in the company of men, so I just listened and picked up the rhythm of their language," she said. "As a kid growing up, a couple of my uncles used to play cards, and I would sit and listen to their language as they flipped cards on the table and bet their money. There was a lot of loose talk. A lot of bragging."

Edwards adores Harlem and said in a *Rose and Thorn* interview that she aspires "to show a different aspect of Harlem through Mali's middle-class sensibilities, to highlight the history of jazz and the famous nightclubs that are no longer there.. . . Harlem shaped my personality, my love of music, especially jazz and blues, and I feel lucky in that I'm able to draw on a store of memories to enhance my stories."

Edwards has found a comfortable niche in the burgeoning mystery genre.

Works by the Author

In the Shadow of the Peacock (1988)
The Viaduct (2003)

Mali Anderson Series

If I Should Die (1997)
A Toast before Dying (1998)
No Time to Die (1999)
Do or Die (2000)

For Further Information

Carroll, Denolyn, "First Person Singular," *Essence* (September 2000).

Cornell, J. M., "Grade F. Edwards, the View from Harlem," *The Rose & Thorn*. *http://www.theroseandthornezine.com/Profile/GraceEdwards.htm* (viewed July 14, 2006).

Grace F. Edwards interview, *Black Ink Online. http://www.randomhouse.com/broadway/blackink/qa_edwards.html* (viewed July 14, 2006).

Grace F. Edwards Web page. *http://members.aol.com/malmystery/homemain.html* (viewed July 14, 2006).

Percival Everett

Mainstream Contemporary Literature, Humor

Benchmark Title: *Erasure*

Fort Gordon, Georgia

1955

Photo credit: F. Everett

About the Author and the Author's Writing

> One night at a party in New York . . . , a tall, thin, rather ugly book agent told me that I could sell many books if I'd forget about writing retellings of Euripides and parodies of French postconstructuralists and settle down to write the true, gritty, real stories of *black* life. I told him that I was living a black life, far blacker than he could ever know.
>
> —from *Erasure*

The author Percival Everett similarly insists on living and writing the black life and has made a success of it in the more than two decades since his first novel saw print.

A South Carolinian by birth, Everett attended the University of Miami and did graduate studies at the University of Oregon. He earned a master of fine arts degree in writing from Brown University. Studying philosophy in college, he related to interviewer Ed Newton, "I was seduced completely by [analytical philosopher Ludwig] Wittgenstein. He still informs my way of thinking. The root for me is matters of language."

Before settling into a life of academia, Everett played in a blues band, worked on a ranch and taught high school math. He has been an instructor at Bennington College, the University of Wyoming, the University of California at Riverside, and the University of Southern California. He and his wife, Francesca, a professor of ancient history at University of California at Riverside, and her two children by a previous marriage split their time between a Los Angeles apartment, a small California ranch, and a farm on Vancouver Island. While he does less rock climbing today than he once did, he likes to fly fish and paint.

Everett sought relief from the routine of academic studies—although he still quite enjoys teaching—by taking a few writing courses and trying his hand at crafting a story. His first novel, *Suder,* was published soon after he completed the graduate writing program at Brown University. In the years since, he has won numerous awards including an American Academy of Arts and Letters Award for Literature in 2003.

The novel *Erasure* depicts the conflicts of college professor Thelonious (Monk) Ellison, who writes novels so obscure, his sister the physician can't read them. He is incensed at the success of a superficial "ghetto" novel by a middle-class woman who, at the most, he believes, spent a few days in Harlem visiting kin. Forced to care for his aging mother, forced to confront the issues that spurred his father to commit suicide several years before, forced to face his standstill writing career, in a burst of creative energy, he writes a biting parody of the urban best seller. When it is published, as *My Pafology* by Stagg R. Leigh, he is acclaimed as a powerful new voice for the oppressed. And that begins a whole new set of problems about Monk's *black* life.

"I see it essentially as a book about the creation of art and all the impediments placed in front of some of us as we set out to do that within this culture," the author told reporter Sean O'Hagan. "What is most interesting to me about Monk is not his colour, but his selfless examination of himself. He does not want to be constrained or reduced by society's demands or expectations. He's alert to that all the time."

Everett thrives on changing themes and styles. *Boston Globe* critic James Sallis observed, "This writer mixes genre and tone with absolute abandon, slops paint from one bucket to another, never does the same song twice, throws African American arealist tropes and retellings of Greek myths together into the same pot, never recooks a meal. He's literature's NASCAR champion, going flat out."

Everett's books are often populated with, well, unusual characters (if dead-end athletes, very short Native American women, and Strom Thurmond count as unusual). With a nod to Mark Twain, he wrote a Western in the vein of Thomas Berger's *Little Big Man* or E. L. Doctrow's *Hard Times,* for example. His *God's Country* relates the tale of gambler and loser Curt Marder and the legendary black tracker Bubba and an orphan boy Jake on a journey of vengeance. The author said the book, set in 1871, is parody, or myth. "It has nothing to do with any reality," he told interviewer Robert Birnbaum. "And how that mythology that was invented for the West is really the American story. Not the story itself but the fact that it was needed."

Everett plays with issues of race. In books such as *God's Country* and *Cutting Lisa,* he does not say whether characters are black. To him, they should be taken simply as people. Of course, the author's photo on the back of the book prompts readers to reassess. To his consternation, most readers assume the characters are white unless described otherwise. "He does not explicitly write race into his work 'unless it's a feature of the story,' " according to Trent Masiki in *Poets & Writers.* He explains, "I refuse to be influenced by a culture that is sick and so perniciously flawed. I'm going to do what I want to do and perceive the world the way I perceive the world, and I don't perceive race as a valid category, unless there is a context in which it does in fact make a difference."

Everett said he has a good relationship with his editors and their ideas. "I like criticism," he said in a FictionAddiction interview. "I see my editor's suggestions as a way to make my work better. Often, I'm too close to the story or novel to see something that's not working. Sometimes criticism is wrong, but it allows me to see something else. My skin is pretty thick."

Everett is reluctant to discuss deeper meanings in his work; he considers it the writer's role to put the material forward and the reader's to interpret it.

Works by the Author

Fiction

Suder (1983)
Walk Me to the Distance (1985)
Zulus (1989)
For Her Dark Skin (1989)
God's Country (1994)
The Body of Martin Aguilera (1994)
Watershed (1996)
Frenzy (1997)
Glyph (1999)
Cutting Lisa (2000)
Grand Canyon, Inc. (2001)
Erasure (2002)
A History of the African American People (proposed) by Strom Thurmond as Told to Percival Everett and James Kincaid (2004), with James Kincaid
American Desert (2004)
Wounded (2005)

Short Story Collections

The Weather and Women Treat Me Fair (1989)
Big Picture (1996)
Damned If I Do (2004)

Poetry

re: f (gesture) (2006)

Contributor

Making Callalo: 25 Years of Black Literature (2002)
Gumbo: A Literary Rent Party to Benefit the Hurston/Wright Foundation (2002), edited by Marita Golden and E. Lynn Harris
The Jefferson Bible by Thomas Jefferson (2003)

Books for Children

The One That Got Away (1992)

Television Movies Based on the Author's Work

Follow Your Heart (1990), based on *Walk Me to the Distance*

For Further Information

Birnbaum, Robert, Percival Everett interview, *identitytheory.com. http://www. identitytheory.com/interviews/bimbaum105.html* (viewed March 6, 2005).

Masiki, Trent, "Irony and Ecstasy: A Profile of Percival Everett," *Poets & Writers* (May–June 2004).

Newton, Ed, "Way with Words," *University of Southern California Trojan Family Magazine* (spring 1999).

O'Hagan, Sean, "Colour Bind," *The Observer* (March 16, 2003).

Percival Everett interview, *FictionAddiction.Net. http://interviews.fictionaddiction. net/percivaleverett.html* (viewed March 6, 2005).

Sallis, James, "The Audacious, Uncategorizable Everett," *Boston Globe* (July 14, 2006).

Aisha Ford

Inspirational Literature

Benchmark Title: *Flippin' the Script*

Missouri

Date of birth not revealed

About the Author and the Author's Writing

Aisha Ford, who lives in Missouri with her parents and younger sister, has found an ever-increasing audience for her inspirational romance novels.

Ford grew up in a Christian home. Thus, it's no surprise that "Christianity is a primary part of my characters' lives, because it's a primary part of who I am," she said on a Walk Worthy Press Web page. "People also tell aspiring writers to write what you know, and I know about being a Christian. I know that praying the prayer of salvation didn't make me perfect overnight (or even twenty-something years later!) I know that Christians experience real emotions and face real problems, and that sometimes, we put on happy faces even though we are hurting inside."

Ford was homeschooled from grade two through high school. "I've been an avid reader since I was a kid," she said on the twbookmark.com Web page. "One of the great things about reading is that when the weather wasn't so great, reading was something I could do regardless of the conditions outdoors." She lists as favorites Louisa May Alcott's *Little Women* and Lucy Maud Montgomery's *Anne of Green Gables* books. She attended college intending to study English but ended up graduating with a degree in ballet and modern dance from Christian Leadership University.

Ford said she hopes her novels comfort readers. "One of my goals for my writing is to write stories that appeal to a wide audience and present an example of how we should live and grow and change as Christians. I also want to write encouraging stories that positively represent African Americans in the growing field of inspirational fiction," she said on her Web page.

The biggest hurdle as a new author, Ford said in an interview with Sandra Moore, "was the fear of doing something wrong—not giving myself time to learn and make mistakes."

A suggestion her mother made, which was to write an hour a day, no matter what, has helped Ford's writing career. "Some days I wrote a lot and went over an hour. Some days I wrote two sentences and couldn't wait to get out of my chair. The result of that experiment was finishing a (rough) manuscript for my first published novel."

Ford said she generally starts with an idea, and jumps in without writing an outline. She tries to keep her characters as believable as possible, to shape them with backgrounds and worries.

The author's first three novels were written for the Barbour Heartsong Presents series. In *Stacy's Wedding,* professional wedding planner Stacy Thompson has seen it all—and never anticipated what it would be like when she enters a whirlwind romance and ends up marrying Max Edwards.

The author contributed a novelette, "The Joy Business," to the collection *Promises to Keep* and another novelette, "Mission: Marriage," to the *Dear Miss Lonely Heart* collection.

Ideas from her books come from the author's life experiences. She doesn't necessarily put a lot of stock in them, but "New Year's Resolutions have intrigued me for a long time," she wrote for another twbookmark.com Web page, "so I chose this yearly tradition as the cornerstone of the plot for *Flippin' the Script*." The story follows Sabrina Bradley, who is determined to succeed in the fast-paced world of television, even if it means keeping an unusual New Year's resolution—not to fall in love.

Ford said she appreciates that most of us need guidance in our lives. "I know how easy it is to get caught up in trying to work everything out on my own," she told *Romance in Color*. "But the Bible reminds me that I am not expected to solve everything in my own power. Matthew 11:28 says, 'Come unto me, all you who are weary and burdened, and I (Jesus) will give you rest.' "

Works by the Author

Missouri Gateways (2003)
Flippin' the Script (2004)

Heartsong Presents Series

362. *Stacy's Wedding* (1999)
405. *The Wife Degree* (2000)
461. *Pride and Pumpernickel* (2001)
Whole in One (2002)

Anthologies

Promises to Keep (2000), with Cecelia Dowdy and Lillian Meredith
Dear Miss Lonely Heart (2001), with Linda Lyle, Pamela Kaye Tracy, and Terry Fowler
Kiss the Bride (2006), with Kristy Dykes, Carrie Turansky, and Vickie McDonough

For Further Information

Aisha Ford biography, Romance in Color. *http://www.romanceincolor.com/Profiles%20-%20AF.htm* (viewed July 14, 2006).
Aisha Ford biography, twbookmark. *http://www.twbookmark.com/authors/88/3058* (viewed July 14, 2006).

Aisha Ford Web page, Walk Worthy Press. *http://www.walkworthypress. net/ford7.html* (viewed Feb. 14, 2005).

Aisha Ford Web site. *http://www.AishaFord.com/* (viewed July 14, 2006).

Ford, Aisha, "The Allure of Making Resolutions, *twbookmark. http://www.twbookmark. com/authorslounge/articles/2004/september/article 19513.html* (viewed Feb. 14, 2005).

Moore, Sandra, "Interview with Aisha Ford," *ACRW. http://www.acrw.net/ interviews/inlh5.shtml* (viewed Feb. 14, 2005).

Gwynne Forster

Romance, Mainstream Contemporary Literature

Benchmark Title: *If You Walked in My Shoes*

North Carolina

Date of birth not revealed

Photo credit: David M. Brown

About the Author and the Author's Writing

Gwynne Forster had a long career as a nonfiction writer—mostly professional papers on demographics or population characteristics—and found the transition to writing romance fiction remarkably smooth.

"I used to joke with a French colleague that when I left the United Nations," she told interviewer Lora McDonald, "I was going to write on-the-edge novels, never dreaming that I was telling the truth." She decided to write women's fiction after purchasing the only English-language novel she could find in a Bangkok hotel—*A Woman of Substance* by Barbara Taylor Bradford.

She began a manuscript in January 1994 and by October had sold it, launching a career that has recently stepped up to mainstream women's contemporary fiction and a contract with Kensington Publishing. She was chosen recipient of the Affaire de Coeur Award for Best Contemporary Ethnic Romance in 1997.

The author was born in North Carolina and grew up in Washington, D.C. After earning college degrees in sociology and economics/demography from Columbia University, she became chief of the Fertility Studies Section of the Population Division of the United Nations. Her husband is also a demographer. She has lectured and given workshops on fiction writing. She is also a freelance nonfiction writer for periodicals including *The Crisis*.

Typical of her novels is *Blues from Down Deep,* in which Regina Pearson yearns to know the family she never had. Regina's parents long ago severed ties with their kin and moved to Hawaii, where Regina grew up. Her father raised her there as a single parent after her mother died in an accident. After her father's death, Regina finds an old letter that leads her to an aunt and maternal grandfather in North Carolina. She aches to become part of her unknown family—only to find squabbling and secret-loving aunts, uncles and cousins. But there's one shining light . . .

Forster's move into the mainstream has enabled her to cut back on her day job as a consultant. "I wish I could write full time," she said in a 2002 GRITS interview. "I still work as a demographer, a profession that sums up as research and the writing of the results for publication. I write fiction . . . from around six to ten mornings, and after dinner until I fall face down on the computer keyboard."

A writer is obligated, she told reporter Carol N. Vu, "to inform as well as entertain.. . . To give constructive information without preaching. If we want preaching, we go to church."

As much as facts inhabit her everyday world, Forster forsakes most research for her novels. "My story is purely fiction," she told Lauretta Pierce of *Literary World,* in discussing *If You Walked in My Shoes.* "I have never met anyone who claimed to have given up a child for adoption. If I interviewed women and told or reflected their stories, a report on that would be a documentary, not fiction, and I have to affirm to my publisher that my novels come from my imagination only, and that all characters are purely fictional."

Forster has also written suggestions for emerging writers. "What makes characters uniquely African American," she observed in *Affaire de Coeur Magazine* in February 1998, "is their perspective of the world around them; their optimism and tenacious pursuit of dreams and goals in the presence of towering social impediments; and their ability to laugh at awesome obstacles, or to ignore them and, often, climb over them."

Works by the Author

Sealed with a Kiss (1995)
Against All Odds (1996)
Ecstasy (1997)
Obsession (1998)
Naked Soul (1998)
Beyond Desire (1999)
Wedding Bells (1999)
Fools Rush In (1999)
Against the Wind (1999)
Swept Away (2000)
Midnight Magic (2000)
Scarlet Woman (2001)
When Twilight Comes (2002)
Once in a Lifetime (2002)
Blues from Down Deep (2003)
Flying High (2003)
Last Chance at Love (2004)
If You Walked in My Shoes (2004)
After the Loving (2005), sequel to *Once in a Lifetime*

Whatever It Takes (2005)
Love Me or Leave Me (2005)
McNeil's Match (2006)
Her Secret Life (2006)
Against the Wind (2006)
When You Dance with the Devil (2006)

Contributor

Silver Bells (1996), with Lynn Emery and Carmen Green
I Do! (1998), with Robyn Amos and Shirley Hailstock
Midnight Clear (2000), with Leslie Esdaile, Carmen Green, Donna Hill, and Monica Jackson
Going to the Chapel (2001), with Rochelle Alers, Donna Hill, and Francis Ray
Destiny's Daughter (2006), with Parry "Ebony Satin" Brown and Donna Hill

For Further Information

Forster, Gwynne, "Culture and Ethnicity in the African American Romance Novel," *Affaire de Coeur Magazine* (February 1998).

Forster, Gwynne, "Don't Just Sit There: Do Something (Getting Started)," *Keynotes* (January 1999).

Forster, Gwynne, "The Road to Publication: Getting Started," *Affaire de Coeur Magazine* (April 1998).

Forster, Gwynne, "A Writer's Eyes and Ears," *Keynotes* (February 1998).

Gwynne Forster interview, GRITS. *http://www.thegritsbookclub.com/Interviews/GwynneForster.html* (viewed July 14, 2006).

Gwynne Forster Web page, African American Literature Book Club. *http://authors.aalbc/com/gwynne.htm* (viewed July 14, 2006).

Gwynne Forster Web page, Literary Times. *http://www.tlt.com/authors/gforster.htm* (viewed July 14, 2006).

Gwynne Forster Web site. *gwynneforster.com* (viewed July 14, 2006).

McDonald, Lora, Gwynne Forster interview, *Romance Reader's Connection. http://www.theromancereadersconnection.com/aotm/authorofthemonthforstergwynne.html* (viewed July 14, 2006).

Pierce, Lauretta, Gwynne Forster interview, *Literary World. http://www.literaryworld.org/GForster3.html* (viewed July 14, 2006).

Vu, Carol N., "Romance novelist to give keynote address," *Northwest Asian Weekly* (April 16, 2005). *http://www.nwasianweekly.com/editorial/romance24.16.htm* (viewed July 14, 2006).

Sharon Ewell Foster

Inspirational Literature, Romance, Historical Literature

Benchmark Title: *Ain't No Mountain*

Marshall, Texas

Date of birth not revealed

Photo credit: Bethany House Publishers

About the Author and the Author's Writing

Texas-born Sharon Ewell Foster grew up in a family with four brothers in East St. Louis, Illinois, and now lives in Baltimore, Maryland. She has two adult children. Until 2000, she worked for the Defense Department variously as an instructor, writer, editor, or logistician. She most recently worked for the Defense Information School at Fort Meade, Maryland. She now writes devotionals for *Daily Guideposts,* short stories, news and feature articles, and novels.

"I write with the hope that the words I give, if they are given in truth, will entertain, uplift, bless, heal, and serve," she said on her African American Literature Book Club Web page. "I write because I hope that my own struggles to live a truer life will help someone else."

Foster said she resisted writing for years. As a single mother, when she finally began to find times early in the mornings to jot down a story in longhand, it brought a great sense of fulfillment. She attended a writers' conference expecting to come away discouraged and ended up making vital contacts with a publisher and an agent and being named most promising writer there.

Her first novel, the Christy-award winning *Passing by Samaria,* follows the journey of Angela, who discovers the lynched body of a classmate, as she flees for her life from Mississippi north to Chicago in the early 1900s. The book was praised for its sensitive look at a vital period in American race relations. It describes the 1919 riots, black troops serving during World War I, and W. E. B. Du Bois. The author said she wrote it to exorcise anger and pain she felt over racism. She has scoffed at expectations of black Christian writers. She said she writes for men as much as women, and will confront issues of Christian racism and classism if it needs confrontation. Her books brim with optimism and happy endings.

Foster's books often have an older woman mentoring a younger woman. This in part is a tribute to her mother. "One of the most profound things she taught me she actually borrowed from William Shakespeare," Foster told a *Good Girls Magazine* interviewer. " 'To thine own self be true,' she would say over and over again. I take that very seriously, trying to be honest with myself, and I'm sure that impacts my writing. God has blessed me to be 'adopted' by lots of wise older women and men. I believe that the wisdom of all these women, and the wisdom of God's Spirit, is present in the characters that come to sit with me."

Ain't No River is something of a reverse trip; the heroes leave their urban environment seeking peace in their old hometown. Garvin Daniels, a lawyer in the District of Columbia, goes back to Jacks Creek, North Carolina, to check on her grandmother, who reportedly is being pursued by a younger man. That younger man is GoGo Walker, a former football star who as a boy spent summers in Jacks Creek and has now returned to the town, charming older women with his slick patter. There are lots of surprises in store for both characters. "Foster writes great, natural-sounding dialogue," praised reviewer Nora Armstrong. *Ain't No Mountain,* winner of the Golden Pen Award, similarly follows a curious trio on a journey of discovery with moments of lightheartedness and moments of emotion.

Riding through Shadows follows a girl, Shirley, grappling with issues during the Vietnam War era. A sequel, *Passing into Light,* follows the characters in modern times. "One of my hopes," Foster told interviewer Marilyn Griffith, "is to write in such a way that it can be shared among generations. I have a heart for young women—really, for young people. Many people from my generation have been so busy working that we haven't had a chance to pass on the mother wit that was given to us to younger people."

Foster swims and participates in other sports, is active in her church, and particularly enjoys reading and music. "Just say 'sing' and I will break out into a song," she said on her Web page.

Works by the Author

Passing by Samaria (2000)
Ain't No River (2001)
Riding through Shadows (2002)
Passing into Light (2003), sequel to *Riding through Shadows*
Ain't No Mountain (2004)
Ain't No Valley (2005)
Abraham's Well (2006)

Contributor

Keeping the Faith: Stories of Love, Courage, Healing and Hope from Black America (2002), edited by Tavis Smiley
The Women of Color Devotional Bible (2003)

For Further Information

Armstrong, Nora, *Ain't No River* review, All about Romance. *http://www. likesbooks.com/cgi-bin/bookReview.pl?BookReviewId=5136* (viewed July 14, 2006).

Griffith, Marilynn, Sharon Ewell Foster interview, *Word Praize. http://www. marilynngriffith./com/wordpraize/interviews/sefoster.html* (viewed Feb. 28, 2005).

Sharon Ewell Foster interview, *Good Girl Magazine. http://www.goodgirlbookclubonline. com/magazine/interviews/content/sefoster.html* (viewed July 14, 2006).

Sharon Ewell Foster Web page, African American Literature Book Club. *http://authors.aalbc.com/sharon_ewell_foster.htm* (viewed July 14, 2006).

Sharon Ewell Foster Web site. *http://www.sharonewellfoster.com/* (viewed July 14, 2006).

Ernest J. Gaines

Mainstream Contemporary Literature

Benchmark Title: *The Autobiography of Miss Jane Pittman*

Oscar, Louisiana

1933

About the Author and the Author's Writing

Ernest James Gaines was born, the last of six children, in 1933 on a plantation called Riverlake in Pointe Coupee Parish near New Roads, Louisiana. He attended school held at the plantation's church. As he grew up with his aunt and worked the cotton fields, he never forgot the stories he heard and the lore he absorbed.

At age fifteen, Gaines moved to San Francisco to live with his mother and stepfather and receive a better education. He experienced the world of literature for the first time. "I went into the library there because I was not allowed to go to the library in New Roads," Gaines told interviewer Faith Dawson. "I read Russian writers, French writers, and American writers, of course. And then I tried to write about the kind of people I knew."

Write about them he did in *The Autobiography of Miss Jane Pittman* and *A Lesson before Dying*. "His stories have been noted for their convincing characters and powerful themes presented within authentic, often folk-like, narratives that tap into the complex world of the rural South," observed Contemporary Authors Online.

Gaines served in the U.S. Army from 1953 to 1955. He attended Vallejo Junior College and earned a bachelor of arts degree from San Francisco State College (now University) in 1957. He did graduate study on a fellowship at Stanford University for the next two years. He has been writer-in-residence at Denison University, Whittier College, Stanford, and University of Southwestern Louisiana, Lafayette, where he also became an English professor in 1983. He has received a National Endowment for the Arts grant and has been a Wallace Stegner, a Guggenheim, and a John D. and Catherine T. MacArthur Foundation fellow. In 1993, he married Dianne Saulney. They have homes in California and Louisiana.

Gaines sold his first short story in 1956. Likened by some to William Faulkner in his creation of a fictional-yet-very-real rural setting for many of his works, Bayonne, the author told interviewer John Lowe, "I must go back to the plantation where I was born and raised. I have to touch, I have to be, you melt into things and you let them melt into you . . . the trees, the rivers, the bayous, the language, the sounds."

If he has consulted history books, Gaines said in conversation with Bill Ferris, it was for background information only. "With Miss Jane, I worked to find and think of events that she might remember from the past, locally, statewide, and nationally.. . . I didn't have any political thought in mind in terms of using a historical novel as a vehicle to rewrite American history."

Gaines wrote two novels and several short stories before *The Autobiography of Miss Jane Pittman* was published and took its grip on the reading public. The main character, who is more than a century old, relates her experiences in a life that spanned slavery through the civil rights movement. Cicely Tyson starred in the television movie based on the novel.

Gaines told a college newspaper, the *Lewis & Clark Chronicle,* that he does not plot his novels in any great detail before he begins to put words to paper. "When I begin writing, I don't know everything about my story. I don't want to know everything. I want to discover along with you, the reader. I try to breed my characters with character—to help me develop my own character and, maybe, the character of the people who read my work."

The author Wallace Stegner once pinned Gaines down on exactly who he wrote for, and he answered that it was for young black people in the South, so they could develop self-identity. And for young white people, so they will realize their lives are shaped by their relationships with blacks. Gaines expressed to *Publishers Weekly,* "But, in fact, I have no intention of addressing any group over another. It's dangerous for writers to think of their audience. I try to write as well as I can, and that's tough enough."

Stagnation of the black population in the South is at the heart of *A Lesson before Dying.* In this book, the main character, a university-educated man who, to fulfill a promise, is teaching at a small plantation school, through circumstance gets to know and ultimately bonds with a death row inmate who, unlike himself, never had a chance to climb out of the dismal existence of many poor blacks in the South. That book won the 1993 National Book Critics Circle Award for fiction.

Gaines sometimes surprises his black students by pointing to writings by a white writer, Ernest Hemingway. "I tell them: 'All Hemingway wrote about was grace under pressure. And he was talking about you. Can you tell me a better example of grace under pressure than our people for the past three hundred years? Grace under pressure isn't just about bullfighters and men at war. It's about getting up every day to face a job or a white boss you don't like but have to face to feed your children so they'll grow up to be a better generation.' "

Works by the Author

Catherine Carmier (1964)
Of Love and Dust (1967)
Blood Line (1968), short stories
A Long Day in November (1971), originally included in *Blood Line*
The Autobiography of Miss Jane Pittman (1972)
In My Father's House (1978)
A Gathering of Old Men (1984)
A Lesson before Dying (1993)

Contributor

Wide Awake in the Pelican State: Sories by Contemporary Louisiana Writers (2006), edited by Ann Brewster Dobie

Nonfiction

Mozart and Leadbelly: Stories and Essays (2005)

Television Movies Based on the Author's Work

The Autobiography of Miss Jane Pittman (1974)
The Sky Is Gray (1980), based on a short story
A Gathering of Old Men (1987)
A Lesson before Dying (1999)

For Further Information

Babb, Valerie, "Conversations with Ernest Gaines," *African American Review* (summer 1998).

"Callahan, John F., "Ernest Gaines: A Man of the Word," *Lewis & Clark Chronicle* (winter/spring 2002).

Dawson, Faith, "A Louisiana Life: Ernest J. Gaines, *NewOrleans.com. http://www.neworleans.com/lalife/17.2-ALouisiana.html* (viewed March 28, 2005).

Ernest J. Gaines biography, Vintage Books. *http://ww.randomhouse.com/vintage/gaines/bio.html* (viewed July 14, 2006).

Ernest J. Gaines entry, Contemporary Authors online, Gale, 2005. Reproduced in Biography Resource Center. Farmington Hills, Mich.: Thomson Gale, 2005. *http://galenet.galegroup.com/servlet/BioRC* (viewed Feb. 26, 2005).

Ernest Gaines Web page, African American Literature Book Club. *http://authors.aalbc.com/ernest.htm* (viewed Feb. 17, 2005).

Ferris, Bill, "Meeting Ernest Gaines," National Endowment for the Humanities. *http://www.neh.gov/news/humanities/1998-07/gaines.html* (viewed March 28, 2005).

Lowe, John, ed. *Conversations with Ernest Gaines.* Jackson: University Press of Mississippi, 1995.

Summer, Bob, "Ernest Gaines: The Novelist Describes His Arduous Efforts to Educate Himself as a Writer," *Publishers Weekly* (May 24, 1993).

Donald Goines

Urban Literature

Benchmark Title: *Dopefiend*

Detroit, Michigan

1937–1974

Photo credit: Courtesy Holloway House

About the Author and the Author's Writing

Aspiring writers are often given the advice: write from experience. That didn't prepare the reading public for Donald Goines, who began writing his gritty, violent urban novels from a prison cell and produced sixteen books in a career that soared and exploded as quickly as a fireworks rocket. Disparaged by most critics in his day, he is now being taught in novels of violence courses in colleges. Goines has been embraced by the hip-hop generation and rappers such as Tupac Shakur and Jay-Z and others who contributed cuts to a 1999 memorial recording, *Black Gangster*.

"The landscapes and character of Donald Goines's stories are not a far cry from the living reality of many of today's black youth," suggested Tracy Grant in *Black Issues Book Review*. "In the poorest sections of large cities where the population is largely African American, employment and quality education are still in short supply, so crime is the economy of the streets. And drugs drive this economy." Goines knew this violent world intimately. And that was his great strength as a writer.

Rapper DMX agreed, in conversation with reporter Lola Ogunnaike: "He was a real storyteller. You read his books and you feel like you're right there."

"Goines sold millions of copies to black America, not in bookstores but in mom-and-pop venues far beneath the radar of traditional publishing houses," explained Marc Gerald. "Today, Goines' novels continue to sell big among black men, a testament to his honest, muscular writing and the lack of any contemporary works that speak to their experiences. However, Goines remains an anathema to critics and scholars who've never given him even a glimmer of recognition."

Goines has been the subject of two major biographies in the past few years. Despite the scrutiny, his life is not well documented. He was born in Detroit, Michigan, in 1937 to a laboring family that owned a dry-cleaning business. He attended parochial school. In the early 1950s, he lied about his age and enlisted in the U.S. Air Force, serving from 1952 to 1955 in Japan. Upon discharge, Goines refused to go into the family business. Addicted to heroine, he lived on the streets, as he wrote about in *Dopefiend.* He pimped. He drove a truck. He labored in a factory. He became a career criminal, as he wrote about in *Inner City Hoodlum.* He robbed a local numbers house, as he wrote about in *Eldorado Red.* He was seven times sentenced to prison and served six years. As he wrote about in *White Man's Justice, Black Man's Grief,* he encountered intense racism in the judicial system. While incarcerated, a fan of cowboy movies, he attempted to write a western.

Serving another sentence, Goines read a book by Iceberg Slim and realized his Wild West was really the wild Midwest; he began to describe urban life. He finished two novels, *Dopefiend* and the semi-autobiographical *Whoreson,* before his release. He sold the books to a small California publisher, Holloway House, and when the paperbacks found a readership, he began to write at a ferocious pace. Living in the Watts section of Los Angeles, he wrote in the mornings, but the afternoons were devoted to his jones—his addiction to heroin. He took the pseudonym Al C. Clark for five novels about a character named Kenyatta, leader of a Black Panther-like group seeking to rid the ghetto of prostitution and crime. The hero dies in the last book.

"Goines's style is unpolished; his language is a combination of Black English and poorly edited American Standard English," in the view of Petri Liukkonen. "The books are populated with pimps, prostitutes, thieves, hit men, and dope addicts. They are people whose survival struggle in ghettos the author knew best." Yet there are emotions and characters in Goines's crude and violent world.

Goines does not glorify the slumtown lifestyle. "The glamour of easy money, fast women, and fine cars, was not coupled with fairy tale endings," said Scott Haskins. "If you're looking for a rainbow in the sky and the pot of gold at the end, you won't find it while reading Donald Goines. His works are as real as a blue sky and honest as a mother's love."

The literary virtue of the Goines books should not be underestimated, in the opinion of critic Greg Goode: "The Goines corpus of crime novels is important because it gives perhaps the most sustained and realistic criminous picture ever created by an author of the lives, activities, and frustrations of one segment of the black ghetto population."

Goines and his common-law wife, Shirley Sailor, died in their Detroit home in 1974, shot to death in an attack that was never solved.

Works by the Author

Dopefiend: The Story of a Black Junkie (1971)
Whoreson: The Story of a Ghetto Pimp (1972)
Black Gangster (1972)
White Man's Justice, Black Man's Grief (1973)
Street Players (1973)
Black Girl Lost (1973)

Eldorado Red (1974)
Swamp Man (1974)
Daddy Cool (1974), as a graphic novel
Never Die Alone (1974)
Inner City Hoodlum (1975)

Written as Al C. Clark

Cry Revenge (1974)
Kenyatta Series
Crime Partners (1974)
Death List (1974)
Kenyatta's Escape (1974)
Kenyatta's Last Hit (1975)

Motion Pictures Based on the Author's Work

Crime Partners (2001)
Never Die Alone (2004)
Whoreson (announced)
Black Gangster (announced)

For Further Information

Allen, Eddie B. Jr. *Low Road: The Life and Legacy of Donald Goines*. New York: St. Martin's Press, 2004.

Gerald, Marc, "My Search for African-American Noir's Lost Legacy," *Salon. http://www.salon.com/march97/noir970307.html* (viewed July 14, 2006).

Goode, Greg, Donald Goines entry, *St. James Guide to Crime & Mystery Writers,* 4th ed., Jay P. Pederson, ed. Detroit: St. James Press, 1996.

Grant, Tracy, "Why Hip-Hop Heads Love Donald Goines," *Black Issues Book Review* (September 2001).

Haskins, Scott, Donald Goines biography, African American Literature Book Club Web page. *http://authors.aalbc.com/donald.htm* (viewed Feb. 17, 2005).

Liukkonen, Petri, Donald Goines biography, *LitWeb.net.* http://www.biblion. com/litweb/biogs/goines_donald.html (viewed July 14, 2006).

Ogunnaike, Lola, "New Popularity for a '70s Pulp-Fiction Sensation," *International Herald Tribune* (March 30, 2004).

Stone, Eddie. *Donald Writes No More: A Biography of Donald Goines*. Los Angeles: Holloway House, 1974, rereleased 2001.

Alex Haley

Historical Literature, Memoir

Benchmark Title: *Roots*

Ithaca, New York

1921–1992

About the Author and the Author's Writing

In 1999, the United States commissioned an Alaska-based cutter in the name of author Alex Haley—the first military vessel to be named for a journalist. Transportation Secretary Rodney Slater remarked, "By seeking his own roots, Alex Haley enlarged the world for millions of Americans, connecting us with a history we thought was lost."

Three years later, the $750,000 Kunta Kinte–Alex Haley Memorial—the only monument in the United States to an enslaved African—was dedicated in Annapolis, Maryland, on the spot where the captured Gambian who inspired the author's landmark novel *Roots* arrived in America in 1767.

All this occurred after a British Broadcasting Corporation documentary in 1997 (which did not air in the United States) resurrected points made in a 1993 article by journalist Philip Nobile in the *Village Voice* that Haley borrowed passages from a 1967 novel *The African* by white author Hal Courlander and erred or fabricated his own pre–Civil War genealogy that purported to be the basis for his Pulitzer Prize–winning novel *Roots*. (The plagiarism challenge was settled out of court; Haley said researchers had provided him with uncredited material.)

Haley's legacy remains a mixed one since his death in 1992. Controversy, however, need not detract from the ambitious and compelling novel and the landmark television miniseries that grew from it.

Alexander Murray Palmer Haley was born in Ithaca, New York, in 1921, the oldest of three brothers. The family soon relocated to Henning, Tennessee, where the children and their mother, Bertha Palmer Haley, stayed while the father, Simon Haley, attended Cornell University to complete his graduate studies in agriculture. The Haleys moved to Alabama where Simon Haley took a teaching position.

After attending State Teachers College in Elizabeth City, North Carolina, and the Alcorn Agricultural and Mechanical College for two years, Alex Haley joined the U.S. Coast Guard as a mess attendant third class. He began writing stories, although it would be several years before any of them saw publication.

Haley was three times married, twice divorced, and had three children.

After twenty years in the service and rising to the position of chief journalist, Haley retired and joined the staff of *Reader's Digest*. Later, as staff writer for *Playboy* magazine, he inaugurated the periodical's extended interview feature. He interviewed Muhammed Ali, Miles Davis, Martin Luther King Jr., and George Lincoln Rockwell, among others. He expanded his interview with Malcolm X into a book: *The Autobiography of Malcolm X: As Told to Alex Haley,* a cornerstone in a library of contemporary black biography.

Recalling stories his maternal grandmother had related about his ancestors including a slave named Toby, Haley began to do research into African customs and his own family origins. He looked into records at the Library of Congress and the British Museum and traveled to a small village in Gambia, West Africa, where he is said to have met a griot, or oral historian, who related the story of seven generations of Mandinka tribal lore. Of this tribe, it was Kunta Kinte, a sixteen-year-old, who went searching for wood to make a drum. He was snatched from the forest by slavers and shipped to the United States in the 1760s. From freedom-yearning Kunta Kinte through his daughter Kizzy through her son Chicken George and George's son Tom down to Cynthia, Haley followed the line through his grandmother, who married Will Palmer in Henning.

Haley's novel and the eight-part, nine Emmy Award–winning 1977 television series sparked what continues to be a widespread fascination with genealogy. Haley with his two brothers established the Kunta Kinte Foundation as a tool to preserve genealogical records of African Americans.

"A major influence on American culture, Haley inspired a generation to seek out its heritage. Roots objectively showed the finality of slavery and the sometimes subtle consequences of assimilation," according to *Contemporary Southern Writers.*

The author said he combined facts with fiction storytelling techniques—he called it "faction"—in writing *Roots,* which won him the National Book Award in 1976 and the Spingarn Medal from the National Association for the Advancement of Colored People as well as the Pulitzer. The book couldn't have been better timed, coming out in the year of America's bicentennial when the country was keen on learning more about itself and its past.

Roots was "the single most spectacular educational experience in race relations in America," in the view of Vernon Jordan, executive director of the National Urban League.

Enslaved blacks clung long and fast to their African culture, passing it along through song and spoken word, with the best humor as could be mustered. "The book showed that the oppressed never became docile; Kunta Kinte suffered amputation of a foot for his repeated attempts to run away," noted a writer on the kirjasto.sci.fi Web page. "He valued his heritage so much that he never accepted the ways of his slave masters and insisted on being called by his real name Kinte, not by his slave name Toby."

Roots also has had its detractors. Beyond credibility of authorship and sources, some critics took issue with the story's authenticity. Dismissing Haley's depiction of a white slave hunter capturing Kunta Kinte, essayist Thomas Sowell wrote, "The tragedy of slavery was of a far greater magnitude than that. People of every race and color were both slaves and enslavers, for thousands of years, all around the world. . . . Slavery existed in the Western Hemisphere before Columbus ever got here."

Apart from his writing, Haley hosted *Alex Haley Presents: Black Men of African Descent* and was a producer of the television program *Palmerstown, USA,* which aired in 1980. He traveled widely as a lecturer. He adjusted well to his fame as a writer. "I don't let it get to me," he told reporter Jacqueline Trescott. "I stay within the bounds of where Sister Scrap Green in Henning used to keep people. Once when my father was pontificating about his fraternity key, Sister Scrap said, 'Fine, 'fessor Haley, but what do it open?' All this is nice. . . . But I have to keep thinking what do it open?"

In 1978, the state of Tennessee purchased and restored Haley's boyhood home, a ten-room bungalow in Henning, and secured its listing on the National Register of Historic Places. It was the first Tennessee-owned site devoted to the legacy of African Americans.

At the time of his death, the author was working on *Queen,* a book about his (Haley's) family experience. The book was completed by David Stevens and published in 1993.

Works by the Author

Fiction and Memoir

> *Roots: The Saga of an American Family* (1976)
> *A Different Kind of Christmas* (1988)
> *Alex Haley's Queen*: *The Story of an American Family* (1993), with David Stevens
> *Mama Flora's Family* (1998), with David Stevens

Nonfiction

> *The Autobiography of Malcom X: As Told by Alex Haley* (1965), with Malcolm X
> *Alex Haley: The Playboy Interviews* (1993), edited by Murray Fisher

Television Programs Based on the Author's Work

> *Roots* (1977)
> *Alex Haley: The Search for Roots* (1977)
> *Roots; The Next Generations* (1979)
> *Palmerstown USA* (1988)
> *Roots: The Gift* (1988)
> *Malcolm X* (1992)

For Further Information

> Alexander, George, " 'Roots' Still Resonates," *Variety* (April 28, 2003).
> Alex Haley biography. *http://www.kirjasto.sci.fi/ahaley.htm* (viewed July 18, 2006).
> Alex Haley biography, History Channel. *http://www.historychannel.com/blackhistory/?page=icons.*
> Alex Haley entry, *Contemporary Black Biography*, Vol. 4. Detroit: Gale Research, 1993.

Alex Haley entry, *The African American Almanac*. Detroit: Gale Research, 1997.

Alex Haley entry, *Contemporary Southern Writers*. Detroit: St. James Press, 1999.

Alex Haley Kunta Kinte Foundation Web site. *http://kintehaley.org* (viewed July 18, 2006).

"Celebrated Roots of a Lie." *http://www.martinlutherking.org/roots.html* (viewed September 14, 2006).

"Coast Guard Cutter Named in Honor of Late 'Roots' Author Alex Haley," *Jet* (Aug. 2, 1999).

Haley, Alex, "In Search of the African," *American History Illustrated* (fall 1974).

Haley, Alex, "My Search for Roots*,*" *Reader's Digest* (May 1974).

Jensen, Susan, "Classic Authors: Alex Haley," Suite101.com (March 28, 2000). *http://www.suite101.com/article.cfm.840/37073* (viewed May 18, 2003).

Jones, David, and John D. Jorgenson, eds., Alex Haley entry, *Contemporary Authors New Revision Series,* Vol. 61. Detroit: Gale Research, 1998.

"Remembering the Past," *Jet* (July 1, 2002).

Schulte, Elizabeth, "25 Years after Alex Haley's 'Roots'," *Socialist Worker* (Feb. 1, 2002).

Shirley, David. *Alex Haley*. New York: Chelsea House, 1994.

Sowell, Thomas, "Alex Haley's 'Roots:' Fact Or Fiction?," *Capitalism Magazine* (Jan. 30, 2002).

Trescott, Jacqueline, "Haley — The Master Storyteller Whose 'Roots' Ran Very Deep," *Washington Post* (Feb. 11, 1992).

Wynn, Linda T., Alex Haley biography. *http://www.tnstate.edu/library/digital/Haley.htm* (viewed July 18, 2006).

Patricia Haley

Inspirational Literature

Benchmark Title: *Nobody's Perfect*

Rockford, Illinois
Date of birth not revealed

Photo credit: Patricia Haley

About the Author and the Author's Writing

When she sat down to make her first serious attempt at writing fiction, Patricia Haley was surprised it came to her so easily. She self-published her first novel *Nobody's Perfect* under the byline Patricia Haley-Brown and used the name Anointed Vision for her publishing venture. She sold nearly 20,000 copies, which, she believed, validated a vision and plan that came from the Lord. The book made many best-seller lists and reached number 1 on the *Essence* chart. Haley soon signed on with a literary agent and found a mainstream publisher.

Since then, she has written what she wanted to read: contemporary fiction addressing real issues and with a spiritual message.

Nobody's Perfect, the author explained on her Web site, "represents everyone I know and no one I know. In essence, aspects of the story are common enough that just about anyone can relate to some part of the story and/or its characters." It is about a thirty-year-old single woman, Rachel, who will settle for only the perfect man as a husband. But she is impatient and falls into a whirlwind romance with Ken, a churchgoing man who, it turns out, has a daughter from a now-ended marriage. Rachel is thrown by this revelation—and ultimately has to reevaluate her stringent, twelve-point list of criteria for the ideal mate.

The author was born in Rockford, Illinois, and today lives in Pennsylvania with her husband, Jeffrey. She earned a bachelor of science degree in engineering from Stanford University and an MBA in marketing and finance from the University of Chicago. She works part time as a consultant and project manager in addition to writing.

She also writes book reviews for *Quarterly Black Review*. She is affiliated with Dominion Christian Center in Rockford and participates in the gospel choir, stewardship programs, budgeting, financial counseling, and building development committees at New Covenant Church in Trooper, Pennsylvania. She also heads a financial mentoring program there with her husband, Jeffrey. She is chaplain for her local chapter of Delta Sigma Theta Sorority. She is also an IRS tax assistance volunteer.

Haley's second book, *No Regrets,* is about Karen and Johnny Clark, married for eighteen years and raising three children, who discover their "perfect marriage" is unraveling. Karen turns to the church for wisdom and strength, and Johnny ultimately discovers what is truly meaningful in his life. "A twist at the end and a hint that the past may pose yet more problems for the Clarks save the story from a pat ending and give it a stronger message," in the view of reader Tracey D. Weaver for *Black Issues Book Review*.

In *Blind Faith,* Courtney isn't as taken with handsome, born-again believer Roger as the rest of her family is. There are a lot of characters in the book, but reviewer Tricia-Anne Blades on the Romance in Color Web site found, "Each character represents a specific thread that makes up the intricate web of *Blind Faith*.. . . The rich dialogue between and among the characters can leave one hungering for more and the belief that with faith nothing is impossible with God."

Haley's career is young, but shows great promise in a growing genre.

Works by the Author

No Regrets (2002)
Blind Faith (2003)
Still Waters (2005)
Let Sleeping Dogs Lie (2006)

Anthology

Blessed Assurance: Inspirational Short Stories Full of Hope & Strength for Life's Journey (2003), with Victoria Christopher Murray, Jacquelin Thomas, S. Thomas Guitard, Terrance Johnson, and Maurice Gray

As Patricia Haley-Brown

Nobody's Perfect (1998)

For Further Information

Blades, Tricia-Anne, *Blind Faith* review, *Romance in Color. http://www. romanceincolor.com/REVIEW_Blind_Faith_Haley_0603.htm* (viewed March 21, 2005).

Haley, Patricia, e-mail from author, June 14, 2005.

Patricia Haley Web page, African American Literature Book Club. *http://authors. aalbc.com/patriciahaleybrown.htm* (viewed July 18, 2006).

Patricia Haley Web site. *http://www.patriciahaley.com/* (viewed July 18, 2006).

Weaver, Tracey D., *No Regrets* review, *Black Issues Book Review* (Nov.–Dec. 2002).

Virginia Hamilton

Young Adult Literature, Children's Literature

Benchmark Title: *M.C. Higgins the Great*

Yellow Springs, Ohio

1936–2002

About the Author and the Author's Writing

Virginia Hamilton was a pioneer in writing young adult and children's books with strong African American themes. Deceptively simple, her books are at the same time remarkably complex.

In examining some of the mechanics of Hamilton's narrators, scholar Roberta Seelinger remarked in *African American Review,* "She has a distinct style, one that is poetic, intricate, and political; indeed, all of her books are informed by her commitment to racial issues."

Hamilton was born in 1936 in Yellow Springs, Ohio, the daughter of a musician and a housewife—both storytellers. The author grew up in a close family of farmers who scratched to make a living during the Great Depression. She took an interest in writing in grammar school.

" I remember *really* writing more than a page or two by the age of nine," said the author in a brochure issued by Harcourt Brace Jovanovich. "I grew up reading as well. I don't remember the moment I knew what words meant, but, one day, I could read—that's what I remember clearly. And a whole world seemed to open before me. It was as if I were sucking life in through my eyes."

Hamilton majored in writing at Antioch College and literature at Ohio State University. She took novel writing courses at the New School for Social Research in New York. Besides writing, Hamilton became a Distinguished Visiting Professor at Queens College and Ohio State University.

In 1960, she married Arnold Adoff, an anthropologist and poet. They lived on the same homestead her grandfather, an ex-slave, had acquired in the 1850s and had operated as a station on the Underground Railroad.

Hamilton published her first young adult novel, *Zeely,* in 1967. John Rowe Townsend described it in *Written for Children* as "a book without bitterness or paranoia . . . it is deeply concerned with black dignity: the splendor of Zeely in contrast with her humble occupation, the associations of night traveling with escape from slavery."

After her initial critical success, Hamilton went on to become the first author to win both the National Book Award and the Newbery Medal, awarded to her for the young adult novel *M.C. Higgins, the Great*. In the story, a country boy toils hard on the ancestral home first farmed by a former slave in the face of numerous challenges.

"Family is an important theme in all of Hamilton's books," said *Contemporary Authors*, "and her strong faith and love of family, along with the fact that she has always considered herself to be a loner, has influenced the characterization in her novels."

Hamilton wrote in *Horn Book* of the writing process: "What's important is expressed by a kind of illumination at the core; better, at the mind's eye of the self. It is like a brief foresight of the all-important source: the experience of living and partly living, to use a T. S. Eliot phrase, that each novelist has and which is unique to each."

The House of Dies Drear and its sequel *The Mystery of Drear House* dramatize events of the Underground Railroad and serve as a tribute to members of her own family. The story was made into an episode of public television children's program *Wonderworks*.

Hamilton also wrote several books of Jahdu tales, in the style of the traditional folktale and incorporating elements of fantasy. One of her last novels was *Bluish,* the reaffirming story of two girls who stretch beyond their inhibitions and befriend a new girl in their school who sits in a wheelchair and wears a knitted hat.

"Virginia Hamilton has heightened the standards for children's literature as few other authors have," summed up Betsy Hearne in *Twentieth-Century Children's Writers*. "She does not address children so much as she explores with them, sometimes ahead of them, the full possibilities of imagination. Even her farthest flung thoughts, however, are leashed to the craft of writing."

Hamilton, a foundation stone of juvenile fiction, died in 2002 of breast cancer.

Works by the Author

Young Adult Fiction

Zeely (1967)

The House of Dies Drear (1968)

The Planet of Junior Brown (1971)

M.C. Higgins, the Great (1974)

Arilla Sun Down (1976)

Sweet Whispers, Brother Rush (1982)

The Magical Adventures of Pretty Pearl (1983)

Willie Bea and the Time the Martians Landed (1983)

A Little Love (1984)

Junius over Far (1985)

The People Could Fly: American Black Folktales (1985)

The Mystery of Drear House: The Conclusion of the Dies Drear Chronicle (1987), sequel to *The House of Dies Drear*

A White Romance (1987)

In the Beginning: Creation Stories from Around the World (1988)

Bells of Christmas (1989)

The Dark Way: Stories from the Spirit World (1990)

Cousins (1990)
Many Thousand Gone: African Americans from Slavery to Freedom (1992)
Drylongso (1992)
Plain City (1993)
When Birds Could Talk and Bats Could Sing: The Adventures of Bruh Sparrow, Sis Wren, and Their Friends (1996)
Second Cousins (1998), sequel to *Cousins*
Bluish (1999)
The Girl Who Spun Gold (2000), with Diane Dillon
Bruh Rabbit and the Tar Baby Girl (2003)

Jahdu Tales

The Time-Ago Tales of Jahdu (1969)
Time-Ago Lost; More Tales of Jahdu (1973)
Jahdu (1980)
The All Jahdu Storybook (1991)

Justice Trilogy

Justice and Her Brothers (1978)
Dustland (1980)
The Gathering (1981)

Nonfiction

W. E. B. Du Bois (1972)
Paul Robeson: The Life and Times of a Free Black Man (1974)
Anthony Burns; The Defeat and Triumph of a Fugitive Slave (1988)

Editor

The Writings of W. E. B. Du Bois (1975)
Many Thousand Gone: African Americans from Slavery to Freedom (1992)

Fiction for Younger Readers

The People Could Fly: American Black Folktales (1985)
Jaguarundi (1994)
Her Stories: African American Folktales, Fairy Tales, and True Tales (1995)
A Ring of Tricksters: Animal Tales from America, the West Indies, and Africa (1997)
Time Pieces: The Book of Times (2002)
Wee Winnie Witch's Skinny: An Original African American Scare Tale (2004)
The People Could Fly: The Picture Book (2004)

Adaptations in Other Media

The House of Dies Drear (1984), for public television's *Wonderworks* series.

For Further Reading

Hamilton, Virginia, "Writing the Source: In Other Words," *Horn Book Magazine* (December 1978).

Hearne, Betsy, Virginia Hamilton entry, *Twentieth-Century Children's Writers,* 3d ed., ed. Tracy Chevalier. Chicago: St. James Press, 1989.

Long, Sidney D., *Time-Ago Lost: More Tales of Jahdu* review, *Horn Book Magazine* (June 1973).

McElmeel, Sharron, Virginia Hamilton entry, *100 Most Popular Children's Authors: Biographical Sketches and Bibliographies.* Englewood, CO: Libraries Unlimited, 1999.

Robinson, Beryl, *M.C. Higgins, the Great* review, *Horn Book Magazine* (Oct. 1974).

Sterling, Dorothy, *The House of Dies Drear* review, *New York Times Book Review* (Oct. 13, 1968).

Sutherland, Zena, *Time-Ago Lost: More Tales of Jahdu,* review, *Bulletin of the Center for Children's Books* (April 1973).

Townsend, John Rowe. *Written for Children: An Outline of English Language Children's Literature.* New York: J. B. Lippincott, 1974.

Trites, Roberta Seelinger, " 'I double never ever never lie to my chil'ren': Inside People in Virginia Hamilton's Narratives," *African American Review* (spring 1998).

Virginia Hamilton entry, *Contemporary Authors*, Vol. 37, revised, James G. Lesniak, ed. Detroit: Gale Research, 1992.

Virginia Hamilton HBJ Profiles. New York: Harcourt Brace Jovanovich, c. 1988.

Virginia Hamilton obituary, *Publishers Weekly* (March 4, 2002).

Virginia Hamilton Web page, African American Literature Book Club. *http://authors. aalbc.com/virginia.htm* (viewed July 18, 2006).

Virginia Hamilton Web site. *http://www.virginiahamilton.com* (viewed July 18, 2006).

Lorraine Hansberry

Drama

Benchmark Title: *A Raisin in the Sun*

Columbia, South Carolina

1930–1965

About the Author and the Author's Writing

That which makes you exceptional, if you are at all, is inevitably that which must also make you lonely.

—from *A Raisin in the Sun*

Although she was, as she said, born black and female, Lorraine Hansberry overcame the dual obstacles to enjoy a bright, if short, career as a dramatist. Her play *A Raisin in the Sun* was the first written by an African American woman to be produced on Broadway. She became the youngest and first black recipient of the New York Drama Critic's Circle Award for Best Play for that work, which ran for 530 performances. She later won an award at the Cannes Film Festival for her *Raisin* (although it was filmed without the additional scenes that she wrote), which featured actors Sidney Poitier, Claudia McNeil, and Ruby Dee.

The three-act play is set in the Chicago slum apartment that Lena Younger shares with her son Walter Lee and his wife, Ruth, and their son, Travis, and with Lena's daughter, Beneatha. Mama anticipates a $10,000 life insurance settlement as the result of her husband's recent passing. She wants to use the money to buy a house in the white suburbs. Walter, chaffing at his dead-end job driving well-to-do whites, hopes the money will buy him a share in a liquor store. Beneatha, who is attending college and aspires to become a medical doctor, supports her mother. All of the characters yearn for a better life.

In contrast to her characters, Lorraine Vivian Hansberry grew up in a more prosperous setting in Chicago in the 1930s. Her mother, Nannie Perry Hansberry, was a teacher and her father, Carl Augustus Hansberry, was a real estate broker. When she was eight, her family relocated to a restricted white neighborhood. The efforts of members of a white neighborhood to pay off Mama Younger so she will move elsewhere is another theme of *A Raisin in the Sun*—and they were forced, with the help of the NAACP, to resort to legal proceedings to substantiate their right to desegregate that neighborhood despite restrictive covenants.

The future playwright attended the University of Wisconsin for two years and Roosevelt University (now called Art School of Chicago). She moved to New York, where she wrote short stories and poetry and reported for Paul Robeson's *Freedom* magazine. At Jefferson School for Social Sciences, W.E.B. Du Bois was one of her instructors in African culture. She also came to know Duke Ellington and Langston Hughes (*Raisin*'s title was inspired by a line from one of his poems.) These creative men helped shape Hansberry's inspiration and direction. *Raisin* was Hansberry's fourth attempt at crafting a play, and the first that she completed.

Buoyant with the success of *Raisin*, and with the eruption of the modern civil rights movement, Hansberry became a popular public speaker.

Hansberry's second play, *The Sign in Sidney Brustein's Window*, although it ran for 101 performances (and closed the night of her death), was not the same critical success as her first play. Among other reasons, it was about white characters. A posthumously produced *Les Blancs,* which explored the quest of colonial Africans to secure their freedom from Europeans, also eluded success.

Producer Dory Schary asked Hansberry to write a screenplay for a series of five productions to air on NBC to commemorate the Civil War centennial. NBC management ultimately nixed the program, but Hansberry turned the project into *The Drinking Gourd.*

"It is believed that *The Drinking Gourd* was inspired in part by stories told to Hansberry by her mother and grandmother," according to *Something about the Author and Artist.* "Hansberry's grandfather, who was a slave, escaped from his master and hid in the Kentucky hills while his mother brought food to him." Hansberry also used extensive research materials to craft her story of dehumanization not only of the enslaved, but of poor whites and slave owners.

In 1953, Hansberry married Robert Nemiroff, a Jewish political activist. They met while on a picket line protesting discrimination at New York University. They lived in Greenwich Village, and later Croton-on-Hudson, New York. Although they divorced after nine years, Nemiroff remained her collaborator and completed Hansberry's unfinished *Les Blancs* after her death from cancer in 1965. He also later fused her writings into a pastiche that became *To Be Young, Gifted and Black.*

Hansberry's *A Raisin in the Sun* is restaged periodically. It was made into a television film in 1989 with Danny Glover, Esther Rolle, and Kim Yancey in the featured roles. Five years later, a *Raisin* revival opened on Broadway with rap performer Sean P. "Diddy" Combs as Walter Lee and Audra McDonald and Phylicia Rashad. Critics found her work as fresh and poignant as it was when it was written.

"In recent years, a feminist revisioning of her plays and some of her unpublished writings affirm her politically progressive views, her sophistication about gender issues, and her sensitivity to homosexuality and opposition to homophobia," according to Margaret B. Wilkerson. "As more of her work is made accessible, the full extent of Hansberry's vision and contribution to American letters will be revealed."

Works by the Author

A Raisin in the Sun (1960), screenplay

To Be Young, Gifted and Black: An Informal Autobiography (1970), edited by Robert Nemiroff

Les Blancs: The Collected Last Plays of Lorraine Hansberry 1972), also includes *The Drinking Gourd* and *What Use Are Flowers?*; retitled *Lorraine Hansberry: The Collected Last Plays* (1983)

Drama

A Raisin in the Sun (produced on Broadway, 1959; musical version *Raisin*, Broadway, 1973)

The Drinking Gourd (1960), teleplay for NBC, unproduced

The Sign in Sidney Brustein's Window (1972), produced on Broadway, 1964; musical version)

Les Blancs (1970), produced on Broadway

To Be Young, Gifted, and Black: A Portrait of Lorraine Hansberry in Her Own Words (1969), adapted by Robert Nemiroff, produced off-Broadway

Adaptations

Laughing Boy by Oliver LaFarge

The Marrow of Tradition by Charles W. Chestnut

Masters of the Dew by Jacques Romain (screenplay)

Anthologies

American Playwrights on Drama (1965)

Black Titan: W. E. B. Du Bois (1970)

Nonfiction

The Movement: Documentary of a Struggle for Equality (1964) (in England as *A Matter of Colour: Documentary of the Struggle for Racial Equality in the U.S.A.,* 1965)

Lorraine Hansberry Speaks Out: Art and the Black Revolution (1972), voice recording

Movies Based on the Author's Work

A Raisin in the Sun (1961)

A Raisin in the Sun (1989), television movie

For Further Information

Abell, Joy L., "Lorraine Hansberry's *Les Blancs* and the American Civil Rights Movement," *African American Review* (fall 2001).

Andrews, William L., Frances Smith Foster, and Trudier Harris, eds. *The Oxford Companion to African American Literature*. New York: Oxford University Press, 1997.

Carter, Steven R. *Hansberry's Drama: Commitment amid Complexity*. Urbana: University of Illinois Press, 1991.

Johnson, Brett, "Recasting a Classic: Lorraine Hansberry's *A Raisin in the Sun*—45 Years Later," *Essence* (June 2004).

Leeson, Richard M. *Lorraine Hansberry: A Research and Production Sourcebook*. Westport, CT: Greenwood Press, 1997.

Lorraine Hansberry entry, *Authors & Artists for Young Adults*, Vol. 25. Detroit: Gale Research, 1998. Reproduced in Biography Resource Center, Farmington Hills, MI: Thomson Gale, 2005. *http://galenet.galegroup. com/servlet/BioRC* (viewed Feb. 26, 2005).

Lorraine (Vivian) Hansberry entry, Contemporary Authors Online, Gale, 2005. Reproduced in Biography Resource Center, Farmington Hills, MI: Thomson Gale, 2005. *http://galenet.galegroup.com/servlet/BioRC* (viewed Feb. 26, 2005).

Lorraine Hansberry, *Voices from the Gaps*. *http://voices.cla.umn.edu/ vg/Bios/entries/hansberry_lorraine.html* (viewed July 18, 2006).

Magill, Frank N., ed. *Masterpieces of African-American Literature*. New York: HarperCollins, 1992.

McKissack, Pat, Frederick L. McKissack, and Patric C. McKissack. *Young, Black, and Determined: A Biography of Lorraine Hansberry*. Los Angeles: Holiday House, 1998.

Wilkinson, Margaret B., Lorraine Hansberry entry, *Oxford Companion to African American Literature,* ed. William L. Andress, Frances Smith Foster, and Trudier Harris. New York: Oxford University Press, 1987.

Gary Hardwick

Mystery, Urban Literature

Benchmark Title: *Executioner's Game*

Detroit, Michigan

1960

About the Author and the Author's Writing

Gary Hardwick, a television series scriptwriter, has begun to write, produce, and direct feature films. At the same time, he has maintained a flow of edgy novels with urban settings.

A Detroit native, Hardwick absorbed the Motor City's gritty rhythms to good stead for his writing. He was one of twelve children in a working-class family. He attended University of Michigan on a scholarship, then Wayne State University (where he was class president) for a law degree. He was admitted to the Michigan Bar in 1985 and later was admitted to the bar in California. He clerked to the presiding justice of the U.S. Bankruptcy Court for Michigan's eastern district for two years, then became a corporate attorney for two years for Michigan Consolidated Gas. After moving to California in 1990, he worked for the U.S. Department of Justice in Los Angeles. In 1988, he married Susan Annette Hall; they have one child.

There was always something of the entertainer in Hardwick; he performed stand-up comedy to help pay his way through college. He wrote his first novel when he was nineteen. Within a year of moving to Los Angeles, he sold a script to Disney. He soon began to write scripts for situation comedies; he also produced one, *In the House*. Since then, he has steadily climbed the success ladder, his films *Deliver Us from Eva* and *The Brothers* grossing several million dollars at theaters. *The Brothers* has been compared by some with *Waiting to Exhale* in its depiction of middle-class characters.

"I knew these people growing up," Hardwick said in a BlackFilm.com interview, describing his youth on Detroit's poor east side and his rise to the middle class. "I think it's important to tell all those stories.. . . I wanted Morris' family to be the centerpiece of the movie; to be a family that started out from humble beginnings and sort of hit the jackpot through hard work."

It hasn't been so easy to move his films in the same way. "The biggest challenge has been trying to move our films from the specialized category into mainstream acceptability," Hardwick told *Jet*'s Nicole Walker, "to have people accept Black actors who do Black characters as human beings first and Blacks second. That's an ongoing struggle for all."

Hardwick's first novel, *Cold Medina,* is about a serial killer who preys on black drug lords in Detroit—against the frenzied backdrop of a mayoral election. Perhaps the first legal thriller featuring a black protagonist, *Double Dead* follows county prosecutor Jesse King as he sorts through the tangled affairs of a murdered Detroit politician—and the murder of lawyer and former lover Karen Blake, for which King is a prime suspect. A reviewer on the African American Literary Book Club Web site said of the author, "Hardwick is one of the rare breed of African-American authors who write mystery/suspense novels with a violent, hard-edged, reality-based style that takes place in the inner city."

In 2005, Hardwick ventured into the international thriller field with *The Executioner's Game,* in which rogue CIA agent Luther Green is sent to cover up new information about the Kennedy assassination. That same year, using a penname, A. A. Clifford, Hardwick established his own publishing company for a science fiction novel, *SexLife.*

Hardwick sees a strong future in writing novels, then selling the rights or producing them as motion pictures. He feels he is in an ideal position in Hollywood, with his legal background. "It has helped that I am very disciplined," he told interviewer Elisabeth Sherwin, adding, "and people are scared of lawyers and that doesn't hurt."

Works by the Author

Cold Medina (1996)
Double Dead (1997)
Supreme Justice (1999)
Bring It On (2000)
Color of Justice (2001), sequel to *Supreme Justice*
Radio (2002), writer and director
Executioner's Game (2005)
Slam the Trick (announced)

Written as A. A. Clifford

Sex Life (2005)

Films and Television Movies

Hangin' with Mr. Cooper (1992), television scriptwriter
Where I Live (1993), television scriptwriter
South Central (1994), television coproducer
Me and the Boys (1994), television scriptwriter
In the House (1995), television scriptwriter
Matt Waters (1996), television scriptwriter
Trippin (1999), writer
Cheer Fever, director
The Brothers (2001), writer and director
Deliver Us from Eva (2003), cowriter and director

For Further Information

Gary Hardwick entry, Contemporary Authors Online, Gale, 2005. Reproduced in Biography Resource Center, Farmington Hills, MI: Thomson Gale, 2005. *http://galenet.galegroup.com/servlet/BioRC* (viewed Feb. 25, 2005).

Gary Hardwick Web site. *http://www.ghard.com/index2.htm* (viewed March 26, 2005).

Morales, Wilson, "It's a Hard Knock Life: An Interview with Gary Hardwick," BlackFilm.com. *http://blackfilm.com/0305/features/i-garyhardwick.shtml* (viewed March 26, 2005).

Sherwin, Elisabeth, Gary Hardwick interview, *Davis Virtual Market. www.dcn. davis.ca.us/go/gizmo/1998/hardwick.html* (viewed Sept. 14, 2006).

Walker, Nicole, "Filmmaker and Writer Gary Hardwick Strives for Humor and Balance in Portrayals of Blacks," *Jet* (June 23, 2003).

E. Lynn Harris

**Mainstream Contemporary
Literature, Gay Literature**

Benchmark Title: *Invisible Life*

Flint, Michigan
1957

Photo credit: Matthew Jordan Smith

About the Author and the Author's Writing

E. Lynn Harris took a major risk on his journey from IBM computer salesman to professional fiction writer. He quit his job and self-published his first novel.

Born in Flint, Michigan, in 1957, Harris grew up in Little Rock, Arkansas, where his unwed mother worked in a factory. In 1977, he graduated with a journalism major from the University of Arkansas; he had been both the school's first black yearbook editor and its first black male cheerleader.

Harris long yearned to write. In the face of a dozen rejections from major publishers, he quit his job after eleven years, hired a printer and with his savings self-published *Invisible Life*. By then living in Atlanta, he made the rounds to black-owned bookstores, groceries, and hair salons to drum up sales. His industriousness eventually brought him an agent and a contract with Doubleday in 1992. In a new edition, that first book along with its sequel sold some 200,000 copies.

While in college, Harris found he was bisexual and that orientation afforded a twist in his prose. He examined, for example, what happens when one partner in a heterosexual marriage discovers the other partner is bisexual or homosexual. They should "realize that the 'coming out' process is very painful," Harris told *Jet*. "They [people coming out] need support more than they need people turning their back on them." He counsels keeping an open mind.

Harris guides his readers through reexamination of relationships. "If it makes women and men take a closer look at the relationships they choose, that's wonderful. These stories don't just affect women. I've heard stories of men who were hurt after a woman came out as a lesbian. It goes both ways," he told *Ebony*.

Invisible Life helped the author work out his emotions. "It helped me to deal with my own sexuality," he told *Entertainment Weekly*. "For me, my 20s and early 30s were spent just hiding and running, because there was no one to tell me that my life had value and the way I felt was okay."

Despite his frequent theme, Harris has generally shunned gay politics, and thus the activist gay and lesbian community was slow to support his writing. This is not to say he's had it easy with the black community, either, which still apparently resents that gay activists often equate their struggle with that of African Americans. "Sixty percent of my audience is black women—straight black women," the author told the *Advocate*. "They're my sisters. They're the smartest, most loyal readers. Another 10% or so is straight black men. The women are reading me. So the men come to find out what's going on. The rest are gay people, mostly black and Latino."

Harris enjoys reading mostly women fiction writers—Terry McMillan, Bebe Moore Campbell, Tina Ansa—and male nonfiction writers—Nathan McCall, Cornel West. Perhaps not surprisingly, his success as a writer has prompted comparisons as the "Luther Vandross of literature" and the "male Terry McMillan" and the "black Jackie Collins."

Harris recently wrote a memoir. It wasn't his first attempt. His original contract with a mainstream publisher was for a memoir, which he completed. "After writing it, I realized that it wasn't a memoir," he said in a *Publishers Weekly* interview with Elizabeth Millard. "It was fiction, because it was how I wanted people to see my life. I was also getting more e-mails and letters from fans around that time, and I decided, for them, I needed to tell the whole truth. So I tore [the first memoir I wrote] up. Doubleday didn't mind. They said it was up to me. I should tell the story when I was ready." He was ready with *What Becomes of the Brokenhearted* in 2003.

More recently Harris's career took another turn. He wrote a screenplay for a proposed remake of the film *Sparkle*. He has sold novel rights for motion picture production. And he has written a pilot for a new dramatic television series.

Works by the Author

Invisible Life (1991)
Just as I Am: A Novel (1994), sequel to *Invisible Life*
And This Too Shall Pass (1996)
If This World Were Mine (1997)
Abide With Me (1999)
Not a Day Goes By: A Novel (2000)
Any Way the Wind Blows: A Novel (2001)
A Love of My Own (2002)
I Say a Little Prayer (2005)
The Greatest Pretender (announced for 2007)
Love Is Stronger than Pride: E. Lynn Harris's New Novella Plus Four Novellas from Debut Authors (announced for 2007)
The Greatest Pretender (announced for 2008)

Contributor

Got to Be Real: Four Original Love Stories (2000)

Editor and Contributor

Gumbo: A Celebration of African American Writing (2003)
Freedom in this Village: Black Gay Men's Writing 1969 to the Present (2004), with Marita Golden

Nonfiction

What Becomes of the Brokenhearted: A Memoir (2003)

For Further Information

Achy, Obejas, "In Profile: E. Lynn Harris," *The Advocate* (June 24, 1997).

"Cruz, Clarissa, "Sex and the Single Guy; With a Screenplay, a Memoir, and Two Film Adaptations of His Books in the Works, E. Lynn Harris—the Chart-Topping Author of Romance Novels about Black Men—Has Got It Going On," *Entertainment Weekly* (Sept. 1, 2000).

E. Lynn Harris entry, Contemporary Authors Online, Gale, 2005. Reproduced in Biography Resource Center. Farmington Hills, MI: Thomson-Gale, 2005. *http://galenet.galegroup.com/servlet/BioRC* (viewed Feb. 26, 2005).

E. Lynn Harris interview, *Black Ink Online. http://www.randomhouse.com/broadway/blackink/qa_harris.html* (viewed Sept. 14, 2006).

E. Lynn Harris interview, *Book Remarks* (Jan. 2001). *http://www.book-remarks.com/elynn_harris.htm* (viewed July 18, 2006).

E. Lynn Harris Web page, African American Literature Book Club. *http://authors.aalbc.com/e.htm* (viewed July 18, 2006).

E. Lynn Harris Web site. *http://www.randomhouse.com/features/elynnharris/about.html* (viewed Sept. 14, 2006).

Millard, Elizabeth, "Writing to Find Some Kind of Peace of Mind: PW Talks with E. Lynn Harris," *Publishers Weekly* (June 16, 2003).

"Q&A with Best-Selling Author E. Lynn Harris," *Ebony* (October 2000).

"Sweet Bi and Bi: E. Lynn Harris Has Twin Best-Sellers with an Ambisexual Hero," *People Weekly* (May 15, 1995).

"What to Do When Your Partner Comes Out of the Closet," *Jet* (Feb. 23, 1998).

Gar Anthony Haywood

Mystery

Benchmark Titles: Aaron Gunner Series

Los Angeles, California

1954

About the Author and the Author's Writing

Gar Anthony Haywood was inspired by the 1950s television show *Peter Gunn,* a program that depicted a jazz-loving Los Angeles private eye who hangs out at a nightclub, when he created his fictional L.A. operative Aaron Gunner and the Acey Deuce Bar. Although he has been overshadowed by Walter Mosley (and his Easy Rawlins series), Haywood caught the attention of critics and he won the 1988 Best First P.I. Novel Contest and the 1996 Shamus and Anthony awards for the Gunner short story "And Pray Nobody Sees You," from the anthology *Spooks, Spies, and Private Eyes.*

Haywood was born in Los Angeles in 1954. As a youth he devoured The Daredevil, the Fantastic Four, and other Marvel Comics heroes and fantasy and science fiction by Robert E. Howard, Larry Niven, and Frank Herbert. He worked as a computer technician for two decades before he began writing. His crime novels were specifically influenced at first by Ross MacDonald and Lawrence Block, later by Martin Cruz Smith, James Lee Burke, and Elmore Leonard.

"Internally, my characters are very much reflections of myself," he said in a Mystery One interview. "They tend to be stronger-willed, though. And I think it would be more accurate to say that I regularly have them do things I could *never* do."

Gunner is a prototypical near-alcoholic private investigator. In *Fear of the Dark,* he tracks down the man who gunned down a bartender and a member of the Brothers of Volition, a black revolutionary group. "The biggest strength here is the vividness and genuineness of the writing," observed a Mystery Guide reviewer. "Haywood is strong and unsentimental in his portrait of what it's like to be down and out in some of the poorest neighborhoods of Los Angeles."

A 180-degree change of pace are Haywood's cozy novels featuring retired cop Joe Loudermilk and his wife, Dottie, who have retired, sold the house, and are traveling the country in their Airstream—for the adventure and to get away from their adult children. In *Going Nowhere Fast,* a corpse turns up in their highway-bound home. "The best thing about the book is Dottie's narration," Mystery Guide observed, "Which is warm and witty in a sentimental, motherly way."

"I wanted to do a second series," Haywood said in an *American Visions* interview, "because I didn't want my character to get stale."

Taking a third spin on crime solving, Haywood launched a third series, issued under the penname Ray Shannon and featuring an executive with a Hollywood production company, Ronnie Deal, who in *Man Eater* tries to evade the aim of a hired killer.

Haywood was intrigued by the possibilities of using a mixed racial cast set against a backdrop of Hollywood's fast-paced, and at times crazy, environment. "But there was no one great inspiration for the story other than maybe the title and I knew that I wanted such a strong female lead that I wanted the term Man Eater to apply to her accurately," he said in a Novel View interview.

This is his second series told from a female perspective, but he has said he makes no radical change in the way he writes the character, other than to make her a little smarter and a little humbler.

Haywood has also written teleplays for two ABC *Movies of the Week* and for the drama programs *New York Undercover* and *The District*. He lives in Los Angeles with his wife and children.

Works by the Author

Aaron Gunner Series

Fear of the Dark (1988)
Not Long for This World (1990)
You Can Die Trying (1993)
It's Not a Pretty Sight (1996)
When Last Seen Alive (1998)
All the Lucky Ones Are Dead (1999)

Joe and Dottie Loudermilk Series

Going Nowhere Fast (1994)
Bad News Travels Fast (1995)

Contributor

Spooks, Spies, and Private Eyes: Black Mystery, Crime, and Suspense Fiction of the 20th Century (1995), edited by Paula L. Woods

Written as Ray Shannon

Ronnie Deal Series
Man Eater (2003)

For Further Information

Aaron Gunner Web page, *Thrilling Detective*. http://www.thrillingdetective. com/gunnera.html (viewed Sept. 14, 2006).
Fear of the Dark review, *MysteryGuide.com*. http://www.mysteryguide.com/ bkHaywooddark.html (viewed Sept. 14, 2006).

Gar Anthony Haywood entry, *Contemporary Black Biography*, Vol. 43. Detroit: Gale Group, 2004.

Gar Anthony Haywood interview, *A Novel View*. *http://www.anovelview. com/chats/ray_shannon_author_of_man_eater.htm* (viewed Feb. 14, 2005).

Gar Anthony Haywood interview, Mystery One Bookstore Web site, spring 2003. *http://www.mysteryone.com/GarHaywoodInterview.htm* (viewed July 18, 2006).

Going Nowhere Fast review, MysteryGuide.com. *http://www.mysteryguide. com/bkHaywoodFast.html* (viewed July 18, 2006).

Tillery, Carolyn, Gar Anthony Haywood interview, *American Visions* (April-May 1997).

Donna Hill

Romance, Mainstream Contemporary Literature

Benchmark Title: *Chances Are*

Brooklyn, New York
1955

Photo credit: Courtesy of the author

About the Author and the Author's Writing

Donna Hill's first fiction was a short story that she sold to *Black Romance* in 1987. Later, after she became an advice columnist for the periodical, her editor encouraged her to write a romance novel. So she did. In 1990, *Rooms of the Heart* was released. The next year, her next novel *Indiscretions* was, according to her Web site, the first African American romance to make the *Essence* best-seller list.

A divorced mother of three, Brooklyn-born Hill attended Pace University. She is a public relations associate for the Queens Borough Public Library system, and she has her own production company, Annod Productions, which arranges author events for cable or television broadcast. Among numerous awards, she was the first recipient of the Trailblazer Award in 2002 for her pioneering work.

It's a juggling act to maintain a home life and two careers, the author says. "I am a single mom, and I have three kids and a grandson who all live with me," she commented in her African American Literature Book Club Web page. "My balance comes from setting goals and priorities, including my children, and by incorporating people in my life who provide me with positive energy and who creatively compliment me. This gives me more energy to stretch myself further."

In a *Romance in Color* interview Hill said she enjoys her craft. "Bringing to the page the warmth, beauty and passions of black men and women and being able to showcase black love in a positive light. Being able to tour the country and tell people that, being interviewed on radio, or television or newspapers and be able to say that."

At least one of her novels has exceeded expectations. Hill said a social agency in Louisiana has patterned a group residence after the one depicted in her novel *Chances*

144

Are. The organization Divas in Society emerged from her novel *Divas, Inc.*, a look at extremely arrogant women.

Rayne Holland, the main character of *In My Bedroom,* struggles to recover from an auto accident that took the lives of her husband and daughter. Her therapist and friends help her on her road to recovery, a major detour being her father's unusual distance. Denise Morrison, at the beginning of *Rockin' around That Christmas Tree* (which Hill cowrote with Francis Ray), decides that since her children are grown and her husband is discouraging her career interest, it's time to get a divorce.

Hill thrives on topicality. "I don't think I could write a novel (intentionally) if I did not feel that passion or drive to put the topic on the page," she said on her Web site. "Whenever I write, I want people to question themselves and each other. I want to be able to give readers a different way of looking at things, find a new approach—but by doing it subtly."

Hill has ventured into the past in her generational novel *Rhythms,* which is set in 1927 Mississippi and examines social barriers, prejudice, life and family.

The author's recent *Getting Hers* spins its suspense plot from a classic movie based on a novel by Patricia Highsmith. Hill poses the question: How far would you go to attain retribution? "I was totally fascinated with [director Alfred] Hitchcock's movie *Strangers on a Train,"* Hill said in an eMediaWire interview. "I wondered how I could use the concept of strangers, mob mentality and a unified goal and add an urban twist. The result was *Getting Hers.*"

Hill maintains a busy writing schedule, producing both novels and, increasingly, novellas for an avid audience.

Works by the Author

Rooms of the Heart (1990)
Indiscretions (1991)
Temptation (1994)
Murder Uptown (1992)
Scandalous (1995)
Deception (1996)
Intimate Betrayal (1997)
A Private Affair (1998)
Shipwreck Season (1998)
Charade (1998)
Chances Are (1998)
Pieces of Dreams (1999)
Interlude (1999)
A Scandalous Affair (2000)
If I Could (2000)
Through the Fire (2001)
Soul to Soul (2001)
Rhythms (2002)
An Ordinary Woman (2002)
Rockin' around That Christmas Tree: A Holiday Novel (2003), with Francis Ray

In My Bedroom (2004)
Say Yes (2004)
Dare to Dream (2004)
Divas, Inc. (2004)
Getting Hers (2005)
In My Bedroom (2006)
Love Becomes Her (2006)
Guilty Pleasures (2006)
Long Distance Lover (2006)
Savin' All Lovin' (2006)
Soul to Soul (2006)

Contributor

Spirit of the Season (1994), with Francis Ray and Margie Walker
Love Letters (1997), with Rochelle Alers and Janice Sims
Rosie's Curl and Weave (1998), with Rochelle Alers, Felicia Mason, and Francis Ray
Winter Nights (1999), with Shirley Hailstock and Francis Ray
Della's House of Style (2000), with Rochelle Alers, Felicia Mason ,and Francis Ray
Welcome to Leo's (2000), with Rochelle Alers, Brenda Jackson, and Francis Ray
Indigo after Dark, Vol. 1 (2001)
Midnight Clear (2000), with Leslie Esdaile, Gwynne Forster, Carmen Green, and Monica Jackson
Going to the Chapel (2001), with Rochelle Alers, Gwynne Forster, and Francis Ray
Sister, Sister (2001), with Carmen Green and Janice Sims
Night Wind Calling (2001), with Dawna Anderson
'Tis the Season (2001), with Rochelle Alers and Candice Poarch
Silk Black Anthology (2002)
Proverbs for the People (2003)
Living Large (2003), with Rochelle Alers, Brenda Jackson, and Francis Ray
Dark Thirst: An Anthology (2004), with Omar Tyree, Angela C. Allen, Monica Jackson, Linda Addison, and Kevin S. Brockenbrough
A Whole Lotta Love (2004), with Brenda Jackson, Monica Jackson, and Francis Ray
Where There's a Will (2004), with Bridget Anderson, Shirley Hailstock, Shelby Lewis, and Margie Walker
Let's Get It On (2004), with Rochelle Alers, Brenda Jackson, and Francis Ray
Big Girls Don't Cry (2005), with Brenda Jackson, Monica Jackson, and Francis Ray
Courageous Hearts (2005)
Destiny's Daughter (2006), with Gwynne Forster and Parry "Ebony Satin" Brown

Screenplay

Fire (2000), cowriter

Author's Works Made into Television Films

Masquerade, based on the short story from *Love Letters*
Intimate Betrayal, based on the 1997 novel
A Private Affair, based on the 1998 novel

For Further Information

Butler, Tamara, *Rockin' around That Christmas Tree* review, *Library Journal* (Nov. 1, 2003).

Donna Hill entry, *Who's Who Among African Americans*, 17th ed. Detroit: Gale Group, 2004.

Donna Hill Web page, African American Literature Book Club. *http://authors. aalbc.com/donna.htm* (viewed Feb. 17, 2005).

Hoffman, LaShaunda, "Author of the Month—Donna Hill," *Romance in Color. http://www.romanceincolor.com/authormthill.htm* (viewed May July 18, 2006).

In My Bedroom review, *Publishers Weekly* (Dec. 8, 2003).

"An Intimate Chat with Author Donna Hill," Donna Hill Web site. *http://www. donnahill.com/* (viewed Sept. 14, 2006).

Let's Get It On review, *Publishers Weekly* (Nov. 8, 2004).

"Three Strangers—A Deadly Pact—The Perfect Crime—Hitchcock Comes to Uptown," *eMediaWire* (April 21, 2005). *http://emediawire.com/releases/ 2005/4/emw231037.htm* (viewed May 13, 2005).

Chester Himes

Mystery, Urban Literature, Mainstream Contemporary Literature

Benchmark Title: *Cotton Comes to Harlem*

Jefferson City, Missouri

1909–1984

About the Author and the Author's Writing

In a quiet moment, you might find the Harlem cops Coffin Ed Johnson and Grave Digger Jones chomping down chicken and black-eyed peas at Mammy Louise's eatery. In a wild episode, you might find the same pair squeezing information out of a jittery informant or punching a confession from a reluctant criminal.

"Folks just don't want to believe that what we're trying to do is make a decent peaceful city for people to live in, and we're going about it the best way we know how," Coffin Ed explains in *The Heat's On*.

Author Chester Bomar Himes was born in Jefferson City, Missouri, in 1909. Although his parents were middle class and educated, they often bickered, in part because of his mother's light and his father's dark skin tones, his mother's demanding personality (she was part white), and his father's genial acceptance (he was the son of a slave). When a work injury afforded a small disability income, Himes attended Ohio State University but was expelled in his sophomore year.

The racism suffered by his mother, guilt from the accidental blinding of his brother during a school science demonstration, the injuries from falling down a hotel elevator shaft from which he never quite recovered—these were among the demons that haunted Chester Himes. He pimped and bootlegged liquor and spent seven and a half years in Ohio State Penitentiary for armed robbery. Then he began to write short stories for African American newspapers and *Esquire,* among other markets. "Himes's achievement as a writer of fiction, indeed, his very existence as an author comes directly from his experience in prison, which shaped his imagination and determined his outlook on American society," said H. Bruce Franklin in *Prison Literature in America*.

In 1937, Himes married Jean Lucinda Johnson. During the Depression, he worked for the Works Progress Administration's Writers Project in Ohio then joined the staff of the *Cleveland Daily News*. During World War II, he worked at a California shipyard. His first novel, *If He Hollers, Let Him Go,* appeared in 1945. It is about black defense plant laborer Bob Jones's humiliation and anger because of the daily racism he faces.

Himes wrote his first three books while living in California. He and Jean divorced in 1951. Two years later, in 1953, he went into self-exile in Europe. There he met a white librarian, Lesley Packard, and they lived together and finally married in 1978. He continued to write.

"Himes used writing as a form of therapy," observed Michael Marsh. "He focused on the struggles of black male characters who ranged from losers or victims defeated by whites to strong men who occasionally triumphed over obstacles. Racial conflict is a central theme."

At the request of the French publisher Gallimard, Himes began to write crime novels. The Coffin Ed and Grave Digger cases appeared first in French-language books under the line La Serié Noire.

"In France (and later in Germany) Himes was accepted as a serious novelist who wrote sociological crime novels," observed Jens Peter Bomar, "but America was wary." Himes won the Grand Prix de Littérature Policiére in 1958 in France for *For Love of Imabelle*. His books in America were marketed as sexy and violent in the spirit of Mickey Spillane, rather than probing and elegiac a la Raymond Chandler.

But Himes is not a Mickey Spillane—he is much more than that. In the view of Jay B. Berry Jr. in *The Armchair Detective,* "He should be recognized as a capable, and at times outstanding, practitioner of the art of detective story writing."

Himes was in his forties when he began writing fiction, and in his fifties when he achieved success with his Harlem crime novels—more urban fiction than police procedural, despite the main characters Coffin Ed and Grave Digger. One can detect in these characters, and in the author himself, an increasing sense of despair that blacks could overcome the oppression-forced, violence-destined rut they were in.

Cotton Comes to Harlem, to give an example, has the duo involved with Deke O'Hara, newly freed conman whose new back-to-Africa scam is fooling a lot of Harlemites—to the tune of $87,000, which is heisted by a white gunman and hidden in a bale of cotton. The story inspired the first of two motion pictures based on Himes's Coffin Ed and Grave Digger books.

"It struck me that sex and writing were my two obsessions," Himes said in *My Life of Absurdity,* "writing because it was my profession, my ambition, my goal and my salvation, and sex because it was my sword and shield against the hurts and frustrations of the other."

"The only time I was happy," he is quoted by his biographer James Sallis, "was while writing these strange, violent, unreal stories." Himes died in Spain in 1984.

Works by the Author

If He Hollers, Let Him Go (1945)
Lonely Crusade (1947)
Cast the First Stone (1952)
The Third Generation (1954)
The Primitive (1955), retitled *The End of a Primitive* (1990)
Dare-dare (1959) (in English as *Run Man Run,* 1966)
Pinktoes (1961)
Mamie Mason; ou, Un Exercise de la bonne volonte (1963)
Black on Black: Baby Sister and Selected Writings (1973), short stories

Une Affaire de viol (1963) (in English as *A Case of Rage,* 1980; *A Case for Rape,* 1985)

Un Menteau du reve? (1982)

The Collected Stories of Chester Himes (1990)

Plan B: A Novel (1993)

Coffin Ed and Grave Digger Jones Series

For Love of Imabelle (1957), revised as *A Rage in Harlem* (1965)

Il pleut des coupe durs (1958) (in English as *The Crazy Kill,* 1959)

Couche dans le pain (1959) (in English as *The Real Cool Killers,* 1959)

Imbroglio negro (1960) (in English as *All Shot Up,* 1960)

Tout pour plair (1959) (in English as *The Big Gold Dream,* 1960)

Ne nous enverons pas! (1964) (in English as *The Heat's On,* 1961; retitled *Come Back Charleston Blue,* 1970)

Retour en Afrique (1964) (in English as *Cotton Comes to Harlem,* 1965)

Blind Man with a Pistol (1969); also titled *Hot Day, Hot Night* (1969)

Nonfiction

The Quality of Hurt (1972), autobiography

My Life of Absurdity (1976), autobiography

Conversations with Chester Himes (1995), edited by Michel Fabre and Robert E. Skinner

Contributor

American Negro Short Stories (1966), edited by John Henrik Clarke

The Best Short Stories by Negro Writers: An Anthology from 1899 to the Present (1969), edited by Langston Hughes

Negro Caravan (1969), edited by Sterling Allen Brown

Black Writers of America (1997), edited by Richard Barksdale and Kenneth Kinnamon

Right On! (2000)

Films Based on the Author's Works

Cotton Comes to Harlem (1970)

Come Back Charleston Blue (1974), based on *The Heat's On*

For Further Information

Becker, Jens Peter, Chester Bomar Himes entry, *St. James Guide to Crime & Mystery Writers*, 4th ed., Jay P. Pederson, ed. Detroit: St. James Press, 1996.

Bell, Bernard W., "Conversation with Chester Himes," *African American Review* (summer 1998).

Berry, Jay R. Jr., "Chester Himes and the Hard-Boiled Tradition," *Armchair Detective* 15, no. 1 (1982).

Chester (Bomar) Himes entry, Contemporary Authors Online, Gale, 2005. Reproduced in Biography Resource Center. Farmington Hills, MI: Thomson Gale, 2005. *http://galenet.galegroup.com/servlet/BioRC* (viewed Feb. 26, 2005).

Chester Himes biography. *http://www.math.buffalo.edu/~sww/HIMES/himes-chester_BIO.html* (viewed Sept. 14 2006).

Chester Himes entry, *St. James Encyclopedia of Popular Culture*. Detroit: St. James Press, 2000.

Franklin, H. Bruce, "Portrait of the Artist as a Young Convict," *Andromeda*. *http://andromeda.rutgers.edu/~hbf/himes.html* (viewed July 18, 2006).

Lundquist, James. *Chester Himes*. New York: Ungar, 1976.

Marsh, Michael, "Harsh Words," *Chicago Reader* (Dec. 4, 1998) reprinted on African American Literature Book Club's Chester Himes Web page. *http://authors.aalbc.com/chesterhimes.htm* (viewed July 18, 2006).

Muller, Gilbert H. *Chester Himes*. Boston: Twayne, 1986.

Ostrowski, Mark, "Life after Chester," *Spike* magazine. *http://www.spikemagazine.com/0899lesleyhimes.php* (viewed Sept. 14, 2006).

Sallis, James. *Chester Himes: A Life*. New York: Walker, 2001.

Siegel, Jeff, "Lonely Crusader: A Few Words about Chester Himes," *Armchair Detective* (fall 1996).

Skinner, Robert E. *Two Guns from Harlem: The Detective Fiction of Chester Himes*. Bowling Green, OH: Bowling Green State University Popular Press, 1989.

Hugh Holton Jr.

Mystery, Fantasy

Benchmark Titles: Larry Cole Series

Chicago, Illinois

1947–2001

About the Author and the Author's Writing

Hugh Holton Jr. wrote police procedural novels with an insider's knowledge; he was, after all, a career police officer.

Popular within the mystery writing fraternity, and eager to share his knowledge, Holton wrote a regular "Cop's Corner" column for *Mystery Scene* magazine. In one essay, as an example, he described what it was like to be a beat cop. He did so with precision useful to other writers: "It is really necessary for the officer to know his or her beat. They should know the rhythms of the beat. What time a certain business closes or when it opens. Who belongs there and who doesn't. How many entrances and exits there are to any structure and which of them are the most frequently used."

And there's your crime.

Holton was born in Chicago in 1947. His father was a military policeman during World War II, then became a grocer, then became a Chicago beat cop, working his way up to commander in the detective division. Is it any surprise Holton the younger followed in his dad's footsteps? He grew up in Woodlawn, on the South Side, and played football at Mount Carmel High School. Although this school had only recently been integrated, Holton told the *Chicago Reader* that he had no recollection of "being any different than anyone else" in the community. From high school he entered the Chicago Police Department's cadet program and enrolled in Lop College. He served in the U.S. Army from 1966 to 1969 and had a tour in Vietnam. Returning stateside, he entered Chicago Police Academy and graduated in 1969. He soon became a plainclothes officer and in 1975 made desk sergeant. He was promoted to lieutenant in 1984.

Holton was married and had one daughter. During the 1980s, he began to moonlight—he wrote several hours each evening until he had several manuscripts, although no prospective publisher. Through a connection with Ed Gorman, mystery writer and editor of *Mystery Scene,* Holton signed on with an agent, and soon he had a publishing contract. His first book came out in 1994, followed by eight more in the police commander Larry Cole series.

"I'm not writing the traditional mystery," Holton said in a *Profiles in Mystery* interview. "If you look at Gar Anthony Haywood and Gary Phillips out on the West Coast, their private detectives are integral parts of a black community, where Larry

Cole is not. Larry Cole is the chief of the Chicago Police Department, who happens to be black."

"I don't think there is a finer rendition anywhere of urban police and detective rituals than in Holton's novels," asserted Lerone Bennett Jr. in a preface to the anthology *Shades of Black*. "Nor, I think, is there a finer rendition of the *structures* of crimes that create drug addicts, criminals, and crime-fighters the same way Detroit assembly lines turn out cars.. . . Hugh Holton knew that his task was not to preach or teach but to *show* the world and to make us freely re-create it and assume responsibility for it."

For example, Holton bent the genre a little in the science fiction vein with his short story "The Thirteenth Amendment" in the anthology *Spooks, Spies, and Private Eyes* and "The Werewolf File" in *Shades of Black*.

"I'm a thriller writer, I'm not a police procedural writer," Holton said in a *Chicago Reader* interview with Michael Marsh. "If I decide I want to drop in a little supernatural or voodoo in there, it's odd, but if it's in keeping with the tone of the story and I could suspend disbelief enough to do it, I'm going to do it. You can't do that in a down-and-dirty, nitty-gritty police procedural."

Holton died in 2001 of colon cancer, having been a police officer for thirty-two years, achieved the rank of captain, and secured a spot on the crime literature bookshelf.

Works by the Author

Larry Cole Series

Presumed Dead (1994)
Windy City (1995)
Chicago Blues (1996)
Violent Crimes (197)
Red Lighting (1998)
The Left Hand of God (1999)
Time of the Assassins (2000)
The Devil's Shadow (2001)
Criminal Element (2002)

Nonfiction

The Thin Black Line (2004)

Contributor

Spooks, Spies and Private Eyes: Black Mystery, Crime, and Suspense Fiction of the 20th Century (1995), edited by Paula L. Woods
Homicide Hosts Presents: A Collection of Original Mysteries (1996)
Shades of Black: Crime and Mystery Stories by African-American Writers (2004), edited by Eleanor Taylor Bland

For Further Information

Bennett, Lerone Jr., Preface, *Shades of Black: Crime and Mystery Stories by African-American Writers,* Eleanor Taylor Bland, ed. New York: Berkley Prime Crime, 2004.

Holton, Hugh, "Cop's Corner," *Mystery Scene* (March/April 1995).

Hugh Holton interview, *Chicago Reader* (Sept. 29, 2000).

Hugh Holton interview, *Profiles in Mystery. http://www.planetpreset.com/HOLTON.htm* (viewed July 18, 2006).

Hugh Holton Jr. entry, *Contemporary Black Biography*, Vol. 39, Ashyla Henderson, ed. Detroit: Gale Group, 2003.

Marsh, Michael, "Books behind the Badge," *Chicago Reader* (Sept. 29, 2000), reprinted on Hugh Holton Web page, African American Literary Book Club. *http://aalbc.com/authors/hugh.htm* (viewed July 18, 2006).

Shufelt, Craig L., *Criminal Element* review, *Library Journal* (Feb. 15, 2002).

Nalo Hopkinson

Science Fiction, Fantasy, Historical Literature

Benchmark Title: *The Salt Roads*

Kingston, Jamaica
1960

Photo credit: David Findlay

About the Author and the Author's Writing

Only when she wanted to enroll in a Ryerson University course in writing taught by science fiction author Judy Merril did Nalo Hopkinson attempt to write a short story. Not enough students signed up to take the course, and it was canceled. But Hopkinson got to know Merril anyway, and because of the author's encouragement, she attended the Clarion Science Fiction and Fantasy Writers' Workshop at Michigan State University in 1995 to learn how to write short prose. Shortly thereafter, Hopkinson submitted a manuscript to the Warner Aspect First Novel Contest—and won. That novel, *Brown Girl in the Ring,* came out in 1998.

"Fantastical literature is something I was always drawn to, even as a child," the author said on the SFSite. "I loved folk and fairy tales—Ananasi stories, for instance. From my father's shelves, I was reading works such as *Gulliver's Travels* and Homer's *The Iliad* and *The Odyssey* at a very young age. I guess I just never outgrew the habit of looking for magical stories."

Nalo Hopkinson was born in Kingston, Jamaica, in 1960, with hints of Jewish and Scottish and Southeast Asian ancestry as well as Caribbean and African. Her father Slade Hopkinson was a poet, playwright, and actor of Guyanese extraction. She lived in Trinidad and Guyana, as well as Connecticut for a time while her father studied at Yale University. In 1977, she relocated permanently to Toronto, Ontario, Canada. She earned a bachelor of arts degree in Russian language and literature and French language from York University in 1982. In 2002, she earned her master's degree in writing popular fiction from Seton Hill College in Greensburg, Pennsylvania.

155

Since 1996, Hopkinson has taught at a number of workshops including ones at the University of Toronto, and she has been writer-in-residence at the University of British Columbia, Howard University, Atkinson College, and Michigan State University.

Her fiction has received numerous awards including *New York Times* Notable Book of the Year for *Midnight Robber* in 2000 and the John W. Campbell Award for Best New Writer in 1999.

Hopkinson's island background both enriched and complicated her writing. *Midnight Robber,* for instance, is about a girl whose story grows to mythical proportions. The author incorporated the real-life codes of Caribbean Creoles. "Caribbean cultures are hybrid cultures," she said in an essay she wrote for ssf.net. "Hybridity was a strategy for survival and resistance amongst the enslaved and indentured people. They all came from different cultures with different languages and then had an alien culture and speech imposed on them. They had to find ways to use elements of all the cultures in order to continue to exist."

Alienation is a common theme in science fiction, Hopkinson noted, but those who are alienated are often conspicuously white and male. Only when a more feminist science fiction emerged in recent years did she connect solidly with the genre. In a SciFi.com interview she said she would love to see even more diversity in science fiction. "Can you see where it might be valuable to get more worldviews on the map? . . . What does a fiction which talks about colonizing other races and spaces become when written by people who've recently—as the history of the world goes—experienced that colonization?"

Everyday challenges are also to be found in the author's work. "Even if I create a character who's a rich, white, North American, straight man, I find myself thinking about how what he is affects the choices he has. Everybody faces limitations in life," she said in a ReadingGroupGuides.com roundtable discussion.

On another note, Hopkinson expressed optimistism about change during an interview with Space.com: "I do think paradigm shifts will happen. I don't know what will bring it about, or when, but the one thing humanity does consistently do (other than to die) is to change."

In a conversation with BookSense.com the author said she's not so much trying to change science fiction and fantasy as to give it a different voice. She said she "came out of a very strong Caribbean literary tradition. In that sense I'm kind of marrying the two, but not in a way of 'trying to go out there and do something new.' I'm like any other writer." Thus Hopkinson has worked folklore into her prose to create something of a Creoles-in-space world. But the use of her diverse background, which also includes hints of Trinidad, can complicate her writing. In another ssf.net essay, Hopkinson said she wanted to use a "soucouyant" in one of her stories, but didn't want to distract the reader by having to explain the nuance of difference between a soucouyant, a succubi, and a vampire. "It's a series of choices I have to make every time I write, weighing speculation against information."

The author's most ambitious work, *The Salt Roads,* is something of a historical fantasy, portraying the lives of three women of African heritage: a Greek-Nubian prostitute of the third century, an eighteenth-century Haitian slave, and a mistress of the French poet Bauedelaire. The women are linked by a connection to Ezili, the Afro-Caribbean goddess of love and sex.

Even as feminism has taken hold in science fiction, it's mostly a young feminism. Middle-aged and older women characters are still missing from the genre. "I once tried to pitch the idea of a multiple-author anthology of fiction about old women kicking butt," she told Nneda Okorafor-Mbachu for *Black Issues Book Review,* "acting up and generally being the revolutionary viragoes that old women can be, but I couldn't get a publisher to bite. I don't quite know what to do about it, but since I plan to be an old black woman some day, I'm going to keep kicking at that particular can."

Works by the Author

Brown Girl in the Ring (1998)
Midnight Robber (2000)
The Salt Roads (2003)
The New Moon's Arms (announced for 2007)

Collections

Skin Folk (2001)

Anthologies

Silver Birch, Blood Moon (1999)
Northern Frights (1999), edited by Don Hutchison
Women of Other Worlds: Excursions through Science Fiction and Feminism (1999), edited by Helen Merrick and Tess Williams
Northern Suns (1999), edited by David Hartwell and Glenn Grant
Tellin' It Like It Is (monologues) (2000), edited by Djanet Sears
Dark Matter: A Century of Speculative Fiction from the African Diaspora (2000), edited by Sheree R. Thomas
Bakkanthology (2002), edited by John Rose
Queer Fear II (2002), edited by Michael Rowe
Dark Matter II: Reading the Bones (2004), edited by Sheree R. Thomas

Editor

Whispers from the Cotton Tree Root (2000), and contributor
Mojo: Conjure Stories (2003), and contributor
So Long Been Dreaming: Postcolonial Science Fiction & Fantasy (2004), with Uppinder Mehan and Samuel R. Delany
Tesseracts Nine (2005), with Geoff Ryman

For Further Information

Aylott, Chris, "Filling the Sky with Islands: An Interview with Nalo Hopkinson," Space.com. *http://www.space.com/sciencefiction/books/hopkinson_intv_000110.html* (viewed July 19, 2006).

Beck, Ervin, "Whispers from the Cotton Tree Root; Caribbean Fabulist Fiction," *World Literature Today* (summer-autumn 2001).

"Black History Month Author Roundtable," Authors on the Web.com. *http://www.authorsontheweb.com/features/0302-bhm/bhm/authors2.asp* (viewed Feb. 14, 2005).

"Conversation with Nalo Hopkinson," SFSite.com. *http://www.sfsite.com/03b/nh77.htm* (viewed July 19, 2006).

Grant, Gavin J., Nalo Hopkinson interview, *BookSense.com. http://www.booksense.com/people/archive/hopkinsonnalo.jsp* (viewed Sept. 14, 2006).

Hopkinson, Nalo, "Code Sliding: About *Midnight Robber* and My Use of Creole in the Narrative," *ssf.net. http://www.sff.net/people/nalo/writing/slide.html* (viewed Feb. 14, 2005).

Hopkinson, Nalo, "Dark Ink: Science Fiction Writers of Colour," *sff.net. http://www.sff.net/people/nalo/writing/writrs.html* (viewed Sept. 14, 2006).

Nalo Hopkinson biography, *sff.net. http://www.sff.net/people/nalo/writing/whome.html* (viewed Feb. 14, 2005).

Nalo Hopkinson entry, *Authors and Artists for Young Adults*, Vol. 40. Detroit: Gale Group, 2001.

Nalo Hopkinson entry, Contemporary Authors Online, Gale, 2005. Reproduced in Biography Resource Center, Farmington Hills, MI: Thomson Gale, 2005. *http://galenet.galegroup.com/servlet/BioRC* (viewed Feb. 25, 2005).

Nalo Hopkinson interview, *twbookmark.com. http://www.twbookmark.com/authors/84/1272/* (viewed July 19, 2006).

Nalo Hopkinson Web page, African American Literary Book Club. *http://authors.aalbc.com/nalo_hopkinson.htm* (viewed Feb. 17, 2005).

Okorafor-Mbachu, Nnedi, "A Traveling Female Spirit," *Black Issues Book Review* (March–April 2004).

Rutledge, Gregory E., "Speaking in Tongues: An Interview with Science Fiction Writer Nalo Hopkinson," *African American Review* (winter 1999).

Soyka, David, "Nalo Hopkinson Uses SF to Probe the Inner and Outer Worlds of Alienation," *SciFi.com. http://www.scifi.com/sfw/issue232/interview2.html* (viewed Sept. 14, 2006).

Langston Hughes

Poetry, Drama, Short Fiction, Young Adult Literature

Benchmark Title: *The Weary Blues*

Joplin, Missouri
1902–1967

About the Author and the Author's Writing

It was a centennial birthday gala for Langston Hughes in 2002. The U.S. Postal Service issued a commemorative postage stamp bearing his image. The Schomburg Center for Research in Black Culture in Harlem, where his ashes lie beneath the foyer to the auditorium, had a big party with Ossie Davis and Ruby Dee, Sonia Sanchez, and others in attendance. And the American Academy of Poets dedicated the month of April to the honor of the man who, although he never held the title officially, will long be thought of as the poet laureate of African Americans.

Hughes was a poet—and much more. One of the first of his race to make a living from his creative writing, he produced novels, plays, short stories, essays, children's stories, and opera lyrics. "He was a mentor and an inspiration to generations of Black writers and entertainers, from Gwendolyn Brooks to contemporary hip-hop," said Charles Whitaker, writing in *Ebony*. Hughes's verse, particularly, reflected the cadence of jazz and blues. His life and work epitomized the dynamic Harlem Renaissance. Even as he became more popular, Hughes wrote directly about and for the common man and woman in black America.

Born James Langston Hughes in Joplin, Missouri, in 1902, he was the son of Carrie Langston Hughes and James N. Hughes. He grew up in Lawrence, Kansas, and then, after his parents divorced, he lived with his grandmother, Mary Langston, in Lincoln, Illinois. (His grandmother's first husband, Sheridan Leary, died in the ill-fated John Brown raid on Harper's Ferry in 1859. Her second husband, Charles Hughes, was brother to one of the most famous African Americans of his day, John Mercer Langston.)

It was in Illinois that Hughes first began to craft verse, taking after his mother, who was an aspiring poet and actress. He eventually returned to the household of his mother and her second husband, who worked in a steel mill in Cleveland, Ohio. After graduating from high school, Hughes spent a year in Mexico (where his businessman father had gone to operate a cattle ranch) and another year at Columbia University. He worked as a cook, laundryman, and busboy. While working as a seaman on a tramp freighter, he saw parts of western Africa as well as Paris. He lived in Washington,

D.C., for a time and completed his education at Lincoln University in Pennsylvania in 1929. In the 1930s, he toured Japan, Haiti, and the Soviet Union.

Hughes's first published poem, "The Negro Speaks of Rivers," appeared June 1921 in the National Association for the Advancement of Colored People *Crisis* magazine edited by W. E. B. Du Bois. Many more of his poems would follow in that periodical. His first book of poetry, *The Weary Blues,* came out in 1926, and his first novel, *Not without Laughter,* appeared four years later. The latter won a Harmon gold medal for literature.

Hughes's writing is deceptively simple, realistic yet fired with passion, and at times politically radical. "To many readers who love verse, and are also committed to the ideal of social and political justice" suggests Arnold Rampersad in the introduction to *The Collected Poems of Langston Hughes,* "he is among the most eloquent American poets to have sung about the wounds caused by injustice. For still other admirers, he is, above all, the author of poems of often touching lyric beauty, beyond issues such as race and justice."

In 1942, Hughes began a weekly column in the *Chicago Defender,* describing exchanges on a variety of topics ranging from racism to alcoholism to politics between Jess B. Semple, or "Simple," and one of his well-educated Harlem neighbors. A transplanted southerner, Semple challenged readers to take a different perspective on things.

"Through Simple, Hughes celebrated the fullness of life—its joys and its sorrows—and distilled some of the nation's most complicated issues during a particularly complicated period: World War II," Donna Akiba Sullivan Harper wrote in *New Crisis.*

Hughes acknowledged a number of influences on his work, beginning with the Bible and Du Bois and including Paul Lawrence Dunbar, Carl Sandburg, and Walt Whitman. Despite the modernism of those last named, Arnold Rampersad, who wrote a two-volume biography of Hughes, acknowledges that some scholars decry Hughes's lack of modernism, of intellectual challenge. To that charge, Rampersad says that Hughes instead set out to reflect all variety of black experience, aspiration, and emotion.

A further controversy developed over Hughes's political leanings, which were leftward, although he denied in a public hearing before Senator Joseph McCartny that he ever belonged to the Communist Party. "Hughes' career hardly suffered from this episode," noted Rampersad in an essay in *Oxford Companion to African American Literature.* "Within a short time McCarthy himself was discredited and Hughes was free to write at length about his year in the Soviet Union." Still, his *Famous American Negroes,* published in 1954, omits mention of Du Bois or Paul Robeson, then both immersed in controversy.

Hughes collaborated with Zora Neale Hurston and Arna Bontemps. In his later years, he turned increasingly to musical theater, although he never quite duplicated the success of his 1947 show *Street Scene,* which provided enough income that Hughes could at last purchase his own home.

The writer died in 1967 in New York, of prostate cancer. His residence at 20 East 127th Street (renamed Langston Hughes Place) is a city landmark.

Works by the Author

Fiction

Not without Laughter (1930)
Tambourines to Glory (1958)

Short Story Collections

The Ways of White Folks (1934)
Simple Speaks His Mind (1950)
Laughing to Keep from Crying (1952)
Simple Takes a Wife (1953)
Simple Stakes a Claim (1957)
The Best of Simple (1961)
Something in Common and Other Stories (1963)
Simple's Uncle Sam (1965)
Thank You, Ma'am (1991)
The Langston Hughes Reader (1968)
The Return of Simple (1995)
Short Stories of Langston Hughes (1996)
Not So Simple: The "Simple" Stories by Langston Hughes (1996), edited by
    Donna Akiba Sullivan Harper

Drama and Opera

Mule Bone (1932) with Zora Neale Hurston
Mulatto (1935)
Little Ham (1936)
When the Jack Hollers (1936)
Front Porch (1937)
Soul Gone Home (1937)
Emperor of Haiti (1938)
Little Eva's End (1938)
Don't You Want to Be Free? (1938)
The Sun Do Move (1942)
For This We Fight (1943)
Street Scene: An Opera in Two Acts (1947) lyrics (book by Elmer Rice, music by
    Kurt Weill)
The Barrier (1950)
Esther (1957)
Simply Heavenly (1959) lyrics and book (music by David Martin)
The Ballad of the Brown King (1961) lyrics and book (music by Margaret Bonds)
Black Nativity (1961)
Five Plays by Langston Hughes (1963), edited by Webster Smalley
Jericho-Jim Crow (1964)

The Prodigal Son (1965)
Three Negro Plays (1987)
The Political Plays of Langston Hughes (2000)

Screenplay

Way Down South (1942)

Librettos

The Barrier
Troubled Legend

Poetry

The Weary Blues (1926)
Fine Clothes to the Jews (1927)
The Negro Mother and Other Dramatic Recitations (1931)
Dear Lovely Death (1931)
The Dream Keeper and Other Poems (1932)
Scottsboro Limited: Four Poems and a Play (1932)
A New Song (1938)
Shakespeare in Harlem (1942) with Robert Glenn
Jim Crow's Last Stand (1943)
Freedom's Plow (1943)
Lament for Dark Peoples and Other Poems (1944)
Fields of Wonder (1947)
One-Way Ticket (1949)
Montage of a Dream Deferred (1951)
Selected Poems (1959)
Ask Your Mama: 12 Moods for Jazz (1961)
The Panther and the Lash: Poems of Our Times (1967)
The Collected Poems of Langston Hughes (1994)
The Block: Poems (1995)
Carol of the Brown King (1997)
The Pasteboard Bandit (1997)

Poetry for Young Adults and Children

The Dream Keeper (1932)
The First Book of Rhymes (1954)
Poetry for Young People: Langston Hughes (2006), edited by David Roessel and
   Arnold Rampersad

Nonfiction

A Negro Looks at Soviet Central Asia (1934)
The Big Sea: An Autobiography (1940)

The Sweet Flypaper of Life (1955) with Roy de Carava

I Wonder as I Wander: An Autobiographical Journey (1956)

A Pictorial History of the Negro in America (1956) with Milton Meltzer; republished as *A Pictorial History of Black Americans* (1983); republished as *A Pictorial History of African Americans* (1995)

Fight for Freedom: The Story of the NAACP (1962)

Black Magic: A Pictorial History of the Negro in American Entertainment (1967) with Milton Meltzer, republished as *Black Magic: A Pictorial History of the African American in the Performing Arts* (1990)

Black Misery (1968)

Good Morning Revolution: The Uncollected Social Protest Writing of Langston Hughes (1973), ed. Faith Berry; reissued as *Good Morning Revolution: Uncollected Writings of Social Protest by Langston Hughes* (1992)

Langston Hughes in the Hispanic World and Haiti (1977), edited by Edward J. Mullen

Arna Bontemps–Langston Hughes Letters, 1925–1967 (1980), edited by Charles H. Nichols

Langston Hughes and the Chicago Defender: Essays on Race, Politics and Culture, 1942–62 (1995), edited by Christopher C. De Santis

Remember Me to Harlem: The Letters of Langston Hughes and Carl Van Vechten, 1925–1964 (2001), edited by Emily Bernard.

Nonfiction for Young Adults and Children

Popo and Fifinia: Children of Haiti (1932) with Arna Bontemps

The First Book of Negroes (1952)

Famous American Negroes (1954)

Famous Negro Music Makers (1955)

The First Book of Jazz (1955), revised as *Jazz* (1982)

The First Book of the West Indies (1956)

Famous Negro Heroes of America (1958)

The First Book of Africa (1964)

Black Misery (1969)

Don't You Turn Back (1969), edited by Lee Bennett Hopkins

Editor

Four Lincoln University Poets (1930)

The Poetry of the Negro, 1746–1949 (1949) with Arna Bontemps, revised as *The Poetry of the Negro, 1746–1970* (1970)

Lincoln University Poets (1954) with Waring Cuney and Bruce M. Wright

The Book of Negro Folklore (1958) with Arna Bontemps

An African Treasury: Articles, Essays, Stories, Poems by Black Africans (1960)

Poems from Black Africa (1963)

New Negro Poets: U.S. (1964)

The Book of Negro Humor (1966)

The Best Short Stories by Negro Writers: An Anthology from 1899 to the Present
(1967)

Translator

Masters of Dew by Jacques Roumain (1947), with Mercer Cook
Cuba Libre by Nicholas Gullen (1948) with Frederic Carruthers
Gypsy Ballads by Frederico Garcia Lorca (1951)
Selected Poems of Gabriela Mistral (1957)

For Further Information

Dickinson, Donald C. *A Bio-Bibliography of Langston Hughes, 1902–1967.*
Hamden, CT: Archon Books, 1972.

Harper, Donna Akiba Sullivan, "Langston Hughes Centennial, 1902–1967:
Langston's Simple Genius," *New Crisis* (January/February 2002).

Haskins, James. *Always Movin' On: The Life of Langston Hughes.* Trenton, NJ:
African World Press, 1993.

Langston Hughes entry, *Authors and Artists for Young Adults*, Vol. 12. Detroit:
Gale Research, 1994. Reproduced in Biography Resource Center.
Farmington Hills, MI: Thomas Gale, 2005. *http://galenet.galegroup/
com/servlet/BioRC*

Meltzer, Milton. *Langston Hughes: A Biography.* New York: Crowell, 1968.

Rampersad, Arnold, Langston Hughes entry, *The Oxford Companion to African
American Literature,* Andrews, William L., Frances Smith Foster and
Trudier Harris, eds. New York: Oxford University Press, 1997.

Rampersad, Arnold. *The Life of Langston Hughes, Volume 1: 1902–1940: I Too
Sing America.* New York: Oxford University Press, 2001.

Rampersad, Arnold. *The Life of Langston Hughes, Volume 2: 1941–1967: I
Dream a World.* New York: Oxford University Press, 2002.

Walker, Alice. *Langston Hughes, American Poet.* New York: Crowell, 1974.

Whitaker, Charles, "Langston Hughes: 100th Birthday Celebration of the Poet
Laureate of Black America," *Ebony* (April 2002).

Zora Neale Hurston

Mainstream Contemporary Literature, Drama, Poetry

Benchmark Title: *Their Eyes
Were Watching God*

Notasulga, Alabama

1891–1960

About the Author and the Author's Writing

Zora Neale Hurston, one of the earliest African American folklorists as well as a novelist, dramatist, and short-story writer during the Harlem Renaissance, influenced writers ranging from Toni Morrison to Gayl Jones, Alice Walker to Toni Cade Bambara. And her light continues to shine for new generations, thanks to Washington, D.C.'s, 2002 Arena Stage production of *Polk County,* the story of Big Sweet, the lumber camp hoodoo woman who carries a pistol; and telefilms such as *Oprah Winfrey Presents: Their Eyes Were Watching God* in 2005 in which Halle Berry starred as Janie, the young woman who yearns for passion and fulfillment.

Hurston was born in 1891 in Notasulga, Alabama, although she claimed she was born a decade later in Eatonville, Florida, the first incorporated all-black community in the United States where she grew up. Her father was a carpenter and Baptist preacher and mayor, her mother a seamstress. After her mother died in 1904, Zora and her siblings were sent to boarding school; eventually they were rejected by her father and new stepmother. Zora had to support herself while she obtained her high school degree from Morgan Academy in Baltimore, Maryland. She attended Howard and Barnard Colleges and Columbia University. She was twice married, to Herbert Sheen in 1927 and to Albert Price III in 1939. She divorced both.

Hurston's first published story was "John Redding Goes to Sea" in a Howard University literary magazine in 1921. While at Barnard, she studied anthropology with Franz Boas. In spurts from 1927 to 1938 she traveled the American South, Jamaica, Haiti, Honduras, and Bermuda to collect folklore. She also taught drama at Bethune-Cookman College in Florida and North Carolina College for Negroes, was a staff writer for Paramount Studios, shelved books as a librarian at Patrick Air Force Base, taught at Lincoln Park Academy, and assisted writer Fannie Hurst. She was a librarian for the Library of Congress for a time. All the while she was a freelance writer and dramatist. She collaborated with Langston Hughes on the comic play *Mule Bone.* Her first published book was *Jonah's Gourd Vine,* a story of two people living in an all-black Florida town. The first of her anthropologic work appeared in the book *Mules and Men.*

Many consider Their *Eyes Were Watching God* to be Hurston's best work, "a classic in African-American and feminist literature for its portrayal of a black woman's quest for fulfillment and freedom from exploitation," according to *Authors and Artists for Young Adults.* "Janie struggles to find an equal, rewarding relationship with a man, despite her grandmother's warning that 'de nigger woman is de mule uh de world' and that love is 'de very prong all us black woman gits hung on.' "

In Harlem, Hurston became part of the literati. "She became well known not only for her writing, but also for her outspokenness, her distinct way of dressing and her refusal to be ashamed of her culture," according to her New York City Women's Biography Web page.

In *Ms. Magazine*, Alice Walker wrote, "Zora was funny, irreverent (she was the first to call the Harlem Renaissance literati the 'niggerati'), good-looking and sexy."

Hurston had a rich style of writing. She infused her prose with myth and folklore. But her optimistic depictions of plain folks clashed with the more political aspirations of writers and critics such as Richard Wright and Harold Peece. "Never in her works did she address the issue of racism of whites toward blacks, and as this became a nascent theme among black writers in the post World War II era of civil rights, Hurston's literary influence faded. She further scathed her own reputation by railing [against] the civil rights movement and supporting ultraconservative politicians," according to her Women in History Web page.

The reception to Hurston's autobiography, *Dust Tracks on a Road,* was mixed. Arna Bontemps complained it oversimplified the black situation. It turned out the publisher omitted three chapters (restored by editor Robert Hemenway in 1984) that discussed issues of race and exploitation. Hurston's success and fame were fading.

In 1950, the *Miami Herald* headlined a news story, "Famous Negro Author Working as Maid Here Just to Live a Little." Hurston was working as a $30-a-week domestic for a Miami, Florida, household—just seven years after publication of her award-winning autobiography.

A decade later in Fort Pierce, Florida, while living in a welfare home, Hurston died. She was largely forgotten until Alice Walker in 1973 sought out her grave and had a marker placed there. Since then, her work has drawn scholarly scrutiny in, for example, Tiffany Ruby Patterson's recent *Zora Neale Hurston and a History of Southern Life*, which closely examines Hurston's depiction of southern black life.

Works by the Author

Jonah's Gourd Vine (1934)

Mules and Men (1935), reissued as *Mules and Men: A Treasury of Black American Folklore* (1989)

Their Eyes Were Watching God (1937)

Moses, Man of the Mountain (1939)

Seraph on the Suwanee (1948)

Spunk: The Selected Stories of Zora Neale Hurston (1985)

The Gilded Six-Bits (1986) story

Drama (partial list)

Color Struck! A Play in Four Scenes (1926), published in *Fire*

The First One: A Play, published in *Ebony and Topaz* (1927), edited by Charles S. Johnson

Fast and Furious with Clinton Fletcher and Tim Moore in *Best Plays of 1931–32* (1931), edited by Burns Mantle and Garrison Sherwood

Stephen Kelen-d'Oxylion Presents Polk County: A Comedy of Negro Life on a Sawmill Camp with Authentic Negro Music (1944)

Mule Bone: A Comedy of Negro Life in Three Acts (1964), with Langston Hughes, published in *Drama Critique* (1991), revised and edited by George H. Bass and Henry Louis Gates Jr.

Spunk (1990), adapted as a play by George C. Wolfe

Polk County (2002)

Collections

I Love Myself When I Am Laughing . . . And Then Again When I Am Looking Mean and Impressive: A Zora Neale Hurston Reader (1979), edited by Alice Walker

The Sanctified Church (1981)

Three Classic Works by Zora Neale Hurston: Their Eyes Were Watching God, Dust Tracks on a Road, Mules and Men (1991)

The Complete Stories (1992)

Complete Works (1995)

Children's Books

The Six Fools (2006)

Nonfiction

Tell My Horse (1938), retitled *Voodoo Gods: An Inquiry into Native Myths and Magic in Jamaica and Haiti* (1939), retitled *Tell My Horse: Voodoo and Life in Haiti and Jamaica* (1989)

Dust Tracks on a Road (1942), retitled and omitted manuscript chapters restored for *Dust Tracks on a Road: An Autobiography* (1984)

Television Film Based on the Author's Works

Oprah Winfrey Presents: Their Eyes Were Watching God (2005).

For Further Information

Bass, Holly, "Better Late Than Never: After 60 Years, Zora Neale Hurston's Flavorful *Polk County* Comes to Life," *American Theatre* (July–August 2002).

Gilbert, Matthew, "A Soulful Berry Brightens 'Eyes,' " *Boston Globe* (March 4, 2005).

Holmes, Marian Smith, "Zora Neale Hurston Out of Obscurity," *Smithsonian* (Jan. 2001).

Hurston, Lucy. Speak So You Can Speak Again: The Life of Zora Neale Hurston. New York: Doubleday, 2004.

Lee, Felicia R., "A Woman's Journey toward Herself," *New York Times Television* (March 6, 2005).

Patterson, Tiffany Ruby. *Zora Neale Hurston and a History of Southern Life.* Philadelphia: Temple University Press. 2005.

Walker, Alice, "In Search of Zora Neale Hurston," *Ms. Magazine* (March 1975).

Zora Neale Hurston biography, *Women in History,* Lakewood (Ohio) Public Library. *http://www.lkwdpl.org/wihohio/hurs-zor.htm* (viewed Sept. 14, 2006).

Zora Neale Hurston entry, *Authors and Artists for Young Adults*, Vol. 15. Detroit: Gale Research, 1995.,

Zora Neale Hurston entry, New York City Women's Biography, City University of New York. *http://www.library.csi.cuny/edu/dept.history/lavender/386/zhurston.html* (viewed Sept. 14, 2006).

Zora Neale Hurston entry, Voices from the Gaps. *http://voices.cla.umn.edu/vg/Bios/entries/hurston_zora_neale.html* (viewed July 19, 2006).

Zora Neale Hurston Web page, African American Literary Book Club. *http://authors.aalbc.com/zoraneal.htm* (viewed July 19, 2006).

Iceberg Slim

Urban Literature

Benchmark Title: *Pimp:
The Story of My Life*

Chicago, Illinois

1918–1992

Photo credit: Courtesy Holloway House

About the Author and the Author's Writing

His heavily autobiographical novels were too intense for a general white audience. They were even discomforting in their day to African Americans, during the Black is Beautiful movement. Iceberg Slim nevertheless developed a cult following and became an inspiration to raw urban fictionalists such as Donald Goines and Omar Tyree, and to rappers such as Ice-T and Ice Cube, who borrowed from his name.

The author's real name was Robert Lee Maupin. He was born in Chicago in 1918 and grew up in a single-parent family in Milwaukee and Rockford, Illinois, before returning to Chicago. He attended Tuskegee Institute in the late 1930s, but was expelled when he was caught bootlegging alcohol. He returned to Chicago's South Side and became a street hustler. Taking the name Iceberg Slim, he ran a stable of prostitutes. He was arrested and convicted, and served two stretches in Leavenworth Prison. But it was ten months of solitary confinement in the Cook County Jail in 1960 that persuaded Slim it was time to change occupations. After his release, he moved to Los Angeles, where he worked a variety of odd jobs. He took the name Robert Beck. He almost collaborated with a college professor on a book about his life of crime. But his share of royalties seemed minuscule, so Slim wrote the book himself and sold it to Holloway House. Right off, its title, *Pimp: The Story of My Life*, limited its distribution.

There was a good deal of misogynist ego in Iceberg Slim's life, as is revealed in this edited excerpt from an interview with Helen Koblin: "Really what is the bedrock of all male aspiration if it isn't [—] and money? Now here the pimp, what has he got? All kinds of beautiful girls, who bring him [—] and money. Kiss and [—] and love him ... on the surface of course, because beneath they really pray for his ruin."

Slim outright declared himself "of superior intelligence" in a conversation with Hollie I. West of the *Washington Post*, and styled himself something of a sociologist in dissecting male-female relationships, allowing only that the pimp's "mauling of the sexual object is perhaps a more severe version of what happens in conventional relationships."

In California, Slim made the acquaintance of Huey Newton and the Black Panthers. "He considered his success as a pimp as a blow against white oppression," noted Patrick Deese. "The Black Panthers, however, had little mutual regard for Slim, considered his former profession as little more than the exploitation of his people for personal gain."

Slim took it in stride. Now married with children, he occasionally accepted college lecture assignments. He recorded an LP of his poetry.

Pimp was optioned for movie production in the early 1970s, at the same time that *The Godfather* became a hit, but it proved more than Universal Pictures wanted to handle. Iceberg Slim died in 1992. But his legend lived on and in 2004, *Pimp* was again slated to become a movie. Ice-T, who had sought the lead role, is quoted on the AllHipHop.com Web site: "Iceberg Slim was true to where he came from. He ruled the streets of Chicago for twenty-five years and he chose not to write about what he didn't know. He knew pimping. He knew hustling. He knew the streets. What he calls 'The Life' is still the same roller-coaster ride it's always been."

Works by the Author

Pimp: The Story of My Life (1967)
Trick Baby: The Story of a White Negro (1967)
Mama Black Widow: A Story of the South's Black Underworld (1969)
The Naked Soul of Iceberg Slim: Robert Beck's Real Story (1971)
Death Wish: A Story of the Mafia (1976)
Long White Con: The Biggest Score of His Life! (1977), sequel to *Trick Baby*
Airtight Willie & Me: The Story of Six Incredible Players (1979)
Doom Fox (1996), written in 1978
The Game for Squares, uncompleted manuscript

Poetry Recording

Reflections (1976)

Film Based on the Author's Work

Trick Baby (1973)

For Further Information

Deese, Patrick, "Biographical Notes for Iceberg Slim aka Robert Beck," Biography Project. *http://www.popsubculture.com/pop/bio_project/iceberg_slim.html* (viewed May 10, 2005).

Friedman, Josh Alan, "A Tribute to Iceberg Slim." *http://www.wfmu.org/LCD/21/ice.html* (viewed July 29, 2006).

"Iceberg Slim's 'Pimp,' " *This American Life,* WBEZ Chicago. *http://www. thislife.org/pages/trax/shows/pimp_anthro.hmtl* (viewed July 29, 2006).

Koblin, Helen, "Portrait of a Pimp," *Los Angeles Free Press* (July 29, 2006).

Muckley, Peter A., *Iceberg Slim: The Life as Art.* Philadelphia: Dorrance Publishing, 2003.

Patton, Phil, "Sold on Ice: Six Million Readers Can't Be Wrong," *Esquire* (October 1992).

Strong, Nolan, "Pras Snags Rights to Iceberg Slim's 'Pimp'," AllHipHop.com. *http://www.allhiphop.com/hiphopnews/?ID=3742* (viewed July 29, 2006).

West, Hollie I., "Sweet Talk, Hustle and Muscle," *Washington Post* (1973). *http://www.popsubculture.com/pop/bio_project/sub/iceberg_slim.2.html* (viewed July 29, 2006).

Brenda Jackson

Romance, Women's Literature

Benchmark Title: *The Midnight Hour*

Jacksonville, Florida

1948

Photo credit: Photo courtesy the author

About the Author and the Author's Writing

Brenda Jackson celebrated the tenth anniversary of her first romance novel, *Tonight and Forever*, on a cruise to the Bahamas. It wasn't just any cruise; it was a package tour, "The Madaris Family Reunion Cruise," with 400 of her reader-fans. And it coincided with publication of the thirteenth entry in her Madaris Family romance series, *Unfinished Business*.

Unfinished Business is about Christy Madaris, an investigative reporter, who gets in deep water while checking into a female slave trading conspiracy. Her longtime family friend, private investigator Alex Maxwell, makes a welcome appearance despite having years before broken her heart. Will love endure this time?

"Jackson is a master at juggling two plots at a time, and *Unfinished Business* proves no exception. A perfect balance of tension and chemistry is created as Christy and the somewhat domineering Alex battle unknown criminals—as well as their unresolved attraction to each other," according to reviewer T.L. Burton in *Romantic Times Book Club Magazine*.

The romance genre doesn't generally lend itself to series; Jackson makes it work by exploring relationships among peripheral members of the Texas family—and brings earlier characters back for a quick glimpse in *Unfinished Business*. Her Web site includes a family tree whereby one can link Dr. Justin Madaris from the first novel with Dex, Jake and other Madarises.

Describing the characters in these books as "strong, fun-loving and positive," Jackson told *Romantic Times Book Club Magazine*, "I am proud to have a crossover group of readers who want a good love story—no matter what the race of the heroes and heroines is."

A native of Jacksonville, Florida, Brenda Streator graduated from William M. Raines High School. She earned a degree in business administration from Jacksonville University. She is a founding member of Women Writers of Color and belongs to First Coast Chapter of Romance Writers of America.

According to Jackson, she began writing fiction at a stressful time in her life. Her husband encouraged her, and sent her to a romance writers conference where she not only gained insight into the craft of writing, but also forged friendships with her peers. She came home brimming with inspiration.

The story of the Madaris men just bubbled from Jackson. "I wanted the brothers' story told," she explained in a *Romance in Color* interview, as they are stable, confident, respectful and dynamic professionals. And most of them are modeled at least a little on her husband. "I want [readers] to have an appreciation and acknowledgment for a strong and loving man."

Jackson has developed other romance series, including books for Harlequin's Silhouette Desire line. *Perfect Timing* in 2002 was her first hardcover novel and *Ties That Bind* falls into the women's fiction category. The author has said she changes direction occasionally not because she wants to fit in other subgenres, but because it pleases her.

Jackson is married to her high-school sweetheart, Gerald Jackson, a machinist, and they have two grown sons. One has to wonder, given her writing output, how Jackson also maintains a full-time job as manager of a State Farm Insurance office. However, to Jackson, writing is not a profession, it is a way to relax.

Works by the Author

Ties That Bind (2002)
Scandal Between the Sheets (2004)
Taking Care of Business (2006)
Ian's Ultimate Gamble (2006)
The Durango Affair (2006)
Night Heat (2006)
Solid Soul (2006)
Dreaming of You (2006)
What a Woman Wants (2006)
Beyond Temptation (2007)
Taking Care of Business (2007)

Bennett Family Series

A Family Reunion (2001)
The Savvy Sistahs (2003)

Madaris Family and Friends Series

Tonight and Forever (1995)
A Valentine Kiss (1996), omnibus with novelettes by Carla Fredd and Felicia Mason

Whispered Promises (1996)
Eternally Yours (1997)
One Special Moment (1998)
Fire and Desire (1999)
Something to Celebrate (1999), omnibus with novelettes by Felicia Mason and Margie Walker
Secret Love (2000)
True Love (2000)
Surrender (2001)
The Best Man (2003), omnibus with novelettes by Cindi Louis, Felicia Mason, and Kayla Perrin
The Midnight Hour (2004)
The Madaris Saga (2004), includes *Tonight and Forever, Whispered Promises,* and *Eternally Yours*
Unfinished Business (2005)

Perfect Series

Perfect Timing (2002)
Perfect Fit (2003)

Playa Series

The Playa's Handbook (2004)
Revised Playa's Handbook (2005)
No More Playas (2005)

Texas Cattlemen Club Series

Strictly Confidential Attraction (2005)

Westmoreland Series

Delaney's Desert Sheik (2002)
A Little Dare (2003)
Thorn's Challenge (2003)
Stone Cold Surrender (2004)
Riding the Storm (2004)
Jared's Counterfeit Fiancée (2005)
Chase's Delicious Cravings (2005)
Ian's Ultimate Gamble (2006)
The Durango Affair (2006)

Anthologies

A Valentine Kiss (1996), with Carla Fredd and Felicia Mason
Something to Celebrate (1999), with Felicia Mason and Margie Walker
Welcome to Leo's (2000), with Rochelle Alers, Donna Hill, and Francis Ray

Let's Get It On (2004), with Joylynn Mossell, Kayla Perin, and Tamara Sneed, sequel to *Welcome to Leo's*
An All Night Man (2005), with Jaylynn Jassel, Kayla Perrin, and Tamara Sneed
Sin City Wedding/Scandal Between the Sheets (2005), with Katherine Garbera
Mr. Satisfaction (2006), with Delilah Dawson, Joy King, and Maryann Reid

Special Woman Series

Living Large (2003), with Rochelle Alers, Donna Hill, and Francis Ray
A Whole Lotta Love (2004), with Donna Hill, Monica Jackson, and Francis Ray
Big Girls Don't Cry (2005), with Donna Hill and Monica Jackson

For Further Information

Brenda Jackson biography, *The Literary Times*. *http://www.tlt.com/authors/bjackson.htm* (viewed March 21, 2005).

Brenda Jackson interview, *Romance in Color*. http://www.romanceincolor.com/authormthjackson.B.htm (viewed March 21, 2005).

Brenda Jackson Web site. *http://www.brendajackson.net/home.htm* (viewed Feb. 14, 2005).

Brenda Streater Jackson entry, Contemporary Authors Online, Gale, 2005. Reproduced in Biography Resource Center; Farmington Hills, MI: Thomson Gale, 2005.*http://galenet.galegroup/com/servlet/BioRC* (viewed Feb. 26, 2005).

Burton, T. L., review of *Unfinished Business*, *Romantic Times Book Club Magazine* (April 2005).

Hoahing, Cheryl A., "Brenda Jackson," *Romantic Times Book Club Magazine* (April 2005).

Beverly Jenkins

Romance, Historical Literature

Benchmark Title: *Night Song*

Detroit, Michigan
1951

Photo credit: Glamour Shots of Michigan

About the Author and the Author's Writing

Voted one of the Top Fifty Favorite African American Writers in the 20th Century by the African American Literature Book Club, Beverly Jenkins has for a decade written popular historical romances.

Born Brenda Hunter in Detroit in 1951, she was the oldest of seven children of a high school teacher and an administrative aide. She discovered her knack with words at a young age when she became editor of her elementary school newspaper. A graduate of Cass Technical High School, she attended Michigan State University where she majored in journalism and English literature. She and her husband, Mark Jenkins, and their family reside in Belleville, Michigan, where she also serves as a lay Eucharistic minister in the Episcopal Church.

As a child Jenkins enjoyed *Alice in Wonderland* and the Grimm tales. Later she devoured Frank Herbert's *Dune* (she says she'd love someday to write a futuristic romance). But, she has noted, her grandfather was an avid reader of Western novels, and she herself enjoyed reading frontier novels by Zane Grey and Louis L'Amour. This combined with an appreciation for black history nurtured by her parents prompted her to write about the century following the Civil War, when much of ethnic accomplishment has been overlooked.

"We're a very, very proud race," she said on Contemporary Authors Online. "And America could not be America without the African-American patches in the American history quilt."

Jenkins said the need for her approach to romance fiction was obvious. "I've been a reader all of my life," she told Jennifer Coates, "but none of the stories had anything to do with me. If we were featured, we would be relegated to the background."

Jenkins crafted her first book, *Night Song,* while working as a librarian and raising a family. It took her thirteen years to finish, but with the help of agent Vivian Stephens, the book found a home with the publisher Avon (and with Doubleday Book Club and Literary Guild). The story relates the experiences of freed blacks in Kansas in the years following the War Between the States. Of course, there are plenty of passages of passion placed against this historical backdrop.

"Romance is a necessary part of life," the author told *People Weekly.* "But so many books about black people are studies in survival. Not everything has to be about the civil rights movement. I'm very proud to bring 'heaving bosoms' and 'throbbing manhoods' to black women all over America!"

For her second novel, *Vivid,* Jenkins pushed expectations even further by creating a medical doctor heroine, Viveca Lancaster, who grabs the opportunity for a new start in rural Michigan. For *Topaz,* her first truly Western title, the author established as heroine a woman newspaper reporter, Kate Love, who is out to expose a stock swindler.

In 2002, Jenkins shifted direction slightly to author her first young adult novel. "Belle and Beau and Josephine and the Soldier were done for a teenage romance line called Avon True Romance," the author told *Shades of Romance Magazine.* "They are both set in 19th century Michigan and revolve around a Black abolitionist family."

She has also written a Christmas novella and a contemporary romance, *The Edge of Midnight,* the first of a planned trio of books. The switch to modern times isn't that difficult, she has said, as long as she keeps control of the appropriate writing voice. Still, she assures readers, she won't wander forever from her historical roots.

Works by the Author

Night Song (1994)
Vivid (1995)
Indigo (1996)
Topaz (1997)
Through the Storm (1998)
The Taming of Jessi Rose (1999)
Indigo (2000)
Always and Forever (2000), sequel to *Through the Storm*
Before the Dawn (2001)
A Chance at Love (2002)
The Edge of Midnight (2004)
The Edge of Dawn (2004)
Something Like Love (2005)
Black Lace (2005)
Winds of the Storm (2006)
Sexy/Dangerous (2006)

Young Adult Fiction

Belle and the Beau (2002)
Josephine and the Soldier (2003)

Anthologies

Gettin' Merry (2002), with Geri Guillaume, Monica Jackson, and Francis Ray

For Further Information

Beverly Jenkins entry, Contemporary Authors Online, Gale 2001. Reproduced in Biography Resource Center, Farmington Hills, MI: Thomson Gale, 2005. *http://galenet.galegroup.com/servlet/BioRC* (viewed Feb. 26, 2005).

Beverly Jenkins Web page, African American Literature Book Club. *http://authors. aalbc.com/beverly.htm* (viewed Sept. 14, 2006).

Coates, Jennifer, "Author of the Month—Beverly Jenkins," *Romance in Color. http://www.romanceincolor.com/authormthjenkins.htm* (viewed Sept. 14, 2006).

"Cover Author Beverly Jenkins," *Shades of Romance Magazine* (Jan./Feb. 2004). *http://www.sormag.com/sourmag201.pdf* (viewed March 9, 2005).

Israel, Betsy, and Nancy Drew, "Heat in Another Color: Writer Beverly Jenkins Combines Breathless Romance and Black History," *People Weekly* (Feb. 13, 1995).

Yolanda Joe

Women's Literature, Mystery

Benchmark Title: *He Say, She Say*

Chicago

1962

Photo credit: Powell Photography

About the Author and the Author's Writing

"I get ideas from songs, from a phrase that I may overhear at the dinner table, any number of ways!" author Yolanda Joe said in a TreasureAve.com interview. Gladys Knight and Marvin Gaye are two of her particular favorite musicians. Her favorite food? She didn't say.

The author did explain that she first builds a plot, then figures out characters, then decides on a setting. Her heroines and heroes may reflect a jumble of physical and personal characteristics of friends and family members, but may just as easily be made up. "I put my fun-loving attitude in all my books and my longing for romance in them, too," she added.

Joe has noted her experience in journalism has both provided inspiration for books and grounded her in narrative and detail. "Broadcasting is fast paced," she told a Black Men in America Web page interviewer. "You must write well and quickly and conversationally. That helps me to meet deadlines and to write dialogue well."

Joe was born in Chicago in 1962. Her parents soon separated and Yolanda and her older sister Donna were raised by their maternal grandparents. Yolanda has said she knew that she needed to express herself by the time she was six and reading *Cat in the Hat*. Later influences included Zora Neale Hurston, Maya Angelou, J. California Cooper, and James Baldwin. She said her grandparents, despite being poor, passed along to her a sense of confidence and faith.

"I always wanted to be a writer," the author said on her Web page. "I was writing poetry at age seven—it wasn't great poetry but praise from my family, my public school teachers, and church members made me believe that I could do anything if I tried."

Joe attended an all-black high school, then went to Yale University, where she graduated with a bachelor of arts degree in English. She spent the summer of her junior year at Oxford in England. She received a master of science degree from Columbia School of Journalism, returned to Chicago and went to join the CBS radio affiliate newsroom. She switched to television news at WBBM and worked as a writer and producer before launching her career writing fiction. Her six fresh, contemporary books found an immediate audience.

The Hatwearer's Lesson, for example, features Chicago city attorney Terri Mills who is thrown for a loop when her fiancé, Derek Houser, has an affair with another woman. Called suddenly to care for her aged grandmother, Terri rues the loss of Derek—it's hard to find a soulmate on her intellectual plane—and is totally oblivious to the interest of rodeo star Lynnwood Conway. With her grandmother's help, the young professional woman works her way through the relationship crisis and, naturally, finds happiness.

In discussing the book with interviewer Sharon Hudson, Joe spoke of her own Louisiana-born grandmother, Bernice Barnett, who "stressed a sense of home, place, and education. I'm first generation college and she encouraged me to go to Yale where I won a scholarship. She was funny and warm, bossy and cranky but everything that is good in my character was shaped by her."

Joe adopted the penname Ardella Garland for a series of mystery novels featuring television journalist Georgia Barnett, her policeman boyfriend Doug, and her blues singer sister Peaches. In *Hit Time,* the amateur detective figures out who killed Hit Time Records producer Fab Weaver.

Joe today writes fiction but keeps a hand in television journalism. "I am a freelance journalist," she said on her publisher Penguin's Web page. "I work for a television network a couple of times a week. I once worked at CBS for more than ten years and I'm trying to keep my toe in. I freelance articles, too. Just wrote a book review for the *New York Times*. And I teach an essay class at a community college. But my real work is being the best novelist I can possibly be."

Works by the Author

Fiction

Falling Leaves of Ivy (1992)
He Say, She Say (1997)
Bebe's By Golly Wow! (1998)
This Just In (2000)
The Hatwearer's Lesson (2003)
My Fine Lady (2004)

Written as Ardella Garland (reissued as by Yolanda Joe)

Georgia Barnett Mysteries

Details at Ten (2000)
Hit Time (2002)
Video Cowboys (2005)

Contributor

Gumbo: A Literary Rent Party to Benefit the Hurston/Wright Foundation (2002), edited by Marita Golden and E. Lynn Harris
Brown Sugar 2 (2003), edited by Carol Taylor

For Further Information

Hudson, Sharon, Yolanda Joe interview, *MyShelf.com. http://www.myshelf.com/haveyouheard/03/joe.htm* (viewed March 9, 2005).

Interview with Yolanda Joe, *Black Men in America. http://www.blackmeninamerica.com/e-spotlight2.htm* (viewed March 9, 2005).

Interview with Yolanda Joe, Penguin Group. *http://www.penguinputnam.com/static/rguides/us/hatwearers_lesson.html* (viewed March 9, 2005).

Interview with Yolanda Joe, *TreasureAve.com. http://www.treasureave.com/shop/authorasp?authNum=3* (viewed March 9, 2005).

Yolanda Joe entry, *Contemporary Black Biography*, Vol. 21, Shirelle Phelps, ed. Gale Group, 1999. Reproduced in Biography Resource Center; Farmington Hills, MI: Thomson Gale, 2005. *http://galenet.galegroup.com/servlet/.BioRC.*

Yolanda Joe Web page. *http://www.yolandajoe.com* (viewed March 9, 2005).

Angela Johnson

Young Adult Literature, Children's Literature

Benchmark Title: *Heaven*

Tuskegee, Alabama

1961

Photo credit: Sam Jackson

About the Author and the Author's Writing

Three-time winner of the Coretta Scott King Award for young adult fiction, most recently for *The First Part Last*, Angela Johnson came a long way from the punk poetry she wrote in her high school years. "At that point in my life," she said on her African American Literary Book Club Web page, "my writing was personal and angry. I didn't want anyone to like it." Today, of course, she hopes her writing "is universal and speaks to everyone who reads it."

Johnson's books for children and young adults emphasize family life—although not perfect family lives. *Heaven*, a Coretta Scott King award recipient, is about fourteen-year-old Marley who has a part-time job at Western Union. She is content in the small town of Heaven, Ohio, until she learns a family secret. Her "parents" are really her aunt and uncle. Her life will never be the same. A character in that book, Bobby, was so popular with readers that the author gave him his own story, *The First Part Last*: Bobby experiences the trials of being a single parent, at age sixteen.

Johnson's books also emphasize character. "Plot hurts me," she said in an interview with Gillian Engberg. "I think sometimes that it makes my editors weep. But I fall in love with the character first. An issue is there, and I have to tell real stories; I can't write fantasy. I have to address issues that surround the kids that I love and the things that have touched my life."

The author was born in Tuskegee, Alabama, in 1961. Her father was an autoworker, her mother an accountant. Inspired by a storyteller who visited her school, Johnson decided to make up her own stories.

She attended Kent State University, then joined the Volunteers in Service to America (VISTA) program and worked in Ohio for two years as a child development worker. She also worked as a nanny, at a day-care center, and at a summer camp. In 1989, she began writing books.

From the start, Johnson wrote about everyday life. In the picture book *Tell Me a Story, Mama*, a girl asks her mother for a bedtime tale but ends up telling most of it herself.

Three generations of black women are depicted in Johnson's first young adult novel, *Toning the Sweep*, another winner of the King honor. Fourteen-year-old Emmie travels to California to visit her grandmother, who is afflicted with cancer. As she videotapes her dying relative, she comes to realize the great opportunity for sharing that can come from a tragic situation.

Johnson's courage to tackle tough issues captivates readers and critics alike. The author's "critical reputation continues to grow," observed Duane Telgen of *Authors & Artists for Young Adults* (2000), "as does her readership."

Although known for writing books about family, Johnson stretches some of the traditional meanings of family. "In recent years the 'family' has been talked about, dissected, redefined," the author said in an article in *Horn Book Magazine* (1997). "The well-meaning and not-so-well-meaning have even gone so far as to wield picket signs over the heads of those whose definition of family did not meld with their own."

Characters in Johnson's books do family things. They celebrate. They argue. They cry. They agree and disagree.

"In an era of teenage pregnancy, divorce, blended families, and a bit too much television baby-sitting," Johnson said in *Horn Book*, "all eyes have turned to the 'family.' It seems everyone is longing for the way it used to be. Mom, Dad, kids and a passel of relatives who hug the kids and give an overall warm fuzzy feeling of home."

While this is a comfortable image, it simply is not the way family life is for everyone, especially today—and Johnson has carved a comfortable place as an author in attempting to promote understanding and tolerance of all lifestyles.

Young Adult Books

Toning the Sweep (1993)
Humming Whispers (1995)
Gone from Home: Short Takes (1998), stories
Heaven (1998)
The Other Side: Shorter Poems (1998), verse
Songs of Faith (1998)
The First Part Last (2003), companion to *Heaven*

Books for Children and Middle Readers

Tell Me a Story, Mama (1989)
Do Like Kyla (1990)
When I Am Old with You (1990)
One of Three (1991)
The Leaving Morning (1992)
The Girl Who Wore Snakes (1993)
Julius (1993)
Joshua by the Sea (1994)

Joshua's Night Whispers (1994), sequel to *Joshua by the Sea*
Mama Bird, Baby Birds (1994)
Rain Feet (1994)
Shoes Like Miss Alice's (1995)
The Aunt in Our House (1996)
Daddy Calls Me Man (1997) .
The Rolling Store (1997)
Songs of Faith (1998)
Those Building Men (1999)
Maniac Monkeys on Magnolia Street (1999)
The Wedding (1999)
Down the Winding Road (2000)
Casey Jones (2001)
When Mules Flew on Magnolia Street (2001), sequel to *Maniac Monkeys on Magnolia Street*
Running Back to Ludie (2001)
Looking for Red (2002)
A Cool Moonlight (2003)
I Dream of Trains (2003)
Just Like Josh Gibson (2003)
Bird (2004)
Violet's Music (2004)
Sweet Smell of Roses (2005)

For Further Information

Angela Johnson biography, *http://www.visitingauthors.com/printable_pages/ johnson_angela_print_info.html* (viewed Sept. 14, 2005).

Angela Johnson entry, *Black Authors & Illustrators of Children's Books*, 2d ed., Barbara Rollock, ed. New York: Garland, 1992.

Angela Johnson entry, *Contemporary Authors, New Revision Series*, Vol. 92. Detroit: Gale, 2001.

Angela Johnson entry, *Dictionary of American Children's Fiction, 1990–1994*, Alethea K. Helbig and Agnes Regan Perkins, eds. Westport, CT: Greenwood Press, 1996.

Angela Johnson interview, *Ohio Authors and Illustrators for Young People. http://green.upper-arlington.k12.oh.us/ohioauthors/johnson,angela.htm* (viewed July 29, 2006).

Angela Johnson Web page, African American Literature Book Club. *http://authors. aalbc.com/angela.htm* (viewed Feb. 17, 2005).

Engberg, Gillian, Angela Johnson interview, U.S. Department of State International Information Programs. *http://usinfo.state.gov/scv/Archive_Index/ The_Booklist_Interview_Angela_Johnson.html* (viewed Sept. 14, 2006).

Gregory, Lucille H., Angela Johnson entry, *Twentieth-Century Children's Writers*, 4th ed. Chicago: St. James Press, 1995.

Johnson, Angela, "Family Is What You Have," *Horn Book Magazine* (March-April 1997).

Parravano, Martha V., *Songs of Faith* review, *Horn Book Magazine* (March-April 1998).

Telgen, Diane, Angela Johnson entry, *Authors & Artists for Young Adults*, Vol. 32, Thomas McMahon, ed. Detroit: Gale, 2000.

Gayl Jones

Mainstream Contemporary Literature, Poetry, Drama

Benchmark Title: *The Healing*

Lexington, Kentucky

1949

About the Author and the Author's Writing

Gayl Jones has been in seclusion in her hometown of Lexington, Kentucky, since 1998 when she was briefly institutionalized for treatment of mental illness.

Her life is as enigmatic and troubling as her novels and poetry.

Born in Lexington in 1949, Jones was known for her shyness and her interest in writing. She earned a bachelor of arts degree from Connecticut College in 1971 and a master's degree in creative writing from Brown University where poet Michael Harper was one of her mentors. While at Brown she wrote and produced a play, *Chile Woman*. In 1975, she completed requirements for a doctorate. After teaching briefly at Wellesley College, she became an assistant professor of English at the University of Michigan. She married Bob Higgins—he took her last name when they wed. Apparently Bob was an unstable individual who in 1976 took a shotgun to an AIDS rally and was arrested. The couple fled the country before the trial and spent a dozen years in Paris, coming back in 1988 when Gayl Jones's mother became ill in Kentucky. Police eventually learned of their return—Bob Jones was outspoken in claiming a conspiracy in his mother-in-law's death—and surrounded the cabin where the couple was living. Bob Jones took his own life. Shortly thereafter, in winter 1998, Gayl Jones was taken to Eastern State Hospital for a short stay.

Does that explain or muddle one's thinking about Gayl Jones's writing? Perhaps a little of both; it does help explain the complexity of Jones's work. From her first novel, *Corregidora*, she challenged her audience with a raw, nightmarish depiction of slavery and racism. Ursa Corregidora, the main character, is troubled in love. She is a 1940s blues singer obsessed with her heritage: The same man fathered her grandmother as fathered her mother.

"In each personal relationship she [Ursa] finds yet again the sickness of the master-slave dynamic," explains *Contemporary Novelists*. "Her short-lived first marriage is convulsive with desire, possessiveness, humiliation, and violence; her second, safer, marriage fails as she cannot forget the first."

Poet David Burn argues that the discomfort level is necessary to confront the institution of slavery. "In the hands of a less gifted author," he wrote, "*Corregidora* would be merely a polemic, for Jones fearlessly exposes ugly truths that must be told, and told again, if our nation is to ever progress toward the advanced, enlightened society we hold up as an ideal."

The author explores a number of themes, including mixed emotions. "I was and continue to be interested in contradictory emotions that coexist . . . ," she told interviewer Claudia Tate. "I think people can hold two different emotions simultaneously."

Jones's next book, *Eva's Man*, probes character Eva Medina Canada's pathological mind against all cultural convention. Canada, imprisoned for killing and mutilating a male friend, feels abused by a hostile society.

In *White Rat*, a collection of stories, the author "displays her unflinching ability to delve into the most treacherous of psyches and circumstances," according to its publisher, Random House Canada.

After that book, with the exception of a novel published only in Germany, the author had no new publications in the United States until her surreptitious return, when she produced two powerful new works.

"Months after reading it, I'm still shivering over Gayl Jones's novel *The Healing . . .* ," observed reviewer Johanna Isaacson. Her reaction was positive: "It's the chills I always get when someone reinvents America for me." The novel, about rock music manager Harlan Jane Eagleton, who has become a faith healer, is relatively straightforward compared with the author's next book, *Mosquito*. Mosquito is a truck driver and teller of stories. Reviewer James A. Miller said *Mosquito* is a novel in name, though not form. "This is a work that steadfastly resists not only any sense of a linear narrative but also the qualities we often associate with well-made fictions: shape, symmetry, proportion, epiphanies. Instead, *Mosquito* is a work that aspires to the condition of 'truth,' of 'experience' in all its formlessness and apparent chaos."

Despite the controversy of and tragedy in her life, Jones's work remains well-respected. "Perhaps most important throughout the psychological developments in the characters [in Jones's works] are their voices which shout from the pages of her work their story, their song, and their truth," said her biographers on the Voices from the Gap Web site. "Her readers cannot wait to hear what will come next from this quiet woman who writes out loud."

Works by the Author

Corregidora (1975)
Eva's Man (1976)
White Rat: Short Stories (1977)
Die Volgelfaengerin (*The Birdwatcher*) (early 1980s in Germany)
The Healing (1998)
Mosquito (1999)

Drama

Chile Woman (1974)

Poetry

Song for Anninho (1981)

The Hermit-Woman (1983)
Xarque & Other Poems (1985)

Nonfiction

Liberating Voices: Oral Tradition in African American Literature (1991)

Contributor

Confirmation (1983)
A Life Distilled: Gwendolyn Brooks, Her Poetry and Fiction (1987)
Presence Africaine: Revue Culturelle du Monde Noir/Cultural Review of the Negro World (1987)
Graywolf Annual Seven: Stories from the American Mosaic (1990)
Black-Eyed Susans/Midnight Birds: Stories By and About Black Women (1990)
Callaloo: A Journal of African -American and African Arts and Letters (1994)

For Further Information

Burn, David, "Scar Tissue: The Painful Beauty of Gayl Jones' *Corregidora*," David Burn Web site. *http://www.davidburn.com/scartissue.php* (viewed July 29, 2006).

Coser, Stelamaris, *Bridging the Americas: The Literature of Paule Marshall, Toni Morrison, and Gayl Jones.* Philadelphia: Temple University Press, 1995.

Eckhoff, Sally, "The Terrible Mystery of Gayl Jones," *Salon.com.* (Feb. 26, 1998). *http://www.salon.com/media/1998/02/26media.html* (viewed Sept. 14, 2006).

Gayl Jones biography, *Voices from the Gaps. http://voices.cla.umn.edu/vg/Bios/entries/jones_gayl.html* (viewed March 16, 2005).

Gayl Jones entry, Contemporary Authors Online, Gale, 2005. Reproduced in Biography Resource Center, Farmington Hills, Mich.: Thomson Gale, 2005. *http://galenet.galegroup.com/servlet/BioRC* (viewed Feb. 26, 2005).

Gayl Jones entry, *Contemporary Novelists*. Detroit: St. James Press, 2001.

Isaacson, Johanna, *The Healing* review, *The Second Circle. http://www.thesecondcircle.com/john/jone.html* (viewed March 18, 2005).

Miller, James A., "A Talker, a Tale-Teller, a Sojourner," *Boston Globe* (Jan. 17, 1999).

Tate, Claudia C., "Ursa's Blues Medley," *Black American Literature Forum* (1979).

White Rat, catalog description, Random House of Canada. *http://www.randomhouse.ca/catalog/display.pperl?0767922131* (viewed July 29, 2006).

Jamaica Kincaid

Mainstream Contemporary Literature

Benchmark Title: *Annie John*

St. Johns, Antigua

1949

About the Author and the Author's Writing

> I couldn't move, and when I looked down it was as if the ground had opened up between us, making a deep and wide split. On one side of the split stood my mother . . . on the other side stood I, in my arms carrying my schoolbooks and inside carrying the thimble that weighed worlds.
>
> — from *Annie John*

That sentence from Jamaica Kincaid's 1985 novel *Annie John* sums up the disaffection felt by the novel's main character—an autobiographical theme which, along with power, sexuality and alienation threads throughout the author's work.

Kincaid was born Elaine Potter Richardson in St. Johns, Antigua, in 1949. She grew up in poverty that worsened when her mother bore more children. Never an affectionate woman, Kincaid's mother distanced herself emotionally from her daughter. Her mother worked as a domestic. Her stepfather was a carpenter. When Kincaid was seventeen, her family sent her to the United States to work as an au pair. Not shy about speaking her feelings, she wore out her welcome with two families, and then found work in a photo agency. She studied at New School for Social Research and Franconia College.

"I started to write because I couldn't hold a job," she told *People Weekly's* Joanne Kaufman. "If I had a job, I would get so outspoken."

Exercising her frustrations and rebelliousness, the six-footer dyed her hair blonde and adopted a distinctive counter-culture wardrobe. She changed her name in 1973, selecting "Jamaica" for its sound, "Kincaid" for the same reason from a George Bernard Shaw story. She gradually began to appear in print in *The Village Voice*. She persuaded an editor at *Ingenue* to assign her to interview Gloria Steinem. An unexpected meeting with *New Yorker* contributor George Trow led to an introduction to that periodical's editor, William Shawn, who began to publisher her essays and stories. She became a staff writer for the weekly. Later, she married Allen Shawn, a composer of classical music and son of the famed *New Yorker* editor. The couple lives in North

Bennington, Vermont, where they have raised their two children. Kincaid has also taught as a visiting professor at Harvard College.

Smarting from her dysfunctional childhood, Kincaid has written about her mother in *Annie John* and *The Autobiography of My Mother*; her brother, Devon Drew, and his struggle with AIDS in *My Brother;* and her natural father, whom she did not meet until she was in her thirties, in *Mr. Potter.*

New York Times writer Leslie Garis suggested the author "has never gotten over the betrayal she felt when she began to suffer from her mother's emotional remoteness." At a young age, she found a haven in reading—so much so that she sometimes stole books or stole money to buy them. "Books brought me the greatest satisfaction to be alone, reading, under the house with lizards and spiders running around," Kincaid told Garis. In another interview, she told *People Weekly* that she chose to write semiautobiographical works to come to understand her family and her past.

Kincaid described her relentless pursuit of truth to journalist Brad Goldfarb: "When I was a child, I was much praised for my memory because it was very precocious. I could remember everything I saw and heard, and I would complete people's stories—everyone thought it was so charming. And then when I kept it up and told people things they didn't want to remember, everyone grew annoyed with me."

Beyond the family, she has attributed her provocative and sometimes unpleasant prose characterizations to her cultural background, nothing that Americans are too anxious for happy endings. She used gardening as an example in a conversation with Marilyn Snell: "Most of the nations that have serious gardening cultures also have, or had, empires. You can't have this luxury of pleasure without somebody paying for it."

Works by the Author

At the Bottom of the River (1983), short stories
Annie John (1985)
Annie, Gwen, Lilly, Pam, and Tulip (1986)
Lucy (1990)
The Autobiography of My Mother (1995)
My Brother (1997)
Mr. Potter (2002)

Contributor

Snapshots: Twentieth-Century Mother-Daughter Fiction (2000)
Whispers from the Cotton Tree Root: Caribbean Fabulist Fiction (2000)

Nonfiction

A Small Place (1988), essays
Poetics of Place (1998)
My Garden (1999)
Talk Stories (2000)
Seed Gathering Atop the World (2002)
Among Flowers: A Walk in the Himalaya (2005)

Editor

My Favorite Plant: Writers and Gardeners on the Plants They Love (1998)
The Best American Travel Writing 2005 (2005)

For Further Information

Garis, Leslie, "Through West Indian Eyes," *New York Times Magazine* (Oct. 4, 1990).

Goldfarb, Brad, "Writing Life," *Interview* (Oct. 1997).

Jamaica Kincaid entry, Contemporary Authors Online, Gale, 2005. Reproduced in Biography Resource Center. Farmington Hills, MI: Thomson Gale, 2005. *http://galenet.galegroup.com/servlet.BioRC* (viewed Feb. 26, 2005).

Jamaica Kincaid Web page, African American Literature Book Club. *http://authors.aalbc.com./jamacia.htm* (viewed July 29, 2006).

Jamaica Kincaid Web page, *Voices from the Gaps. http://voices.cla.umn.edu/vg/Bios/entries/kincaid_jamaica.html*(viewed July 29, 2006).

Kaufman, Joanne, "Jamaica Kincaid: An Author's Unsparing Judgments Earn Her an Unwanted Reputation for Anger," *People Weekly* (Dec. 15, 1997).

Kreilkamp, Ivan, "Jamaica Kincaid: Daring to Discomfort," *Publishers Weekly* (Jan. 1, 1996).

McLarin, Kim, "BIBR Talks with Jamaica Kincaid," *Black Issues Book Review* (July-Aug. 2002).

Snell, Marilyn, "Jamaica Kincaid Hates Happy Endings," *Mother Jones* (Sept./Oct. 1997).

Sandra Kitt

**Romance, Mainstream
Contemporary Literature**

Benchmark Title: *The Color of Love*

New York, New York
1947

Photo credit: John Penderhughes

About the Author and the Author's Writing

Sandra Kitt didn't set out to write romances. Rather, she said in a *Wonderful World of Color* interview, she wanted to write stories about relationships—between men and women, between parents and children, between siblings. "Yes, I wanted to have a love relationship in my books, but I never considered them strictly romances. I guess the early influences were 'gothic' writers like Mary Stewart and Victoria Holt even though their stories were suspenseful. There was more than just romance going on in their books." Kitt admires the writing of Janet Dailey, for her realistic, ordinary characters; she also admires Kathleen Eagle, Tess Gerritson, Chassie West, and Elizabeth Berg.

Kitt didn't sell her first book the conventional way. A professional artist and librarian, she wrote in her spare moments, ending up with two manuscripts. At first she didn't consider trying to have them published. Then after reading in the newspaper one day that a major publisher, Harlequin, had opened a New York office, she phoned an editor there, arranged an appointment, showed her work—and went home with a contract. Within a month, she sold two other manuscripts and her second career was off and running.

Kitt was born in Harlem in 1947. She graduated from the Music & Art High School in New York and earned an associate's degree from Bronx Community College of the City University of New York. She also earned a bachelor of arts degree from City College of the City University of New York in 1969, and a master's degree in fine arts from the same institution in 1975. She attended the School of Visual Arts, the New School for Social Research and the University of Guadalajara. When she was twenty-one she hitchhiked across Canada, and she has since traveled to China, Japan, and the former Soviet Union. Now divorced, she lives in New York.

Kitt worked as an art assistant for Philip Gips Studios, a teacher in the Cloisters Workshop Program, a staff member of the Children's Art Center, a teacher at Printmaking Workshop, and a librarian for the city of New York before joining the American Museum of Natural History in New York in 1992. She worked there as manager of library services at the Richard S. Perkin Library, Hayden Planetarium. She has also taught a creative writing course at County College of Morris in New Jersey. At the same time, she has been a freelance graphic artist, (illustrating two of Isaac Asimov's books and one of her own, *Love Everlasting*), a greeting card designer for UNICEF, and a printmaker. And she has been a writer of romance and suspense novels.

Considering her workload, Kitt fortunately is a fast worker, generally completing a manuscript in less than six months. "I have to be disciplined," she said in an African American Literary Book Club interview, explaining she has had to prepare better outlines as her contractual obligations have grown. "Each book gets more detailed. Now I write a synopsis that acts as a guidepost or map to guide me."

Although Kitt has become popular for her works depicting African Americans, her very first book was about Caucasians. She has explored a variety of themes, many of them revolving around relationships between races. *She's the One* is about a woman whose friend has become the guardian of her biracial daughter, and at the same time is falling in love with a man from a lower economic class. *The Color of Love* looks at interracial relationships, *Between Friends* at a character's experience as the child of a mixed marriage. In *Close Encounters*, an innocent Black woman is wounded by a white undercover cop.

The author explains that she really is simply writing about people who have different skin colors and are accepting of change. With the cultural mix of New York City—Asians, Middle Easterners, Hispanics, mixed-race—it is obvious the nation's complexion is rapidly changing.

"I guess to some extent I'm a selfish writer, in that I want to write what I want to write. . . . What motivates me is always trying to understand the complex nature of what brings people together, to either love or hate each other," the author said in an All About Romance interview. "I do believe in a 'positive' and upbeat ending."

Kitt generally starts formulating a novel with the characters' personalities, adding physical details, establishing conflicts and building the plot later. She puts a great deal of attention on visual description. She carefully paces her books; there are no scenes of intimacy in the first half, as by her observation, people just getting to know each other usually hold off on sex. Her characters, she asserts, are not perfect; they have the same flaws as most everyone has.

Kitt hopes her reputation will spur other Black writers. "I've always considered myself a writer who's Black, rather than a Black writer, because I always wanted to make sure I had the options of writing anything and being seen capable of doing more than just another 'Black' work."

She's not likely to run out of ideas soon. "For many years I've had an idea I've wanted to write about an African American woman and an American Indian man," she said in a New People interview. "I happen to believe that the spirituality between the two groups are very similar, and I think there is much that we share. I'm also particularly interested because of my own American Indian background from both my mother and father's family."

With all of her ideas, talent, and ambition, Kitt has enormous opportunity ahead.

Works by the Author

Fiction

All Good Things (1984)
Love Everlasting (1993)
Serenade (1994)
The Color of Love (1995)
Sincerely (1995)
Significant Others (1996)
Suddenly (1996)
Between Friends (1998)
Family Affairs (1999)
Close Encounters (2000)
She's the One (2001)
First Touch (2004)
Beyond the Rapture (2005)
The Next Best Thing (2005)
Adam and Eve (2006)

Harlequin American Romance Series

48. *Rites of Spring* (1984)
86. *Adam and Eva* (1984)
97. *Perfect Combination* (1985)
112. *Only with the Heart* (1985)
148. *With Open Arms* (1987)
280. *An Innocent Man* (1989)
327. *The Way Home* (1990)
399. *Someone's Baby* (1991)

Anthologies

Friends, Families and Lovers (1993)
Baby Beat (1996)
For the Love of Chocolate (1996)
Merry Christmas, Baby (1996)
Sisters (1996)
Girlfriends (1999)
Valentine Wishes (2001)
Back in Your Arms (2006)
Have a Little Faith (2006)

Illustrator

Asimov's Guide to Halley's Comet by Isaac Asimov (1985)
Beginnings: The Story of Origin . . . by Isaac Asimov (1986)

For Further Information

"Interview with Author Sandra Kitt," *Wonderful World of Color Page. http://www.geocities.com/bellesandbeaux/Kitt.html* (viewed May 24, 2003).

"Interview with Sandra Kitt," *Your Interracial e-Mag. http:newpeople/. weblogger.com/feature* (viewed May 24, 2003).

Mendoza, Sylvia, "Sandra Kitt; Bringing 'The Color of Love' to Romance Novels." *http://www.sylvia-mendoza.com/SDWMSep97.htm* (viewed May 24, 2003).

Sandra Kitt entry, *Contemporary Authors, New Revision Series*, Vol. 91, Peacock, Scot, ed. Detroit: Gale, 2000.

Sandra Kitt interview, AALBC. *http://www.aalbc.com/authors/sandrakitt.htm* (viewed May 24, 2003).

Sandra Kitt interview. *http://www.writersandpoets.com/newsletter/sandra_kitt_interview.htm* (viewed Aug. 1, 2006).

Sandra Kitt Web page. *http://www.sandrakitt.com* (viewed Aug. 1, 2006).

"Sandra Kitt: A Matter of Hope," *All About Romance* (Sept. 11, 2000). *http://www.likesbooks.com/sandrakitt.html* (viewed Aug. 1, 2006).

Julius Lester

Mainstream Contemporary Literature, Children's Literature

Benchmark Title: *To Be a Slave*

St. Louis, Missouri

1939

Photo credit: Milan Sabatini

About the Author and the Author's Writing

"Obviously, literature is the royal road that enables us to enter the realm of the imagination," Julius Lester explained in *Horn Book Magazine*. "Literature enables us to experience what it is like to be someone else. Through literature we experience modes of being. Through literature we recognize who we are and who we might be."

Born in St. Louis, Missouri, in 1939, Julius Bernard Lester experienced segregation and racism firsthand during a childhood in Kansas City, Kansas, and Nashville, Tennessee, with Arkansas summers thrown in. He said on the Finding His True Voice Web site. "The forties and fifties were not pleasant times for blacks and I am offended by white people who get nostalgic for the fifties. . . . I have no nostalgia for a time when I endangered my life if, while downtown shopping with my parents, I raised my eyes and accidentally met the eyes of a white woman. Black men and boys were lynched for this during my childhood and adolescence."

Lester has said he was not a good writer in his younger years and never dreamed he would one day take home major awards for his writing. He first began to dabble with words after discovering a book of Japanese haiku poetry. He studied the haiku tradition, and from there, Zen Buddhism.

In 1960, Lester earned a bachelor of arts degree in English from Fisk University. He joined the civil rights movement, and took charge of the photo department for the Student Non-Violent Coordinating Committee (SNCC).

He also played guitar. He recorded two albums and performed with Pete Seeger, Phil Ochs, and Judy Collins. He was a radio announcer in New York. He directed the

Newport Folk Festival in Rhode Island from 1966 to 1968. And he lectured for the New School for Social Research in New York. From time to time he has written about music—how-to works and biographies.

In 1968, Lester joined the faculty of University of Massachusetts at Amherst and was professor of Afro-American studies from 1971 to 1988. He held other positions with the university and was also writer-in-residence at Vanderbilt University in Nashville, Tennessee. He hosted "Free Time," a television show for WNET-TV in New York.

The author, his wife Milan Sabatini, and her child from a previous marriage live in western Massachusetts.

Lester's first book for younger readers was *To Be a Slave*, a Newbery Honor Book. "This book received this recognition during the decade in which the Civil Rights Movement was significant," explained Harold Nelson. "Also, during this decade, historians . . . had begun to consult original sources and, on the basis of these sources, to challenge accepted historical truths. In *To Be a Slave*, Lester challenged the assumption prevalent at the time that African-American history is relatively important in American history. . . . ."

Lester's interest in slavery was heart-felt: Three of his great-grandparents had worn shackles. He told teacher.scholastic.com, "I became intrigued by the challenge of trying to imagine what it was like to have been a slave. I wanted to communicate to others that those we call slaves were really human beings, human beings pretty much like us."

Lester did this by interspersing primary documents with his own writing. "Thus, the reader can better understand what it meant to be a slave; to be owned like a piece of property that could be sold at will; to be used as an object to plow fields;" suggested Laura M. Zaidman in *Authors & Artists for Young Adults*, "cook food, or nurse others' babies; and to be cruelly punished for the slightest offense."

Lester wrote other books in this vein and was a National Book Award finalist for *Long Journey Home: Stories from Black History* (1972). He converted to Judaism, and wrote of the experience in *Lovesong: Becoming a Jew* (1988).

He went on to retell some of our most popular stories and folktales. He rewrote Helen Bannerman's *Little Black Sambo* and, with illustrator Jerry Pinkney, gave it a new, modern, fantasy twist. He has also rewritten the stories of John Henry and Uncle Remus. These new visits to old characters have not been published without controversy. But as he told interviewer Janice Del Negro, reworking icons, even stereotypes, is difficult. "There are white people who have great love for the Uncle Remus tales as Joel Chandler Harris wrote them and feel they should not be touched, and there are black people who are antagonistic to the stories because of slavery. The frightening thing about doing the stories was that sense of responsibility to the culture, both past and present, as well as future. . . ."

His recent young adult novel, *When Dad Killed Mom*, alternates the perspectives of a brother and sister whose father has killed their mother and been sent to prison. While a single parent's complaint about strong language got the book banned at a Wyoming school library, reaction to the book was generally positive, he told Downhomebooks.com: "I have gotten a couple of letters from adults who were children when their father killed their mother and that has been very moving to hear from them that *When Dad Killed Mom* reflected their experience."

"I write because the lives of all of us are stories," the author said on the Virginia Hamilton Conference Web site. "If enough of those stories are told, then perhaps we will begin to see that our lives are the same story. The differences are merely in the details."

Works by the Author

Young Adult Fiction

To Be a Slave (1969)
Black Folktales (1969)
The Knee-High Man and Other Tales (1972)
Two Love Stories (1972)
When Dad Killed Mom (2001)
Pharaoh's Daughter: A Novel of Ancient Egypt (2000)
The Autobiography of God (2004)
Cupid: A Tale of Love and Desire (2007)

Children's Fiction

Tales of Uncle Remus: The Adventures of Brer Rabbit (1987)
More Tales of Uncle Remus: The Further Adventures of Brer Rabbit, His Friends, Enemies, and Others (1988)
Further Tales of Uncle Remus: The Misadventures of Brer Rabbit, Brer Fox, Brer Wolf, the Doodang, and Other Creatures (1990)
The Last Tales of Uncle Remus (1994)
John Henry (1994)
The Man Who Knew Too Much: A Moral Tale from the Baile of Zambia (1994)
Sam and the Tigers: A New Telling of Little Black Sambo (1996)
Black Cowboys, Wild Horses (1998)
From Slave Ship to Freedom Road (1998)
Albidaro and the Mischievous Dream (2000)
Ackamarackus: Julius Lester's Sumptuously Silly Fantastically Funny Fables (2001)
Why Heaven Is Far Away (2002)
Shining (2003)
Day of Tears (2005)
Time's Memory (2006)

Poetry

Who Am I? (1974)

Nonfiction

12-String Guitar as Played by Leadbelly (1965), with Pete Seeger
Seventh Son: The Thoughts and Writings of W. E. B. DuBois (1971), two volumes
Long Journey Home: Stories from Black History (1972)

All Is Well: An Autobiography (1976)
Lovesong: Becoming a Jew (1988)
Othello: A Novel (1995)
Blues Singers: Ten Who Rocked the World (2001)
Let's Talk About Race (2005)

For Further Information

"About Julius Lester." *http://www.scils.rutgers.edu/special/kay/cool6.html* (viewed Aug. 1, 2006).

Del Negro, Janice, Julius Lester interview, *Booklist* (Feb. 15, 1995).

Julius Lester entry, *Black Authors and Illustrators of Children's Books*, 2d ed., edited by Barbara Rollock. New York: Garland, 1992.

Julius Lester entry, *Contemporary Authors, New Revision Series*, Vol. 43. Detroit: Gale, 1994.

Julius Lester entry, *Eighth Book of Junior Authors and Illustrators*, Connie C. Rockman, ed. New York: H.W. Wilson, 2000.

Julius Lester entry, *Meet Authors and Illustrators. http://www.childrenslit.com/ f_lester.html* (viewed Aug. 1, 2006)

Julius Lester interview, *Downhomebooks.Com. http://www.downhomebooks. com/ lester.htm* (viewed Aug. 1, 2006).

"Julius Lester," Virginia Hamilton Conference. *http://dept.kent.edu/ virginiahamiltonconf/lester.htm* (viewed Aug. 1, 2006)

"Julius Lester: Finding His True Voice." *http://www.facing.org/* (viewed March 23, 2001).

"Julius Lester's biography," Resource Finder. *http://teacher.scholastic.com/* (viewed March 23, 2001).

Lester, Julius, "Re-imagining the Possibilities," *Horn Book Magazine*, May-June 2000.

Lodge, Sally, "Julius Lester: Working at His Creative Peak," *Publishers Weekly* (Feb. 12, 2001).

Nelson, Harold, Julius Lester entry, *Twentieth Century Young Adult Writers*, Laura Standley Berger, ed. Detroit: St. James Press, 1994.

"Q&A with Julius Lester." *http://wildes.home.mindspring.com/OUAL/int/ lesterjulius.html* (viewed March 23, 2001).

Zaidman, Laura M., Julius Lester entry, *Authors & Artists for Young Adults*, Vol. 12, Kevin S. Hile, ed. Detroit: Gale, 1994.

Zaidman, Laura M., Julius Lester entry, *Writers of Multicultural Fiction for Young Adults: A Bio-Critical Sourcebook*, M. Daphne Kutzer, ed. Westport, CT: Greenwood Press, 1996.a

Paule Marshall

Mainstream Contemporary Literature, Poetry

Benchmark Title: *Brown Girl, Brownstones*

Brooklyn, New York

1929

About the Author and the Author's Writing

Paule Marshall could cite traditional writers she has enjoyed reading. But as she explained in an essay for the Making of a Writer series for the *New York Times Book Review,* the greatest influences on her writing career were the "poets in the kitchen," the housewives, including her mother, who gathered around a table in the kitchen of the Brooklyn brownstone where she grew up. "They talked—endlessly, passionately, poetically, and with impressive range. No subject was beyond them. . . . [T]his is why the best of my work must be attributed to them; it stands as testimony to the legacy of language and culture they so freely passed on to me in the workshop of the kitchen," she wrote.

Author Paul Lawrence Dunbar was a guiding figure in her writing as well. "I sensed that what Paul Lawrence Dunbar was doing with his use of dialect was like what my mother and friends were doing when they talked—trying to process language on their own terms," she said in *Essence.*

The author was born Vlenza Pauline Burke in Brooklyn, New York, in 1929. Her parents were from Barbados, West Indies, and returned there when she was nine years old. Her exposure to that community enriched her education. More formally, she studied social work at Hunter College, but had to take a year off because of a nervous breakdown. Her father had long before left the household to become a disciple of Father Divine in Harlem.

She graduated cum laude with a bachelor's degree in English literature from Brooklyn College in 1953. She had married psychologist Kenneth Marshall in 1950, and they had a son. From 1953 to 1956, she worked as a librarian for the New York Public Library. During that time, she also became a staff writer for *Our World.* She taught creative writing at Yale University, Columbia University, the University of Iowa, and the University of California at Berkeley. In 1963, she was divorced; and in 1970, she married Nourry Menard.

Marshall's first book was *Brown Girl, Brownstones.* It is about Selina, who grows up in an African-Caribbean community that is struggling to keep its traditions alive. Selina's mother Silla is an all-powerful and controlling matron. "In her attempts at resisting Silla's influence, in her fears of being or becoming like Silla, and in her

200

ability to reach a kind of peace with her, Selina establishes her individuality and her relationship to her ethnicity," explains essayist Martin Japtok.

Recognition of Marshall and her work has been bountiful. She received a Guggenheim Fellowship in 1961 and a National Endowment for the Arts grant in 1966. The author's collection *Soul Clap Hands and Sing* garnered her the National Institute of Arts Award while *Praisesong for the Widow* earned a Columbus Foundation American Book Award. According to the Voices from the Gaps Web site, "She feels as though her work serves not only as a career but also as a means of healing for herself—a vehicle through which she is able to work through issues and recurring themes in her own personal odyssey." One repeating theme is the search for one's identity, as in the novel *Brown Girl, Brownstones*.

The novel *The Chosen Place, The Timeless People* is about American sociologists who encounter an unknown people living in Bournehills (an area resembling the Caribbean islands). The book examines implications of natural versus technical lives. "The politics of the novel are conservative in a way that is unknown in parliaments or organized parties," observes *Contemporary Novelists*. "This conservative politics grows from knowledge that the configurations of character and the complex relationships of love or resentment gain their shape from historical cultures."

The author's *The Fisher King* came after a gap of nearly a decade. The main character Sonny, born in Paris, lives in Brooklyn and comes to meet and reconcile cultural and other differences with members of his extended family.

"I'm a very slow, painstaking, fussy writer," Marshall explained to Bella Stander. "One of my struggles has been to accept my pace because the pressure is so great to produce a novel every three to five years."

Her readers are eager for new works—however long it may take her to produce them the way she wants.

Works by the Author

Brown Girl, Brownstones (1959)
Soul Clap Hands and Sing (1962), short stories
The Chosen Place, the Timeless People (1970)
Praisesong for the Widow (1983)
Reena and Other Stories (1983), short stories; reissued as *Merle: A Novella and Other Stories* (1985)
Daughters (1991) (published in Britain as *Serpent's Tail*, 1992)
The Fisher King (2000)

Nonfiction

Language Is the Only Homeland: Bajan Poets Abroad (1995)

For Further Information

Japtok, Martin, "Paule Marshall's *Brown Girl, Brownstones*: Reconciling Ethnicity and Individualism—African American Woman Author's Semi-Autobiographical Novel," *African American Review* (summer 1998).

Marshall, Paule, "From the Poets in the Kitchen," *New York Times Book Review* (Jan. 9, 1983).

Paule Marshall biography, *Voices from the Gaps. http://voices.cla.umn.edu/vg/Bios/entries/marshall_paule.html* (viewed Aug. 1, 2006).

Paule Marshall entry, Contemporary Authors Online, Gale, 2005. Reproduced in Biography Resource Center, Farmington Hills, MI: Thomson Gale, 2005. *http://galenet.galegroup.com/servlet/BioRC* (viewed Feb. 26, 2005).

Paule Marshall entry, *Contemporary Novelists*, 7th ed. Detroit: St. James Press, 2001.

Paule Marshall entry, *Heath Anthology of American Literature*, 4th ed., Paul Lauter, ed. *http://college.hmco.com/english/lauter/heath/4e/students/author_pages/contemporary/marshall_pa.html* (viewed Aug. 1, 2006).

Stander, Bella, "A Conversation with Paule Marshall," *Albemarle* (Feb./March 2001).

Washington, Elsie B., "Paule Marshall: Merging Our Cultures," *Essence* (Oct. 1991).

Felicia Mason

Romance, Inspirational Literature

Benchmark Title: *Body and Soul*

Pennsylvania

1963

About the Author and the Author's Writing

Felicia Mason has been widely praised for her romance novels. She twice earned the Romantic Times Best Multicultural Romance of the Year honor.

Born in about 1963, the daughter of a Baptist minister, Mason grew up in Pennsylvania and later lived in Virginia. Mason has said she began to jot stories in a notebook at a very young age and begged relatives to listen as she read them. She created her own scripts for popular television programs while in junior high. In high school, she wrote news stories for the student paper.

In 1984, Mason graduated from Hampton University with a major in mass media arts. Since then, she has taught Sunday school, worked as a recruiter of newsroom staff for the Newport News *Daily Press*, and taught at the college level. She is a motivational speaker and also enjoys travel, particularly to the mountains or water. Mason has a house full of books (favorite authors are Langston Hughes, Raymond Carver, Ernest Hemingway, James Baldwin, and Edna St. Vincent Millay) and is an avid collector of blue and white porcelain, letter openers, and ink pens. To relax, she enjoys watching old romantic movies.

Mason's novels draw from her experience. Her novelette in the collection *Heart Songs* is about the Rev. T.C. Holloway of the Peaceful Rest Church, a televangelist who has a second chance at love when he is reunited with old friend Carys Shaw.

In *Sweet Devotion*, old adversaries Amber Montgomery and Police Chief Paul Evans reevaluate their opinions of each other when they chaperone a church youth group camping trip. "The interplay of characters with the themes of fear and love is heart-rending," in the opinion of reviewer Tricia-Anne Blades.

There's a strong inspirational aspect to Mason's novelette, "The First Noel," in the anthology *Something to Celebrate*. The heroine, Kia Simmons, lost her faith in God when her sister died. But when Franklin Williams, a man of strong faith, comes into her life, the spark returns.

Mason admittedly writes for readers who want an escape. "The reason you pick up a novel is to go away for a while," she told the *Virginian Pilot-Ledger Star*. "Novels are places people go to experience something else."

She said it is easier to write about places she imagines, rather than places she's actually been, as she then has control of everything. Sometimes, however, her experiences work their way into her books. "I do a lot of traveling," she said on the Steeple Hill Web page, "so I frequently use those places as secondary settings. For example, in my Steeple Hill series based in Wayside, Oregon (a fictional town outside Portland), the hero in the first book, *Sweet Accord*, was from Louisiana. So I included just a touch of that even though the primary setting for the novel was Oregon."

She's not too keen on the isolation of the writer's life, though, and often writes her first drafts in public places such as restaurants. Finish work, however, must be done in her home office where it is quiet and isolated.

Whatever challenges come with her craft, Mason said she thrills at being able to write in the will of God.

Works by the Author

Body and Soul (1995)
For the Love of You (1995)
Seduction (1996)
Rhapsody (1997)
Foolish Heart (1998)
Forbidden Heart (2000)
Testimony (2002)
Sweet Accord (2003)
Sweet Harmony (2004)
Sweet Devotion (2004)
Enchanted Heart (2004)
Gabriel's Discovery (2004)
How Sweet the Sound (2005)
What Anna Mae Left Behind (2005)
Enchanted Heart (2005)

Collections

Seductive Hearts (2005), includes *Body and Soul, For the Love of You,* and *Seduction*

Anthologies

A Valentine Kiss (1996), with Carla Fredd and Brenda Jackson
Man of the House (1998), with Adrianne Byrd and Doris Johnson
Rosie's Curl and Weave (1999), with Rochelle Alers, Donna Hill, and Francis Ray
Something to Celebrate (1999), with Margie Walker and Brenda Jackson
Della's House of Style (2000), with Rochelle Alers, Donna Hill, and Francis Ray
Island Magic (2000), with Rochelle Alers, Shirley Hailstock, and Marcia King-Gamble
Island Bliss (2002), with Rochelle Alers, Carmen Green, and Marcia King-Gamble
The Best Man (2003), with Brenda Jackson, Cindi Louis, and Kayla Perrin
How Sweet the Sound (2005), with Francis Ray and Jacquelin Thomas

Film Based on the Author's Work

Rhapsody (2000)

For Further Information

Blades, Tricia-Anne, *Sweet Devotion* review, *Romance in Color. http://www. romanceincolor.com/REVIEW_Sweet_Devotion_Mason_TB_0204.htm* (viewed Aug. 1, 2006).

Felicia Mason biography, *Virginia Romance Writers. http://www. virginiaromancewriters.com/Authors/Mason/mason.html* (viewed March 21, 2005).

Felicia Mason entry, *Contemporary Black Biography*, Vol. 31, Ashyla Henderson, ed. Detroit, MI: Gale Group, 2001.

Felicia Mason profile, *Virginian Pilot-Ledger Star* (June 22, 1997).

Felicia Mason Web page. *http://www.geocities.com/Paris/Gallery/9250/* (viewed Aug. 1, 2006). *http://www.steeplehill.com/authors/AuthorDetail. aspx?id=1800016&t=Interview* (March 21, 2005).

Terrones, Claudia S., *Something to Celebrate* review, *All About Romance. http://www.likesbooks.com/claudia76.html* (viewed March 21, 2005).

James McBride

Historical Literature, Memoir

Benchmark Title: *Miracle at St. Anna*

New Jersey

1957

About the Author and the Author's Writing

A real-life World War II episode inspired James McBride's historical novel *Miracle at St. Anna*. Although he had crafted a well-received, award-winning memoir, *The Color of Water: A Black Man's Tribute to His White Mother*, this was his first work of fiction.

Which is not to say McBride had no experience with words. He was a journalist, working stints as staff writer with the *Boston Globe, People* and the *Washington Post*. He was and is also a jazz musician (playing saxophone and leading a twelve-member band) and composer.

McBride attended Oberlin Conservatory of Music and earned a master of arts degree from Columbia University in 1979. He also holds honorary doctorates from Whitman College and The College of New Jersey. He and his wife, Stephanie, and their three children live in Bucks County, Pennsylvania, and he commutes to an office in Manhattan.

"To be a good writer, you really have to have your ear to the ground and listen to the buffalo," McBride said in an interview with Ronald Kovach for *The Writer*. "And I felt like I was losing that when I was in journalism."

It was only as an adult that McBride and his siblings came to realize that the light-skinned mother who raised them in the Red Hook projects of Brooklyn was, in fact, Jewish and the daughter of a rabbi. His Polish-born mother, Ruth McBride, was a a housekeeper, and had left Virginia where she grew up and moved to Harlem. She met and married a black man, Andrew McBride. She established a Baptist church and saw that each of her twelve children went to college. McBride had to know more, and after fourteen years of digging, interviewing family friends, and questioning his mother, he crafted a dual memoir, of himself and his mother.

"She initially resisted so I reported around her . . . ," McBride told Bill Zimmerman, regarding his experiences speaking to his mother. "I interviewed my father's friends, my stepfather's friends until I had enough detail I could walk up to her and say . . . 'I thought you said the courthouse was right across the street.' 'No, it was. . .' I'd sort of spin her into it."

McBride was ready for a lot of things, but discovering that his rabbi grandfather had molested his mother was not one of them. That information Rachel Shilsky (her birth name) had to write out on paper, she was so ashamed.

McBride also heard a lot of war stories from his uncle, Henry, a veteran of World War II, and he set out to write a novel about black soldiers with the 92nd Division in Italy.

"Originally I wanted to write a book about a group of black soldiers that liberate a concentration camp in Hungary, but after researching it, I just didn't feel qualified to write about the Holocaust," he said in an interview with Dave Welch on Powells.com. He made another stab with three spec chapters of a book with a story similar to *Miracle at St. Anna*. He learned Italian, went to Italy, and began to interview anyone he could find who knew something about a German SS massacre of more than 500 Italians at the little village called St. Anna di Stazzema.

Miracle at St. Anna is the story of a Negro soldier in Italy during World War II—a member of the 92nd Infantry (Buffalo) Division—who befriends a young Italian kid he finds on a battlefield. As a result of their meeting, he and three other men from his squad end up in a small village in the mountains of Tuscany. There they encounter a miracle. "What it's really about is the communality of the human experience," the author said in a Powells.com interview. The main characters, a giant, illiterate black soldier and a six-year-old boy who is struck mute by the sight of an atrocity, are both victims. So too was a German soldier, one of the several who refused to take part in the massacre, who was killed on the same battlefield.

The author likened his approach to words to his approach to jazz notes: there may be improvisational parts, but they flow toward a planned conclusion. The writer/musician knows the key dramatic points and continually arcs the story/composition back to them. "Writing fiction is like playing jazz," he said on his Web site. "There are no foreseen rules, no maps, no music to read; the audience doesn't understand harmony, theory, chord changes. They only know what works for them because the ear doesn't lie."

Works by the Author

Miracle at St. Anna (2002)

Memoir

The Color of Water: A Black Man's Tribute to His White Mother (1996)

For Further Information

Color of Water Reading Guide, Penguin Group. *http://www.penguinputnam. com/static/rguides/us/color_of_water.html* (viewed Aug. 1, 2006).

"Conversation with James McBride," *Miracle at St. Anna*, James McBride Web site. *http://www.jamesmcbride.com/conversation.htm* (viewed April 3, 2005).

Fretts, Bruce, " 'Miracle' Worker: *The Color of Water's* James McBride Makes an Impressive Foray into Fiction with a Multi-Shaded WWII Tale," *Entertainment Weekly* (March 1, 2002).

James C. McBride entry, Contemporary Authors Online, Gale, 2005. Reproduced in Biography Resource Center. Farmington Hills, MI: Thomson Gale, 2005. *http://galenet/galegroup.com/servlet/BioRC* (viewed Feb. 27, 2005).

James McBride interview, BookBrowse. *http://www.bookbrowse.com/index.cfm?page=author&authorID=271&view=interview* (viewed Feb. 28, 2005).

Kovach, Ronald, "James McBride: Illuminating the Past—and Going Beyond It," *The Writer* (June 2003).

Mason, George, "*The Color of Water*: A Black Man's Tribute to His White Mother," *The Christian Century* (Nov. 19. 1997).

Mudge, Alden, "Real-Life Episode Inspires James McBride's WWII Novel," *BookPage. http://www.bookpage.com/0202bp/james_mcbride.html* (viewed Feb. 28, 2005).

Welch, Dave, "James McBride Stays in Tune," Powells.com. *http://www.powells.com/authors/mcbride.html* (viewed Aug. 1, 2006).

Zimmerman, Bill, "An Interview with the Author of *The Color of Water*," Stony Brook University. *http://www.sunysb.edu/writernet/communitytext/mcbrideinterview.html* (viewed Feb. 28, 2005).

James McEachin

Historical Literature

Benchmark Title: *Tell Me a Tale*

Pennert, North Carolina

1930

About the Author and the Author's Writing

James McEachin—you would recognize him if you saw his face on television. He has appeared in dozens of programs and in more than 200 roles, including the title character in NBC's *Tenafly* from 1973 to 1974, and Lt. Brock in more than a dozen Perry Mason television movies in the 1980s. He also appeared in *Hill Street Blues, Matlock, Diagnosis: Murder, Dragnet, Emergency, Quincy, Six Million Dollar Man, St. Elsewhere, First Monday, Murder She Wrote,* and *I'll Fly Away.* This is in addition to a film career that since 1968 has included *The Undefeated, Buck and the Preacher, 2010,* and *Guess Who's Coming for Christmas?*

McEachin was born in Pennert, North Carolina, in 1930. He served with the 24th Infantry Regiment and the 2nd Infantry Division during the Korean War. His heroic actions earned him a Purple Heart. His wounds ended his thoughts of becoming a career soldier, and he worked as a firefighter, police officer, and music producer before finding a niche as an actor. But he always really wanted to write.

His first novel, *Tell Me a Tale*, takes place in the South just after the Civil War. Moses, age seventeen and a former slave, returns to the plantation where he had been born. His parents were the plantation's white owner and one of his slaves. Passing himself off as a journalist looking for stories about the good old days before Reconstruction, he confronts individuals from his past who shatter his dream—fire destroyed the plantation he stood to inherit.

McEachin told *Contemporary Authors* the novel is a "trip back into the lives of a small community, Red Springs, North Carolina . . . offering a picture of the innocence of a young boy with a spirit that triumphs over evil men who live small, petty, and empty lives."

Publishers Weekly observed, "The subtext of McEachin's stunning first novel is the moral rot of slavery, its harmful effects on both white and black and its lingering legacy in deep-rooted prejudice."

McEachin's second historical novel, *Farewell to the Mockingbirds*, jumps ahead a half century to depict the all-black 24th Infantry Regiment, Company K, during World War I. Just as they were about to ship overseas from Texas, the all-volunteer soldiers, under the leadership of Sgt. Obie McLellan, were instead reassigned to grunt duty at an isolated outpost in Houston. They were harassed by the city's police until McLellan organized them into an armed protest to free some of their number who had been jailed. McEachin served in Korea in the same unit he depicts in this gripping episode from the earlier war.

The author's next two works are crime novels. In *The Heroin Factor*, it's Los Angeles in the 1990s and Lt. Wyatt McKnight of the narcotics division investigates the murder of an undercover officer. He is on the outs with his superior, who assigns a visiting German policeman as his partner on the case. *Say Goodnight to the Boys in Blue* takes place in New Jersey in the 1950s. There are satirical elements to its depiction of the fumbling police department in a dead-end town. "In this delightfully loony and suspenseful story, everybody gets what they deserve," said a *Publishers Weekly* reviewer.

In his most recent work, McEachin turns to outdoor adventure for *The Great Canis Lupis*, which weaves the story of black cowboys in the 1800s and a wily wolf.

Although it might not put his Hollywood career on hold, McEachin's writing has given him a promising second career.

Works by the Author

Tell Me a Tale: A Novel of the Old South (1996)
Farewell to the Mockingbirds (1997)
The Heroin Factor (1999)
Say Goodnight to the Boys in Blue (2001)
The Great Canis Lupis (2001)

Nonfiction

Pebbles in the Roadway: Tales and Essays, Bits and Pieces (2003)
Voices: A Tribute to the American Veteran (2005)

For Further Information

"Actor, Author, Korean War Vet to Speak at Mobile Dedication," Department of Defense 50th Anniversary of the Korean War Commemoration Committee news release. *http://korea50.army.mil/media/newsrelease/newsrelease_02-31.html* (viewed August 1, 2006).

Farewell to the Mockingbirds review, *Publishers Weekly* (Aug. 11, 1997).

Heroin Factor review, *Publishers Weekly* (June 21, 1999).

James McEachin entry, Contemporary Authors Online. The Gale Group, 2005. Reproduced in Biography Resource Center. Farmington Hills, MI: Thomson Gale, 2005. *http://galenet.galegroup.com/servlet/BioRC* (viewed Feb. 21, 2005).

James McEachin Web page, *Emergencyfans.com*. *http://www.emergencyfans.com/people/james.mceachin.htm* (viewed Feb. 15, 2005).

Say Goodnight to the Boys in Blue review, *Publishers Weekly* (Aug. 21, 2000).

Tell Me a Tale: A Novel of the Old South review, *Publishers Weekly* (Jan. 8, 1996).

Bernice L. McFadden

Mainstream Contemporary Literature, Erotica

Benchmark Title: *Sugar*

Brooklyn, New York
1966

Photo credit: Peter Chin

About the Author and the Author's Writing

Frustrated with dead-ends in the corporate world, Bernice L. McFadden wagered everything on a major career change into writing—her Zora Neale Hurston Society award and others have proven it a sound decision.

McFadden was born in Brooklyn in 1966. Her mother came from the South, and the author has said there was a strong tradition of storytelling in her family. She attended P.S. 161 in Brooklyn and St. Cyril Academy in Pennsylvania before enrolling in the Laboratory Institute of Merchandising. Aspiring to become an international clothing buyer, she went to work for Bloomingdale's and later for Itokin. Dissatisfied with her employment, she took a travel and tourism course at Marymount College. After a daughter was born in 1988, she joined the staff of Rockresorts. When the company was sold, she was laid off and out of work for a year. In those twelve months, she did a lot of reading (favorite authors include Alice Walker, Toni Morrison, and J. California Cooper) and she began writing. She also took courses in African American history, and writing and literature at Fordham University. Still frustrated with her work in the travel industry, she finally quit her next job and spent half a year writing in earnest. In 1999, she signed on with an agent who placed her first novel, *Sugar*, with Dutton.

McFadden has written a novel a year since.

Sugar takes place in Bigelow, an imagined Arkansas town, in the 1950s. Pearl Taylor, who has just lost her young daughter, finds solace in her church. Free-spirited young Sugar moves in next door and they begin a tentative acquaintance, which grows into friendship. That friendship remains firm, even after neighbors learn that Sugar is a prostitute.

211

"McFadden captures the full character of small-town life and the strengths and weaknesses of its people," praised Ellen Flexman in *Library Journal. Sugar* earned the Black Caucus of the American Library Association's Fiction Honor Award.

"I take my relationships with women very seriously," the author said in a *Reading Group Guides* interview. "I come from a family of women, so my respect for them is quite extraordinary. Friendships between women are sacred because we understand and feel for each other on levels that men are just not equipped to do."

McFadden followed her first novel with *The Warmest December*, a novel that takes place in Brooklyn. Kenzie Lowe tells her story, beginning with growing up in the 1970s with an abusive and alcoholic father. As time passes, Kenzie holds various jobs and yearns for the bottle. Though at first she can't believe it, she feels compelled to visit her dying father in the hospital. Gradually she learns what created his miserable personality—and ultimately puts that knowledge to work in pulling herself together.

McFadden said on her African American Literature Book Club Web page that she was drawn to this subject "to help someone choose love, sanity and life," and to show that something good can be drawn from the bad.

McFadden has said she finds her role as an author one of simply finding the characters then sitting back and letting them reveal the story. *Contemporary Black Biography* said she has been "widely praised for her sensuous prose and her ability to vividly depict harrowing experiences and emotional pain."

Her recent *Camilla's Roses* examines another character with a troubled childhood: a character who refuses to look back until a diagnosis of cancer shakes her to the core and forces her to pursue reconciliation with those she has rejected. Under the penname Geneva Holliday, McFadden is writing a trilogy for Broadway Books in a genre she calls urban erotica, with a light touch. The books explore the sexual experiences of four characters who grew up together in New York City and ended up with very different lives. One is rich, one gay. One is in serious trouble and one is still stuck in the projects. While most McFadden fans have given the new series a warm reception, according to the author, "it's a little like walking in on your parents having sex." However, she admitted to reporter Celia McGee of the *New York Daily News* that she doesn't at all mind writing sex scenes: "No, I laugh out loud. Sex is such a natural part of life. And I also wanted to show that there's humor in what I write."

McFadden is just beginning to explore all the possibilities of the world of fiction.

Works by the Author

Sugar (2000)
The Warmest December (2001)
This Bitter Earth (2002), sequel to *Sugar*
Loving Donovan (2003)
Camilla's Roses (2004)
Nowhere Is a Place (2006)

Contributor

Black Silk: A Collection of African-American Erotica (2002), edited by Retha Powers

Gumbo: A Literary Rent Party to Benefit the Hurston/Wright Foundation (2002), edited by Marita Golden and E. Lynn Harris

Brown Sugar 2 (2003), edited by Carol Taylor

Written as Geneva Holliday

Groove (2005)

Fever (2006)

For Further Information

Bernice L. McFadden entry, *Contemporary Black Biography*, Vol. 39, Ashyia Henderson, ed. Detroit: Gale Group, 2003.

Bernice L. McFadden Web page, African American Literature Book Club. *http://authors.aalbc.com/bernicemcfadden.htm* (viewed Aug. 1, 2006).

Bernice L. McFadden Web site. *http://www.bernicemcfadden.com* (viewed Aug. 1, 2006).

Bernice McFadden biography, *ReadingGroupGuides.com.http://www.readinggroupguides.com/guides3/this_bitter_earth2.asp* (viewed Aug. 1, 2006).

Flexman, Ellen, *Sugar* review, *Library Journal* (December 1999).

Geneva Holliday Web site. *http://www.genevaholliday.com* (viewed Aug. 1, 2006).

McGee, Celia, "5 minutes with Geneva Holliday," *New York Daily News* (July 25, 2005).

Aaron McGruder

Comics

Benchmark Title: *Boondocks*

Chicago, Illinois

1975

About the Author and the Author's Writing

Artist Ted Shearer's Quincy razzes the preacher. Ray Billingsley's Curtis lays into his dad periodically to quit smoking. But few newspaper comic strip characters —the exception being Garry Trudeau's Doonesbury, and he's white—have lashed out at everyone from President Bush to gangsta rappers with the biting ferocity of Aaron McGruder in his *Boondocks*.

Aaron Vincent McGruder was born in Chicago in 1975. His family moved to Columbia, Maryland, six years later. He graduated from the University of Maryland, where he took courses in African American studies. While in college, he created his comic strip for an Internet site and later published it in a college newspaper, *The Diamondback*, in 1996, and in *The Source* in 1997. Several syndicates turned down the strip, but in 1999 Universal Press Syndicate signed McGruder. *Boondocks* landed on the funny pages with 160 initial subscribers, and that number has more than doubled since. However, there have been occasional evacuees as some newspaper publishers found the content too strong for their tastes.

"Some black readers have accused it of perpetuating stereotypes, while naysayers thought that it bashed them and others charged McGruder with ridiculing interracial marriage with his portrayal of Jazmine, the biracial daughter of a liberal white woman and a bourgie black man," *Newsweek* reported shortly after the comic's debut.

The main character—he is yet to smile—is Huey Freeman, a well-read and radical ten-year-old; his smarts-shy brother Riley; their Granddad, who moved them from the inner city to this weird place, the white suburbs; and their young neighbors, flying-haired Jazmine and dreadlocked Michael Caesar.

McGruder said in *Editor & Publisher* he "never sought controversy for its own sake." But, "when my strip is at its best, it brings you up to the brink of being offended and pulls back at the last minute."

McGruder won the NAACP's Chairman's Image Award in 2002, uncomfortably sharing the stage with one of his prime targets, then National Security Advisor Condoleezza Rice (who won the same organization's President's Award).

The terrorist attacks in September 2001 proved a turning point for the artist, who until then had largely patterned his characters and panels after Berke Breathed, Bill

214

Watterson, and Trudeau. "I knew on that tragic day that many more tragic days were to follow, and I made the decision that I would use my little space to scream out louder against the great injustices the U. S. government was about to unleash upon the planet," McGruder said in the introduction to *A Right to Be Hostile*. This he did immediately with a faux comic featuring two unusual characters, Flagee and Ribbon, a talking stars and stripes and ubiquitous twisted yellow band—symbolic of what McGruder considered bloated and false patriotism. McGruder's Thanksgiving episodes in which the strip apparently compared Osama bin Laden with (an unnamed) George W. Bush (both from a "wealthy oil family," both "bomb innocents") struck a nerve as well.

Naturally a few newspapers, including the *New York Daily News,* canceled the strip.

"I tried to be really careful to not make light at all of the death and suffering, which, like everybody else, I feel really bad about," McGruder told reporter Jennifer A. Carbin. "But I have a different perspective on things than what the media's putting out, and I thought it was important to voice that, and if it meant losing the New York papers, I think it was worth it."

McGruder has often expressed his very strong concerns about the loss of civil liberties in the United States. "It's not temporary. Once you give up rights, they're not going to give them back," he said in an interview on the Web site Refuse & Resist. "This is a war that will never end. When are they going to say they've defeated terrorism?"

Despite his success, McGruder has said he finds the comic strip in many ways confining. In 2005, a graphic novel, *Birth of a Nation*, cowritten by McGruder and film producer Reginald Hudlin, with art by Kule Baker, afforded a different satirical take on the country: What if East St. Louis seceded and became a sovereign state? That same year, McGruder was hard at work readying *Boondocks* for the television world, with a program which in autumn 2005 began to air over Cartoon Network's late-night Adult Swim.

Although it intensified McGruder's workload, the television show in no way lessened the bite of his comic strip (although at the time of this writing, it was on hiatus).

Works by the Author

The Boondocks: Because I Know You Don't Read the Newspaper (2000)
Fresh for '01 . . . You Suckas: Boondocks Collection (2001)
A Right to be Hostile: The Boondocks Treasury (2003)
Birth of a Nation: A Comic Novel (2005), with Reginald Hudlin, illustrated by Kyle Baker
Public Enemy No. 2: An All-New Boondocks Collection (2005)
All the Rage: The Boondocks Past and Present (2007)

For Further Information

"Aaron McGruder, the Pen Is a Tool of Strength!" *African American Registry. http://www.aaregistry.com/african_american_history/2648/Aaron_McGruder_the_pen_is_a_tool_of_strength* (viewed Aug. 1, 2006).
Aaron Vincent McGruder entry, *Contemporary Black Biography*, Vol. 28, Ashyia Henderson, ed. Detroit: Gale Group, 2001.

Aaron McGruder Web page, African American Literature Book Club. *http://authors.aalbc.com/aaron.htm* (viewed Aug. 1, 2006).

Arnold, Andrew D., "Black Humor: A New Comic Novel Boldly Takes on Politics and Race," *Time* (Aug. 2, 2004).

Astor, Dave, " 'Boondocks' Screen Deal," *Editor & Publisher* (July 14, 2003).

Astor, David, " 'Boondocks' Artist Still Living on the Edge of Controversy: Aaron McGruder Comes to Canada to Talk about His High-Profile Comic," *Editor & Publisher* (Oct. 9, 1999).

Astor. Dave, "Off Center: 'The Boondocks' Comic Strip Causes Post Sept. 11th Controversy," *Editor & Publisher* (Dec. 10, 2001).

Bates, Karen Grigsby, "Aaron McGruder's Greatest Hits," *Black Issues Book Review* (Sept.-Oct. 2003).

"Boondocks," *Entertainment Weekly* (Jan. 21, 2005).

"*Boondocks* Dives into Adult Swim," *USA Today,* Nov. 4, 2005.

Carbin, Jennifer A., "Boondocks Speaks: An Interview with Aaron McGruder," *Philadelphia City Paper,* Nov. 5, 2001. *http://www.alternet.org/story/11859* (viewed Aug. 1, 2006).

"Comic Strip's Black Characters Take on Racists, Bush, BET," NPR, Oct. 13, 2003. *http://www.npr.org/templates/story/story.php?/storyId=146214* (viewed April 11, 2005).

Justice, Steve, "Apesheet Interview: Aaron McGruder." *http://www.theapesheet.com/archivesix/mcgruder.html* (viewed Aug. 1, 2006).

Lemons, Stephen, "Interview with Aaron McGruder—Boondocks Cartoonist," Refuse & Resist! *http://www.refuseandresist.org/newresistance/121001mcgruder.html* (viewed Sept. 18, 2006).

McGrath, Ben, "Why Do Editors Keep Throwing 'The Boondocks' Off the Funnies Page?" *New Yorker* (April 19, 2004).

"Unfunny Business: A Political Cartoonist Finds His Satirical Strip Banned in New York," *Entertainment Weekly* (Oct. 19, 2001).

"What's the Color of Funny? 'The Boondocks' Riffs on Race—and Stirs Up Controversy," *Newsweek* (July 5, 1999).

Diane McKinney-Whetstone

Women's Literature, Mainstream Contemporary Literature

Benchmark Title: *Tumbling*

Philadelphia, Pennsylvania

Date of birth not revealed

About the Author and the Author's Writing

Diane McKinney-Whetstone grew up in Philadelphia, the daughter of a two-term state senator. She still lives in Philadelphia with her husband, Greg. They have two grown children. She is a 1975 graduate of the University of Pennsylvania and teaches creative writing. For the first decade after she received her degree in English, she worked for the Philadelphia City Council and the Forest Service. She has been a frequent contributor to periodicals such as *Philadelphia Magazine, Essence,* and *Philadelphia Inquirer.*

Terry McMillan, Toni Morrison, and James Baldwin are among the writers who have most influenced McKinney-Whetsone. She said in a *Writers Write* interview that she was inspired to write fiction when her fortieth birthday approached. "I had written poetry in school, but creative writing was one of those things I always told myself I really wanted to do. Because I read a lot, it inspired me to want to do the same type of writing." She took a writing course and joined a writers' group.

McKinney-Whetsone uses her home city, with some imaginative liberties, as background for her novels. "I really need to know the place where my characters live before I know who the characters are," she told *Essence*. "Place informs character. I know Philly. It's provincial, a neighborhood city. When I was growing up, it was very territorial. People thought they knew things about you based upon the section of the city where you lived."

McKinney-Whetstone writes about the Philadelphia of a generation ago, so she recruited family members to help her gather anecdotal information to flesh out her first book. "My daughter came running over to me and said, 'Mommy, they were wearing Mary Jane shoes,' and my son would tell me the Negro Leagues were playing at such and such a place," the author told Philadelphia citypaper.net.

Tumbling takes place in South Philly in the 1940s and 1950s and relates the love story of club-hopping Herbie and church-attending Noon. In *Tempest Rising*, which takes place in the west side of the city in the early 1960s, three sisters who grow up in a well-to-do household are jolted into fending for themselves when their father's catering business fails. *Blues Dancing* is set both in the 1970s and in contemporary time. Verdi, a spoiled young Southerner, enrolls in a Philadelphia college and is attracted to street-savvy Johnson. A sympathetic professor falls in love with Verdi and helps her withdraw from drug addiction. And *Leaving Cecil Street* revisits the late 1960s to tell the story of several residents of one city block.

The message she hopes readers take from this last book, McKinney-Whetstone said in an interview on her Web site, is the closeness of community. "So much is made of the negatives of African American communities—the crime, the drugs, the poverty —and I am not suggesting that those conditions do not exist . . . all over the country there have been African American communities that thrive, that are desirable places to live."

That said, the author in a ReadingGroupGuides.Com author roundtable stated she feels there is great pressure on black writers to create characters who are role models, even if it is at the expense of believable characterizations. She gave as an example Herbie in *Tumbling*, who runs around on his wife. She said she didn't set out to create the character that way; but because of her organic style of writing, that was the course the character obviously was meant to follow. She then found ways to bring the flawed character to a realization of what he was doing and to grow as a human being.

McKinney-Whetstone said on the roundtable that her writing obviously derives from who she is: an African American woman. "My fictional worlds are all created from the unique vantage point of one who has seen and felt discrimination based on race and gender. It doesn't end there though. Since I have also seen, felt certain triumphs, my stories have a sense of hope, a bluesy quality that hums."

Works by the Author

Tumbling (1996)
Tempest Rising: A Novel (1998)
Blues Dancing (2000)
Leaving Cecil Street (2004)

Contributor

Bluelight Corner: Black Women Writing on Passion, Sex, and Romantic Love (1998), edited by Rosemary Robotham
Best Black Women's Erotica (2001), edited by Blanche Richardson
Mending the World: Stories of Family by Contemporary Black Writers (2002), edited by Rosemary Robotham

For Further Information

"Blues Dancing," *Essence* (Aug. 2000).
Dellasega, Cheryl, "Mothers Who Write: Diane McKinney-Whetstone," *Writers Write*. *http://www.writerswrite.com/journal/oct00.whetstone.htm* (viewed Feb. 14, 2005).
DeLombard, Jeannine, "All In the Family: The Story Behind Local Novelist Diane McKinney-Whetstone's Dazzling Debut," *Philadelphia citypaper.net*. *http://citypaper.net/articles/040496.article027.shtml* (viewed March 14, 2005).

Diane McKinney-Whetstone entry, Contemporary Authors Online, Gale, 2005. Reproduced in Biography Resource Center. Farmington Hills, MI: Thomson Gale, 2005. *http://galenet.galegroup.com/servlet/BioRC* (viewed Feb. 26, 2005).

Diane McKinney-Whetstone profile, *Black History Month Author Roundtable,* ReadingGroupGuides.Com. *http://www.authorsontheweb.com/features/ 0302-bhm/bhm-authors2.asp* (viewed Aug. 1, 2006).

Diane McKinney-Whetstone Web site. *http://www.mckinney-whetstone.com* (viewed Aug. 1, 2006).

Terry McMillan

Women's Literature

Benchmark Title: *Waiting to Exhale*

Port Huron, Michigan
1951

Photo credit: Darien Davis

About the Author and the Author's Writing

Terry McMillan made believers out of publishers who doubted there was an audience for a fresh, vibrant black voice in literature. Her third novel, *Waiting to Exhale,* was months on the *New York Times* bestseller list, and when it was made into a motion picture, it became a major event.

Terry McMillan was born in 1951 in Port Huron, Michigan, the oldest of five children. During her childhood, the only book in the house was a Bible. Her parents divorced when she was thirteen, and her father, a sanitation worker and an abusive alcoholic, died three years later. McMillan attended public schools. Only when she took a job shelving books at a local library did she encounter the magic of literature—she was in awe of women writers such as the Bronte sisters and Louisa May Alcott, and of black writers including James Baldwin and Langston Hughes. Reading Ring Lardner, she realized the humor to be found in tragedy.

In 1979, McMillan received a bachelor of arts degree in journalism from the University of California at Berkeley. During her college years, her first short story, "The End," was published. After moving to New York, she studied film at Columbia University and earned her master of fine arts degree. She worked as a word processor and took a workshop at the Harlem Writers Guild. In the early 1980s, she had a child. She also struggled with alcohol and drug abuse.

McMillan worked hard to promote her first novel, *Mama*, published in 1987. "[C]ritics praised McMillan for her realistic detail and powerful characterization of her heroine, Mildred Peacock," according to Voices from the Gaps. "They loved Mildred's energy and zest for life...."

Added *Contemporary Novelists*, "The character of Mildred provides a counter-image to these stereotypes [of the black "welfare queen"]: she is complex, dignified, and committed to raising her children to be capable, responsible adults."

Two years later, McMillan followed the novel of a strong woman struggling to keep her family together with *Disappearing Acts*. Her son's father took exception to the way he was portrayed in the book and sued McMillan for slander. His suit was dismissed in court. Nevertheless, McMillan has frequently been criticized for her negative depictions of black men.

"I do extensive profiles of my characters before I write the stories," the author told *Essence* in 2001. "I ask my characters questions: Do you lie? Do you have a secret? If so, what is it? Do you pay your bills on time? If you could change something about yourself, what would it be, and why?"

Of decisions made by men and women, McMillan said in a Bookbrowse.com interview, "[H]ow many of us are actually 'smart' when it comes to relationships? We do what we want to and suffer the consequences later."

Critic Andrew B. Presler noted the author's close examination of cultural expectations and relationships which cross professional, gender, and family lines: "*Mama* depicts an acceptance by an intellectual daughter of her flawed mother. *Disappearing Acts* follows a love affair between a professional, responsible woman and an uneducated tradesman. *Waiting to Exhale* builds an ambitious collage of images from all three types of relationships."

From 1987 to 1990, McMillan was an instructor at the University of Wyoming in Laramie, then became a professor at the University of Arizona in Tucson for two years. In 1988, she held a National Endowment for the Arts fellowship. She edited an anthology of black fiction, *Breaking Ice*, in 1990, the same year she was a judge for the National Book Award for fiction. She now lives in Danville, California.

McMillan's big break came with her publication of *Waiting to Exhale*. It energized the black reading community, not only establishing McMillan's career, but opening doors for other writers of color. McMillan disputes this latter categorization as simply good marketing; there were many active ethnic writers before she came on the scene, she asserts.

The story of four middle class, smart, hip women, *Waiting to Exhale* "told the world that not all Black people live in ghettos," said BBC World Service. "Displaying a level of determination and ambition, McMillan's characters could have been created in the author's own image. . . . Depicting sexy, determined, black women is unsurprisingly McMillan's forte as she openly admits that she enjoys writing about her own 'evolution.' "

The author intended to follow *Exhale* with *A Day Late and a Dollar Short*, a depiction of a loving mother. But in 1993 her own mother, to whom she felt extremely close, died following an asthma attack. On top of this, one of McMillan's best friends, novelist Doris Jean Austin, died of cancer the following year. Devastated, the grieving McMillan traveled to Jamaica to find healing.

The largely autobiographical *How Stella Got Her Groove Back* was published in 1996. The main character is a professional woman in her forties, raising a son as a single parent, who travels to Jamaica, meets and falls in love with a younger man—just as McMillan did, marrying a twenty-four-year-old hotel management student named Jonathan Plummer. This novel was longer in gestation than McMillan was accustomed to, the writing disrupted by personal issues; nonetheless it was a success and was also made into a film.

"I am a fast writer," she said on her PenguinPutnam Web page. "My drafts usually come quickly, in a rush. *Mama* took about a month; *Disappearing Acts*, two weeks; *Exhale*, a few months. These are just rough drafts, the versions you don't dare show a soul. The rewriting and revisions took close to a year."

A Day Late and a Dollar Short, which came out in 2001, examines the dynamics of family life through all generations—children are still children to their parents even as the children age through the years. "I've come to realize that people don't tell everything," the author told interviewer Esther Iverem. "As much as you love your siblings, there are things you just don't share. You think, this is my sister or brother they tell me everything, and then you realize they don't tell you everything. And maybe they shouldn't. Maybe some things shouldn't be shared."

"McMillan writes intimately, sometimes mockingly, about a middle-class black experience in which white America is largely irrelevant," summarizes *Newsweek's* John Leland. "Her best work captures the foibles and rhythms around her in lusty vernacular. . . ."

In McMillan's recent *The Interruption of Everything*, Marilyn Grimes has a husband, three kids and a lot of postponed dreams which life has a strange way of keeping unfulfilled. The book met a ready audience, as reviewer Joanne Skerrett noted in the *Boston Globe*: "[S]he continues to write about headstrong black women, pleasing an increasingly diverse audience, which seems to grow hungrier for her sassy prose with each novel."

In an article in *The Writer*, McMillan stated why she loves her craft: "I write because the world is an imperfect place, and we behave in an imperfect manner. I want to understand why it's so hard to be good, honest, loving, caring, thoughtful and generous. . . . I want to understand myself and others better, so what better way than to pretend to be them?"

Works by the Author

Fiction

Mama (1987)
Disappearing Acts (1989)
Waiting to Exhale (1992)
How Stella Got Her Groove Back (1996)
A Day Late and a Dollar Short (2001)
The Interruption of Everything (2005)

Screenplays

Waiting to Exhale (1996), with Ronald Bass

Contributor

Gumbo: A Literary Rent Party to Benefit the Hurston/Wright Foundation (2002), edited by Marita Golden and E. Lynn Harris

Editor

Breaking Ice: An Anthology of Contemporary African-American Fiction (1990)

Nonfiction

It's OK If You're Clueless: and 23 More Tips for the College Bound (2006)

Contributor

Five for Five: The Films of Spike Lee (1991)

Films Based on the Author's Works

Waiting to Exhale (1996)
Disappearing Acts (2000)
How Stella Got Her Groove Back (1998)

For Further Information

Bass, Patrik Henry, "Terry McMillan's Triumphant Return," *Essence* (Jan. 2001).

Iverem, Esther, "Interview with Terry McMillan," *Seeingblack.com.* (Sept. 26, 2002). *http://www.seeingblack.com/x092602/mcmillan.shtml* (viewed Aug. 1, 2006).

Leland, John, "How Terry Got Her Groove," *Newsweek* (April 29, 1996).

"McMillan Finally Exhales," *Time* (Sept. 21, 1996).

Patrick, Diane, *Terry McMillan: The Unauthorized Biography*. New York: St. Martin's Press, 1999.

Presler, Andrew B., Terry McMillan entry, *American Ethnic Writers*, Vol. 2, David Peck, ed. Pasadena, CA: Salem Press, 2000.

Richards, Paulette, *Terry McMillan: A Critical Companion*. Westport, CT: Greenwood Press, 1999.

Skerrett, Joanne, " 'Interruption' Is Vintage McMillan," *Boston Globe* (July 14, 2005).

"'Stella' in South Africa: Still Looking for Her Groove, Best-Selling Author Terry McMillan Reveals New Details of Art-Imitating-Life Love Affair," *Ebony* (December 1996).

"Terry McMillan," *The Writer* (Aug. 2001).

Terry McMillan biography, *Voices from the Gaps*. http://voices.cla.umn.edu/vg/Bios/entries/mcmillan_terry.html (viewed Aug. 1, 2006).

Terry McMillan entry, *Contemporary Authors New Revision Series*, Vol. 60, Daniel Jones, and John D. Jorgenson, eds. Detroit: Gale Research, 1998.

Terry McMillan entry, *Contemporary Novelists*, 7th ed. Detroit: St. James Press, 2001.

Terry McMillan interview, *Bookbrowse. http://www.bookbrowse.com/index.cfm?page=author&authorID=542&view=interview* (viewed March 13, 2005).

Terry McMillan interview, *BookPage. http://www.bookpage.com/0102bp/.terry_mcmillan.html* (viewed March 31, 2003).

Terry McMillan Web page, African American Literature Book Club. *http://authors.aalbc.com/terry.htm* (viewed Feb. 17, 2005).

Terry McMillan Web page. *http://us.penguingroup.com/static/html/author/terrymcmillan.html* (viewed Sept. 18, 2006).

Wilkerson, Isabel, "On Top of the World," *Essence* (June 1996).

Mary Monroe

Women's Literature

Benchmark Title: *God Don't Like Ugly*

Toxey, Alabama
1951

Photo credit: Sigrid Estrada

About the Author and the Author's Writing

Mary Monroe crafts stories about conflict and struggle, determination and victory. They are rooted in Christian faith, with strong characters and sound stories.

The author is the daughter of poor but devotional sharecroppers and domestic workers. Born Mary Nicholson in 1951 in Toxey, north of Mobile, Alabama, she grew up there and in Ohio, where the family moved after her father died and her mother remarried. Mary found a great sense of community in her Baptist church. She was the first member of her family to finish high school—Alliance (Ohio) High School. In 1973, she moved to California; and she has lived in Oakland since 1984. She has been married and divorced and has two daughters.

An early effort at writing was a 400-page biography of an elderly woman her mother was caring for. She soon began to write (and sell) confessions to monthly periodicals such as *Bronze Thrills* and *True Confessions*. Because these were made-up stories, it was a short step for Monroe to write a novel—which she did at the urging of one of her editors. After numerous submissions, the gothic-styled *The Upper Room* found a receptive editor at St. Martin's Press and was published in 1985.

There followed fifteen years without another book sale. Monroe worked as a secretary, picked beans and apples, washed cars, and was a dog-sitter. She continued to write. But as she explained to *Contemporary Black Biography,* her manuscripts were riddled with typographic errors and misspellings. Then she found an editor at Kensington Books willing to work with her to smooth her prose, dialogue, and characterizations. Beginning in 2000, she has produced a novel a year for Kensington's Dafina line. One novel, *God Don't Like Ugly*, earned her the PEN/Oakland Josephine Miles Award and prompted a sequel. The books are the frightful yet amusing tales of

225

two young women as they emerge into adulthood in the 1950s South. One girl, Annette, sexually abused by a family boarder, overeats. Another girl, Rhoda, has a dark secret.

"I get my ideas from a variety of sources: my own experiences, old movies, current events, even dreams," the author said in an e-mail. "My characters are all composites of people I know (including myself). I write a detailed outline of a novel first. Then I do at least four drafts, writing each draft on a computer. I don't have an organized writing schedule, but I do write something every day, whether it's just a few sentences or several hundred pages.

"I HAVE to read at least two books a week for creative nourishment," she continued. "I read books by everybody from Steinbeck and Stephen King to Toni Morrison and Carl Weber. One of the many things I enjoy about writing is that it can be done anywhere. I finished two of my novels stretched out on beaches in Mexico and Hawaii."

Monroe's editor, Karen Thomas, told *Publishers Weekly* the author is "a true storyteller who can take dark subject matter and make you laugh about it. In *Red Light Wives*, someone dies, but you find yourself laughing. You love all of the women and you feel sorry for Clyde."

Works by the Author

The Upper Room (1985)
God Don't Like Ugly (2000)
Gonna Lay Down My Burdens (2002)
Gods Still Don't Like Ugly (2003), sequel to *Gods Don't Like Ugly*
Red Light Wives (2004)
In Sheep's Clothing (2005)
God Don't Play (2006)

For Further Information

Abbott, Charlotte, "Two Marys Mix It Up," *Publishers Weekly* (July 26, 2004).

Baker, John F., "African-American Novelist (and Essence Bestseller) Mary Monroe Has Signed for Four New Books with Kensington . . .," *Publishers Weekly* (Nov. 15, 2004).

Mary Monroe entry, Contemporary Authors Online. Gale, 2005. Reproduced in Biography Resource Center. Farmington Hills, Mich.: Thomson Gale, 2005. *http://galenet.galegroup.com/servlet/BioRC* (viewed Feb. 26, 2005).

Mary Monroe entry, *Contemporary Black Biography*, Vol. 35, Ashyla Henderson, ed. Detroit: Gale Group, 2002.

Mary Monroe Web site. *http://www.marymonroe.org/author.html* (Sept. 22, 2006).

Mary Monroe, e-mail to author (Aug. 14, 2005).

Toni Morrison

Mainstream Contemporary Literature

Benchmark Title: *Beloved*

Lorain, Ohio

1931

About the Author and the Author's Writing

Toni Morrison not only has a huge popular following, she has also won literature's top awards—the National Book Critics Circle Award for *Song of Solomon*, the Pulitzer Prize for *Beloved,* and the Nobel Prize for Literature (1993). She was the first African American woman so honored—for her stories of survival, endurance, and self-growth.

The author was born Chloe Anthony Wofford in Lorain, Ohio, in 1931. She grew up in the small industrial town in a close community which, as she has explained, gave greater measure to wise and mature actions than to the accumulation of material wealth. Storytelling was a tradition in her home. She earned an English degree from Howard University, where she began going by the nickname, "Toni" (which comes from her middle name). She completed requirements for a master's degree in English literature from Cornell University, writing a thesis on William Faulkner and married architect Howard Morrison. In 1955, she became an English instructor at Texas Southern University, two years later shifting to Howard, where she stayed until 1964. (The author later taught at Princeton University, Yale University, Bard College, Rutgers University, Harvard University, and Trinity College.)

When her marriage ended in 1964, Morrison and her sons moved to New York City, and she became an editor at Random House until 1985. As the firm's textbook editor, she developed books to meet new standards for the teaching of race and diversity such as *Contemporary African Literature*. She told *Black Issues Book Review*'s Susan McHenry that her work on this volume proved a revelation. "I realized that with all the books I'd read by contemporary black American writers—men that I admired, or was sometimes disturbed by—I felt they were not talking to me. I was sort of eavesdropping as they talked over my shoulder to the real (white) reader. Take Ralph Ellison's *Invisible Man*: That title alone got me. Invisible to *whom?*"

Morrison nurtured the careers of writers such as Toni Cade Bambara and Gayl Jones while at the same time working on her own prose. Her efforts have paid off. Many critics have observed the strong morality that pervades her novels, the search for identity, and the struggle to overcome tradition.

227

Morrison has always set her sights high, expecting the most from her readers, scoffing when (white) critics find her difficult. "We're a very complicated people," she said in an interview for *Essence*. "Nothing is more complicated than jazz, or even the nuances of the blues. We're accustomed to very complicated art forms, we really are. It's only in literature that we think we're supposed to skim, probably because of the way in which we've been educated."

When she received news of the Nobel Prize for Literature, Morrison said, "I am of course profoundly honored. But what is most wonderful for me, personally, is to know that the Prize at last has been awarded to an African-American. Winning as an American is very special—but winning as a Black American is a knockout."

Beloved, Morrison's fifth novel, centers on a shocking act: at the close of the Civil War, an enslaved woman named Sethe travels from her old Kentucky plantation to Cincinnati to live with her daughter, Denver. They live in a house haunted by a mean-spirited apparition, Beloved. Sethe is troubled by her past. Paul D., another former slave, drives the ghost away only to have it take human form to torment and break apart Sethe and Denver and Paul D. Beloved, it turns out, is the spirit of a daughter Sethe killed years before rather than see the child become a victim to slave life.

"I'm interested in the way in which the past affects the present," the author said in a *Time.com* interview, "and I think that if we understand a good deal more about history, we automatically understand a great deal about contemporary life."

Morrison raises many issues in this novel of long-suppressed guilt and love's redemptive powers. But "she offers no solutions to problems, nor does she simplify the complex realities of the past or present. Instead, out of respect for the cultural knowledge that black people bring to life and living, she uses the power and majesty of her imagination to address them and anyone interested in the stories that have created a permanent place for her among America's greatest writers," in the view of Marilyn Sanders Mobley in *Oxford Companion to African American Literature*.

Morrison revisits familiar themes in her recent *Love*, which *Newsweek*'s David Gates said is "a dense, dark star of a novel, seemingly eccentric, secretly shapely, with Faulknerian passions and Nabokovian layers of lies and misdirection, the 19th century device of a disputed will and some 20th-century social history—and with Morrison . . . writing at the top of her game."

Morrison's dynamic writing career has traversed a wide range of genre and great depth of emotion and craft.

Works by the Author

The Bluest Eye (1970)
Sula (1974)
Song of Solomon (1977)
Tar Baby (1981)
Beloved (1987)
Jazz (1992)
Jazz/Beloved/Song of Solomon (1994), omnibus
Toni Morrison Boxed Set (1999), omnibus
The Dancing Mind (1997)
Paradise (1998)
Love (2003)

Drama

Dreaming Emmett (1986)

Children's Books

Remember: The Journey to School Integration (2004)

Written with Slade Morrison

The Big Box (2002)
The Book of Mean People (2002)
The Book of Mean People Journal (2002)

Who's Got Game? Series

The Lion or the Mouse? (2003)
The Ant or the Grasshopper? (2003)
The Poppy or the Snake? (2004)
The Mirror or the Glass? (2005)

Nonfiction

Case for Black Reparations (1972), with Boris I. Bittker
Playing in the Dark: Whiteness and the Literary Imagination (1992)
Nobel Speech Acceptance (1994)
Memoirs (2005)

Editor

The Black Book (1974)
Race-ing Justice, En-Gendering Power: Essays on Anita Hill, Clarence Thomas, and the Construction of Social Reality (1992)
To Die for the People: The Writings of Huey P. Newton (1995)
Deep Sightings and Rescue Missions: Fiction, Essays, and Conversations (1996), by Toni Cade Bambara
Birth of Nationhood: Gaze, Script, and Spectacle in the O.J. Simpson Case (1997), with Claudia Brodsky Lacour

Contributor

Immigration: The Debate Over the Changing Face of America, edited by Nicolaus Mills (1994)

Film Based on the Author's Works

Beloved (1998)

For Further Information

Gates, David, "Another Side of the August Ms. Morrison," *Newsweek* (Sept. 1, 2003).

Jaffrey, Zia, "The Salon Interview—Toni Morrison," *Salon.com. http://dir.salon. com/books/int/1998/cov_si_02int.html* (viewed April 11, 2005).

McHenry, Susan, "Lady Laureate," *Black Issues Book Review* (Nov.-Dec. 2003).

"McKinney-Whetstone, Diane, "The Nature of Love," *Essence* (Oct. 2003).

Mobley, Marilyn Sanders, Toni Morrison entry, *Oxford Companion to African American Literature*, William L. Andrews, Frances Smith Foster, and Trudier Harris, eds. New York: Oxford University Press, 1997.

Toni Morrison entry, Contemporary Authors Online, Gale, 2005. Reproduced in Biography Resource Center. Farmington Hills, MI: Thomson Gale, 2005. *http://galenet.galegroup.com/servlet/BioRC* (viewed Feb. 26, 2005).

Toni Morrison entry, *Essential Black Literature Guide*, Roger M. Valade III, ed. Detroit: Visible Ink, 1996.

Toni Morrison interview, *Time.com,* Jan. 1, 1998. *http://www.time.com/time/ community/transcripts/chattr012198.html* (viewed Sept. 21, 2005).

Walter Mosley

Mystery, Science Fiction

Benchmark Titles: Easy Rawlins Series

Los Angeles, California
1952

Photo credit: Vincent Laforet

About the Author and the Author's Writing

Walter Mosley learned a lot about the craft of prose writing while in a poetry program at City College. "[S]tudying poetry taught me the major things I needed to know about fiction," he said in a *BookPage* interview with Alden Mudge. "I already had a narrative voice, and I already loved characters and character development. But the other stuff I had to think about was condensation, the music in language, how simile works, how metaphor works, how to make a sentence say one thing and mean other things also."

Walter Ellis Mosley was born in 1952 in Los Angeles, California. He was an only child of a black man from Louisiana and a Jewish woman—thus he felt the influence of two cultures when growing up, southern black American and Eastern European. His father served in the military during World War II—an experience that brought him to realize, when German soldiers were shooting at him, that no matter his skin color, he was an American. Similarly, Walter Mosley went through an epiphany following the September 11, 2001, terrorist attacks—when the airplanes smashed into the World Trade Center, they were attacking all of America, regardless of skin color.

"My father always taught by telling stories about his experiences," Mosley relates in his memoir *What Next*. "He told me what it meant to be a man and to be a Black man. He taught me about love and responsibility, about beauty, and how to make gumbo. My father's instructions have sustained me in the complex life we live here in America. Some of his lessons I'm still working out over forty years later."

After graduating from Hamilton High School in 1970, Mosley attended Goddard College in Vermont. In 1977, he received a political science degree from Johnson State

College. He attended the University of Massachusetts at Amherst and City College of the City University of New York. In 1987, he married dancer and choreographer Joy Kellman. They later divorced. He now lives in Greenwich Village.

Mosley worked as a potter, caterer, and computer programmer before becoming a writer. (He briefly considered becoming a nurse but didn't because he's troubled by the sight of blood.) He wrote a coming-of-age story of a black man and, as he has said, because it was before Terry McMillan had achieved popularity, it found no publisher. McMillan opened doors for black authors, as Mosley did in turn when President Bill Clinton said Easy Rawlins was one of his favorite fictional characters.

Although author Chester Himes paved the way for black crime writers, Mosley read the Himes books only after he began writing his own. Among Mosley's favorite novels are *One Hundred Years of Solitude, The Adventures of Huckleberry Finn,* and *Their Eyes Were Watching God.*

Mosley has been president of Mystery Writers of America, a member of PEN American Center's executive board and a member of the National Book Awards board of directors. He won a Grammy award in 2002 for best liner notes for a boxed set of Richard Pryor recordings.

Best known are his Ezekiel "Easy" Rawlins noir crime novels—the first one, *Devil in a Blue Dress,* won the Private Eye Writers of America Shamus Award in 1990 for best first P.I. novel. The Easy Rawlins stories are set in post–World War II Los Angeles in which a just-discharged soldier ends up a detective. Time moves ahead a few years with each new novel. Rawlins acquires real estate and a new job, finds a mate and starts a family, and befriends an ex-gangster named Mouse Alexander. The series will take Rawlins through the 1960s, according to the author.

Mosely develops a complex relationship in the books between Rawlins and his son Juice. "What I write about are black, male heroes," the author said in an interview on his Web page. "A big part of being a hero in a community is raising children from one way or another. I don't have any kids. But I know this role from my own father. I wanted to write it specifically, which this book *Bad Boy Brawly Brown* does, and it talks about black men and their sons and their friends' sons."

"[T]he books are really about Black life in Los Angeles," the author said in an *Armchair Detective* interview, "[T]here are all these important events since WWII, contemporary, historical events which Black people have been edited out of. I'm talking about, for instance, in *A Red Death* the juxtaposition of the lives of Black people and the lives of those people who were destroyed by McCarthy. So there's all this important history."

Mosley enjoys a strong and diverse readership. Black men read his books, the author has said, "because I won't embarrass them," and black women read him because he addresses important issues such as racism, sexism, and discrimination.

How do the stories come together? The author does not outline before he starts writing. "I never have the plot worked out when I start writing," he said in a *NYTimes.com* chat. "My ideal situation is to have a first sentence that captures the voice of my story—with that I don't need anything else." He continues to edit and polish his manuscript until he reaches the point where he no longer knows how to fix things.

Mosley has also launched two other series characters, ex-con Socrates Fortlow and bookseller Paris Minton. In reviewing the second book in the series, *Fear Itself,*" Jeanne Russell of the *Montreal Gazette* remarked on the author's ability to investigate the darker side of racism: "The contrast evoked by two close male friends helps underscore and explain the tension of being black in 1950s Los Angeles."

Mosley has also written a science fiction novel, *Blue Light*, and brought out a collection of imaginative stories, *Futureland*. "The best thing that science fiction can do," he said in an *onlineSciFi.com* chat, "is to break you out of ruts in the way you see the world and to shatter one's illusions about progress. It should not make people feel cozy but it should make people question their good fortune about being born at any one moment in time."

Mosley has taken the hardboiled private detective of Dashiell Hammett and Raymond Chandler into new and interesting directions, deftly weaving in social commentary.

"All his works share an abiding interest in the moral dimensions of everyday life," observed reviewer Ben Greenman in the *New Yorker.*

"For blacks who emigrated to the west and north," the author said in a *BookPage* discussion with Robert Fleming, "there was a deep concern for one another. There was a strong bond among blacks during the days of Jim Crow. They realized there was no chance of help coming from outside the community. They knew they were only a hair's breadth from misfortune happening to any one of them if they didn't help each other. I'm very interested in this quality."

Are there other genres Mosley still wants to explore? "I might, one day, write a western," he told *Black Issues Book Review*. "But I'm not dying to do it. I have pretty much done most things I've wanted to."

Works by the Author

Fiction

RL's Dream (1995)
Blue Light (1998)
The Greatest (2000)
Whispers in the Dark (2000)
The Man in My Basement (2004)
The Wave (2005)
Fortunate Son (2006)

Easy Rawlins Series

Devil in a Blue Dress (1990)
A Red Death (1991)
White Butterfly (1992)
Black Betty (1994)
A Little Yellow Dog (1995)
Gone Fishin' (1996)
Bad Boy Brawly Brown (2002)
Little Scarlet (2004)
Cinnamon Kiss (2005)

Paris Minton and Fearless Jones Series

Fearless Jones (2001)
Fear Itself (2003)

Socrates Fortlow Series

Always Outnumbered, Always Outgunned (1997)
Walkin' the Dog (1999)

Collections

Futureland: Nine Stories of an Imminent World (2001)
Six Easy Pieces (2003)

Editor

Black Genius (1999)
The Best American Short Stories 2003 (2003)

Contributor

The New Mystery (1993)
Constable New Crimes 2 (1993)
The Plot Thickens (1997)
Best American Mystery Stories 1998 (1998), edited by Sue Grafton
Gumbo: A Literary Rent Party to Benefit the Hurston/Wright Foundation (2002), edited by Marita Golden and E. Lynn Harris
Dark Matter II: Reading the Bones (2004), edited by Sheree R. Thomas
Best American Mystery Stories 2003 (2003), edited by Michael Connelly
Transgressions (2005), edited by Ed McBain

Young Adult Fiction

47 (2005)

Nonfiction

Working on the Chain Gang: Shaking Off the Dead Hand of History (1999)
What Next: A Memoir toward World Peace (2003)

Motion Pictures Based on the Author's Work

Devil in a Blue Dress (1994)
Always Outnumbered (1998)

For Further Information

Benson, Christopher, "What's Behind the Boom in Black Mystery Writers?," *Ebony* (Sept. 2003).

"Easy Rawlins," *Thrilling Detective. http://www.thrillingdetective.com/rawleasy.html* (viewed Sept. 22, 2006).

Fleming, Robert, "Interview with Walter Mosley," *BookPage.com. http://www.bookpage.com/9607bp/mystery/littleyellowdog.html* (viewed Sept. 22, 2006).

Greenman, Ben, "What Lies Beneath: Subterranean Homestead Blues in Walter Mosley's New Novel," *New Yorker* (Jan. 19, 2004).

"How My Father Shaped My Life," *Ebony* (June 2003).

"In His Own Words," *twbookmark.com. http://www.twbookmark.com/features/waltermosley/article.html* (viewed May 24, 2003).

Lindsay, Tony, "BIBR Talks with Walter Mosley," *Black Issues Book Review* (July-Aug. 2002).

Mosley, Walter, "Writers on Writing: For Authors, Fragile Ideas Need Loving Every Day," *New York Times* (July 3, 2000).

Mudge, Alden, "New Crime Fiction with a Twist from Noir Master Walter Mosley," *BookPage. http://www.bookpage.com/0106bp/walter_mosley.html* (viewed Sept. 22, 2006).

Petersen, James R., "Easy Does It," *Playboy* (Aug. 2002).

Russell, Jeanne, "Hot Reads: Paris Minton and Fearless Set Out on a Wacky Tale," *Montreal Gazette* (Aug. 30, 2003).

Silet, Charles L. P., "The Other Side of Those Mean Streets," *Armchair Detective* (fall 1993).

"10 Questions for ... Walter Mosley," *NYTimes.com* (April 14, 2003). *http://www.nytimes.com/2003/04/14/readersopinions/15MOS1.html* (viewed April 20, 2003).

Villinger, Binti L., *Six Easy Pieces* review, *Black Issues Book Review* (Jan.-Feb. 2003).

Walter Mosley entry, *Contemporary Authors New Revision Series,* Vol. 57, Chapin, Jeff, and John D. Jorgenson, eds. Detroit: Gale Research, 1997.

Walter Mosley interview, *Sci.Fi.com. http://www.scifi.com/transcripts/2001/mosley_chat.html* (viewed Sept. 22, 2006).

Walter Mosely page. *http://www.wwnorton./com/catalog.featured/mosley/welcome.htm* (viewed May 24, 2003).

Walter Mosley Web page. *http://www.twbookmark.com/features/waltermosley/bookshelf.html* (viewed May 24, 2003).

Weeks, Linton, "Of Life and Depth: For Mystery Writer Walter Mosley, Easy Rawlins Is Just the Beginning of the Intrigue," *Washington Post* (Aug. 5, 2002).

Williams, Juan "Walter Mosely: 'What Next,' National Public Radio (March 17, 2003). *http://www.npr.org/display_pages/features/feature_1192760.html* (viewed Sept. 22, 2006).

Walter Dean Myers

Photo credit: Courtesy HarperCollins

**Young Adult Literature,
Historical Literature,
Memoir, Poetry**

Benchmark Title: *The Glory Field*

Martinsburg, West Virginia

1937

About the Author and the Author's Writing

"I am a product of Harlem and of the values, color, toughness, and caring that I found there as a child," Walter Dean Myers said on his African American Literature Book Club Web page. "I learned my flat jump shot in the church basement and got my first kiss during recess at Bible school. I played the endless street games kids played in the pre-television days and paid enough attention to candy and junk food to dutifully alarm my mother."

Myers uses positive experiences from his childhood to make points to his teen readers. "But he doesn't look through rose-colored glasses when he writes about the dangerous and dead-end reality of Harlem—the gangs (such as he depicts in *Scorpions*), drugs, school dropout," *Twentieth Century Children's Writers* noted.

Myers often intertwines contemporary issues with a school sports setting. In *Bad Boy: A Memoir*, as he explained to *teenreads.com*, he demonstrates "that it is acceptable to be an African American from the inner city, a basketball player *and* a voracious reader and I've reached an age at which I needed to say to young people. These 'different' identities are too often considered mutually exclusive."

Myers has both won prestigious awards and been challenged for his honesty. His 1999 young adult novel *Monster*, about a sixteen-year-old boy charged as an accomplice in the murder of a drugstore owner, won the Michael L. Printz Award for excellence in literature for young adults. *Fallen Angels*, his 1988 story of soldiers in Vietnam, so enraged parents in several states because of its profane language that they sought to ban it from library shelves.

The author, descended from Southern slaves, was born Walter Milton Myers in 1937 in Martinsburg, West Virginia. His mother died when he was three. He and two of seven siblings grew up with a foster family named Dean in Harlem. His foster father, he recalled, loved to tell ghost stories and stories of creatures from the sea, stories which at times scared the youngster.

"Books have always played a central role in my life," Myers said in *Books I Read When I Was Young,* "The stories of Langston Hughes . . . introduced me to a joyous style of writing which I have loved since first reading the book. Hughes had treated the Black experience with a style and dignity which I had felt, and he had done so without resorting to a literature of rage."

Myers began writing in school, composing read-aloud poems that avoided certain sounds that, because he had a speech difficulty, prompted laughs from schoolmates.

The author joined the army at age seventeen and learned radio repair. He returned to New York and a succession of jobs. He married, worked for the U.S. Postal Service, and raised a family. His first marriage ended in divorce. He wed a second time.

Myers is a natural storyteller. "I wrote for magazines," he said on a Scholastic Web page. "I wrote adventure stuff. I wrote for the *National Enquirer.* I wrote advertising copy for cemeteries. Then I saw that the Council on Interracial Books for Children had a contest for black writers of children's books. I won the contest and that was my first book—*Where Does the Day Go?* Eventually I got into writing for teenagers." His young adult novel *Fast Sam, Cool Clyde and Stuff* found a receptive publisher in 1975. From then on, writing became his life.

"When I began writing for young people, I was only vaguely aware of the problem with children's books as far as blacks were concerned," he said in a piece for *New York Times Book Review.* "The pain was not so much that the images of my people were poor, but that the poor images were being made public."

"Considered an important black writer, he is often praised for his appealing characterizations, natural dialogue, exciting plots, successful integration of topic, and superior use of details," according to *Children's Literature Review.* Myers also tackles historical subjects. *The Glory Field,* for example, follows five generations of a family, from Africa to New York City.

"I enjoy writing for young people because the forms are less constricting, more forgiving to the stretched imagination," he told *Authors & Artists for Young Adults.* "I particularly enjoy writing about the city life I know best. Ultimately what I want to do with my writing is make the connection—reach out and touch the lives of my characters and share them with a reader."

Myers says he writes with a positive outlook. He said in *Romantic Times,* "The trick, of course, is understanding that there is no inherent fairness in life, and that ultimately we are our own salvation."

Works by the Author

Young Adult Fiction

Fast Sam, Cool Clyde, and Stuff (1975)
Mojo and the Russians (1977)
Victory for Jamie (1977)

It Ain't All for Nothin' (1978)
The Young Landlords (1979)
The Legend of Tarik (1981)
Hoops (1981)
Won't Know Till I Get There (1982)
The Nicholas Factor (1983)
Tales of a Dead King (1983)
Motown and Didi: A Love Story (1984)
The Outside Shot (1984), sequel to *Hoops*
Sweet Illusions (1986)
Crystal (1987)
Shadow of the Red Moon (1987)
Scorpions (1988)
Fallen Angels (1988)
The Young Landlords (1989)
Mouse Rap (1991)
Somewhere in the Darkness (1992)
Darnell Rock Reporting (1994)
The Glory Field (1994)
Slam (1996)
The Journal of Scott Pendleton Collins (1999)
Monster (1999)
The Journal of Joshua Loper, a Black Cowboy: The Chisholm Trail, 1871 (1999)
African Princess: At Her Majesty's Request (1999)
145th Street (2000), short stories
Journal of Biddy Owens: The Negro Leagues, Birmingham, Alabama, 1948 (2001)
Somewhere in the Darkness (2002)
Dream Bearer (2003)
The Beast (2003)
Shooter (2004)
Autobiography of My Dead Brother (2005)
Street Love (2006)
Jazz (2006)

Arrow Series

Adventure in Granada (1985)
The Hidden Shrine (1985)
Duel in the Desert (1986)
Ambush in the Amazon (1986)

18 Pine St. Series (created by Myers, written by Stacie Johnson)

1. *Sort of Sisters* (1992)
2. *The Party* (1992)

3. *The Prince* (1992)
4. *The Test* (1993)
5. *Skyman* (1993)
6. *Fashion by Tasha* (1993)
7. *Intensive Care* (1993)
8. *Dangerous Games* (1993)
9. *Cindy's Baby* (1994)
10. *Kwame's Girl* (1994)
11. *The Diary* (1994)
12. *Taking Sides* (1994)

Anthologies

What We Must See: Young Black Storytellers (1971), edited by Orde Coombs
We Be Word Sorcerers: Twenty-five Stories by Black Americans (1973), edited by Sonia Sanchez
On the Wings of Peace: Writers and Illustrators Speak Out for Peace in Memory of Hiroshima and Nagasaki (1995)

Nonfiction for Young Adults

The World of Work: A Guide to Choosing a Career (1975)
Social Welfare (1976)
Now Is Your Time: The African-American Struggle for Freedom (1991)
The Righteous Revenge of Artemis Bonner (1992)
Malcolm X: By Any Means Necessary (1993)
A Place Called Heartbreak: A Story of Vietnam (1993)
Amistad Affair: A Long Road to Freedom (1998)
Greatest: Muhammad Ali (2000)
Bad Boy: A Memoir (2001)
Antarctica: Journeys to the South Pole (2004)
Patrol: An American Soldier in Vietnam (2005)

Fiction for Younger Readers

Where Does the Day Go? (1969), as Walter M. Myers
The Dragon Takes a Wife (1972)
The Dancers (1972)
Fly, Jimmy, Fly! (1974)
Brainstorm (1977)
The Black Pearl and the Ghost; or, One Mystery after Another (1980)
The Golden Serpent (1980)
Mr. Monkey and the Gotcha Bird (1984)
Me, Mop, and the Moondance Kid (1988)
Won't Know till I Get There (1988)
The Mouse Rap (1990)
Mop, Moondance and the Nagasaki Knights (1992)

Brown Angels: An Album of Pictures and Verse (1993)
The Righteous Revenge of Artemis Bonner (1994)
The Story of the Three Kingdoms (1995)
How Mr. Monkey Saw the Whole World (1996)
Smiffy Blue, Ace Crime Detective: The Case of the Missing Ruby and Other Stories (1996)
Blues of Flats Brown (2000)
Handbook for Boys (2002)
Blues Journey (2003)

Nonfiction for Younger Readers

Young Martin's Promise (1993)
One More River to Cross: An African American Photograph Album (1996)

Poetry

Brown Angels: An Album of Pictures and Verse (1993)
Harlem: A Poem (1996)
Here in Harlem: Poems in Many Voices (2004)

Film Based on the Author's Work

The Young Landlords

For Further Information

Cullinan, Bernice, and M. Jerry Weiss. *Books I Read When I Was Young: The Favorite Books of Famous People*. New York: Avon, 1980.

Davis, Kenneth C., *The Glory Field* review, *New York Times Book Review* (Nov. 13 1994).

Fader, Ellen, *Somewhere in the Darkness* review, *Horn Book Magazine* (May-June 1992).

Fischer, Marilyn, Carol Levandowski, Carol Marlow, and Barbara Snyder with Kaye E. Vandergrift, "Learning about Walter Dean Myers." *http://www.scils.rutgers.edu/~kvander/myers.html* (viewed Sept. 22, 2006).

Foerstal, Herbert N. *Banned in the USA: A Reference Guide to Book Censorship in Schools and Public Libraries*. Westport, CT: Greenwood Press, 1994.

Forman, Jack, Walter Dean Myers entry in *Twentieth Century Children's Writers*, 3d ed, Tracy Chevalier, ed. Chicago: St. James Press, 1989.

Myers, Walter Dean, "I Actually Thought We Would Revolutionize the Industry," *New York Times Book Review* (Nov. 9 1986).

Walter Dean Myers, Author of the 1989 Newbery Honor Book Scorpions. New York: Harper Junior Books Group, 1989.

Walter Dean Myers biography and interview, Scholastic Books. *http://www2.scholastic.com/teachers/authorsandbooks/authorstudies/authorhome.jhtml?authorID=67&collateralID=5250&displayName=Biography* (viewed Sept. 22, 2006).

Walter Dean Myers entry, *Authors & Artists for Young Adults*, Vol. 4, Agnes Garrett and Helga P. McCue, eds. Detroit: Gale Research, 1990.

Walter Dean Myers entry, *Children's Literature Review,* Vol. 16, Gerard J. Senick, ed. Detroit: Gale Research, 1989.

Walter Dean Myers entry, *Fifth Book of Junior Authors & Illustrators*, Sally Holmes Holtze, ed. New York: Wilson, 1983.

Walter Dean Myers profile, *Romantic Time Bookclub Magazine* (April 2005).

Walter Dean Myers profile, *teenreads.com. http://www.teenreads.com/authors/ au-myers-walterdean.asp* (viewed Sept. 22, 2006).

Walter Dean Myers, TeenReads, *Romantic Times* (April 2005).Walter Dean Myers Web page, African American Literature Book Club. *http://au-thors.aalbc.com/walter1.htm* (viewed Sept. 22, 2006).

Gloria Naylor

Mainstream Contemporary Literature

Benchmark Title: *The Women
of Brewster Place*

New York, New York

1950

About the Author and the Author's Writing

Author Gloria Naylor won the American Book Award immediately out of the gate, with her 1982 debut novel, *The Women of Brewster Place*.

This novel follows seven African American women, women who are diverse, but who also share common fears, weaknesses, and strengths, as they go through love, grief, sex, and birth. "Her women feel deeply, and she unflinchingly transcribes their emotions. . . . Vibrating and undisguised emotion, *The Women of Brewster Place* springs from the same roots that produced the blues. Like them, her book sings of sorrows proudly borne by black women in America," remarked reviewer Diedre Donohue.

Noting Naylor's novels center on enclosed black communities with characters coming to grips with themselves and their environments, Christine H. King further observed, "Naylor's powerful settings combine elements of the ordinary with the otherworldly, allowing for magical events and mythic resolutions."

The author was born in 1950 in New York City, the daughter of a master framer/transit worker and a telephone operator. Her parents had been sharecroppers in Mississippi who relocated to the North. She credits her mother with opening her eyes to the wonderful world of books. Her mother gave her a blank diary when she was twelve, and that's where she wrote down those emotional things she otherwise had a hard time articulating.

After graduating from high school in 1968, Naylor was baptized a Jehovah's Witness and became a minister in that faith. Still living at home, she worked as a switchboard operator for six years before venturing to North Carolina and Florida as a full-time worker for her religion. In 1975, she left the Jehovah's Witnesses, suffered a nervous breakdown, recovered and began taking nursing courses at Medgar Evers College. She discovered the work of feminist advocates and saw the emergence of a black literature from Zora Neale Hurston, Toni Morrison, and others. She transferred to Brooklyn College of CUNY to study English and earned a degree in 1981, the same

242

year she divorced after a year of marriage. With encouragement from an editor at *Essence* magazine, she wrote *The Women of Brewster Place*.

"The novel began with my using, in an odd way, the sort of confessional writing that I began with in my diary," the author said in a National Book Foundation interview. Feeling anxious over a relationship, "I just felt I was going to die. So I said to myself, what could make another woman hurt the way I'm hurting? That's when I invented 'Luciella' Louise Turner. It wasn't my situation, but I imagined a woman who loses her husband, loses her unborn child and loses her toddler."

From there, Naylor conceived the characters of the other six women in the book, variations on the experiences of black women in this country. Naylor comes from a large, close extended family, so she naturally explores family issues.

"Naylor's success," suggests *Contemporary Novelists*, "lies, in part, in the intensity of her presentation of such social issues as poverty, racism, discrimination against homosexuals, the unequal treatment of women, the value of a sense of community among blacks, and the failure of some upper middle-class educated blacks to address racial problems and social injustice."

In 1983, Naylor received a master of arts degree in African American studies from Yale University; the novel *Linden Hills* was her master's thesis. She was writer-in-residence at Cummington Community of the Arts and a visiting lecturer at George Washington University that year. In 1985, Naylor was a National Endowment for the Arts fellow and scholar-in-residence at the University of Pennsylvania the year after. She was a visiting lecturer at Princeton University (1986) and Boston University (1987) and senior fellow in the Society for Humanities at Cornell University in 1988. She also received a Guggenheim fellowship in 1988.

Her next two books, *Mama Day* and *Bailey's Café*, completed an interrelated sequence, the accomplishment of which, the author said in *The Writer*, gave her great satisfaction. "When I finished the last of that quartet, it was an exciting, exciting moment for me, to realize that I had set that goal and achieved it. You know, a whole lot can happen in 10 years of an adult life, and I had written through all of that."

Today Naylor has her own film production company, One Way Productions, which promotes a positive African American image.

She nevertheless continues to explore her themes and write powerful fiction. *The Men of Brewster Place* (1998) responds to queries from readers about where the men were. "Like many in this country I was profoundly moved by the Million Man March and the images of all those black men calling themselves to task, promising to return home and be better citizens by concentrating on being better fathers and brothers," the author said on her Penguin Putnam's Web page. "It has taken me these many years to decide finally that I wanted to give the men who had appeared briefly in *The Women* a voice of their own."

Works by the Author

The Women of Brewster Place: A Novel in Seven Stories (1982)
Linden Hills (1985)
Mama Day (1988)
Bailey's Café (1992)
The Men of Brewster Place (1999)
1996 (2005)

Contributor

Gumbo: A Literary Rent Party to Benefit the Hurston/Wright Foundation (2002), edited by Marita Golden and E. Lynn Harris

Play

Bailey's Café (1992)

Editor

Children of the Night: The Best Short Stories by Black Writers, 1967 to the Present (1995)

Nonfiction

Centennial (1986)

Revolution of the Heart: A New Strategy for Creating Wealth (1996), with Bill Shore

Anthology

The Writing Life: Writers on How They Think and Work (2003), edited by Marie Arana

Film Based on the Author's Work

The Women of Brewster Place (1989)

For Further Information

Awkward, Michael, *Inspiring Influences: Tradition, Revision, and Afro-American Women's Novels.* New York: Columbia University Press, 1991.

Denison, D.C., "Interview with Gloria Naylor," *The Writer* (Dec. 1994).

Donahue, Diedre, review of *The Women of Brewster Place*, *Washington Post* (Oct. 21, 1983).

Edwards, Tamala, "Conversation with Gloria Naylor," *Essence* (June 1998).

Felton, Sharon, and Michelle Loris, eds., *Naylor: The Critical Response to Gloria Naylor.* Westport, CT: Greenwood Press, 1997.

Fowler, Virginia, *Gloria Naylor: In Search of Sanctuary.* New York: Twayne, 1996.

Gloria Naylor biography, *Voices from the Gaps.* http:// *http://voices.cla. umn.edu/vg/Bios/entries/naylor_gloria.html* (viewed August 10, 2006).

Gloria Naylor entry, *Contemporary Novelists*, 7th ed. Detroit: St. James Press, 2001.

Gloria Naylor interview, National Book Foundation. *http://www.nationalbook. org/authorsguide_gnaylor.html* (viewed Aug. 10, 2006).

Hall, Chekita T., *Gloria Naylor's Feminist Blues Aesthetic*. New York: Garland, 1998.

Harris, Trudier, *The Power of the Porch: The Storyteller's Craft in Zora Neale Hurston, Gloria Naylor, and Randall Kenan*. Athens: University of Georgia Press, 1996.

Kelley, Margot Anne, ed., *Gloria Naylor's Early Novels*. Gainesville: University Press of Florida, 1999.

Peacock, Scot, ed., Gloria Naylor entry, *Contemporary Authors New Revision Series*, Vol. 74. Detroit: Gale Research, 1999.

King, Christine H., Gloria Naylor entry, *American Ethnic Writers*, Vol. 2, David Peck, ed. Pasadena, CA: Salem Press, 2000.

Montgomery, Maxine Laura, *Conversations with Gloria Naylor*. Jackson: University Press of Mississippi, 2004

Unofficial Gloria Naylor Homepage. *http://www.lythastudios.com/gnaylor/chron.html* (viewed May 27, 2003).

Whitt, Margaret Earley, *Understanding Gloria Naylor*. Columbia: University of South Carolina Pres, 1999

Women of Brewster Place Reading Guide. *http://www.penguinputnam.com/static/rguides/us/women_of_brewster_place.html* (viewed Aug. 10, 2006).

Barbara Neely

Mystery

Benchmark Title: *Blanche on the Lam*

Lebanon, Pennsylvania
1941

Photo credit: Marion Ettlinger

About the Author and the Author's Writing

Barbara Neely makes no bones about fiction being a convenient vehicle to express her activist views. "I realized the mystery genre was perfect to talk about serious subjects and it could carry the political fiction I wanted to write," she told *Uncommon Detectives*.

Neely was born in Lebanon, a Dutch community in Pennsylvania, in 1941. She attended a Catholic elementary school, the only black student as well as the only fluent speaker of English. She earned a master's degree in urban and regional planning at the University of Pittsburgh. Since then, Neely has long worked in the public sector. She designed and directed the first community-based corrections facility for women in Pennsylvania. She managed a YWCA branch, coordinated family services for ABCD Head Start, and served as a consultant to non-profit organizations. She also served on a research team at the Institute for Social Research and was executive director and co-chairwoman of the board of directors for Women for Economic Justice. She helped found Women of Color for Reproductive Freedom. She was a radio producer for African News Service and a staff member of Southern Exposure Magazine. And she hosted *Commonwealth Journal*, a radio news program.

Neely also dabbled in writing fiction, selling a story to *Essence*. She wrote the draft of a novel and set it aside. "In the middle of working on that novel I started playing around with this character Blanche and thought, 'I'd like to write something about race and class that was funny,' but for a good part of the book I was just doing it for my own amusement," she explained on the Voices from the Gaps Web site. An agent and an editor both took an interest in her middle-aged domestic worker, Blanche White, and so was published *Blanche on the Lam*. When we first meet the heroine, she is

246

scrambling away from jail and a bad check investigation—thanks to her no-use white employers. She enters into service with a wealthy white family only to find crime recognizes no racial bounds when there's a murder to be solved.

That novel garnered Neely three major crime writing awards. Some have likened Neely's amateur crime solver Blanche White to Langston Hughes's Jesse B. Semple—plain, honest, and earnest.

"*Blanche on the Lam* is noteworthy in several respects," according to Pearl G. Aldrich. "Neely took a giant step into unknown territory for a crime novel and succeeded brilliantly. Although racism is not new to fiction, the viewpoint of a domestic worker is. Although Blanche is not the first African American protagonist—not even the first black woman detective—she is the first of her type. And she is a formidable character."

There's also murder in Maine, where Blanche, thanks to the generosity of her Boston employers, is a guest at an all-black resort, Amber Cove. She's surprised to find class divisions within that community. On her first evening she discovers that she's obviously not an "insider": "For a moment, the whole room stared at her as though she were a horse in their bathroom." Blanche scoffs at the idea of a "talented tenth"—a phrase coined by activist W.E.B. Du Bois—but finds she is better capable than they are of solving a suspicious suicide and a murder.

Publishers Weekly's anonymous reviewer found the book a little heavy on the bigotry issue, calling the books "a message with a bit of mystery."

"Blanche is a very strong character," in the view of Jean Swanson and Dean James, "and her voice is distinctive. Throughout the books, Blanche ruminates on what it is like to be female and black in contemporary American society."

There's always room for stories told with compassion and a sense of humor—hallmarks of Neely's work.

Works by the Author

Blanche White Mystery Series

Blanche on the Lam (1992)
Blanche among the Talented Tenth (1994)
Blanche Cleans Up (1998)
Blanche Passes Go (2000)

Contributor

Things That Divide Us (1985), edited by Faith Conlon, Rachel da Silva, and Barbara Wilson
Speaking for Ourselves: The Black Women's Health Book (1994)
Constellations: A Contextual Reader for Writers (1997), edited by John Schilb, Elizabeth A. Flynn, and John Clifford
Literature: Reading and Writing the Human Experience (1997), edited by Richard Abcarian, Marvin Klotz, and Peter Richardson
Breaking Ice: An Anthology of Contemporary African-American Fiction (1990), edited by Terry McMillan

Best Black Women's Erotica (2001), edited by Blanche Richardson
Tar Heal Dead (2005), edited by Sarah R. Shaber

Editor

Prevailing Voices: Stories of Triumph and Survival (1982), with Marc Miller and
    Bob Hall

For Further Information

Aldrich, Pearl G., Barbara Neely entry, *St. James Guide to Crime & Mystery
    Writers*, 4th ed., Jay P. Pederson, ed. Detroit: Gale, 1996.

Barbara Neely biography, *Uncommon Detectives. http://www.neiu.edu/~mystery/
    neely2.html* (viewed Aug. 10, 2006).

Blanche Neely biography, *Voices from the Gaps. http://voices.cla.umn.edu/
    vg/Bios/entries/neely_barbara.html* (viewed Aug. 10, 2006).

Barbara Neely entry, Contemporary Authors Online, Gale, 2005. Reproduced in
    Biography Resource Center, Farmington Hills, MI: Thomson Gale, 2005.
    http://galenet.galegroup.com/servlet/BioRC.

Barbara Neely entry, Murder and Mayhem African American Mystery Writers,
    Evanston Public Library. *http://www.evanston.lib.il.us/library/bibliographies/
    murder.html* (viewed Aug. 10, 2006).

Barbara Neely Web page, African American Literature Book Club. *http://
    authors.aalbc.com/blanche.htm* (viewed Aug. 10, 2006).

Barbara Neely Web site. *http://www.blanchewhite.com* (viewed Feb. 15, 2005).

Blanche among the Talented Tenth review, *Publishers Weekly* (July 18, 1994).

Heising, Wiletta L., *Detecting Women*, 3d ed. Dearborn, MI: Purple Moon Press,
    2000.

Klett, Rex, review of *Blanche Passes Go. Library Journal* (July 2000).

Swanson, Jean, and Dean James, *By a Woman's Hand: A Guide to Mystery Fic-
    tion by Women*, 2d ed. New York: Berkley Prime Crime, 1996.

Evelyn Palfrey

Mainstream Contemporary Literature, Romantic Suspense

Benchmark Title: *Everything in Its Place*

Texarkana, Arkansas

1950

About the Author and the Author's Writing

What better judge of character than a judge?

—Evelyn Palfrey

Born in Texarkana, Arkansas, the author attended Southern Methodist University where she earned a bachelor of arts degree in 1971. A decade later she received her juris doctorate from University of Texas Law School. She and her husband, Darwin McKee, have two children. Palfrey is active in civic and social organizations. She has been a municipal court judge in Austin, Texas, since 1989 and a novelist since 1995.

"I write stories that have middle-age heroes and heroines because I believe that romance is just as beautiful with a little gray at the temples," Palfrey said on her Web site.

A nominee for *Romantic Times* magazine's Career Achievement Award, Palfrey is unpredictable in her plots. In *The Price of Passion*, a husband of two decades one day brings home his illegitimate baby and expects his wife to raise it as if nothing were wrong. In *Three Perfect Men*, three women of different races and ages meet three rugged men and solve a bizarre pine woods murder. *In Everything in Its Place*, an elementary school principal struggles with wooing an ex-army officer, the future of a granddaughter she has raised, and the demands of a drug-addicted daughter. In this last book, wrote reviewer Harriet Klausner on AllReaders.Com, Palfrey "avoids turning the plot into a simplistic tear jerker by making her key cast seem real by filling each one with compassion yet struggling with distrust and a need to overcome flaws."

Long an avid consumer of romance fiction, Palfrey said she found an increasing disjuncture in books that appealed to her. All the heroines were in their twenties. She was forty-five. "Women my age have different issues," she said in a chat with Sisters in Spirit Book Club. "Not better, not worse. Just different. I sat down to write a little story, just to entertain myself. In 90 days, that little story became a book—*Three Perfect Men*. A lot of other women found it entertaining, too—and I was hooked on writing." She self-published her first novel and it was successful enough to be picked up by a major publisher.

Typically in her books, middle-aged women who have given up their dreams in order to please and support their husbands reach a point where they must reevaluate. The author is not shy about discussing topics ranging from menopause and "boomerang" children to domestic violence and loneliness.

As Palfrey develops a book, she said, she allows her heroine to become an imaginary friend; in that way she gets to know her characters inside and out. They become her friends.

"As an attorney, I have been trained to observe and to listen," she told Natasha Brooks-Harris. "I'm sure that plays some part in my being able to describe my friends and their emotional upheavals for the reader."

Her most embarrassing experience as a writer—but one that became instructive —was when she blindly provided pages from a book going into press for review at a local writers' organization. A good friend dissected the sample upside and down. Palfrey ruminated on the editor's suggestions, incorporated as many as she could into the work and, in her view, became a stronger writer because of it.

If the use of motor homes sometimes shows up in Palfrey's novels, it's no wonder. She's on her fourth RV—something she carried on from her outdoors-loving parents. Since the terrorist attacks of September 11, she has preferred highways to skyways as she travels the country to promote her books.

Works by the Author

Three Perfect Men (1996)
The Price of Passion (2000)
Dangerous Dilemmas (2001)
Everything in Its Place (2002)

Contributor

Chicken Soup for the African American Soul (2004), edited by Jack Canfield, Mark Victor Hansen, and Lisa Nichols
Chicken Soup for the African American Woman's Soul (2006), edited by Jack Canfield, Mark Victor Hansen, and Lisa Nichols

For Further Information

Brooks-Harris, Natasha, "An Interview with Evelyn Palfrey," *Romance in Color*. *http://www.romanceincolor.com/authormthpalfrey.htm* (viewed Aug. 10, 2006).

Evelyn Palfrey interview, Sisters in Spirit Book Club. *http://www.geocities.com/ SistersInSpiritBookclub/pages/interviewarchives.htm#epalfrey* (viewed Aug. 10, 2006).

Evelyn Palfrey McKee entry, *Who's Who among African Americans*, 17th ed. Gale Group, 2004. Reproduced in Biography Resource Center. Farmington Hills, MI: Thomson Gale, 2005. *http://galenet.galegroup.com/servlet/ BioRC* (viewed Feb. 26, 2005).

Evelyn Palfrey Web page. *http://www.evelynpalfrey.com* (viewed Aug. 10, 2006).

Klausner, Harriet, review of *Everything in Its Place*, *AllReaders.Com*. *http://www.allreaders.com/Topics/info_13531.asp?BSID=13026971* (viewed Sept. 14, 2006).

Alexs D. Pate

Mainstream Contemporary Literature, Historical Literature, Poetry

Benchmark Title: *Losing Absalom*

Philadelphia, Pennsylvania

1950

About the Author and the Author's Writing

Alexs D. Pate is determined to improve—or at least explain—the image of the contemporary black man. "I focus on the interior lives of black men. While African-American men are almost de rigueur iconography, we don't know anything about them! We don't know the mind-set of the absentee father. We don't know the mind-set of Colin Powell. We only have symbols," he told reporter Kristal Zook of *USA Weekend*.

Pate was born in 1950 in Philadelphia. His mother made sure Alexs had a wide variety of reading to choose from, and he devoured the poetry of Langston Hughes and the prose of Charles Johnson, Ralph Ellison, and Richard Wright. These writers instilled in Pate a desire to achieve the technical virtuosity to write in their realm.

Pate is an associate professor of African-American and African studies at the University of Minnesota, where he teaches English, fiction writing and literature—including a class in the poetry of rap. He has written essays for the *Minneapolis Star Tribune*, *USA Weekend,* and the *Washington Post,* and his verse has shown up in print in a variety of periodicals. In addition, he is a performance artist.

In his first novels, the author explores issues of fatherhood on two levels. In *Losing Absalom*, the title character, Absalom Goodman, is dying of brain cancer, to the distress of his wife and two children.

Through Absalom's last floating thoughts and flashbacks, Pate recreates the life of a sensitive, substantial man. Reviewer Barbara L. J. Griffin said, "Pate's novel succeeds because of the resonating presence of Absalom superimposed upon the story, whispering into the conscience of his children and compelling them to hear him. . . . Not since John Oliver Killens's 1954 novel *Youngblood* have we seen in fiction a more appealing representation of the African American family."

In *Finding Makeba*, Ben Crestfield has abandoned his wife and daughter in order to pursue a career as a writer and now attempts reconciliation when his daughter is an adult. The second novel, Pate told Katherine Line for *African American Review,* was written "as a letter to my children. I wanted them to know that even though I wasn't with them, I loved them and was unprepared to deal with the concept of absenteeism."

251

West of Rehoboth takes place in the early 1960s and follows twelve-year-old Edward Massey as his Philadelphia family flees to a beach in Delaware each summer for relief not only from the stifling heat of summer, but from racial tensions in the city. The author examines male values through the character of an Uncle Rufus, whose past is one of darkness and sadness.

The Multicultiboho Sideshow is as frantic as its title; Ichabod Word has the right name to succeed as a writer. But he's an utter failure, and he kidnaps a police officer in a bizarre ploy to tell the world of his frustrations. "Pate combines elements of a classic whodunit with the best qualities of stinging social satire," said *Publishers Weekly*, "venturing beyond formula and genre."

With *Amistad*, Pate ventures a century and a half into the past to examine the true 1839 mutiny on a Spanish slave ship circling Long Island. For a change of pace, Pate wrote a short story, "The Rumor," for *After Hours: A Collection of Erotic Writings by Black Men*.

Pate has witnessed in the last three decades both the emergence of a strong black literature and a growing popular black literature. But, as he suggested in *Essence*, that development has come to a critical point: "I don't think we're paying enough attention to character and the context in which the lives of the characters are constructed. . . . I try to tell the truth in my writing, the way my characters see and feel it."

Works by the Author

Losing Absalom: A Novel (1994)
Finding Makeba (1997)
Amistad: A Novel (1997), with David Franzoni and Steven Zaillian
The Multicultiboho Show (1999)
West of Rehoboth (2001)

Contributor

Gumbo: A Literary Rent Party to Benefit the Hurston/Wright Foundation (2002), edited by Marita Golden and E. Lynn Harris
After Hours: A Collection of Erotic Writing by Black Men (2002), edited by Robert Fleming
The Cotillion; or, One Good Bull Is Half the Herd (2002), by John Oliver Killens

Editor

With and Without: Black Fathers Speak to and about Their Children (1997)

For Further Information

Alexs D. Pate entry, Contemporary Authors Online, Gale, 2005. Reproduced in Biography Resource Center. Farmington Hills, MI: Thomson Gale, 2005. *http://galenet.galegroup.com/servlet/BioRC* (viewed Feb. 21, 2005).
Alexs D. Pate Web page, African American Literature Book Club. *http://authors.aalbc.com/alexsdpate.htm* (viewed Aug. 10, 2006).
"Alexs Pate: Novelist/Performer," *Skyway News* (Sept. 13, 1994).

Griffin, Barbara L. J., review of *Losing Absalom*, *Melus* (summer 1998).

Link, Katherine, "Illuminating the Darkened Corridors": An Interview with Alexs Pate, *African American Review* (winter 2002).

Multicultiboho Sideshow review, *Publishers Weekly* (Aug. 30, 1999).

West of Rehoboth review, *Essence* (Sept. 2001).

Zook, Kristal, "Literature: Charles Johnson and Alexs D. Pate," *USA Weekend* (Feb. 17, 2001).

Gary Phillips

Mystery

Benchmark Titles: Ivan Monk and Martha
Chainey Series

Los Angeles, California

1955

Photo credit: Chris Voelker

About the Author and the Author's Writing

Gary Phillips's community activism in Los Angeles over a quarter century—
on issues ranging from affordable housing to gang intervention to neighborhood
empowerment—served him well when he began writing crime novels.

Phillips was born in Los Angeles in 1955, the son of a mechanic and a librarian.
Early on he discovered the writers Arthur Conan Doyle, Ellery Queen, Ross Macdonald, Richard Wright, Rod Serling, comic book artist Jack Kirby, Zora Neale Hurston,
Donald Goines, Joyce Carol Oates, and pulp writers Kenneth Robeson (creator of Doc
Savage) and Walter Gibson (creator of The Shadow). From 1972 to 1973, he attended
San Francisco State University, and in 1978, he earned a bachelor of arts degree from
California State University, Los Angeles. Since then, he has worked as a union organizer, political campaign coordinator, radio talk show host, and teacher. He has written
op-ed pieces for the *L.A. Times Magazine, San Francisco Examiner, Washington Post,
Baltimore Sun, Miami Herald* and other newspapers. He has also served as co-director
of the MultiCultural Collaborative.

While Phillips had long dabbled in writing and comic book drawing, it was only
when he was let go from a job with the American Federation of State and County Municipal Employees that he took a class in how to structure a mystery novel with writer
Robert Crais. Students were required to write fifty pages of a proposed mystery, which
Phillips did. The course ended, but Phillips wasn't satisfied. He completed the manuscript, but it found no takers among publishers. When rioting in Los Angeles followed
the acquittal of Los Angeles police officers in the videotaped beating of black motorist
Rodney King, Phillips wrote a new book, *Violent Spring*, and set the action against the

true-life backdrop of the riots. Thus was launched his Ivan Monk private detective series. Reviewers often slotted this and subsequent Monk books as more "whydunits" than "whodunits," because they involved social, racial, and class issues.

The first three Monk titles were published through a cooperative, West Coast Crime, in which Phillips was a financial and sweat-equity participant. Berkley Prime Crime picked up the series and printed the earlier as well as later books.

In an interview for Mystery Guide, Phillips denied that he modeled his detective on himself. "He is, like all (hopefully good) literary PI figures, searching for something bigger than what his cases are—although he might not ever consciously be aware of it, or he might not even admit that to anybody. But Monk is certainly somebody who ultimately is an optimist, who is trying to find those good qualities that are in most people."

The author further stretched mystery novel traditions with another series, featuring a black woman. In *High Hand,* Martha Chainey is a retired showgirl now running money for a Las Vegas mobster. She has to recover $7 million that has been stolen from her. The story is rich in suspense. "An air of heightened tension marks this novel from the outset," said reviewer Rex E. Klett in *Library Journal.*

Not all of Phillips's books are series. *The Perpetrators* is about Marley, a self-appointed expediter who agrees to escort a key witness to a major drug trial in Los Angeles (reviewer Ted Fitzgerald called it a "larger-than-life hoot"). *Bangers* is a violent depiction of an elite Los Angeles anti-gang police team which runs afoul of a woman assistant district attorney when a gang leader is killed while in custody.

Phillips explained the appeal of the violent hero in an essay for *Mystery Scene*: "Part of it is the anti-hero is by definition less concerned with nuance and the rules. For them it's about how to traverse the straight line between where they're at and where they want to get."

In another essay, for *The American Prospect*, Phillips gives an overview of crime and espionage fiction and notes the prescience of authors such as Edward Zwick, whose 1998 novel *The Siege* depicts Muslim agents smashing an airplane into a skyscraper. Phillips speculates on how the literary world will handle issues of race in light of the 2001 terrorist attacks, and he suggests prose writers as well as journalists need to "excavate beneath the surface of the official story line for motivation and, subsequently, richer insight" into suicide bombers and street-fighting rebels. He concludes, "Writers who embrace such complexities—and whose formulas are accordingly tweaked—will go beyond recording our reality and actually shape it. Or as the Continental Op says in Dashiell Hammett's *Red Harvest*, 'Sometimes just stirring things up is all right—if you're tough enough to survive.' "

◆ Works by the Author

The Jook (1999)
Tyson (2001), unpublished novella
The Perpetrators (2002)
Bangers (2003)

Ivan Monk Series

Violent Spring (1996)
Perdition U.S.A. (1996)
Bad Night Is Falling (1997)
Only the Wicked (2000)
Monkology (2004), short stories

Martha Chainey Series

High Hand (2000)
Shooter's Point (2001)

Anthologies

Spooks, Spies, and Private Eyes: Black Mystery Crime and Suspense Fiction (1995), edited by Paula Woods
The Shamus Game (2000), edited by Robert J. Randisi
Flesh and Blood: Erotic Tales of Crime and Passion (2001), edited by Max Allan Collins and Jeff Gelb Warner
World's Finest Crime and Mystery II (2001), edited by Ed Gorman
The Blue and the Gray Undercover: All New Civil War Spy Adventures (2001), edited by Ed Gorman
Sudden Death: Football Mysteries (2002), edited by Otto Penzler
Guns of the West (2002), edited by Ed Gorman and Martin Greenberg
Measures of Poison (2002)
After Hours: A Collection of Erotic Writing by Black Men (2002), edited by Robert Fleming
Flesh and Blood III (2003), edited by Max Allan Collins and Jeff Gelb Warner
Shades of Black: Crime and Mystery Stories by African-American Writers (2004), edited by Eleanor Taylor Bland (Martha Chainey short story)
Show Business is Murder (2004), edited by Stuart M. Kaminsky
Creature Cozies: A Menagerie of All-New Mysteries (2005), edited by Jill M. Morgan
Retro Pulp Tales (2006), edited by Joe R. Lansdale
Dublin Noir: The Celtic Tiger vs. The Ugly American edited by Ken Bruen (2006)

Comic Book Series

Shot Callerz (Oni Comics)
Midnight Mover (Oni Comics)
Angeltown (DC Comics)
The Envoy (Moonstone Comics)

Editor

The Cocaine Chronicles (2005), with Jervey Tervalon

For Further Information

Bangers review, *A Novel View*. *http://www.anovelview.com/bookreviews/bangers_by_gary_phillips.htm* (viewed April 2, 2005).

Fitsgerald, Ted, review of *The Perpetrators*, *Drood Review of Mystery* (Nov./Dec. 2002).

Gary Phillips biography, Do-Not Press. *http://www.thedonotpress.com/titles/jook.html* (viewed Aug. 10, 2006).

Gary Phillips biography, Kensington Books. *http://www.kensingtonbooks.com/kensington/catalog.cfm?dest=dir&linkid=1585&linkon=subsection* (viewed Aug. 10, 2006).

Gary Phillips entry, Contemporary Authors Online, Gale, 2005. Reproduced in Biography Resource Center. Farmington Hills, MI: Thomson Gale, 2005. *http://galenet.galegroup.com/servlet/BioRC* (viewed Feb. 26, 2005).

Gary Phillips interview, *Mystery Guide*. *http://www.mysteryguide.com/phillips.html* (viewed August 10, 2006).

Gary Phillips interview, *Mystery News*. *http://www.blackravenpress.com/phillips.htm* (viewed April 2, 2005).

Gary Phillips interview, *A Novel View*. *http://www.anovelview.com/chats/gary%phillips%20august%202003.htm* (viewed April 2, 2005).

Gary Phillips Web site. *http://gdphillips.com* (viewed August 10, 2006).

Klett, Rex, review of *Bangers, Library Journal* (Oct. 1, 2003).

Klett, Rex, review of *High Hand, Library Journal* (Nov. 1, 2000).

Lachman, Marvin, review of *Violent Spring, Armchair Detective* (summer 1994).

Phillips, Gary, "Bada Bing!" *Mystery Scene* (winter 2003).

Phillips, Gary, e-mail to author, June 18, 2005.

Phillips, Gary, "Pulp Culture: History, Hard-Boiled," *The American Prospect* (March 11, 2002).

Connie Porter

Young Adult Literature

Benchmark Titles: Addy Walker Series

New York City

1959

Photo credit: American Girl

About the Author and the Author's Writing

Connie Porter's first fiction, interwoven stories for adult readers, drew praise and was even compared to the writings of Toni Morrison. *All-Bright Court*, selected by the American Library Association as one of the Best Books of 1991, follows the lives of a black family, the Taylors, who lived in the urban north during the John F. Kennedy era.

"Ms. Porter is an original who knows the tenement life and the characters she describes," declared reviewer Sam Cornish in *Plowshares* journal. "She is aware of the absurdity and humor (which is often lacking in modern fiction) in the African-American experience."

Connie Rose Porter was born in New York City and grew up in Lackawana, New York. She graduated from City Honors High School in Buffalo. She earned a degree from State University of New York at Albany in 1981. While working toward a master in fine arts degree in creative writing at Louisiana State University, she wrote a short story on assignment. Feeling the urge to say more, she expanded it into her first novel—*All-Bright Court*.

Porter attended the Bread Loaf Writers' Conference and was a regional winner in Granta's Best Young American Novelist competition. She has taught English and writing at Milton Academy and Emerson College, both in Massachusetts, and at Southern Illinois University at Carbondale. She now lives in Pittsburgh.

Porter was a regular patron of the bookmobile when she was growing up and avidly read books by Lois Lensky and Beverly Cleary. She once declared to her mother that she wanted to become a writer. "My mother didn't pay me any attention," she remembered for reporter V.R. Peterson in *Essence*. "She was cooking." Porter had the opportunity to offer her own story recipe for middle readers with the American Girl Addy Walker series about a nine-year-old slave girl growing up on a North Carolina plantation during the Civil War era. After her father and older brother are sold, Addy and her mother escape through a series of safe houses until they are able to settle in relative security in Philadelphia. The books were recognized with the 1994 International Reading Association Children's Award and the Children's Book Council's Choice Award. Later book themes echo the American Girl company's family of publications set in various time periods in American history.

"I wanted children to see African-American people as part of strong, loving families, caught up in slavery, doing what they had to do to survive," Porter said on the Children's Literature Web site. *Publishers Weekly* noted *Meet Addy* was among the ten best-selling new children's books of 1993.

Porter did considerable research before she began the Addy series. She also gave a lot of thought to her own family members of generations past, their trials, sacrifices, bravery, and hard work. "I wanted these books to be a tribute to them, so I dedicated the first Addy books to my grandmothers," she said on the Kids Reads Web site.

"The biggest challenge of the Addy books was trying to explain a very complex idea—slavery—to younger readers. I also wanted the books to be entertaining; I didn't want to bore kids to death with information," she added.

Porter's second adult novel, *Imani All Mine*, is an insightful portrayal of fifteen-year-old Tasha Dawson and her baby daughter Imani as they cope with school, poverty and the ghetto in the 1990s. While Tasha may sound stereotypical, she isn't to the author's mind: "Never have I lost sight of the fact that as a child, because of my class and color," she said on her Houghton Mifflin Web page, "some people actually did stereotype me as doomed to fail. . . . Of course, I'm talking about a time twenty-five, thirty years in the past, but I don't feel much of a shift in attitude today."

Works by the Author

All-Bright Court (1991)
Imani All Mine (1998)

Fiction for Middle Readers

American Girls Addy Walker Series

Meet Addy: An American Girl (1993)
Addy Learns a Lesson: A School Story (1993)
Addy's Surprise: A Christmas Story (1993)
Happy Birthday, Addy! A Springtime Story (1993)
Addy Saves the Day: A Summer Story (1994)
Changes for Addy: A Winter Story (1994)
High Hopes for Addy (1999)
Addy's Little Brother (2000)
Addy's Wedding Quilt (2001)
Addy's Story Collection (2001), includes first six books

Addy Studies Freedom (2002)
Addy's Summer Place (2003)

Contributor

Gumbo: A Literary Rent Party to Benefit the Hurston/Wright Foundation (2002), edited by Marita Golden and E. Lynn Harris

For Further Information

Connie Porter biography, *Children's Literature. http://www.childrenslit.com/ f_connieporter.htm* (viewed Aug. 10, 2006).

Connie Porter biography, *KidsReads.com. http://www.kidsreads.com/authors/ au-porter-connie.asp* (viewed Aug. 10, 2006).

Connie Porter biography, *Uncrowned Queens. http://wings.buffalo.edu/ uncrownedqueens/files_2003/porter_connie.htm* (viewed Aug. 10, 2006).

Connie Rose Porter biography, Houghton Mifflin Web site. *http://www. houghtonmifflinbooks.com/catalog/authordetail.efm?textType=interviews& authorID=1244* (viewed Aug. 10, 2006).

Connie Porter interview, *Read In. http://www.readin.org/authors/archives/ 1997/porter.html* (viewed Feb. 14, 2005).

Connie (Rose) Porter entry, Contemporary Authors Online, Gale, 2005. Reproduced in Biography Resource Center, Farmington Hills, MI: Thomson Gale, 2005. *http://galenet.galegroup.com/servlet/BioRC.*

Connie Rose Porter interview, Houghton Mifflin Web site. *http://www. houghtonmifflinbooks.com/readers_guides/porter.shtml* (viewed Aug. 10, 2006).

Cornish, Sam, review of *All-Bright Court, Ploughshares* (fall 1991).

Meet Addy review, *Publishers Weekly* (July 5, 1993).

Peterson, V. R., "Connie Porter: Writing about Home," *Essence* (September 1991).

Jeffrey A. Poston

Western

Benchmark Title: *A Man Called Trouble*

Date and location of birth unknown

Photo credit: Courtesy of the author

About the Author and the Author's Writing

The proliferation of paperback Western series in the 1970s introduced a wide range of lawmen, bounty hunters, mountain men, ranchers, outlaws, vaqueros, cowgirls, Native Americans—even a magician detective and kung fu cattle ropers. But African American cowboys, despite their sizable numbers historically, were scarce in literature, and only appeared at the hands of white wordsmiths such as William R. Cox's Coco Bean in his Buchanan books (written under the penname Jonas Ward), Douglas Thorne's Whitton in his Rancho Bravo series, and Strong in J. D. Sandon's pseudonymous British series, The Gringos.

Today Hiram King and Charles Goodman have given voice to range riders of African descent, and so has Jeffrey Poston.

A former literary agent, Poston works as an advocate for youth literacy as executive director of Write-Read-Succeed. "Writing and reading are the fundamental skills for success," he asserted in a news story in *New Mexico Business Weekly*. His life testifies to that statement.

Poston is an amateur historian who knew when he first began writing his revisionist Westerns he would have to be dead-on with details. His writing, he said on his Web page, "dispels a lot of previously accepted roles of blacks in history." He also notes that *The Peacekeeper* is the only Western novel written by an African American and featuring an African American hero to be published by a major New York publisher (Walker; the first book had been published by Holloway House).

Poston said he was the only African American at a conference of Western writers, and another author suggested he should wear a cowboy outfit to look the part. He replied that he was a writer (and city-bred at that), not a cowboy.

Poston describes some of his historical findings on his Web site, including the estimate that including settlements of freed slaves in Texas and Oklahoma, "as many as one in three cowboys were black cowboys." There were also all-black towns and black-owned ranches and farms. "The freed slaves that migrated west had to go somewhere and do something," he wrote. "Some took jobs in ranching and farming, and some made jobs by starting ranches and farms. Some developed settlements that became incorporated towns with almost exclusively black populations. There were dozens of 'black towns' that sprang up across the frontier between 1870 and 1900, and almost a dozen survived into the early 20th century."

Poston's novels have been praised by members of the Western-writing community including authors Elmer Kelton and Norman Zollinger.

His series protagonist is Jason Peares, a half-black, half-white reformed outlaw who doesn't have to go out of his way to find trouble—it finds him. In *The Peacekeeper,* with his work on a cattle drive ended, the hero reluctantly signs on as lawman in Bronco, Texas, and ends up in a homestead war. His interest in the pretty Marabelle Hopkins soon determines which side he will land on.

In *A Man Called Trouble*, Jay Peares repays a debt owed the woman who cleared him of killing charges years before. In *Gallagher*, he helps defend a Colorado town against the menacing Strange Scalpers. Even as Pinkerton operatives are on his path in *Courage on Trial*, the hero falls for a seductive French woman. In The Indeh, Peares hires on with Buffalo Soldiers in New Mexico.

Poston has shown determination—and a facility with history—in bringing the black hero into the sagebrush setting.

Works by the Author

Jason Peares Series

A Man Called Trouble (1992)
The Peacekeeper (1997)
Gallagher
Courage on Trial
The Indeh (2005)

For Further Information

"PNM Foundation Donates Writing and Reading Program Grant," *New Mexico Business Weekly* (Feb. 12, 2004).
Jeffrey Poston Web site. *http://www.jeffreyposton.com* (viewed Aug. 10, 2006).

Francis Ray

Romance, Suspense, Historical Literature, Mainstream Contemporary Literature

Benchmark Title: *The Turning Point*

Texas

1944

Photo credit: Courtesy of the author

About the Author and the Author's Writing

Francis Ray's novels have consistently drawn praise. Eric Jerome Dickey, for instance, said the author "creates characters and stories that we all love to read about. Her stories are written from the heart."

Born in Texas in 1944, Ray still lives in the Lone Star State with her husband and daughter. She is a graduate of Texas Woman's University and works as a school nurse practitioner with the Dallas Independent School District.

She wrote and sold sixteen confession stories to publications such as *Black Romance* magazine. After reading and enjoying Kathleen Woodiwiss's *Shanna*, she decided to write a novel. "The book captivated me," she told a *Wonderful Women and Men of Color* interviewer. "I didn't know such wonderful love stories existed. The next day I went out and bought every book I could find by her. By the third book I knew I wanted to create similar stories of monogamous relationships with strong, sensitive, and dependable men and the equally strong, caring and independent women they loved."

Once she found a publisher for her first manuscript, Ray continued to represent herself through nine more books and four novellas for collections. Her first imprint, Odyssey, a pioneer in bringing out romances specifically for the black market, went out of business after her first book, and she had to find other book publishers. Her decision in 1999 to move into mainstream fiction prompted her to engage an agent.

Some of Ray's plots come from actual experiences, such as *The Turning Point*, which grew from her macular surgery and slower-than-anticipated recovery. She created the character of ace neurosurgeon Adam Wakefield, who fears he is going blind.

Lilly Crawford, another featured character, is dealing with her own issue of suddenly being penniless.

Once she has her characters in mind, the author said, she generally writes a description of several pages, then comes up with a "what if?"

"Since I try to start each book with conflict," she told Alvin Romer, "I have to know why my characters act or don't react, what makes them who they are. I pay particular attention to their childhood. I strongly believe that this is where we are shaped."

Ray found an unusual plot twist for *I Know Who Holds Tomorrow*. After the loss of her child, television talk show host Madison Reed finds herself withdrawn from her TV correspondent husband Wes Reed. When Wes and a woman companion die in a car accident, Wes reveals in his last breath that he has been unfaithful to Madison and has a nine-month-old daughter. Overwhelmed, Madison struggles with Wes's last request—to raise the other woman's child.

Ray's novels sometimes require a good deal of research, such as *Until There Was You*, for which the author had to learn about the Santa Fe Highway Patrol, and *The Turning Point,* for which she consulted a head trauma specialist. Even though she has a full-time job, she generally can complete a novel in four months, a novella for an anthology in three weeks.

The author said she believes the publishing industry has come to recognize the market for her type of book. "I feel my greatest accomplishment has been creating stories that touch people's lives and impact them in a positive way," she said in a Romance in Color interview. "African-Americans do have love and romance in their lives, and we do live happily ever after."

Works by the Author

Fiction

Fallen Angel (1992)
The Bargain (1995)
Undeniable (1995)
Incognito (1997)
Silken Betrayal (1997)
The Turning Point (2001)
I Know Who Holds Tomorrow (2002)
Someone Knocking at My Door (2003)
Like the First Time (2004)
Troubles Don't Always Last (2004)
Any Rich Man Will Do (2005)
Solid Soul (2006)
Irresistible You (2007)
In Another Man's Bed (2007)

Taggart/Falcon/Grayson Series

Forever Yours (1994)
Only Hers (1996)

Heart of the Falcon (1998)
Break Every Rule (1998)
Until There Was You (1999)
Falcon Saga (2004) omnibus
You and No Other (2005)
Dreaming of You (2006)

Anthologies and Collections

Spirit of the Season (1994)
Winter Nights (1998)
Rosie's Curl and Weave (1999)
Della's House of Style (2000)
Welcome to Leo's (2000)
Going to the Chapel (2001)
Gettin' Merry (2002)
Living Large (2003)
First Touch (2004), with Sandra Kitt and Eboni Snoe
Chocolate Kisses (2006), with Maryann Reid and Renee Luke

Television Movies Based on the Author's Work

Incognito

For Further Information

"Author of the Month—Francis Ray," *Romance in Color. http://www. romanceincolor.com/authormthray.htm* (viewed Aug. 5, 2006).

Francis Ray interview, *Wonderful Women and Men of Color Page. http://www .geocities.com/bellesandbeaux/Ray.html* (viewed June 2, 2003).

Francis Ray Web page. *http://www.francisray.com/bio.htm* (viewed Aug. 5, 2006).

I Know Who Holds Tomorrow review, *Publishers Weekly* (April 29, 2002).

I Know Who Holds Tomorrow review, *Reading Group Guides. http://www. readinggroupguides.com/guides3/i_know_who_holds_tommorow1.asp* (viewed June 5, 2003).

Osborne, Gwendolyn, review of *Break Every Rule, The Romance Reader. http:// www.theromancereader.com/ray-break.html* (viewed Aug. 5, 2006).

Peacock, Scot, ed., Francis Ray entry, *Contemporary Authors*, Vol. 180. Detroit: Gale Research, 2000.

Ramsdell, Kristen, review of *Until There Was You, Library Journal* (Aug. 1999).

Romer, Alvin, Francis Ray interview. *http://myshelf.com/haveyouheard/01/ ray.htm* (viewed Aug. 5, 2006).

Winter Nights review, *Publishers Weekly* (Oct. 26, 1998).

Ishmael Reed

Mainstream Contemporary Literature, Poetry

Benchmark Title: *Mumbo Jumbo*

Chattanooga, Tennessee

1938

About the Author and the Author's Writing

Ishmael Scott Reed is innovative, dynamic, challenging, and controversial.

"Praised for his irreverence and his postmodern experimentation early on in his career," observed Samuel Ludwig, "he was later criticized as a misogynist for some of his opinions . . . and as a bourgeois apologist for his praise of a black middle-class work ethic and his satirical exposure of empty radical rhetoric. . . . Nowadays, Ishmael Reed is well respected by the scholarly establishment and his literary achievements are unquestioned."

That statement is not an exaggeration. Reed has won a National Endowment for the Humanities fellowship and a Guggenheim Award and was twice nominated for a National Book Award.

"I see life as mysterious, holy, profound, exiting, serious, and fun," he is quoted in the *Heath Anthology of American Literature*.

The author is not easily pigeonholed; he as often challenges black literary traditions as white ones. His first novel, *The Freelance Pallbearers* in 1967, parodied Ralph Ellison's *Invisible Man*. "For Reed to be seen as satirizing the black literary tradition in a period of Black Power and the long overdue recuperation and reassessment of that very tradition was not likely to endear him to either white liberals or black cultural nationalists," observed Robert Elliot Fox in *The Oxford Companion to African American Literature*.

Reed was born in 1938 in Chattanooga, Tennessee, with Cherokee, Irish and African ancestry. He grew up in a working class neighborhood in Buffalo, New York. He wrote a jazz music column for a regional newspaper, the *Empire State Weekly*. He attended the University of New York at Buffalo. In New York City, he established an independent newspaper, the *East Village Other*, and wrote his first novel. In 1968 he relocated to Oakland, California. Reed has actively participated in the publication of *Quilt* volumes, which were devoted to minority literature; and in the Before Columbus Foundation, which promotes the work of unknown black and other ethnic writers.

266

Associated with several major universities, Reed is now a senior lecturer at the University of California at Berkeley. Twice married, he has three children. His second wife, Carla Blank, collaborated with him on the bicentennial play, *The Lost State of Franklin.*

Reed has also crafted a literary theory that he called the Neo-Hoodoo Aesthetic. African Hoodoo essentially absorbs the most useful of other beliefs and moral systems to strengthen its own folk origins and enable its adherents to find empowerment in a supernatural force to overcome stultifying social conditions. As this translates into literature, Reed employs a certain argot and rhythm—absorbed from classical literature or street jargon—to take a new slant on things. Strong on parody, Reed's *Yellow Back Radio Broke-Down* jabs at Western fiction (the hero is the Loop Garoo Kid, a black werewolf). *Flight to Canada* jibes slave narratives.

And *Mumbo Jumbo*, probably Reed's most well-known work, upends detective novels. "In the course of the narrative, Reed constructs his history of the true Afro-American aesthetic and parallels the uniting of Afro-American oral tradition, folklore, art, and history with a written code, a text, a literate recapitulation of history and practice," suggests Contemporary Authors Online.

Reed stands strong for the black male, who is in much of the world a pariah. "That also gives you an advantage," Reed told interviewer Reginald Martin. "Because there's a certain desperation, a certain creativeness, originality, that comes from being at the bottom. A lot of our great art comes from the Afro-American male experience. Just think of all the great male jazz musicians. They're innovators, these guys are hungry."

Works by the Author

The Freelance Pallbearers (1967)
Yellow Back Radio Broke-Down (1969)
Mumbo Jumbo (1972)
Neo-HooDoo Manifesto (1972)
The Last Days of Louisiana Red (1974)
Flight to Canada (1976)
Reckless Eyeballing (1986)
Japanese by Spring (1993)

Terrible Trilogy

The Terrible Twos (1982)
The Terrible Threes (1989)

Contributor

Nommo: An Anthology of Modern Black African and Black American Literature (1972)
Cutting Edges: Young American Fiction for the '70s (1973)
Superfiction: or, The American Story Transformed: An Anthology (1975)

Poetry

Conjure: Selected Poems, 1963–1970 (1972)
Chattanooga: Poems (1973)
Secretary to the Spirits (1978)
New and Collected Poetry (1988)
New ands Collected Poems 1964-2006 (2006)

Contributor

American Poets in 1976 (1976)

Editor

From Totems to Hip-Hop (2003)

Drama

The Lost State of Franklin (1976), with Carla Blank and Suzushi Hanayagi
Hell Hath No Fury (1980)
Savage Wilds (1988)
Hubba City (1988)
The Preacher and the Rapper (1994)

Nonfiction

Shrovetide in Old New Orleans (1978)
God Made Alaska for the Indians: Selected Essays (1982)
Writing Is Fighting: Thirty-Seven Years of Boxing on Paper (1988), revised and
    expanded as *Writing Is Fighting: Forty-three Years of Boxing on Paper*
    (1998)
Tell My Horse: Voodoo and Life in Haiti and Jamaica (1990)
Airing Dirty Laundry (1993)
Oakland Rhapsody: The Secret Soul of an American Downtown (1994), with
    Richard Nagler
The Reed Reader (2000)
Another Day at the Front: Dispatches from the Race War (2002)
Blues City: A Walk in Oakland (2003)

Contributor

Amistad I: Writings on Black History and Culture (1970)
The Black Aesthetic (1971)

Editor

19 Necromancers from Now (1970)
Yardbird Lives! (1978), with Al Young
Calafia: The California Poetry (1979)

Before Columbus Foundation Fiction Anthology: Selections from the American Book Awards 1980–1990 (1992), with Kathryn Trueblood and Shawn Wong

Multi-American: Essays on Cultural Wars and Cultural Peace (1997)

African-American Literature: A Brief Introduction & Anthology (1997), with Al Young

Asian-American Literature: A Brief Introduction & Anthology (1997), with Shawn Wong

Hispanic-American Literature: A Brief Introduction & Anthology (1997), with Nicolas Kanellos

Written as Emmett Coleman

The Rise, Fall, and . . . of Adam Clayton Powell (1967)

For Further Information

Boccia, Michael, Ishmael Reed entry, *Heath Anthology of American Literature.* *http://college.hmco.com/english/lauter/heath/4e/students/author_pages/ contemporary/reed_is.html* (viewed Aug. 6, 2006).

Fox, Robert Elliot, Ishmael Reed entry, *Oxford Companion to African American Literature.* William L. Andrews, Frances Smith Foster, and Trudier Harris, eds. New York: Oxford University Press, 1997.

Ishmael Reed entry, Contemporary Authors Online, Gale, 2005. Reproduced in Biography Resource Center. Farmington Hills, MI: Thomson Gale, 2005. *http://galenet.galegroup.com/servlet/BioRC* (viewed Feb. 26, 2005).

Ludwig, Samuel, Ishmael Reed entry, *Literary Encyclopedia. http://www. litencyc.com/php/speople.php?rec=true&UID=3731* (viewed Aug. 6, 2006).

Martin, Reginald, "An Interview with Ishmael Reed," July 1983, Center for Book Culture.org. *http://www.centerforbookculture.org/interviews/interview_ reed.html* (viewed Aug. 6, 2006).

Singh, Amritjit, and Bruce Dick, *Conversations with Ishmael Reed,* Jackson: University Press of Mississippi, 1995.

John Ridley

Mystery, Science Fiction, Urban Literature, Mainstream Contemporary Literature

Benchmark Title: *Stray Dogs*

Milwaukee, Wisconsin

1965

Photo credit: Courtesy of the author

About the Author and the Author's Writing

Comedian, screenwriter, producer, actor, director. John Ridley is all these and also a novelist.

Ridley, already writing movie screenplays and scripts for television comedies such as *The John Laroquette Show* and *The Fresh Prince of Bel-Air*, yet with time available, decided to try his hand at novels. *Stray Dogs* was his first. Although none of its characters was identifiably black, Ridley made sure in subsequent works that it was obvious they were African American. *Stray Dogs* is about a Las Vegas gambler who gets caught up in a double-cross. It was filmed as *U-Turn*. Ridley's next books were *Love Is a Racket,* about a conman trying to wiggle out of debt, and *Everybody Smokes in Hell*, a look at music hustle and murder in Hollywood.

Ridley was born in Milwaukee in 1965. He received a bachelor's degree from New York University. After struggling with stand-up comedy in New York, he went to Hollywood to write scripts. That blossomed into other roles in television and motion picture production. He is married to Gayle Yoshida, a script coordinator and professional gambler.

Recent writing assignments for Ridley have been with NBC's *Third Watch* (for which he was also a supervising producer), the UPN drama *Platinum,* and the animated series *Undercover Brother.*

Ridley's directing credits include *Cold around the Heart,* which he also wrote. The author has said there are always problems with movie production. He wrote the initial script for *Three Kings,* for example, but it was enormously changed (not the least, the lead character was supposed to be black, not white) and Ridley received only a "story by" credit. "The difference between writing books and movies is like the difference between flying and crawling over broken glass," the writer told Benjamin Svetkey for *Entertainment Weekly*. "Screenplays are just really, truly hard." Novels, by comparison, are easy, or at least allow more artistic control, says Ridley.

His novel *A Conversation with the Mann* is set in the 1950s and 1960s and depicts a stand-up comic, Jackie Mann, who followed Ridley's own early career path—only in a different time period. "As a stand-up comedian I had a love of the history of stand-up comedy," the author told Dan Epstein for *Spike* magazine. "It was fun to create a world that was both fictional and real at the same time. Jackie Mann meets real luminaries like Frank Sinatra which is fun for me to go back and write real life characters that I have a fascination for and make them a part of the story." The decade it took him to write the book, Ridley said, allowed him to do deeper research and strengthen its sociological overtones.

The Drift, also released in 2002, rides the rails with contemporary hobo Brain Nigger Charlie, who tries to help a friend's niece break her drug habit and find a decent life. Little does he anticipate having to face a power-mad neo-Nazi and a Hispanic serial killer.

Ridley's recent *Those Who Walk in Darkness* is a futuristic story about a Los Angeles tactical police officer, "Bullet" O'Rourke, who tries to bring a semblance of order to a world of superhuman criminals. Will her ill-advised shooting of a healing woman bring on a last clash between humans and mutants? "The cinematic writing style, fast plot, and loose dialog construction make for quick visual reading," said reviewer Devon Thomas. "Part noir thriller and part sf dystopia, this is a timely entry on the hate and fear that fuel war."

With his versatility, Ridley's writing future is wide open with possibilities.

Works by the Author

Stray Dogs (1997)
Love Is a Racket (1998)
Everybody Smokes in Hell (1999)
A Conversation with the Mann (2002)
The Drift (2002)
Those Who Walk in Darkness (2003)
What Fire Cannot Burn (2005)

Screenplays

U-Turn (1997), adapted from *Stray Dogs*
Cold around the Heart (1997), also director
Undercover Brother (2002), with Michael McCullers
Three Kings by David O. Russell (1999), based on Ridley's story
Undercover Brother (2002), with Michael McCullers
Those Who Walk in Darkness (2003)
Positively Fifth Street (2005)
Let Me Take You Down (2005)

For Further Information

Conversation with the Mann review, *Publishers Weekly* (April 8, 2002).

Drift review, *Publishers Weekly* (Aug. 26, 2002).

Epstein, Dan, "A Real Comedian," *Spike* magazine. *http://www.spikemagazine. com/1002johnridley.php* (viewed Aug. 6, 2006).

John Ridley biography, *Now with Bill Moyers* Web page. *http://www. pbs.org/now/politics/ridley.html* (viewed Aug. 6, 2006).

John Ridley entry, Contemporary Authors Online, Gale, 2005. Reproduced in Biography Resource Center. Farmington Hills, MI: Thomson Gale, 2005. *http://galenet.galegroup.com/servlet/BioRC* (viewed Aug. 6, 2006).

John Ridley entry, *Internet Movie Database. http://www.imdb.com/name/ nm0725983/* (viewed April 19, 2005).

John Ridley Web page. *http://www.twbookmark.com/authors/0/2475* (viewed Aug. 6, 2006).

Svetkey, Benjamin, "Easy Writer: He Wrote the Original *Three Kings* Screenplay, So Why Didn't John Ridley Get the Credit?" *Entertainment Weekly* (Oct. 8, 1999).

Thomas, Devon, *Those Who Walk in Darkness* review, *Library Journal* (June 1, 2003).

Kimberla Lawson Roby

Inspirational Literature, Women's Literature

Benchmark Title: *Too Much of a Good Thing*

Rockford, Illinois

1965

About the Author and the Author's Writing

The veteran of several national book tours, you'd hardly imagine best-selling author Kimberla Lawson Roby self-published her first inspirational romance. She brought out *Behind Closed Doors* on her own Lenox Press imprint. It was a Blackboard bestseller for four months in 1997 and earned a First-Time Author Award from Chicago's Black History Month Book Fair and Conference. That was more than sufficient to attract the attention of an established publishing house.

Roby was born in 1965 in Rockford, Illinois, where she and her husband, Will, reside. She is former co-host of The Wordplayers Club, a monthly radio book club for WKPO in Janesville, Wisconsin.

She said she admires a number of writers, among them Terry McMillan, Connie Briscoe, Eric Jerome Dickey, Barbara Delinsky, Danielle Steel, and Walter Mosley. She encourages aspiring writers to put words down every day, whether in a manuscript or diary.

The author has woven diverse themes into her novels. *"Behind Closed Doors* is about gambling addiction and infidelity; *Here and Now* looks at single motherhood and sibling rivalry. *A Taste of Reality* centers on racial discrimination in the workplace with subplots dealing with gender discrimination, friendship betrayal, and marital infidelity," she said in a *Sisters of Romance Magazine* interview.

"I always write about very real issues," she elaborated in a conversation with PeopleWhoLoveGoodBooks.com, "those that can or have affected everyone some time or another. Some of my topics are controversial and even taboo, but I am inspired by what I see happening to others and in some cases what I have experienced personally."

A graduate of Cardinal Stritch University with a bachelor of arts degree in business administration, cum laude, Roby was working in community development in Rockford when she began writing fiction in 1995. She only received rejection letters from the major publishers and agents she submitted samples to. With the encouragement of her mother and her husband, and her own business background, she brought out the book *Behind Closed Doors* on her own and sold 10,000 copies in the first six months.

"I knew that if we keyed in on the Black market, the book would be successful," she said in an article she wrote for *Essence*. "We scheduled a major tour of about 12 cities that focused on doing book signings at Black bookstores. We held signings at Black churches, and at sorority and fraternity houses."

Roby said in an interview with Black Book Network that she anchors her characters in reality, whether the upper middle-class best friends of *Behind Closed Doors* or the struggling single parent in *Here and Now*. "Marcella is an example of so many women in America," she said, "that's why I created her character. Then there's the other sister, Racquel, who basically has everything, the American dream. But at the same time, she's not able to have children—the thing she wants most."

One Roby character was too good to forget. The charismatic, if roguish pastor, Curtis Black, has appeared in two books and is destined for a third, according to the author. In something of a twist on traditional inspirational works, Roby, a Baptist, believes there is some corruption to be found in the church. She said she expected more negative reaction than she ended up getting. In fact, letters from spouses of clergymen inspired her to write the sequel, *Too Much of a Good Thing*, which a *Publishers Weekly* reviewer called "about being bad but making good."

Roby has brought a strong voice to inspirational fiction.

Works by the Author

Behind Closed Doors (1997)
Here and Now (1999)
Casting the First Stone (1999)
It's a Thin Line (2001)
A Taste of Reality (2003)
Too Much of a Good Thing (2004), sequel to *Casting the First Stone*
The Best-Kept Secret (2005)
Changing Faces (2006)
Lovers and Lies (2007)

For Further Information

Kimberla Lawson Roby entry, Contemporary Authors Online, Gale, 2005. Reproduced in Biography Resource Center. Farmington Hills, MI: Thomson Gale, 2005. *http://galenet.galegroup.com/servlet/BioRC* (viewed Feb. 25, 2005).

Kimberla Lawson Roby interview, *BlackBookNetwork.com*. *http://www.blackbooknetwork.com/interview~roby.htm* (viewed March 31, 2005).

Kimberla Lawson Roby interview, *People Who Love Good Books.* *http://peoplewholuvgoodbook.tripod.com/id15.html* (viewed Aug. 6, 2006).

Kimberla Lawson Roby interview, *Shades of Romance Magazine* (Jan./Feb. 2003). *http://www.sormag.com/14roby.html* (viewed Aug. 6, 2006).

Kimberla Lawson Roby Web page, African American Literature Book Club. *http://authors.aalbc.com/kimberla.htm* (viewed Aug. 6, 2006).

Roby, Kimberla Lawson, "How I Did It," *Essence* (October 1997).

Too Much of a Good Thing review, *Publishers Weekly* (Nov. 24, 2003).

Sister Souljah

Urban Literature, Memoir

Benchmark Title: *The Coldest Winter Ever*

Bronx, New York

1964

About the Author and the Author's Writing

Lisa Williamson was born in the Bronx, New York, in 1964, to an impoverished family. She had no hint of what would become a whirlwind of creative activity.

Longing to overcome the destitution of being on welfare, she worked hard as a student, doing extra research when she felt insufficient attention was being given in history class to African Americans. She became a legislative intern. She won an American Legion Constitutional Oratory Contest. She attended Cornell University's Advanced Summer Program on scholarship and spent a semester abroad at the University of Salamanca in Spain. At Rutgers University, she majored in American history and African studies, wrote for the student newspaper and spoke out on campus for social justice.

The future author and activist began a varied career: as an organizer and program developer for the Rev. Benjamin Chavis of the United Church of Christ Commission for Racial Justice. Working at a medical center, she helped the impoverished in Zimbabwe and in refugee camps in Mozambique. Back in this country, she was among those at the podium at the Million Women March in Philadelphia.

As executive director of Sean "Puffy" Combs's Daddy's House Social Programs, she lectures widely to young black women. At the University of Rochester in 2005, she told an audience in her typical fashion, "It is possible for you to be academically advanced and culturally retarded," and entreated the women students to empower themselves by returning to the female ideal from African, not current American, culture.

Williamson recorded a hip-hop record as Sister Souljah. On her CD *360 Degrees of Power* she rapped that blacks were at war with whites. In 1992, she remarked to the *Washington Post,* "If black people kill black people every day, why not take a week and kill white people?" After saying this, she later elaborated in the *New Republic*, that "she was expressing not her own views but the views of a black person who ordinarily kills black people. 'I was just telling the writer that . . . if a person would kill their own brother, or a baby in a drive-by, or a grandmother, what would make white people think that [he] wouldn't kill them, too?' "

Whatever her intention, Bill Clinton, then running for the Democratic nomination for president, did what has come to be known as the Sister Souljah Moment. At one of

Jesse Jackson's Rainbow Coalition events, Clinton deviated from his usual liberal message to blast the rap performer for promoting a cycle of hatred. Clinton's statement separated him from the rest of the candidates, separated him politically from Jackson, and garnered him many Southern white votes. Sister Souljah was unrepentant.

Sister Souljah's first book is the quasi-autobiographical *No Disrespect*. "I never said I was an angel," she wrote. "Nor am I innocent or holy like the Virgin Mary. What I am is natural and serious and as sensitive as an open nerve on an ice cube. I'm a young black sister with an unselfish heart who overdosed on love long ago."

Explaining to *Jet* the circumstances that inspired her political activism, she said, "As a youth organizer, I was always very critical. I felt that adults did not properly train brothers and sisters to be able to understand their purpose and role in life. Parents had a habit of trying to raise their children off of slogans, like 'do the right thing' or 'be a good boy.'"

The author's coming-of-age novel *The Coldest Winter Ever* is credited with sparking a revival of ghetto realism fiction. It is about pampered young Winter Santiago, whose life in a Long Island mansion crumbles when her mother is shot to death and her father is jailed. Winter and her three sisters are placed in foster care. She becomes addicted to drugs, and is arrested for transporting narcotics and sent to jail for fifteen years. "Sister Souljah herself appears as a character," according to Nancy Pearl in *Library Journal*, "urging Winter and other young black women to stand up to the men in their lives, abstain from drugs, and practice safe sex."

Sister Souljah writes in a hip-hop, vernacular style of urban drugs, sex, crime, disjointed relationships. It's no wonder many find her controversial. The author scoffed to reporter Cindy Fuchs, "America still has a lot of unspoken racial laws. Saying what you think if you're black is still considered uppity."

Works by the Author

No Disrespect (1995)
The Coldest Winter Ever (1999)

For Further Information

Bowman, James, "Plain Brown Rappers," *National Review* (July 20, 1992).

Coldest Winter Ever review, *Literature, Arts, and Medicine Database*. http://endeavor. med/nyu.edu/lit-med/lit-med-db.webdocs.webdescrips/souljah12022-des. html (viewed Feb. 25, 2005).

Elder, Sean, *Coldest Winter Ever* review, *Salon Books*. http://www.salon.com/ books/review/1999/04/12/souljah/ (viewed Aug. 6, 2006).

Fuchs, Cindy, Sister Souljah interview, *Philadelphia City Paper* (May 20, 1999).

Kinsley, Michael, "Speaking in Tongues," *New Republic* (July 13, 1992).

Miller, Alissa, "Sister Souljah Speaks to Inspire," *Campus Times Online* (University of Rochester) (April 14, 2005). *http://www.campustimes.org/media/ storage/paper371/news/2003/03/20/News/Sister.souljah.Speaks.To. Inspire-396092.shtml?norewrite200608060929&sourcedomain=www. campustimes.org* (viewed Aug. 6, 2006).

Mitchen, Tameeka, Sister Souljah biography, *Harlemlive.org. http://www.harlemlive.org/shethang/profiles/sistahsouljah/souljah.html* (viewed Feb. 25, 2005).

Pearl, Nancy, review of *Coldest Winter Ever*, *Library Journal* (April 15, 1999).

Sister Souljah biography, Lycos Music. *http://music.lycos.com/artist/bio.asp?QT=A&QW=Sister+Souljah&AN=Sister+Souljah&MID=54114&MH=* (viewed April 20, 2005).

Sister Souljah biography, *Voices from the Gaps. http://voices./cla.umn.edu/newsite/authors/SOULJAHsister.htm* (viewed Feb. 28, 2005).

Sister Souljah entry, *St. James Encyclopedia of Popular Culture*. Detroit: St. James Press, 2000.

"Sister Souljah Tells Her Life Story in New Book, *No Disrespect*," *Jet* (Feb. 27, 1995).

Sister Souljah Web site. *http://www.sistersouljah.com/pages/2/pages2.html?refresh=1112302862706* (viewed April 20, 2005).

Younis, Saleh A.A., "Demarcation of Eritrean Politics," *Awate.com. http://www.awate.com/artman/publish/article_3926.shtml* (viewed Aug. 6, 2006).

Eboni Snoe

Women's Literature

Benchmark Title: *A Sheik's Spell*

Date and location of
birth not revealed

Photo credit: Courtesy of the author

About the Author and the Author's Writing

Danielle Steel's got nothin' on Eboni Snoe, who matches the queen of literary glitz with her own fictional scheming women, brutish men, opulent settings and wild plots.

Snoe's first novel, *A Sheik's Spell*, is about hydrologist Felicia's struggle to reconcile her western upbringing with the different ways of the oh-so-passionate (and royal) Berber Ra'im Raoul Rahman.

With that novel, Snoe helped launch Kensington Publishing's Arabesque imprint in 1994, a series featuring African American characters. Her second book, *Beguiled*, was the first Arabesque title to go to a second printing. (The book line became so successful it was sold to Black Entertainment Television in 1998.)

Eboni Snoe, of course, is not the author's real name. She's really Gwyn F. McGee. She took on the new name to prove a point. "I was told by agents and people in the industry that no one wanted to read about black people in romantic relationships," she told Fahizah Alim. "And I was told by African Americans that I should be writing about serious matters, anyway."

That made her all the more determined. As she explained on her Web site, "I decided I wanted people to know, Black people, people of color, were missing from novels that simply held a story that a reader could get lost in for imagination's sake."

Thus the imaginative penname—placing side-by-side the ends of the racial spectrum to make a point: Her stories are inclusive.

"With black people, you picked up books with white people on the covers all the time," she told reporter Christy Karras. "I want people to know that yes these books have black people in them, and they're for white people as well as black people."

Snoe adores heroines who are adventurous, fearless, and are still looking to find themselves. The popular Legend of the Stone Keeper series matches Sienna Russell with the love of her life, Hennessey "Hawk" Jackson, as they encounter intrigue in such locations as Martinique, Costa Rica and Kaua'i.

As have many writers before and since, Snoe wrote the type of novel she wanted to read but couldn't locate. Finding the books became something of an issue when, the author explained, two of her books, *Wishin' on a Star* and *Followin' a Dream*, were characterized as general fiction and shelved separate from her earlier romances. Other stores placed them in their African American sections. Her recent *When Everything's Said and Done* is again and with certainty labeled mainstream fiction.

That book looks at the Robinson sisters: brainy Brenda, wild middle child Cora, and protected baby sister Annette, their relationship with each other, and their love for the same man. Serving as a one-person Greek chorus is the mystic healer Nebia, who observes all that happens with an all-knowing certainty of tragedy to come.

Carrying through with her Eboni Snoe persona, in personal appearances and publicity photographs the author appears in black and white and wears flamboyant hats, also making a statement about the ability of African Americans to be just as glamorous as anyone else.

A world traveler, Snow was a resident of Guangzhou, China, for a year. She also lived in Tennesse, and worked there in radio and television journalism . She lives in Salt Lake City, Utah, with her husband and their children. She told interviewer Lora McDonald, "I like to explore other cultures and their belief systems. I am a person of deep faith and an explorer of life's mysteries."

Works by the Author

A Sheik's Spell (1992)
Beguiled (1994)
Tell Me I'm Dreamin' (1998)
A Chance on Lovin' You (1999)
Wishin' on a Star (2000)
Followin' a Dream (2001)
More Than You Know (2004)
When Everything's Said and Done (2004)
Something Deep in My Bones (2005)

Legend of the Stone Keeper Series

The Passion Ruby (1995)
Emerald's Fire (1997)
A Diamond Allure (2003)

Arabesque Family Reunion Series

3. *The Ties That Bind* (2002)

Anthology

First Touch (2004), with Sandra Kitt and Francis Ray

For Further Information

Alim, Fahizah, "A Revolution in Romance: Stories with Black Characters Tap into the Booming Literature of Love," *Sacramento Bee* (Nov. 16, 2004).

Eboni Snoe Web site. *http://www.ebonisnoe.com* (viewed Aug. 6, 2006).

Karras, Christy, "The Colorblind Heart: Eboni Snoe Breaks down Racial Barriers in Romance Genre," *Salt Lake Tribune* (Feb. 12, 2005).

McDonald, Lora, "Author of the Month: Eboni Snoe," *Romance Reader's Connection.* *http://www.theromancereadersconnection.com/aotm/authorofthemonthsnoeeboninov04.html* (viewed Aug. 6, 2006).

Vickie M. Stringer

Urban Literature

Benchmark Title: *Let That Be the Reason*

Detroit, Michigan
1970

About the Author and the Author's Writing

From ex-con to publishing CEO, Vickie M. Stringer's journey has been a rapid and fascinating one. The Detroit-born street-hip author told HarlemLive, "I was able to reflect on the decisions I made, passionately put my story on paper and welcomed God into my life. I live without regret because everything happens for a reason."

Born in 1970, the daughter of a school teacher and a General Motors engineer, Victoria M. Stringer attended Western Michigan University for a year, met a man who turned out to be a narcotics dealer, went astray, bore a son, separated, became a madam and dealt drugs, was arrested in 1994, was tried, and went to prison for seven years. While behind bars, she began to write a novel about a woman named Pamela who starts an escort service, falls in love with bad guy Chino and has his child, and is lured into becoming a dealer.

Out of prison, and with a folder full of twenty-six publisher rejections, Stringer borrowed $2,500 and printed 1,000 copies of her book, *Let That Be the Reason*. Accounts vary as to how many copies she sold—one claim is as many as 100,000, a number detractors say is ridiculously high—but in any case, the book came to the attention of the publisher Atria, which bought rights to her second novel, *Imagine This*, a sequel which follows Pamela's life in prison. Soon Stringer's fledgling Triple Crown Publishers was agent for more than a dozen books by other authors such as K'wan, Nikki Turner, Victor Martin, KaShamba Williams, Trustice Gentles, TuShonda Williams, Joylynn Jossel, and Stringer's husband and copublisher, Shannon Holmes.

Triple Crown also revived interest in the ghetto fiction of Donald Goines and Iceberg Slim.

"We know our market," Stringer told *Black Issues Book Review*. "What we write is not urban fiction. It's not street fiction. It's hip-hop. We have addressed an audience that has said to the world, 'This is the music we want to listen to, this is the way we want to dress.' Now they're saying, 'This is what they want to read.' " Stringer's prose has an attitude but with an underlying positive sensibility.

Stringer insists the books have an important mission, even if they at times lack in grammar or plot consistency. Far from being stereotypical, they express reality, she said. Far from glamorizing street life, they set off alarms. About her critics, she told the *Christian Science Monitor,* "They haven't read the book. There's nothing glorifying, because [the main character] goes to jail in the end."

"The mainstream publishers forgot the African-American market, that will buy books that wants to buy books," she told Dinitia Smith for the *New York Times*. "What I wanted to read, you didn't have in your store."

Stringer's gamble paid off. "Now, 'gangsta lit' or 'hip-hop lit' as it's been dubbed, is one of the fastest growing genres in publishing," according to *Maclean's*, "and every major player from Random House to St. Martin's Press is clamoring to get a piece of its fan base—primarily 15- to 25-year-old African Americans. They saw our books on the shelves outselling theirs and suddenly wanted to give my authors multiple book deals,' said Stringer."

Stringer's high-charged assault on the literary world, though just beginning, shows great promise.

Works by the Author

Let That Be the Reason (2002)
Imagine This (2003), sequel to *Let That Be the Reason*
Dirty Red: A Novel (2005)

Nonfiction

How to Succeed in the Publishing Game (2005)

For Further Information

Benoit, Kevin, "Author Vickie Stringer Speaks," *HarlemLive. http://www. harlemlive.org/community/peeps/stringer%20speaks/Stringer.html* (viewed Aug. 6, 2006).

Campbell, Kim, "Gritty 'Street Lit' Makes Noise in the 'Hood," *Christian Science Monitor* (Sept. 9, 2004).

George, Lianne, "Bringing the Bling to the Book Biz," *Maclean's* (July 12, 2004).

Murray, Victoria Christopher, "Triple Crown Winner," *Black Issues Book Review* (May-June 2004).

Reid, Calvin, "Street Publisher Started Small, Thinks Big," *Publishers Weekly* (July 19, 2004).

Smith, Dinitia, "Unorthodox Publisher Animates Hip-Hop Lit," *New York Times* (Sept. 8, 2004).

Mildred D. Taylor

Young Adult Literature

Benchmark Title: *Roll of Thunder, Hear My Cry*

Jackson, Mississippi

1943

About the Author and the Author's Writing

Mildred D. Taylor is a signal writer, in the opinion of critic Robert Con Davis-Undiano in *World Literature Today*: "I mean that she is a writer whose work has marked a huge cultural shift in the lives of many American families who have suffered the indignities of poverty and racial discrimination. Taylor has been the quintessential social critic—better yet, social-studies teacher—introducing morality and social awareness in American schools for almost three decades."

Taylor was one of the first authors to push children's fiction out of the all-white realm. She depicts black family life in the rural South beginning in the 1930s—her family's life, in fact.

"I grew to know the South—to feel the South—through the yearly trips we took there and through the stories told," Taylor said in accepting Boston Globe-Horn Book award in 1988. "In those days, before the civil rights movement, I remember the South and how it was. I remember the racism, the segregation. . . . But I also remember the other South—the South of family and community."

Ironically, when Taylor first began writing her young adult novels, they were criticized by some white parents who denied that such extreme racism could have existed. A quarter-century later, the writer has said she's found it is sometimes black parents who don't want their children to hear the "n" word and the truth about segregation.

Taylor was born in 1943 in Jackson, Mississippi. Her family moved to a newly integrated town in Ohio when she was ten. She was the only black child in her class. She received degrees from University of Toledo and University of Colorado. After graduating, she joined the Peace Corps and spent two years in Ethiopia. She taught English and history, worked as a recruiter, a study skills coordinator, a proofreader, and an editor. Her work resurrected an old urge to write.

"Taylor excelled in school," according to *Children's Books and Their Creators*, "but from an early age realized that the history books she read did not represent the dignity, the courage, and the achievements of the people she knew about from stories told in her family."

In 1977, Taylor's book *Roll of Thunder, Hear My Cry* earned the American Library Association's Newbery Award. Emily R. Moore explained the book "describes a year during which Cassie Logan learns to handle the indignities inflicted upon herself, her family, and neighbors. She also learns the importance of her family's struggle to keep their land and their economic independence. . . . Throughout the book, the reader is moved to tears by Ms. Taylor's vibrant, exquisite, and simple style."

Taylor's young adult prose about the Logan family creates a generations-spanning tapestry. She has said she was long fascinated by the stories told in her family about her great-grandfather, who came out of slavery to buy and work his own land and confront discrimination. "What I have always tried to do in my books," the author told Hazel Rochman, "is to have the reader walk in the shoes of my characters. . . . If they had to go down into a segregated South, as I did as a child, they would know that what I show is the truth."

Taylor's work has not gone unnoticed. She has received the Coretta Scott King Award for young adult fiction three times, for *Let the Circle Be Unbroken* (in which a friend of the Logan family is tried on a murder charge), *The Friendship* (in which Cassie and her brothers learn a lesson in black-white relations), and *The Land* (in which Paul Logan, the son of a slave and her white master, struggles to realize he will never be fully accepted by either family).

" 'A natural writer' is an overused expression I don't particularly like," said Phyllis J. Fogelman in *Horn Book Magazine*, "but in speaking of Mildred Taylor it seems absolutely appropriate. Mildred's words flow smoothly, effortlessly, it seems, and they abound in richness, harmony, and rhythm. Her stories unfold in a full, leisurely way, well suited to and evocative of her Southern settings. Her ability to bring her characters to life and to involve her readers is remarkable."

Taylor's heart-felt depictions of Southern life, which resonate with anecdote and dialect, have earned a permanent spot in most library collections.

Works by the Author

The Gold Cadillac (1987)
The Friendship (1987)

Logan Family Series

Song of the Trees (1975)
Roll of Thunder, Hear My Cry (1976)
Let the Circle Be Unbroken (1981)
Mississippi Bridge (1990)
The Road to Memphis (1990)
The Well: David's Story (1995)

The Land (2001)
Logan (2004)

Television Miniseries Based on the Author's Work

Roll of Thunder, Hear My Cry (1978)

For Further Reading

Davis-Undiano, Robert Con, "Mildred D. Taylor and the Art of Making a Difference," *World Literature Today* (May-Aug. 2004).

Fogelman, Phyllis J., "Mildred D. Taylor," *Horn Book Magazine* (Aug. 1977).

Greenlaw, M. Jean, *A Teacher's Guide to* Song of the Trees, The Friendship *and* The Gold Cadillac *by Mildred D. Taylor*. New York: Bantam Doubleday Dell, no date.

Mildred D. Taylor Web page. *http://www.olemiss.edu/mwp/dir/taylor_mildred/* (viewed Aug. 10, 2006).

Mildred Taylor entry, *Children's Books and Their Creators,* Anita Silvey, ed. Boston: Houghton Mifflin, 1995.

Moore, Emily R., review of *Roll of Thunder, Hear My Cry, Interracial Books for Children Bulletin,* 7, no. 7 (1976).

Rochman, Hazel, Mildred D. Taylor interview, *Booklist. http://archive.ala.org/booklist/v98/se2/69interview.html* (viewed Aug. 10, 2006).

Taylor, Mildred D., Newbery Award acceptance speech, *Horn Book Magazine* (Aug. 1977).

Omar Tyree

Urban Literature, Mainstream Contemporary Literature

Benchmark Title: *Just Say No!*

Philadelphia, Pennsylvania

1969

Photo credit: Courtesy of the author

About the Author and the Author's Writing

Omar Rashad Tyree jumped track after his first year at college. The world lost a potentially great pharmacist and gained a dynamic writer of urban fiction—some of it self-labeled as hardcore—which has found a solid female audience.

Tyree was born in Philadelphia in 1969, and grew up in a strict household with his pharmacist mother and his stepfather. He thrived on Kung fu movies as a youth—and exposure to movies gave him his first inklings of characterization and narrative. Reaching college age, he entered the University of Pittsburgh and majored in pharmaceutical science. He played on the track and football teams. As he began his second year, he became a member of the Phi Eta Sigma honor society and he lost his passion for dosages and bottles.

Tyree scored unusually high on a reading comprehension test and realized he had the urge to express himself. He wrote an article, "The Diary of a Freshman," for a college publication, then enrolled in a writing course. Although he generally disdained classical literature—Richard Wright is his favorite writer—he loved the use of words. In his junior year, Tyree transferred to Howard University in Washington, D.C. and became a journalism major. By the time he graduated in 1991, he had two manuscripts: *Colored, On White Campus* and *Flyy Girl*. With no publishing prospects, he became his own publisher (MARS Productions). The books soon caught the attention of a Simon & Schuster editor, who signed the writer and reissued his self-published books. *Library Journal* said of *Flyy Girl*, "The author captures growing up in the Eighties with a subtle and finely rendered backdrop of songs and mischief reminiscent of the era."

Tyree didn't immediately make a living from his creative writing. After college, he joined the staff of *Capital Spotlight*, in Washington, D.C., and later was chief reporter for *News Dimensions*, another weekly. He also wrote as a free-lancer. Tyree appeared on the pilot for the talk show *For Black Men Only* for Black Entertainment Television (BET) in 1992, and answered questions from host Julian Bond in an episode of *America's Black Forum*. He appears frequently as a college and community lecturer and performance poet. Today he lives in Delaware with his fiancée, Karintha Randall, and their son.

Simon & Schuster has brought out a new Tyree book each year since 1995, and though some titles have made the *New York Times* bestseller list, reviews in that and other periodicals have been rare. Tyree follows pioneering black novelists Iceberg Slim in his portrayal of street life, and Langston Hughes and Zora Neale Hurston in the use of vernacular language. Some reviewers have complained of Tyree's tendency toward didacticism in his prose, but grudgingly notice each work has been better than the one before. A *Kirkus* reviewer, for example, found *A Do Right Man* focused "less on Afrocentric theorizing and more on character—resulting in a good deal more engaging read."

His recent *Leslie* follows the burnout of an intelligent nineteen-year-old when her father loses his high-paying job and the family is plunged into poverty. "I wanted to write a story about a dysfunctional family and poverty and stress and a girl who snaps out of it all," the writer told *Ebony* magazine.

To the author's chagrin, his fiction appeals primarily to women—the same as E. Lynn Harris and Eric Jerome Dickey. "You know how humiliating that is?" he asked, only half jokingly, to interviewer Brett Johnson, who observed, "Throughout his decade-long writing career, Tyree has juggled a balancing act of wanting to increase his male readership while not alienating his female following." Recent American Booksellers Association statistics found that 75 percent of the nearly 10 million black adults who regularly purchased books were female. "It's torture, man," said Tyree, who yearns to reach his male peers.

Tyree's books take on today's issues. "I won the NAACP Image Award for *The Love of Money*, where I broke down the dilemma of art versus money, that we all struggle with as artists," the writer explained in an *Awareness* magazine interview. *Just Say No!*, Tyree explained to theurbangriot.com, is "about two lifelong friends and the hurdles, downfalls, jealousy, success, and triumphs, but also about how insidious drugs are and why it is important that we understand how these rich and seemingly affluent people can fall into this trap. . . . It's universal and it's sad."

His recent *Boss Lady* resumes the story of Tracy Ellison Grant begun in *Flyy Girl*, as the character rises from the Philadelphia streets to the mansions of Hollywood.

In 2001, Tyree received the NAACP Image Award; that same year he took the open alias Urban Griot—though he's not the only one to use the traditional African term (pronounced gree-oh) meaning a wise storyteller—for a new series of contemporary explorations of life on the edge. He hopes these novels, along with a spoken/rap CD, find him a greater audience of men. The plots are a bit edgier, and the recordings give an added musical appeal to the set.

One Crazy-A** Night, typically, is about a black couple trapped and in the hand of white supremacists in rural Pennsylvania. *Cold Blooded* follows gun-for-hire Warren "Molasses" Hamilton's ill-fated flirtation with a dangerous college psychology major, Janeia Goode.

"I'm here to investigate what brothers are feeling," Tyree declared in a blackauthors.com interview. "It's time for African-American literature to regain its masculinity and become less compromising than the character-driven, social-based stories that cater to non-political women readers."

Works by the Author

Fiction

Colored on White Campus: The Education of a Racial World (1992), reissued as
    Battle Zone: The Struggle to Survive the American Institution (1994)
A Do Right Man (1997)
Single Mom (1998)
Sweet St. Louis (2000)
Just Say No! (2001)
Leslie (2002)
Diary of a Groupie (2003)
What They Want: A Novel (2006)

Tracy Ellison Grant Series

Flyy Girl (1993), reissued (1996)
For the Love of Money (2000)
Boss Lady (2005)

Nonfiction

Capital City: The Chronicles of a D.C. Underworld (1994), reissued (1997)

Written as The Urban Griot

Fiction

The Underground (2001)
College Boy (2002)
One Crazy A** Night (2003)
Cold Blooded (2004)

Anthology

Dark Thirst: An Anthology (2004)

For Further Information

"Author Spotlight: Omar Tyree," Ebony (Nov. 2002).
Do Right Man review, Kirkus Review (Oct. 1, 1977).
Johnson, Brett, "Omar Tyree: Raw and Uncut," Black Issues Book Review
    (July-Aug. 2002).

Omar Tyree entry, Contemporary Authors Online. Reproduced in Biography Resource Center. Farmington Hills, Mich. Thomson Gale, 2005. *http://galenet.galegroup.com/servlet/BioRC* (viewed Feb. 26, 2005).

Flyy Girl review, *Library Journal* (Sept. 15, 1996).

Omar Tyree interview, *Awareness* magazine. *http://www.awarenessmagazine.net/ckelly.pdf* (viewed March 4, 2005).

Omar Tyree interview, Black Authors.com. *http://www.blackauthors.com* (viewed March 4, 2005).

Omar Tyree interview, The Urban Griot. *http://www.theurbangriot.com/links/interviewhtm* (viewed March 4, 2005).

Omar Tyree page, African American Literature Book Club. *http://authors.aalbc.com/omartyree.htm* (viewed Aug. 10, 2006).

Alice Walker

Mainstream Contemporary Literature, Poetry

Benchmark Title: *The Color Purple*

Eatonton, Georgia

1944

About the Author and the Author's Writing

Alice Walker's life story is almost unbelievable; she made the unlikely leap from growing up in a sharecroppers' shack to winning the Pulitzer Prize.

Born in 1944, the youngest of eight children of an impoverished family in Eatonton, Georgia, Alice Malsenior Walker at the age of eight was blinded in one eye by an errant BB shot. It didn't slow her education a bit and she became class valedictorian in high school. In fact, it has been suggested her half-eyesight forced Walker to withdraw from her peers and become a keen observer. Thanks to a scholarship, she attended Spelman College for two years and became active in the civil rights movement. She spent her junior year in Africa as an exchange student, then attended Sarah Lawrence College where she completed requirements for a bachelor of arts degree in 1965.

After graduating, Walker worked at everything from voter registration in Georgia to Head Start in Mississippi to the welfare department in New York City as she developed a reputation as a poet and writer. She became writer in residence and Black Studies teacher at Jackson State College in academic year 1968–69 and at Tougaloo College in 1970–71. Walker married Melvyn Leventhal, a Jewish civil rights attorney, and says their struggle as the only interracial couple in the Mississippi town where they lived strained their relationship, and they subsequently divorced. She became close friends with writer Robert Allen, though they did not marry. She currently lives near San Francisco.

In 1972–73, Walker lectured at Wellesley College and the University of Massachusetts, Boston, and was distinguished writer in Afro-American studies at the University of California, Berkley, in 1982. She was Fannie Hurst Professor of Literature at Brandeis University that same year. She has also been a trustee of Sarah Lawrence College.

Her first scribblings, she has said, were as a child on pages of a Sears, Roebuck catalog. She was drawn to poetry, she told interviewer Alvin P. Sarnoff, explaining "I've suffered from depression a lot. The most horrible feeling is not wanting to live and not being able to act. At those times, poetry would come galloping up with the energy of action—the energy to move a pen across the page or to get up and go looking for a pen."

Walker went on to say she treats verse as historical artifact; it is very representative of the time when it was written. Thus she is reluctant to change it after it has been published.

Walker's growing up years permeate her writing. In her prose, Walker from the beginning examined sexual and racial issues within the black community.

The Color Purple is her literary gem, an epistolary work rich in black vernacular and heavy in the oppression of slavery's legacy. Because of its negative depiction of males, the book angered some critics. For starters, fourteen-year-old Celie is repeatedly raped by her stepfather and has two children by him; then she's married off to a violent, cruel husband, Mister. Her salvation is in her relationships with women.

Other critics hailed the work. Debra Walker King in *The Oxford Companion to African American Literature* observed, "It embodies Walker's womanist views without being reduced to a mere platform for ideological rhetoric. In this novel, Walker's writing reveals the transformative power of female bonding and female love." *The Color Purple* won a Pulitzer Prize and the American Book Award.

Still, the book's depiction of lesbian and bisexual relationships offended some parents, who sought to have it removed from public school libraries. This attempt at censorship prompted the Northern California Independent Booksellers Association to distribute free copies of the book (and another, by Annie Dillard) to California's public high schools.

"I think the most chilling thing to me about the response to *The Color Purple* was that people said, 'This doesn't happen,' " Walker told interviewer Charles Whitaker in *Ebony*. "They said this was totally an anomaly. This is all Alice's problem. But what was really upsetting was the total lack of empathy for the woman."

The controversy flared anew when Stephen Spielberg turned the book into a major motion picture. Again it was attacked as being anti-male, pro-lesbian, too thick in dialect—and as being a Jewish man's vision of a black world. After a decade had passed, Walker wrote a new book about the experience, *The Same River Twice*. "What happened to me during that period was very complex," she told *Essence's* Evelyn C. White, "and it's taken me a while to fully understand it. In terms of the criticism, I just wasn't going to stand for it. Anybody who thought otherwise obviously hasn't been paying close attention to me or my work."

The author expanded in a conversation with Esther Iverem on SeeingBlack.com: "I think that the book did help to bring in greater freedom for people to express how they view life. And I'm very happy about that. Because you really can't, you know, be a good artist if you can't say what you really feel. And people may be offended, but that's how you feel, and that is your right and that is your gift as well."

The terrorist attacks of 2001 had enormous emotional impact on Walker, and brought her back to poetry with *Absolute Trust in the Goodness of the Earth*. "I don't think there is a limit to what people can say about grief," she told *Black Issues Book Review's* Evette Porter. "And I don't think there's a limit to what one can say about the need to sit ourselves down and talk about what kind of future we want, if indeed we have one."

Walker has gone on to demonstrate her deftness as a poet, a children's book author, a writer of non-fiction, and a fictionalist. However, her first story deservedly won't let go. In 2004, director Gary Griffin adapted the novel to the stage and held a premiere at the Alliance Theatre in Atlanta, Georgia, before moving it to New York in 2005.

Works by the Author

The Third Life of Grange Copeland (1970)
Meridian (1976)
The Color Purple (1982)
Alice Walker Boxed Set—Fiction: The Third Life of Grange Copeland, You Can't Keep a Good Woman Down, and In Love and Trouble (1985)
The Temple of My Familiar (1989)
Possessing the Secret of Joy (1992)
By the Light of My Father's Smile (1998)
The Way Forward Is with a Broken Heart (2000)
Now Is the Time to Open Your Heart: A Novel (2004)

Collections

In Love and Trouble: Stories of Black Women (1973)
You Can't Keep a Good Woman Down (1981)
Everyday Use (1994), edited by Barbara Christian
Alice Walker: The Banned Works (1996), edited by Patricia Holt

Poetry

Once: Poems (1968)
Five Poems (1972)
Revolutionary Petunias and Other Poems (1973)
Goodnight, Willie Lee, I'll See You in the Morning (1979)
Horses Make a Landscape Look More Beautiful (1984)
Alice Walker Boxed Set—Poetry: Once: Poems, Revolutionary Petunias and Other Poems, and Goodnight, Willie Lee, I'll See You in the Morning (1985)
Her Blue Body Everything We Know: Earthling Poems 1965–1990 Complete (1991)
Sent by Earth: A Message from the Grandmother Spirit after the Attacks on the World Trade Center and the Pentagon (2001)
A Poem Traveled Down my Arm: Poem and Drawings (2002)
Absolute Trust in the Goodness of the Earth: New Poems (2003)

Editor

Langston Hughes: American Poet (1974)
I Love Myself When I'm Laughing . . . and Then Again When I Am Looking Mean and Impressive: A Zora Neale Hurston Reader (1979)
The Same River Twice: Honoring the Difficult; a Meditation of Life, Spirit, Art, and the Making of the Film "The Color Purple," Ten Years Later (1996)

Children's Fiction

To Hell with Dying (1988)

Finding the Green Stone (1991)
Langston Hughes: American Poet (2002)
There Is a Flower at the Top of My Nose Smelling Me (2006)

Nonfiction

In Search of Our Mothers' Gardens: Womanist Prose (1983)
Living by the Word: Selected Writings, 1973–1987 (1988)
Warrior Marks: Female Genital Mutilation and the Sexual Blinding of Women (1993) with Pratibhas Parmar
Anything We Love Can Be Saved: A Writer's Activism (1997)
Dreads: Sacred Rites of the Natural Hair Revolution (1999), with Francesco Mastalia and Alfonse Pagano
We Are the Ones We Have Been Waiting for: Light in a Time of Darkness (2006)

Film Based on the Author's Work

The Color Purple (1985)

For Further Information

Alice Walker profile, *Voices from the Gap. http://voices.cla.umn.edu/newsite/authors/WALKERalice.htm* (viewed Aug. 10, 2006).

Alice Walker Web page, African American Literature Book Club. *http://authors.aalbc.com/alice.htm* (viewed Aug. 10, 2006).

Behrens, Web, "Sistah? The Color Purple Returns as a Broadway-Bound Stage Musical," *Advocate* (Oct. 26, 2004).

Bloom, Harold, ed., *Alice Walker.* New York: Chelsea, 1989.

Hopward, Lillie P., ed., *Alice Walker and Zora Neale Hurston: The Common Bond.* Westport, CT: Greenwood, 1993.

Iverem, Esther, "An Interview with Alice Walker," *SeeingBlack.com. http://www.seeingblack.com/2003/x022803/walker.shtml* (viewed March 20, 2005).

King, Debra Walker, Color Purple entry, *The Oxford Companion to African American Literature*, William L. Andress, Frances Smith Foster, and Trudier Harris, eds. New York: Oxford University Press, 1997.

Kramer, Barbara, *Alice Walker: Author of* The Color Purple. Berkeley Heights, NJ: Enslow, 1996.

Porter, Evette, "Absolute Alice," *Black Issues Book Review* (March-April 2003).

Sanoff, Alvin P., "The Craft of Survival," *U.S. News & World Report* (June 3, 1991).

White, Evelyn C., *Alice Walker: A Life.* New York: Norton, 2004.

Winchell, Donna H., *Alice Walker.* New York: Twayne, 1992.

Zinn, Howard, "Lit Chat: Alice Walker," *Salon.com. http://www.salon.com/09/departments/litchat1.html* (viewed Aug. 10, 2006).

Carl Weber

Mainstream Contemporary Literature, Urban Literature

Benchmark Title: *The Preacher's Son*

Queens, New York

Date of birth not revealed

About the Author and the Author's Writing

Carl Weber's business background held him in good stead as an author. A graduate of Virginia State University with a BA in accounting and an MBA in marketing, he taught accounting until one day he decided to follow a business model created by his students. He opened a mail-order bookstore that eventually became the African American Bookstore with several stores in Queens and environs. In 2000, Weber earned the Blackboard Bookseller of the Year Award.

"I am a lifelong reader and wanted to write," he said on his Web site, "but I wasn't the best English student." As more and more African American fiction began to show up in publishers' catalogs, he knew the time was right. "I wanted to write a book about ordinary people who have crazy things happen to their lives."

The result was *Lookin' for Luv*, a relationship novel from the male perspective that held the top spot on *Essence's* bestseller list for five months. The main character, Kevin, who gave up an opportunity to play in the National Basketball Association to coach delinquents, despairs of finding a woman. He reluctantly dials a 900 number that promises to find him a true love.

Weber's next novel, *Married Men*, expanded his exploration of relationships from the male perspective (one of the characters, Kyle, doesn't want his beauty supply clients to know about his wife). Then for his third novel, *Baby Momma Drama*, he took a woman's point of view. Postal supervisor Jasmine has made a bad choice in dating Derrick, a drug dealer. Just when he is released from jail, Jasmine has a fling with her ex. Her younger sister Stephanie, meanwhile, has found a stable Army sergeant who is willing to marry her and adopt her young daughter. She hopes.

"The crazier things get, the more Jasmine and Stephanie realized how much they actually have in common—and how much they have to learn from one another," the author told *Shades of Romance Magazine*. "Because when it comes to sorting out life and love, no sister is perfect, but real sisters are forever."

Weber says he learned his writing style from reading other authors. To create dialogue, he listens to the way people around him speak. To create tension, he creates at least one unlikable character per book.

"I write my stories so they're fast-paced, like a movie," the author said in a *Book Remarks* interview. "I love to write about drama and from the reaction of my fans, they love to read it."

Weber shrugs his shoulders at the criticism his novels are often sensational. "We have to realize that not everything is going to be Toni or Cornell West," he told interviewer Leah Mullen.

Weber's 2005 release, *The Preacher's Son*, mixes religion and politics and family turmoil. Bishop T.K. Wilson, who pastors the largest African American church in Queens, takes his message of family values into his campaign for borough president. But while his family's public image shines, behind the scenes his children are giving in to temptation.

Weber is founder and publisher of the Urban Books imprint for Kensington, where, according to the publisher's Web page, he "is setting the tone for what is hot and happening among African-American book buyers." The first two Urban Books that captured the publisher's prescribed "urban edginess" were Sister Souljah's *The Coldest Winter Ever* and Teri Woods' *True to the Game*.

Of the Urban Books line, Weber told reporter Angela P. Dodson, "A new generation of African American readers has emerged. They're seeking more drama-filled stories. What we're trying to do is fill a void."

Works by the Author

Lookin' for Luv (2000)
Married Men (2001)
Baby Momma Drama (2003)
Player Haters (2004) sequel to *Married Men*
The Preacher's Son (2005)
So You Call Yourself a Man (2005)
She Ain't the One (2006), with Mary B. Morrison
The First Lady (2007)

Anthology

A Dollar and a Dream (2003), with La Jill Hunt and Dwayne S. Joseph

For Further Information

Carl Weber Web page, Kensington Books. *http://www.kensingtonbooks.com/finditem/cfm?itemid=8337* (viewed April 2, 2005).

Carl Weber Web site. *http://www.carlweber.net/authorBio.htm* (viewed Aug. 10, 2006).

Dodson, Angela P., "Hip-Hop Lit," *Black Issues Book Review* (Jan.-Feb. 2004).

"Meet the Author: Carl Weber," *Shades of Romance Magazine*. *http://www.sormag.com/14weber.html* (viewed Aug. 10, 2006).

Mullen, Leah, "Carl Weber Gives 'Best Selling' Author a New Meaning," Carl Weber Web page, African American Literature Book Club. *http://authors.aalbc.com/carlweber.htm* (viewed Aug. 10, 2006).

"Questions and Answers with Carl Weber," *Book Remarks. http://www.book-remarks.com/Carl_Weber2.htmm* (viewed Aug. 10, 2006).

Valerie Wilson Wesley

Mystery, Women's
Literature, Mainstream
Contemporary Literature,
Children's Literature

Benchmark Titles: Tamara Hayle Series

Connecticut

1947

Photo credit: Dwight Carter

About the Author and the Author's Writing

It shouldn't come as a surprise to learn that Valerie Wilson Wesley, author of the Tamar Hayle mysteries, as a teen enjoyed reading Edgar Allan Poe and Agatha Christie. (These days, P. D. James, Walter Mosely, Ruth Rendell, Iris Murdoch, and Toni Morrison are among her favorite writers, says the winner of the 2004 Author of the Year Award from Amigirls Book Club.)

Born in Connecticut, Wesley attended high school in Madrid, Spain. She earned a bachelor's degree from Howard University, then master's degrees from both the Bank Street College of Education and the Columbia Graduate School of Journalism. After graduating, she married Richard Wesley, a screenwriter and playwright, and they raised two daughters. They live in Montclair, New Jersey.

Wesley, who was executive editor with *Essence*, initially wrote non-fiction, a collective biography of famous African Americans with Wade Hudson. She followed that with *Where Do I Go From Here?*, a young adult novel about a black student who receives a scholarship to a white boarding school but finds it difficult to fit in with her more wealthy classmates. The American Library Association gave it a Best Books for Reluctant Readers citation.

The author has also served on the board of Sisters in Crime and has written more than a half-dozen cases in the popular Tamara Hayle series. *Dying in the Dark*, as is typical in this series, finds the heroine fed up with racism and sexism in the Newark Police Department. She quits and starts up her own detective agency, and one of her first clients is a gangsta named Cecil Jones, who wants her to find out who killed his mother, who was Tamara's good friend in high school. A week later, Jones himself is dead.

In addition to her work for adult and young adult readers, the author has written several books for children, including *Willimena and the Cookie Money*, the first in a series about a seven-year-old. In this book the heroine spends the $25.75 she earned from selling Girl Scout cookies and has nothing to turn in to the troop. Actually, she spent it helping several people in need. With the help of her older sister Tina, she tries a number of unsuccessful efforts to raise the money before figuring out how to handle the problem.

Wesley has also ventured into relationship fiction with *Ain't Nobody's Business if I Do*, which garnered the Best Fiction for 2000 award from the Black Caucus of the American Library Association. "I wanted to write a love story with a happy ending," she told reporter Martha Southgate for *Essence*. "My having written mysteries was very helpful in writing this book. I learned how to plot the events, because that's how a mystery is built. What was difficult with this book was writing from so many points of view."

Another mainstream contemporary novel, *Playing My Mother's Blues*, explores how a moment of rage—Maria's shooting of her lover and spending twenty years in prison—affects not only her life but those of her two daughters, who were raised by their father and his sister, Lucille.

At another end of the literary spectrum, the author has contributed a story to the *Best Black Women's Erotica* anthology.

Wesley's novel *Always True to You in My Fashion* takes place in a black artistic community and focuses on upper-middle-class and middle-aged characters. "The reality is that happiness is much more than money," the author said in an interview with *Black Issues Book Review*. "It's connections to people; it's love. You can actually do with very little if you have these essentials: know yourself and enjoy life."

This versatile writer is well-equipped to venture into new literary territory.

Works by the Author

Freedom's Gifts (1997)
Ain't Nobody's Business If I Do (1999)
Blue Dancing (1999)
Always True to You in My Fashion (2002)
No Way of Dying (2004)
Playing My Mother's Blues (2005)

Tamara Hayle Series

When Death Comes Stealing (1994)
Devil's Gonna Get Him (1995)
Where Evil Sleeps (1996)
No Hiding Place (1997)
Easier to Kill (1998)
The Devil Riding (2000)
Dying in the Dark (2004)

Contributor

Bluelight Corner: Black Women Writing on Passion, Sex and Romantic Love (1998), edited by Rosemarie Robotham

Room to Grow: Twenty-Two Writers Encounter the Pleasures and Paradoxes of Raising Young Children (2000), edited by Christina Baker Kline

Best Black Women's Erotica (2001), edited by Blanche Richardson

Gumbo: A Literary Rent Party to Benefit the Hurston/Wright Foundation (2002), edited by Marita Golden and E. Lynn Harris

For Young Adult Readers

Where Do I Go from Here? (1993)

For Younger Readers

Freedom's Gifts: A Juneteenth Mystery (1997)

Willimena Rules! Series

Willimena and the Cookie Money (2001)
Willimena and Mrs. Sweetly's Guinea Pig (2002)
Tales of Willimena (2003)
How to Lose Your Class Pet (2003)
How to Fish for Trouble (2004)
How to Almost Ruin Your Class Play (2005)
23 Ways to Mess Up Valentine's Day (2005)

Nonfiction

The Afro-bets Book of Black Heroes from A to Z: An introduction to Important Black Achievers for Young Readers (1988), with Wade Hudson

For Further Information

Jones, Lynda, "BIBR Talks to Valerie Wilson Wesley," *Black Issues Book Review* (Nov.-Dec., 2002).

Southgate, Martha, "No Business Like Wesley's Business," *Essence* (October 1999).

Valerie Wilson Wesley biography, *Voices from the Gaps. http://voices.cla. umn.edu/vg/Bios/entries/wesley_valerie_wilson.html* (viewed Aug. 10, 2006).

Valerie Wilson Wesley Web page, African American Literature Book Club. *http://authors.aalbc.com/valeriewilsonwesley.htm* (viewed Aug. 10, 2006).

Valerie Wilson Wesley Web site. *http://tamarahayle.com/biography.htm* (viewed Aug. 10, 2006).

Wesley, Valerie Wilson, letter to author, June 21, 2005.

Chassie L. West

Mystery, Romance, Young Adult Literature

Benchmark Title: *Sunrise*

Date and location of birth not revealed

Photo credit: Amy Jones Photography

About the Author and the Author's Writing

A veteran writer of romance and young adult novels, Chassie West garnered an Edgar Award nomination for best original paperback for her first adult mystery, *Sunrise*, and Edgar and Anthony Award nominations for its sequel, *Killing Kin*.

The Columbia, Maryland, resident who holds a bachelor of arts in drama from Howard University is no stranger to awards; she had several years before garnering two Romantic Times Career Achievement Awards.

Active in community and regional theater, West began her writing career under one of the most famous of young adult pennames: Carolyn Keene. In the late 1980s, she wrote two entries in the Nancy Drew Files series. Of all her books, she said, those are the most remarked upon by readers, so enduring is the series about the teen detective.

That she started writing young adult novels is perhaps no surprise, considering that's the age at which she discovered the joys of mystery (Helen MacIness) and science fiction (Robert Heinlein and Isaac Asimov) in the library of her East Orange, New Jersey, middle school.

When she switched to adult romantic suspense, her *Unforgivable* was one of the first in which the publisher Silhouette featured African American characters. She received the Romantic Times 1989-1990 Lifetime Achievement Award for New Series Romantic Mystery Author and the periodical's 1990-1991 Career Achievement Certificate of Excellence for Series Romantic Fantasy.

The author has said she's enjoyed writing since high school. In fact, it was a college creative writing teacher-friend who gave the last necessary nudge to get her to begin her career as a novelist. It took a decade before one of her manuscripts found a home. With her young adult romance novels, she explained, she often worked in elements of suspense.

West claims she has little in common with her peppy crime series heroine, Leigh Ann Warren. "I suspect the only thing we have in common is the way we express ourselves," the Northern-born author told Between the Pages interviewer Susan McBride. "The eleven years I lived in North Carolina as a teenager had a great influence on my use of language. I was exposed to a generation of senior citizens whose turns of phrase absolutely captivated me."

West said she created the character to see what impact, emotionally as well as physically, an on-the-job shooting injury might have on a District of Columbia police officer. Forced to retire because of a knee injury, the protagonist Warren went back to her hometown, hoping it would bring back simpler times. It didn't. It brought her a crime to solve.

"The books are infused with warmth, lively characters you'd want to meet and an unhurried pace . . . ," said reviewer Sarah Weinman of *Killer Chameleon*. "West has stated in interviews that she finds plotting to be 'as hard as pulling an impacted wisdom tooth' but there's no evidence of any difficulty here."

Plots for her mystery novels tend to pop up from nowhere, the author said, as "what ifs." The "what if" in *Killer Riches* involves the heroine's missing war medal, a death threat and ransom demand. "There's none better than Chassie West at drawing readers into her stories and keeping them turning the pages," in the view of McBride. "The dialogue flows and is peppered with homey Southern dialect that adds flavor to *Killer Riches* like butter to grits."

The author, a widow since the death of her husband Robert West, lives in Columbia, Maryland. His passing has meant big adjustments in her life.

In an interview with Maria Y. Lima on Amazon.com she said it wasn't intentional, but her mysteries tend to show personal growth on the part of her heroine, Warren, and Warren's amateur detective partner, Troy Burdette. "I wanted to remind readers that behind the badge of every officer of the law and/or amateur sleuth is a thinking, feeling person. What better way than to present them with a life-changing conundrum?"

While she has demonstrated facility in several genres, West appears poised to abandon all her earlier pennames and devote her future writing efforts to the mystery genre.

Works by the Author

Loss of Innocence (1997)

Leigh Ann Warren Mystery Series

Sunrise (1994)
Killing Kin (2000)
Killer Riches (2001)
Killer Chameleon (2004)

Anthology

Bark M. For Murder (2006)

Written as Joyce McGill

Silhouette Intimate Moments Series

347. *Through the Looking Glass* (1990)
368. *A Loving Touch* (1991)
441. *Unforgivable* (1992)

Young Adult Fiction

Written as Carolyn Keene

Nancy Drew Files
  15. *Trial by Fire* (1987)
  21. *High Marks for Malice* (1989)

Written as Chassie L. West

Charisma Series
  4. *Desperado* (1988)
Magic Micro Adventure Series
  3. *Million Dollar Gamble* (1984)
  9. *Dead Ringer* (1985)

Written as Joyce McGill

Hurra! Sie Liebt Mich (1990)

Silhouette Keepsake Series

Love Song (1988)

Written as Tracy West

Silhouette Crosswinds Series
  The Butterflies of Freedom (1988)
Silhouette First Love Series
  Lesson in Love (1982)
  Lovetalk (1984)
  The Other Langley Girl (1985)
  Country Boy (1985)
  Soap Opera (1986)
  Promises (1986)
  Here We Go Again (1986)
  Diamond in the Rough (1987)

For Further Information

Chassie West Web site. *http://www.chassiewest.com/* (viewed Aug. 10, 2006).

Lima, Maria Y., "Chassie West: From Carolyn Keene to Carolina Mysteries," Crescent Blues interview, Amazon.com. *http://www.crescentblues.com/ 3_4issue/chassie_west.shtml* (viewed Aug. 10, 2006).

McBride, Susan, "Between the Pages Past: Chassie West Interview." *http://www.myshelf.com/betweenthepages/01/west.html* (viewed Aug. 10, 2006

Weinman, Sarah, review of *Killer Chameleon*, *Baltimore Sun* (Dec. 26, 2004).

John Edgar Wideman

Urban Literature, Historical,
Mainstream Contemporary
Literature, Memoir

Benchmark Title: *Brothers and Keepers*

Washington, D.C.

1941

Photo credit: Jean-Christian Bourcart

About the Author and the Author's Writing

John Edgar Wideman is a two-time recipient of the PEN/Faulkner Award for fiction: the first time for *Sent for You Yesterday* (1984), the second for *Philadelphia Fire* (1990). He has also earned the Rea and O. Henry awards for short stories (1998 and 2000, respectively) and the American Book Award for Fiction (1990), among other awards. In 1993, he received a MacArthur Foundation fellowship.

The teacher of a graduate writing seminar at Brown University, Wideman was born in Washington, D.C., in 1941. When he was still an infant, the family moved to an African American community that provides the backdrop for much of his later fiction, Homewood, PA, near Pittsburgh. Wideman attended the University of Pennsylvania on a Benjamin Franklin scholarship; while there, he won a creative writing prize and membership in Phi Beta Kappa. In athletics, he won All-Ivy League status as a basketball forward. He also competed in track. He was featured in *Look* magazine in 1963. With a bachelor of arts degree in English from that school the same year, he won a Rhodes scholarship and attended Oxford University's New College to major in philosophy. Back in the United States, he spent a year as a Kent Fellow at the University of Iowa's Writers' Workshop, where he completed his first novel, *A Glance Away*, published in 1967. Since then, he has taught at Pennsylvania State, the University of Wyoming, and the University of Massachusetts at Amherst.

That's the positive picture. On the negative, Wideman has a brother and a son in prison, both convicted of murder. He married his college girlfriend, Judith Goldman, an attorney, but they divorced after 30 years and three children.

305

"Life is pretty touchy," the author said in a *Pages* interview. "We find ourselves assembling forces to bear burdens that we didn't expect, so how do you get ready for that? How does any individual person get ready for that? It may be kind of a metaphor for being alive. We're being tested all the time."

Wideman's 1984 memoir, *Brothers and Keepers*, a nominee for a National Book Critics Circle Award, tells of his relationship with his brother Robby, who was convicted in 1976 for his role as an accomplice in a robbery-murder. Also serving a life sentence is Wideman's emotionally troubled son Jacob, who in 1986 at age sixteen was convicted of stabbing a camping partner in Arizona. The author vented his feelings about the inadequacies of the judicial system in a novel, *Philadelphia Fire*.

And still he is working out his feelings. The author's recent collection of short stories includes one, "What We Cannot Speak about We pass over in Silence," which depicts a man's struggle to make sense of his own world with his son in prison. "His technical virtuosity is on display on every page . . . ," said reviewer Clay Evans. "*God's Gym* shows Wideman pushing himself, sampling different techniques, mulling notions."

That said, Wideman is not obsessed with the theme. He has written love stories, for example, *The Cattle Killing*, though of course it has an edge. And his Homewood Trilogy depicts the travails of the Lawson family and changes and growth in their community. In a Salon interview, Wideman likened the relationship of blacks and America to unrequited love. "We came here like all the other immigrants. We were fascinated by the land and wanted to make a home, to raise families . . . But that love has never been fully answered or accepted. 'Yes, it's nice that you love us. Go off and fight for us and do this for us.' Then the old finger of admonition comes up and it's touch and go."

As much as his prose appears to be autobiographical, Wideman cautioned the Salon reporter that he presents only as much of himself as he wants; there are also things he holds back, and he doesn't necessarily appreciate anyone making judgment calls solely on what he has written.

"Throughout Wideman's work, he examines the connections between family and history," said *Contemporary Novelists*, in summing up the author's career. "Committed to making certain that 'all the stories' are told, Wideman infuses his writing with the style of jazz. His novels are polyphonic and improvisational; genres and discourses blend; and stories and characters are repeated, but played a different way each time. Wideman's riffing style illuminates the diversity of African-American experience, and the inadequacies of traditional narrative in capturing that experience."

Works by the Author

A Glance Away (1967)
The Lynchers (1986)
Reuben (1988)
Philadelphia Fire (1990)
The Homewood Books (1992)
Identities: Three Novels (1994), omnibus
The Cattle Killing (1997)
Two Cities (1998)
The Island (2003)

Homewood Trilogy

Sent for You Yesterday (1983)
Damballah (1984), short stories
Hiding Place (1984)

Collections

Fever: Twelve Stories (1989)
The Stories of John Edgar Wideman (1992)
All Stories Are True (1993)
God's Gym: Stories (2005)

Contributor

The New Gothic: A Collection of Contemporary Gothic Fiction (1991)

Editor

The Best American Short Stories (1997), with Annie Proulx
My Soul Has Grown Deep: Classics of Early African American Literature (2001)
20: The Best of the Drue Heinz Literature Prize (2001)

Nonfiction

Brothers and Keepers (1984), memoir
Fatheralong: A Meditation on Fathers and Sons, Race and Society (1994)
Ancestral House: The Black Short Story in the Americas and Europe (1998)
Conversations with John Edgar Wideman (1998), edited by Bonnie Tu Smith
Chronicles of the Civil War: An Illustrated History of the War between the States (1999)
Hoop Roots: Basketball, Race, and Love (2001)

For Further Information

Evans, Clay, "Wideman's Stories Reflect a Life of High Times, and a Lot of Pain," *Waterbury* (CT) *Sunday Republican* (March 6, 2005).

Hume, Kathryn, "Black Urban Utopia in Wideman's Later Fiction," *Race and Class* (Jan.-March 2004).

John Edgar Wideman entry, *Contemporary Novelists*, 7th ed. Detroit: St. James Press, 2001.

Klein, Julia M., "Darkness and Light," *Pages* (March-April 2005).

Miller, Laura, John Edgar Wideman interview, *Salon.com. http://www.salon. com/nov96/interview961111.html* (viewed Aug. 10, 2006).

Rushdy, Ashref H. A., "Conversations with John Edgar Wideman," *African American Review* (fall 2000).

John A. Williams

Mainstream Contemporary Literaute, Science Fiction, Poetry

Benchmark Title: *The Man Who Cried I Am*

Jackson, Mississippi

1925

About the Author and the Author's Writing

Journalist, novelist, and poet John A. Williams became a rich black voice of literature in the Black Arts Movement of the 1960s. And his work has endured.

Born in Jackson, Mississippi, in 1925, he became a pharmacist's mate in the U.S. Naval reserves from 1943 to 1946, serving in the Pacific. Stateside, he earned a bachelor of arts degree in English and journalism from Syracuse University in 1950 and began a career as a journalist. He worked for *Ebony*, *Jet*, *Newsweek*, and CBS. He also taught at City University of New York, University of California at Santa Barbara, La Guardia Community College, College of the Virgin Islands, University of Hawaii, and Boston University.

He began his book-writing career with a trio of novels, *The Angry Ones*, *Night Song*, and *Sissie*, in which he depicted the African American experience in this country. The first of the novels, for example, looks at how racism intrudes in a black man's experiences both in the ultra-hip, professional world of publishing, and in his personal life and relationship with a white woman.

With his novel *The Man Who Cried I Am*, which involves a plot against the unification of black Africa, Williams attained international recognition. The author continued his venture outside the mainstream with two more speculative novels. *Sons of Darkness, Sons of Light* (1969) describes how a lone act of vengeance can shatter the future of an entire nation. *Captain Blackman* offers perspective on all American wars through the eyes of a 200-year-old man who participated in all of them.

These three science fiction works "are revolutionary fiction, or 'awful warning' stories," according to *St. James Guide to Science Fiction Writers*. "He writes at a high

308

level of prestige in the mainstream of American fiction. His principal characters are African Americans. The three novels in question present a progress of plots and themes from warning story to virtually apocalyptic race revolution triumph."

The Man Who Cried I Am focused in part on 1950 legislation, the McCarran Internal Security Act, which allowed for mass incarceration of dissidents at the order of the president. Sections of that act were repealed four years after Williams' novel came out, but the issue resonates again in the twenty-first century, post the September 11 terrorist attacks on New York City and Washington, D.C.

In 1990 Williams was named Paul Robeson Professor of English at Rutgers University. He received the Syracuse University Centennial Medal for Outstanding Achievement and the 1998 American Book Award for Safari West.

Even as he received these honors, however, Williams felt he experienced discrimination. He was awarded a grant in 1961 to the American Academy in Rome, based on the merits of *Night Song*. The award was withdrawn, however. Williams believes it was because he was black and was believed to be engaged to a white woman—an assertion that Alan Dugan, the poet who received the award in his stead, confirmed.

In 1994, Williams retired from teaching and began focusing exclusively on his writing. He and his wife live in Teaneck, N.J. They have three adult sons.

Williams explored a little-known aspect of history in the novel *Clifford's Blues* (1999), which is about an African American soldier named Clifford Pepperidge who is captured and imprisoned at Dachau by the Nazis, organizes a jazz band, and plays at the officers' club. By working as a house servant to an S.S. officer, he escapes the worst of that facility's tortures. In 1995, Williams told interviewer Dennis A. Williams he was abandoning fiction. "I've always looked at fiction as being a corrective force, an enabling art form focused on an angle of truth. I feel now that that's a view that is not popular."

The author returned to an early love, poetry. *Safari West* (1998) collects verse written over the period 1953 to 1979, revisiting themes both new and familiar.

"Although Williams's writing explores racial themes," sums up Contemporary Authors Online, "he has stated that he dislikes being categorized as a black author. In his view, that label only facilitates the segregation of black writers and their work from the rest of American literature . . . 'I like the idea of being a writer. I am very proud to be a writer.' "

Works by the Author

The Angry Ones (1960), retitled *One for New York* (1975)
Night Song (1961)
Sissie (1963), in England as *Journey Out of Anger* (1965)
The Man Who Cried I Am (1967)
Sons of Darkness, Sons of Light: A Novel of Some Probability (1969)
Captain Blackman (1972)
Mothersill and the Foxes (1975)
The Junior Bachelor Society (1976)
!Click Song (1982)
The Berhama Account (1985)

Jacob's Ladder (1987)
Clifford's Blues (1999)

Poetry

Safari West: Poems (1998)

Nonfiction

Africa: Her History, Lands, and People (1962)
This Is My Country Too (1965)
The Most Native of Sons: A Biography of Richard Wright (1970)
The King God Didn't Save: Reflections on the Life and Death of Martin Luther King, Jr. (1970)
Flashbacks: A Twenty-Year Diary of Article Writing (1973)
Minorities in the City (1975)
I Stop I'll Die: The Comedy and Tragedy of Richard Pryor (1991), with Dennis A. Williams

Editor

The Angry Black (1962), retitled *Beyond the Angry Black* (1966)
Amistad I (1970), with Charles F. Harris
Amistad II (1971), with Charles F. Harris
Yardbird No. 1 (1979), by Ishmael Reed
The McGraw-Hill Introduction to Literature (1985)
Bridges: Literature across Cultures (1994)
Approaches to Literature (1994)

Television Scripts

The History of the Negro People: Omowale—The Child Returns Home (National Education Television, 1965)
The Creative Person: Henry Roth (National Education Television, 1966)

Drama

Last Flight of Ambo Ber (1981)

Written as J. Dennis Gregory

The Protectors: The Heroic Story of the Narcotics Agents, Citizens and Officials in Their Unending, Unsung Battles Against Organized Crime in America and Abroad (1964), with Harry J. Anslinger

Works Adapted for Television

Sophisticated Gents (NBC 1981), based on *The Junior Bachelor Society*

For Further Information

John A(lfred) Williams entry, Contemporary Authors OnlineGale, 2005. Reproduced in Biography Resource Center. Farmington Hills, MI: Thomson Gale, 2005. *http://galenet.galegroup.com/servlet/BioRC* (viewed Feb. 21, 2005).

John A(lfred) Williams entry, *St. James Guide to Science Fiction Writers*, 4th ed. Detroit: St. James Press, 1996.

John A. Williams Web page, African American Literature Book Club. *http://authors.aalbc.com/johna.htm* (viewed Aug. 10, 2006).

John Alfred Williams Web page (Oct. 2001). *http://www.olemiss.edu/mwp/dir/williams_john_a/* (viewed Aug. 10, 2006).

Safari West:Poems review, *African American Review* (fall 2001).

Williams, Dennis A., "An Interview with John A. Williams," *Forkroads* (winter 1995).

Paula L. Woods

Mystery

Benchmark Titles: Charlotte Justice Series

Los Angeles, California
1953

Photo credit: Robert Yager, Robert Yager
Photography

About the Author and the Author's Writing

A Los Angelino through-and-through—she was born there in 1953—novelist Paula L. Woods was shaken by the Rodney King riots in that city in 1992, and she subsequently wove her first mystery around them.

"The 1992 riots were the most devastating event to happen in LA in the 20th century," she said in an interview on her Web site. "The rebuilding effort was supposed to stimulate the renaissance of the city, and a lot of people's hopes and dreams were hanging on the outcome." There were many, however, called "poverty pimps" by Woods' fictional series heroine Charlotte Justice, who found a way to exploit this rebirth. "After having witnessed some of those people operating after the Watts riots in 1965, seeing it again in the '90s made me want to critique it from a fictional standpoint."

Woods is far from being the only writer of Los Angeles crime stories—or even the only black writer of LA crime stories. "I've had people say, 'You're a female Walter Mosley,' and that's a nice compliment, but I'm offering a different take on the territory," she told *Los Angeles Times* reporter Anne-Marie O'Connor.

The mystery series is a handy tool for exploring the modern history of Los Angeles, the author said on her Web site.

As with many professional authors, Woods's path to writing a mystery series was roundabout. Her mother died when she was a college senior at the University of Southern California, and while she was close to her father, she went through an emotional period of depression. She worked as a telephone operator for Martin Luther King Jr.

Hospital and took a keen interest in its trauma center. When she was forty-five, she enrolled in graduate school and completed requirements for a master's degree in hospital administration. She and her husband, Felix H. Liddell, established a hospital consulting firm with clients such as Kaiser Permanente and Cedars-Sinai Medical Center. Woods and Liddell also collaborated on books that collect African-American stories: *I, Too, Sing America: The African American Book of Days*, *I Hear a Symphony: African Americans Celebrate Love*, and *Merry Christmas, Baby: A Christmas and Kwanzaa Treasury*. On her own the author compiled an anthology of historic African American crime fiction, for which she uncovered the first mystery by a black writer, "Talma Gordon," which appeared in *Colored American Magazine* in 1900. "The extent of the black presence in mystery fiction has yet to be 'discovered' by many mystery enthusiasts," she wrote in the introduction to *Spooks, Spies, and Private Eyes*, "regardless of race, or by many mystery scholars. To see Pauline Hopkins's use of the locked room mystery device pioneered by Edgar Allan Poe in 'The Murders in the Rue Morgue' raises tantalizing questions about that mystery master's influence on early black experimenters in the genre."

The next logical step, of course, was for Woods to write her own mystery story. And she wanted it to be about a black policewoman. Through a contact, she interviewed several black women officers in the Los Angeles Police Department. The King riots gave her the background hook. As powerful as that episode was, the author said she worked hard to avoid stereotypes. "I don't want to get into that dehumanizing business of, 'All blacks do this, all Latinos do this, all whites do this,' " she told Edvins Beitiks of the *San Francisco Examiner*.

Rather, she prefers plain confrontation of issues. In *Inner City Blues,* Charlotte Justice puts it this way: "I learned from my mother's experiences that life in America was a game called Pigmentocracy, color a card you played. So if my 'high yellow' color lulled my white superiors in the Department into thinking I was somehow safer and less militant than my darker sisters and brothers, then that was their mistake, not mine."

"Woods expected some criticism for such passes," reported Malcolm Jones in *Newsweek*. "Instead, 'I get an amazed response from whites,' she says, 'and a nod from blacks. Almost everyone is grateful.' "

On the lighter side of the novels, Woods noted in *Mystery Readers International:* "One of my inspirations for the Charlotte Justice series is the music of Charlotte and her family's life and times, from the 1940s onward. From the titles of the mysteries to the use of music in key scenes and chapter titles, music for me is one of the unifying themes of the series."

There may be some advantages to a black mystery series character, the author related in a conversation with reporter Lawrence Donegan: "The thing about the black detective is he or she is the ultimate outsider. Here they are on the side of law and order when often the victims of crime are black and sometimes the perpetrators are too. . . . [T]he black detective has a unique perspective."

Works by the Author

Charlotte Justice Mystery Series

Inner City Blues (1999)
Stormy Weather (2001)
Dirty Laundry (2003)
Strange Bedfellows (2006)

Editor

I, Too, Sing America: The African American Book of Days (1992), with Felix H. Liddell
I Hear a Symphony: African Americans Celebrate Love (1994), with Felix H. Liddell
Spooks, Spies, and Private Eyes: Black Mystery, Crime, and Suspense Fiction of the 20th Century (1995)
Merry Christmas, Baby: A Christmas and Kwanzaa Treasury (1996), with Felix H. Liddell

For Further Information

Beitiks, Edvins, "Creating Poetic Justice," *San Francisco Examiner* (Feb. 28, 2000), reproduced on Paula L. Woods Web site. *http://www. woodsontheweb.com/Bio/creating_poetic_justice.htm* (viewed Aug. 10, 2006).

Donegan, Lawrence, "Skin Deep in Crime," *The Observer* (Aug. 4, 2002).

Jones, Malcolm, "It's Black, White and Noir," *Newsweek* (June 24, 2003).

O'Connor, Anne-Marie, "New Read on L.A.: Novelists Now View the Sprawling City with an Insider's Eye," *Los Angeles Times* (July 6, 2004).

Paula L. Woods entry, Contemporary Authors Online, Gale, 2005. Reproduced in Biography Resource Center. Farmington Hills, Mich.: Thomson Gale. 2005. *http://galenet.galegroup.com/servlet/BioRC* (viewed Feb. 25, 2005).

Spooks, Spies, and Private Eyes review, *Publishers Weekly* (Sept. 11, 1995).

"*Stormy Weather* Q&A with Paula L. Woods," Paula L. Woods Web site. *http://www.woodsontheweb.com/Books/stormy_weather_q_a.htm* (viewed Aug. 10, 2006).

Sweets, Ellen, "A Master of Mystery," *Dallas Morning News* (Feb. 10, 1999).

Woods, Paula L., "Murder to a Motown Beat," *Mystery Readers International* (fall 2003).

Jacqueline Woodson

Young Adult

Benchmark Title: *Locomotion*

Columbus, Ohio
1964

Photo credit: Courtesy Penguin Young
Readers Group

About the Author and the Author's Writing

Jacqueline Woodson often writes about characters on the margins of society who are overlooked but nonetheless important.

"I have chosen to write for young adults with an emphasis on children-of-color to enlighten them to the different issues we as people of color continually struggle with," Woodson said in *Black Authors & Illustrators of Children's Books*. "Issues such as nurturing the gifted black child, racism, classism, and homophobia play major roles in my writing. These are issues that were absent in the literature I read growing up; issues I want my own children to grow up enlightened to."

The author was born in Columbus, Ohio, in 1964. As a child she lived in South Carolina and New York City. She has said she never felt she fully belong in either one. Her family's religious beliefs as Jehovah's Witnesses further kept her apart from children in school.

"Of course, I was always finding ways to do what I wasn't allowed to do (Except go to war, which I still don't believe in.)," she said in *Eighth Book of Junior Authors and Illustrators* (2000). She particularly recalls patriotic songs such as "America the Beautiful." "Maybe I loved them so much because I wasn't allowed to sing this type of song."

Woodson's political views crystallized when Richard Nixon resigned in 1974. She began to challenge the way things were. And she began to write poetry.

"I used to write on everything," she said in a Random House Web site interview. "It was the thing I liked to do the most. I never thought I could have a career as a writer—I always thought it was something I would have to do on the side."

While taking a creative writing class at college, Woodson came out as a lesbian. In 1985, she received a bachelor of arts degree in English from Adelphi University. Later she studied creative writing at New School for Social Research. An associate faculty member at several colleges including Goddard, Eugene Lang, and Vermont, she later became a writer-in-residence for the National Book Foundation. She also worked as an editorial assistant and a drama therapist before becoming a full-time writer in 1997.

"There are all kinds of people in the world," the author said on a teachers@random Web site, "I want to help introduce readers to the kinds of people they might not otherwise meet."

Her first novel, *Last Summer with Maizon*, is about eleven-year-old friends in Brooklyn who are split apart when one goes away to school. Margaret, sorely missing Maizon, finds she has a talent for writing. Maizon, disliking the mostly white boarding school, aches to return home. Later books continue the trilogy.

"Girls rarely get discussed in books and films," the author elaborated for teachers@random, "and I want to do 'girl stories' that show strong, independent people. I think girls are often disregarded in this society and taught to be dependent. I want to show young people that there are other ways to be."

She spoke on the Web site of her book *I Hadn't Meant to Tell You This*: "I really wanted to write about friendship. I really wanted to write about people crossing racial lines to be friends, and people crossing class lines. I wanted to write about what it meant to be a girl in this society, in a society where self-esteem seems to go down when you reach a certain age. And the characters just started coming to me." The characters were so rich, the author continued their story in *Lena*.

Woodson has also written non-fiction children's books and scripted videos. Two of her books for younger readers are *The Other Side*, a story of segregation and friendship despite racial differences, and *Sweet, Sweet Memory*, in which a girl attends her grandfather's funeral. Her *Autobiography of a Family Photo*, a coming-of-age story of a girl living in a dysfunctional family, is intended for an adult audience.

The author, who has received numerous awards for her work including the Coretta Scott King Award for *Miracle's Boys*, always pushes herself. *Locomotion*, the story of an orphaned brother who is sent to a foster home while his sister is adopted by a wealthy family, is told largely in poetry. "I hated poetry growing up," Woodson told interviewer Heidi Henneman. "I think it was more that I was afraid of it. I didn't understand it until I started getting rid of the line breaks."

Contending with censorship by some school libraries, Woodson said in *Black Issues Book Review* that blindness won't make important issues go away. "People say that they're censoring in the guise of protecting the children, but if they'd open their eyes they'd see that kids are exposed to this stuff everyday, and we need a venue by which to talk to them about it and start a dialogue. My writing comes from this place, of wanting to change the world. I feel like young people are the most open."

Works by the Author

Autobiography of a Family Photo (1996)

Contributor

Black Like Us: A Century of Lesbian, Gay and Bisexual African American Fiction (2002), edited by Devon W. Carbado, Dwight A. McBride, and Donald Weise

Young Adult Novels

The Dear One (1991)
I Hadn't Meant to Tell You This (1994)
From the Notebooks of Melanin Sun (1995)
The House You Pass on the Way (1997)
If You Come Softly (1998)
Lena (1998), sequel to *I Hadn't Meant to Tell You This*
Miracle's Boys (2000)
Hush (2002)
Behind You (2004)
Feather (2007)

Contributor

Am I Blue? Coming Out from the Silence (1994), edited by Marion Dane Bauer
Girls Out Game: Sports Stories and Poems (2001), edited by Sue Macy
One Hot Second: Stories about Desire (2003), edited by Cathy Young
Absence: 12 Stories about Loss and Hope (2003), edited by James Howe

Books for Younger Readers

We Had a Picnic This Sunday Past (1997)
Sweet, Sweet Memory (2000)
The Other Side (2001)
Our Gracie Aunt (2002)
Visiting Day (2002)
Locomotion (2003)
Coming on Home Soon (2004)
Show Way (2005)

Ghostwriter Series

Book Chase (1994)

Maizon Series

Last Summer with Maizon (1990)
Maizon at Blue Hill (1992)
Between Madison and Palmetto (1993)

Nonfiction

Editor

A Way Out of No Way: Writing about Growing Up Black in America (1996)

For Further Information

Bashir, Samiya A., "Tough Issues, Tender Minds," *Black Issues Book Review* (May-June 2001).

Day, Frances Ann, Jacqueline Woodson entry, *Lesbian and Gay Voices: An Annotated Bibliography and Guide to Literature for Children and Young Adults*, Westport, CT: Greenwood Press, 2000.

Haydn, Judith A., Jacqueline Woodson entry, *Writers for Young Adults, Supplement 1*, Ted Hipple, ed. New York: Scribner's, 2000.

Henneman, Heidi, "Poetry in Motion," *BookPage. http://www.bookpage.com/0302bp/jacqueline_woodson.html* (viewed Aug. 10, 2006).

Hile, Janet L., Jacqueline Woodson entry, *Authors & Artists for Young Adults*, Vol. 21, Thomas McMahon, ed. Detroit: Gale, 1997.

Merson, Martha, "Jacqueline Woodson: A Lesson Idea or Two," *Readers Talk to Writers. http://alri.org/pubs/woodsonlessons.html* (viewed Aug. 10, 2006).

"Jacqueline Woodson," *teachers@random. http://www.randomhouse.com/teachers/authors/wood.html* (viewed March 9, 2001).

Jacqueline Woodson entry, *Black Authors and Illustrators of Children's Books*, 2d ed., Barbara Pollock, ed. New York: Garland, 1992.

Jacqueline Woodson entry, *Contemporary Authors, New Revision Series*, Vol. 87. Detroit: Gale, 2000.

Jacqueline Woodson entry, *Eighth Book of Junior Authors and Illustrators*, Connie C. Rockman, ed. New York: H. W. Wilson, 2000.

Jacqueline Woodson Web site. *http://www.jacquelinewoodson.com* (viewed Aug. 10, 2006).

McCafferty, Megan, ed., *Jacqueline Woodson: The Real Thing*. Lanham, MD: Rowman & Littlefield, 2003.

Quattlebaum, Catherine T., review of *The Other Side*, *School Library Journal* (Jan. 2001).

Saalfield, Catherine, Jacqueline Woodson entry, *Contemporary Lesbian Writers of the United States: A Bio-Biographical Critical Sourcebook*, Sandra Pollock and Denise D. Knight, eds. Westport, CT: Greenwood Press, 1993.

Saccardi, Marianne, review of *Sweet, Sweet Memory*, *School Library Journal* (April 2001).

Woodson, Jacqueline, "Who Can Tell My Story?" *Horn Book Magazine* (Jan./Feb. 1998).

Alice Wootson

Romance

Benchmark Title: *Snowbound with Love*

Rankin, Pennsylvania
1937

Photo credit: Courtesy of the author

About the Author and the Author's Writing

Pretty pilot Jeanine Stewart has her hands full when her helicopter crashes. She suspects a replacement part was faulty. And there's the less-than-forthcoming government agent. And she has a healthy (and hunky) cosurvivor, Chris Harris. All this is in Alice Wootson's rapid-paced romantic suspense novel *Aloha Love*.

Born Alice Greenhowe in 1937 in Rankin, Pennsylvania, near Pittsburgh, she is the daughter of a steelworker and his homemaker wife.

"I began writing poetry when I was in grade school," the author said on her Web site, "and I still do. In fact, an agent told me that my work was too poetic to sell commercially. (Two days later I received a call from Karen Thomas at Arabesque asking if my manuscript was still available because she liked it.)

Wootson earned bachelor of science and master's in education degrees from Cheyney State University and obtained certification as a reading specialist from the University of Pennsylvania. She also attended Temple University in Ambler, and Goddard College. She married Isaiah Wootson, a teacher, in 1960. From 1964 until 1992, she taught school in Chester and Philadelphia, Pennsylvania.

When her children grew older, she was drawn to write romances, the author has said, to overcome at times depressing national and world news. She could give the characters in her novels happy resolutions.

"I have been writing poetry and short stories for years," she said in a *Literary World* interview. "For as long as I can remember I have been an avid reader. One day I finished reading a book and said, 'I can write this.' While my first novel, *Snowbound with Love*, was the first contemporary novel that I wrote, I have two historicals that have not sold as yet."

In *Dream Wedding*, Melissa Harrison and Jimmy Scott are an item during their high school years in South Carolina. But the two break up at the end of school. Missy earned a full scholarship to college and left town. Jimmy studies auto mechanics and starts his own garage. Years later, on her way back to her hometown to take a new job and marry her beau, Walter Wilson, Missy's car breaks down. Guess who comes to roadside rescue?

"My primary motivation for writing is that I have these people in my head prodding me, asserting themselves, making a pure nuisance of themselves," she told Contemporary Authors Online. "The only way to quiet them is to tell their stories. I am a voracious reader, as were my parents and grandparents. My reading appetite is quite eclectic. I try to emulate excellent writing."

Works by the Author

Snowbound with Love (2000)
Dream Wedding (2001)
Home for Christmas (2001)
Trust in Me (2002)
To Love Again (2003)
Escape to Love (2003)
Kindred Spirits (2004)
Aloha Love (2005)
Perfect Wedding (2005)
Ready to Take a Chance (2006)

For Further Information

Alice (G.) Wootson entry, Contemporary Authors Online, Gale, 2005. Reproduced in Biography Resource Center. Farmington Hills, MI: Thomson Gale, 2005. *http://galenet.galegroup.com/serviet/BioRC* (viewed Feb. 26, 2005).

Alice Wootson Web site. *http://www.alicewootson.net/* (viewed Aug. 10, 2006).

Pierce, Lauretta, Alice Wootson interview, *The Literary World* (May 1, 2003). *http://www.literaryworld.org/AliceWootsontrust.html* (viewed Aug. 10, 2006).

Courtni Wright

Romance, Children's Literature

Benchmark Title: *Journey to Freedom*

Washington, D.C.

1950

About the Author and the Author's Writing

Courtni Crump Wright says she began her writing career because she perceived a gap in African American history in textbooks that she was using in classes she taught. With only the experience of compiling a non-fiction study of women in plays by Shakespeare, she submitted a proposal to Holiday House. The publisher accepted her proposal but split it into three children's books. *Jumping the Broom* takes place on a Southern plantation and describes the anticipated wedding of two slaves. *Journey to Freedom* follows escapees along the Underground Railroad. And *Wagon Train* describes the hazards encountered by a family venturing into the frontier. The books were well received and were adopted into the Core Knowledge curriculum.

Wright was born in Washington, D.C., in 1950. She attended Trinity College and earned a master's degree in education from Johns Hopkins University in 1980. Except for a brief stint as an account executive with C&P Telephone, she has worked as a middle and high school English teacher since then. She has also been a fellow of the Council for Basic Education and the National Endowment for the Humanities, and a consultant to the National Geographic Society on educational films about Harriet Tubman, the black West, Kwanzaa, and other topics. She and her husband and son live in Maryland, where she teaches at Montgomery County Public Schools.

As a teacher, Wright nurtures young writers every day. "I tell my students not to lose heart when revisions are demanded and to set aside time in their lives to write," she told Contemporary Authors Online. "I try to follow my own advice. . . . During school vacations, I dedicate a minimum of eight hours each day to either researching a topic for a book or doing some element of the writing process, either creating or revising. While teaching, I devote as much of my free time as possible to the creative process, often roughing in a manuscript and putting it aside for editing until later."

With a solid case of the writing bug, Wright has recently abandoned children's writing for adult romances for BET/Silhouette. The first book, *Blush*, is about a young woman struggling to prove herself in the business world. Wright followed that with *It Had to Be You*, the story of recent Harvard Law School graduate Jenna Cross as she begins work at a leading Washington law firm. Jenna cautiously falls for one of the senior partners, Mike Matthews, the son of a federal judge and well above her in social status. However, Jenna aspires to some day become a Supreme Court justice—and marriage isn't one of the steps up the ladder. Reviewer Gwendolyn Osborne for Romance Reader found the story was stronger on sensual details than legal ones.

Wright said in a *Voices from the Gaps* interview that her characters "have often experienced the same feelings, frustration, pain, anger or happiness that I have. I know them intimately."

That fascination with people will hold the author in good stead in future writing.

Works by the Author

Blush (1997)
It Had to Be You (1998)
Paradise (1999)
A Sure Thing (1999)
All That Matters (2000)
A New Beginning (2000)
A Forgotten Love (2000)
Recipe for Love (2001)
Uncovered Passion (2002)
A Charmed Love (2002)
The Music of Love (2003)
The Last Christmas Gift (2003)
Summer Breeze (2004)
Espresso for Two (2004)
Windswept Love (2005)
Love under Construction (2006)

Anthologies

Season's Greetings (1999), with Roberta Gayle and Margie Walker
A Very Special Love: A Heartwarming Collection of Mother's Day Romances (2000), with Kayla Perrin and Janice Sims

Nonfiction

The Women of Shakespeare's Plays: Analysis of the Role of the Women in Selected Plays with Plot Synopses and Selected One-Act Plays (1993), written as Courtni C. Wright

Children's Books, as Courtni Crump Wright

Jumping the Broom (1994)
Journey to Freedom (1994)
Wagon Train: A Family Goes West in 1865 (1995)

For Further Information

Courtni Wright biography, *Voices from the Gaps. http://voices.cla.umn. edu/vg/Bios/entries/wright_courtni.html* (viewed Aug. 10, 2006).

Courtni Wright entry, Contemporary Authors Online, Gale, 2005. Reproduced in Biography Resource Center, Farmington Hills, MI: Thomson Gale, 2005. *http://galenet.galegroup.com/servlet/BioRC.*

Courtot, Marilyn, Courtni Wright biography, *Children's Lit.com. http://www. childrenslit.com/f_wright.html* (viewed Aug. 10, 2006).

Osborne, Gwendolyn, review of *A Sure Thing, Romance Reader. http://www. theromancereader.com/wright-sure.html* (viewed Aug. 10, 2006).

Osborne, Gwendolyn, review of *All That Matters, Romance Reader. http://www. theromancereader.com/wright-all.html* (viewed Aug. 10, 2006).

Osborne, Gwendolyn, review of *It Had to Be You, Romance Reader. http://www. theromancereader.com/wright-you.html* (viewed Aug. 10, 2006).

Richard Wright

Mainstream Contemporary Literature, Memoir

Benchmark Title: *Native Son*

Natchez, Mississippi

1908–1960

About the Author and the Author's Writing

A keystone in African American literature mid-twentieth-century, Richard Wright enthralled his own generation and influenced the next with his richly honed stories of alienation and struggle.

Wright was born on a plantation near Natchez, Mississippi, in 1908, the son of an illiterate sharecropper and a schoolteacher. The family moved to Memphis when he was three, and his father left soon after. Wright's childhood was one of poverty. After his long-ill mother died, he lived with his grandmother in Jackson, Mississippi, until he was seventeen. He attended a Seventh Day Adventist school and also public school. Although he had minimal education in his younger years, Wright became an active reader. In Chicago, he worked for the U.S. Post Office until he was laid off during the Great Depression. During that time, he began writing and in 1924, his story, "The Voodoo of Hell's Half Acre," appeared in a black newspaper, the *Southern Register*.

Working at a number of menial jobs, Wright became intrigued with the philosophy of the American Communist Party and became a member in 1933. After moving to New York City, he worked briefly as editor of the *Daily Worker*. A decade later, he resigned his membership not because he lost his radical beliefs, but because he had become disillusioned that the organization would ever help his people. *Uncle Tom's Children* and *Native Son* both take the party to task for its diversions from true Marxism.

Wright briefly edited a literary magazine, *New Challenge*. His first completed novel, published posthumously, was *Lawd Today* (originally called *Cesspool*). It describes a day in the life of an angry postal worker.

Eventually, he found a publisher for four novellas about Southern racial oppression, *Uncle Tom's Children*. He wrote compellingly of the Jim Crow era and how it felt to be a black man living in fear of his life. Reception to the book was such that in 1939, Wright received a Guggenheim Fellowship, enabling him to complete *Native Son*, the story of a black man who accidentally kills a white woman. The book was a critical and popular success.

"The importance of his works comes not from his technique and style, but from the impact his ideas and attitudes have had on American life," observes Matthew

Duffus on the Mississippi Writers Web site. "Wright is seen as a seminal figure in the black revolution that followed his earliest novels."

"The significance of the novel's publication lay in the new and daringly defiant character of its content and in its adoption by the Book-of-the-Month Club, which signaled for the first time since the nineteenth-century fugitive slave narratives the willingness of a mainstream reading public to give an ear to an African American culture," explained Donald B. Gibson in *Oxford Companion to African American Literature*, adding that Wright's prose laid the groundwork for the American black social protest of the 1960s.

In 1945 the author's autobiographical *Black Boy* came out, solidifying his position as a major writer.

Wright was twice married, first to Rose Dhimah Meadman, whom he divorced in 1940, and then to Ellen Poplar. There were two children from the second marriage.

Earnings from his writing enabled Wright to move with his family to France in 1947, to get away from Mississippi racism. He remained in Europe the rest of his life, though in ill health and often in meager financial circumstance. In 1960, he died of a heart attack.

Works by the Author

Uncle Tom's Children: Four Novellas (1938), expanded edition *Uncle Tom's Children: Five Long Stories* (1940)
Bright and Morning Star (1938)
Native Son (1940)
The Outsider (1953)
Savage Holiday (1954)
The Long Dream (1958)
Eight Men (1961), short stories
Lawd Today (1963)

Nonfiction

How "Bigger" Was Born: The Story of Native Son (1940)
12 Million Black Voices: A Folk History of the Negro in the United States (1941)
Black Boy: A Record of Childhood and Youth (1945)
Black Power: A Record of Reactions in a Land of Pathos (1954)
The Color Curtain: A Report on the Bandung Conference (1956)
Pagan Spain (1957)
White Man, Listen (1957)
Letters to Joe C. Brown (1968)
American Hunger (1977)

Drama

Native Son (1941), written with Paul Green
Daddy Goodness (1968), adaptation written with Louis Sapin

Screenplays

Native Son (1950)
Native Son (1986)

For Further Information

Duffus, Mathew, Richard Wright biography, *Mississippi Writers. http://www. olemiss.edu/depts/english/ms-writers/dir/wright_richard/* (viewed Aug. 10, 2006).

Gibson, Donald B., Richard Wright entry, *Oxford Companion to African American Literature*, William L. Andrews, Frances Smith Foster, and Trudier Harris, eds. New York: Oxford University Press, 1997.

Richard Wright chronology, Richard Wright, *Black Boy* Web page. *http:// www.itvs.org/RichardWright.chron.html* (viewed April 11, 2005).

Richard Wright entry, *Essential Black Literature Guide*, Roger M. Valade III, ed. Detroit: Visible Ink, 1996.

Richard Wright—A Webpage by Richard Hancuff. *http://home.gwu.edu/~cuff/ wright/* (viewed Aug. 10, 2006).

Williams, John A., and Dorothy Sterling. *The Most Native of Sons: A Biography of Richard Wright.* Garden City, NY: Doubleday, 1970.

Frank Yerby

Historical Literature, Romance, Mainstream Contemporary Literature, Western, Poetry

Benchmark Title: *The Foxes of Harrow*

Augusta, Georgia

1916–1991

About the Author and the Author's Writing

Frank Yerby was one of the most popular and prolific African American authors of the 1940s and 1950s. But he received little critical respect, and often today is taken to task for not continuing the strong threads of social protest which marked some of the novels of his middle years, such as *Speak Now* or *The Dahomean*, both of which had black protagonists.

Yerby's response to criticism about his lack of racial consciousness, according to the *New Georgia Encyclopedia*, was to argue that "the novelist hasn't any right to inflict on the public his private ideas on politics, race, or religion." Some of his later novels such as *The Garfield Honor* and *Griffin's Way* did, in fact, discuss race and southern culture.

Yerby was the first black writer with a bestseller and the first to sell film rights to a Hollywood studio. What accounted for sales of some 50 million copies of his thirty-some books? Critic Earl F. Bargainnier in *Twentieth-Century Romance & Historical Writers* suggests, "Readers can sense an ethical underpinning to the exciting action and sexy romance. His heroes are nearly always idealists or skeptics, and often the idealists become skeptics, if not stoics, thus fulfilling the theme that most of man's problems have no solutions. This existential view, however bleak, pervades the novels and accounts for the frequent less-than-happy endings." Nevertheless, and perhaps because it was so different, readers were enthralled with the adventure, the characters and the themes.

Yerby was born to a Scots-Irish mother and an African American father in Augusta, Georgia, in 1916. He attended Haines Institute and earned a bachelor of arts degree in English from Paine College in 1937. After completing a master's degree in English from Fisk University the next year, he began work on a Ph.D. at the University of Chicago. He taught briefly at Florida A&M and Southern University in Baton Rouge, Louisiana. In 1944, his short story about racial injustice in the steel industry, "Health Card," won him the O. Henry Memorial Award for best first fiction and launched his career. During World War II, he worked for Ford Motor Company and Ranger Aircraft.

During this time he wrote. His southern novels were repeatedly rejected by publishers, so he cynically decided to write the worst historical novel he could. Half way through, he admitted years later, he became caught up in the story and revised it considerably. It was *The Foxes of Harrow*. Because of his success, he wrote a series of titles along these lines.

His protagonists were generally white (to satisfy publishers), the action intense, and the settings gay and romantic. While the books had colorful plots and multiple complex characters, they were somewhat formulaic and often ended with a turn of luck.

Decades of research went into Yerby's ambitious *Judas, My Brother: The Story of the Thirteenth Disciple*, in which he attempted to demythologize aspects of Christ's life on earth. Still, some critics considered it a costumed melodrama.

Yerby often explored ancient Greece and crusades as backdrops for his novels. However, *The Dahomean* is about the leader of an African tribe. Yerby told Contemporary Authors, "I seem to have changed many critics' minds [with this book]. Pleasantly surprising was the high praise bestowed upon this novel by the critics of the South African papers. Needless to say, black critics immediately removed me from the list of 'non-conductors' and welcomed me back into the fold like a sinner redeemed by faith."

Yerby was twice married, first to Flora Helen Claire Williams in 1941 (they divorced), and then to Blanca Calle Perez in 1956. There were four children from the first marriage. Yerby and his second wife left the United States in 1956, and lived in self-decreed exile in Spain and France for the rest of his life. He died in 1991.

"Yerby adapted protest fiction to suit the medium of popular fiction," summarized James L. Hill. "Enlarging his protest motives and taking aim at inaccuracies in southern history, he became one of America's greatest debunkers of historical myths."

Works by the Author

The Foxes of Harrow (1947)
The Vixens (1947)
The Golden Hawk (1948)
Pride's Castle (1949)
Floodtide (1950)
A Woman Called Fancy (1951)
The Saracen Blade (1952)
The Devil's Laughter (1953)
Benton's Row (1954)
Bride of Liberty (1954)
The Treasure of Pleasant Valley (1955)
Captain Rebel (1956)
Fairoaks (1957)

The Serpent and the Staff (1958)

Jarrett's Jade (1959)

Gillian (1960)

The Garfield Honor (1961)

Griffin's Way (1962)

The Old Gods Laugh: A Modern Romance (1964)

An Odor of Sanctity (1965)

Goat Song: A Novel of Ancient Greece (1968)

Judas, My Brother: The Story of the Thirteenth Disciple (1969)

Speak Now (1969)

The Dahomean: An Historical Novel (1971), in Great Britain retitled *The Man from Dahomey* (1971)

The Girl from Storyville: A Victorian Novel (1972)

The Voyage Unplanned (1974)

Tobias and the Angel (1975)

A Rose for Ana Maria (1976)

Hail the Conquering Hero (1978)

A Darkness at Ingraham's Crest (1981)

Western: A Saga of the Great Plains (1982)

Devilseed (1984)

McKenzie's Hundred (1985)

Contributor

The Best Short Stories by Negro Writers: An Anthology from 1899 to the Present (1967), edited by Langston Hughes

The Poetry of the Negro, 1746–1970 (1970), edited by Langston Hughes and Arna Bontemps

Backlash (1970), edited by Stewart H. Benedict

The African American West: A Century of Short Stories (2000), edited by Bruce A. Glasrud and Laurie Champion

Films Based on the Author's Works

Pride's Castle (episode of *Philco Playhouse*, 1949)

The Foxes of Harrow (1951)

The Golden Hawk (1952)

The Seracen Blade (1954)

For Further Information

Bargainnier, Earl F., Frank (Garvin) Yerby entry, *Twentieth-Century Romance & Historical Writers*, 2d ed., Lesley Henderson, ed. Chicago: St. James Press, 1990.

Frank G(arvin) Yerby entry, Contemporary Authors Online, Gale, 2005. Reproduced in Biography Resources Center. Farmington Hills, MI: Thomson Gale, 2005. *http://galenet.galegroup.com/servlet/BioRC* (viewed Feb. 21, 2005).

Frank Garvin Yerby Web page, African American Literature Book Club. *http://authors.aalbc.com/frankyerby.htm* (viewed Aug. 10, 2006).

Frank Yerby biography, *African American Registry. http://www.aaregistry. com/african_american_history/1132/Frank_Yerby_was_an_award_winning_novelist* (viewed Aug. 10, 2006).

Frank Yerby biography, *HistFiction.net. http://www.histfiction.net/display. php?author=209* (viewed April 12, 2005).

Frank Yerby biography, New Georgia Encyclopedia. *http://www. georgiaencyclopedia.org/nge/Article.jsp?id=h-523* (viewed Aug. 10, 2006).

Hill, James L., Frank Yerby entry, *The Oxford Companion to African American Literature*, William L. Andrews, Frances Smith Foster, and Trudier Harris, eds. New York: Oxford University Press, 1997.

Smiles, Robin V., "Uncovering Frank Yerby," *Black Issues in Higher Education* (Nov. 4, 2004).

Valade, Roger M., III, ed., Frank Yerby entry, *The Essential Black Literature Guide*. Detroit: Visible Ink, 1996.

Zane

Photo credit: Dante Feenix

Erotica

Benchmark Title: *Addicted*

Location of birth not revealed

1966

About the Author and the Author's Writing

Zane didn't invent the subgenre of black erotica—Miriam Decoasta Willis, Reginald Martin, and Roseann Bell broke the ground with their 1992 anthology *Erotique Noire*—but she has taken sexy black fiction to a new level of mass-market appeal. Today, her works have been translated into Swedish, Greek, and Japanese.

Zane is Kristina LaFerne Roberts, the daughter of a theologian father and a school teacher mother. She is a graduate of Howard University. She worked as a sales executive in the paper industry. She and her environmental designer husband and three children live in suburban Washington, D.C. About her pen name, she explains that Zane is the Hebrew word for "God will nourish."

She said in a GRITS interview she has long been an eager reader, and writing was a natural result. "While the suggestions of my English teachers and other supporters fell on deaf ears during my youth, I started writing seriously in November 1997. I honestly cannot imagine doing anything else because the storylines and dialogue haunt me day and night and I cannot make enough time to get it all down on paper."

Zane initially wrote and distributed stories over the Internet, selling 50-page manuscripts for $10 each. In 2000, she self-published three novels that reportedly sold more than 250,000 copies. That caught the attention of major publisher Simon & Schuster's Atria imprint, which began to distribute her works and those of the twenty-eight writers she brought in under the umbrella of her Strebor Books (her last name spelled backwards). In June 2005, she sold the publishing company's backlog to Simon & Schuster outright, retaining ownership of the imprint and responsibility for new acquisitions. That transaction, Zane told reporter Wayne Dawkins of *Black Issues Book Review*, will now enable her to catch up on a backlog of writing ideas.

"I have a childlike imagination," the author told *Entertainment Weekly*. "I just add sex to it." With the novel *Afterburn*, Zane came into public view for the first time to promote her writing, and to discredit fraudulent Zanes who were showing up at book signings in her name.

Her novels adapt to many settings. *Addicted* she calls a psychological thriller about a nymphomaniac. *Skyscraper* takes place in the corporate world. *Nervous* is about a woman with a split personality—one repressed, one oversexed.

The author writes quickly. She said she wrote *Shame on It All* in ten days, *Addicted* in twenty, with an additional day to change the ending at the publisher's suggestion. "I tend to write fast because I become so absorbed in the characters that it bothers me when it is not finished," she told GRITS.

The *New York Times* best-selling author's stories about a college sorority, APF (standing for Alpha Phi Fuckem), were so popular when they appeared in earlier collections that she based a novel on their adventures. The heroines include Mary Ann, the naive daughter of a South Dakota chicken farmer, who at college is taken under the wing of resident manager Patricia and introduced to "the ranks of the sexiest secret society ever: the sisters of APF."

As well as writing, Zane has edited anthologies such as *Chocolate Flava* and *Breaking the Cycle* (which in a departure looks at domestic abuse and other social issues).

While some critics have decried the graphic sexuality of her writing, Zane's editor, Blanche Richardson, commended the author to *Boston Globe* staff writer Vanessa E. Jones and noted her ability to overcome severe obstacles to climb to the top in the world of popular literature. One of those obstacles has been sexual denigration since times of slavery: "We've been hesitant to speak openly about our sensuality even though we know everybody does it. On us it looks a little different. We're looked at as easy, bad, sluts. We tend not to verbalize it or reinforce it in our literature lest we play into those stereotypes."

Zane explained to *Jet* writer Margena A. Christian, "All of my characters are either already very liberated and empowered or they become that way during the book. When I sit down and write each book, I have something different in mind of what I'm trying to get across . . . I do it in a comedic and in a sexual way, but I always have a deeper purpose."

Works by the Author

The Sex Chronicles: Shattering the Myth (2000), short stories
The Heat Seekers (2000)
Shame on It All (2001)
Addicted (2001)
Getting Buck Wild: Sex Chronicles 2 (2002), short stories
The Sisters of APF: The Indoctrination of Soror Ride Dick (2003)
Nervous (2003)
Skyscraper (2003)
Afterburn (2004)

Addicted With a Twist (2005)
It Is What It's: Shame on It All Again (2005)
Vengeance (2005)
Dear G-Spot (2006)

Editor

Blackgentlemen.com (2003)
Chocolate Flava: The Eroticanoir.com Anthology (2004)
Breaking the Cycle (2005)
Caramel Flava: The Eroticanoir.com Anthology (2006)

Contributor

Love Is Never Painless (2005), with V. Anthony Rivers and Eileen M. Johnson

For Further Information

Christian, Margena A., "Meet Zane, the Queen of Erotic Novels," *Jet* (Oct. 4, 2004).

Dawkins, Wayne, "Buying Zane," *Black Issues Book Review* (Sept.-Oct., 2005).

Jones, Vanessa E., "Zane Uncovered," *Boston Globe* (Sept. 6, 2004).

Polk, Felicia, and Robin Gree-Cary, "How to Get Your Literary Freak On—Erotic Fiction—Bibliography," *Black Issues Book Review* (Jan.-Feb. 2003).

Wheat, Alynda, "The Erogenous Zane," *Entertainment Weekly* (Aug. 13, 2004).

Zane interview, *GRITS-dot-com. http://www.thegritsbookclub.com/Interviews/Zane.html* (viewed Aug. 10, 2006).

Zane Web page, African American Literature Book Club. *http://authors.aalbc.com/zane.htm* (viewed Aug. 10, 2006).

Zane Web sites, *www.eroticanoir.com and www.streborbooks.com* (viewed April 14, 2005).

Zimmerman, Sacha, review of *Afterburn, New Republic Online. http://www.powells.com/review/2005_02_17.html* (viewed Aug. 10, 2006).

Author/Title Index

Genre Index

About the Author

BERNARD A. DREW is a freelance writer/editor and book author of numerous articles and books, including *100 Most Popular Young Adult Authors* (Libraries Unlimited, 2002) and *100 Most Popular Genre Authors* (Libraries Unlimited, 2005).